BED AND BREAKFASTS OF
CHARACTER AND CHARM
IN FRANCE

While every care has been taked to ensure the accuracy of the information in this guide, time brings change, and consequently the publisher cannot accept responsibility for errors that may occur. Prudent travelers will therefore want to call ahead to verify prices and other "perishable" information.

Published in the United States by Fodor's Travel Publications, Inc.
Published in France by Payot/Rivages

Fodor's is a registered trademark of Fodor's Travel Publications, Inc.

ISBN 0-679-02873-0
First Edition

**Bed and Breakfasts
of Character and Charm in France**
Translator: Christina Thistlethwayte, Anne Norris
Rewriting: Marie Gastaut
Creative director: Fabrizio La Rocca
Front cover photograph: La Borde (Burgundy), photo by François Tissier;
back cover: Moulin de Labique (Aquitaine)

Special Sales
Fodor's Travel Publications are available at special discounts for bulk purchases for sales promotions or premiums. Special editions, including personalized covers, excerpts of existing guides, and corporate imprints, can be created in large quantities for special needs. For more information, contact your local bookseller or Special Markets, Fodor's Travel Publications, 201 E. 50th Street, New York, NY 10022.

Manufactured in Italy by Litho Service
10 9 8 7 6 5 4 3 2 1

Fodor's RIVAGES

BED AND BREAKFASTS
of Character and Charm
IN FRANCE

Founding editors

Véronique de Andreis, Jean and Tatiana de Beaumont,
Bénédicte Darblay, Anne Deren

Editorial director

Véronique de Andreis

Fodor's Travel Publications, Inc.

New York • Toronto • London • Sydney • Auckland

INTRODUCTION

Now available in the U.S for the first time, this fifth edition of the popular Rivages Guide has been entirely updated. It contains 493 bed-and-breakfast establishments—known as *maisons d'hôtes*—including 94 new addresses. Each year, we travel all over France to select or inspect these houses for their exceptional charm, authenticity, atmosphere, location, modern accommodations, surroundings and, of course, the owners' hospitality.

B&Bs are more popular than ever in France. Their growing numbers make our choice more difficult; however, while we wish to propose a larger selection, our standards in choosing them must remain high. The owners of these privately owned houses will be delighted to welcome you for an evening, a weekend, or a more lengthy vacation. We feel that you will be as delighted as we were to discover these houses, which range from magnificent chateaux (real chateaux as well as spacious mansions) and beautiful country houses to charming old mills, mountain chalets and farmhouses, some of which still operate as farms.

Our selection is very varied and each house has its own charm and personality.
Their owners all know their regions well and they will be delighted to share their touristic and gastronomic discoveries with you.

When you travel with the *Guide to B&Bs of Character and Charm in France*, you also profit from the experience of people who love their region and who are anxious to preserve it from mass tourism.

Whether you enjoy independence or the company of other travelers, rustic or elegant places to stay, modern or simple accommodations, this Guide gives you a wide choice.
Whatever your desires or your pocketbook, you will find the perfect B&B whether you are a couple, a family or a group of friends. Prices vary from l80 F to more than l000 F per day for two people for room and breakfast.

You will find that some owners are more reserved than others. Some may very well become friends. But all will want to help you enjoy a comfortable and pleasant stay.
You should let the owners know of any special needs or preferences. Above all, they are anxious for you to feel at home in their house.

Don't forget, however, that these are private homes and not hotels; the service is not the same and everyone's privacy should of course be respected during the time that you and your hosts spend together.

Advice on reserving

Always reserve in advance; the number of bedrooms is often limited. You will usually be asked to send a letter of confirmation or a down-payment.

If you intend to come as a family or a group of friends, ask about the possibilities of *chambres d'appoint*, spare bedrooms.

When you reserve, indicate whether or not you wish the *table d'hôte* dinner and it is preferable to confirm this reservation in writing.

Arrive on time or notify the owner if you are delayed. Otherwise, you might find no one at home when you arrive.

In the country, houses are often guarded by dogs in the owners' absence. It is thus preferable to let them know of your comings and goings.

Ask the owner for the best itinerary from your departure point.

In case of cancellation

When you reserve, ask what advance notice you should give in case you have to cancel, and if your deposit can be returned.

The *table d'hôtes*

The *table d'hôtes* evening meal is usually served around the family dining table. It gives you the opportunity to get to know your hosts and to meet other travelers who, like you, are looking for different and interesting places to stay.

In some houses, dinner may be served at independent tables. This possibility is indicated for each address given.

Table d'hôtes dinners are generally served at a communal table with the owners and the other guests. They are served at fixed times. If the hostess does not join you, it is because she prefers to devote her time to preparing the meal.

Traditional regional cuisine made with fresh local produce is generally served in these *maisons d'hôtes*, but some also offer excellent gourmet cuisine.

While some *tables d'hôtes* meals are informal and family-style, others are elaborate, with refined cuisine served at a beautiful, festive table. In this regard, prices depend on the various services provided and are thus very variable.

Reserve your table as soon as possible. B&Bs keep little food on hand and meals are made with fresh products. Please note that *table d'hôtes* meals are not necessarily served every evening.

For the houses which do not offer *table d'hôtes* meals, we have indicated the distance to the closest restaurant which is recommended by the B&B owner. They will be happy to give you further addresses.

Bedrooms

Their style and decoration are as varied as the choice of the houses we have selected. Some are simple, while others are truly luxurious.

We have generally included only bedrooms with private bathrooms and toilets. If there are none, this is indicated. These exceptions concern spare rooms which can often be occupied in addition to the main bedroom and which are practical if you are traveling with children or friends.

The rooms generally are cleaned and the beds made regularly or daily. In some rare cases, room cleaning is done on request or by the guests. We have indicated this in the practical information for each address.

The bedrooms all have their own personality and you will often be surprised by their spaciousness. Note the descriptions we give for each house.

But here, too, rooms vary with the house and the price. Some large houses are difficult to heat in winter. Reserve in advance or ask the owners to heat the room when you arrive.

The telephone

Some houses have a *Point-Phone* coin-operated telephone which you are free to use.

Some bedrooms are provided with a direct telephone. Otherwise, it is difficult to use the house telephone which usually does not have a meter.

The salon or living room

In most houses you can use the salon. A living area reserved for guests is sometimes available. This point is indicated for each house.

Prices

The prices indicated have been given to us for 1995. They are occasionally changed by the owners during the year.

Some houses also propose special rates for a weekend, a longer stay or rates for *demi-pension*, or half board (room, breakfast and one meal, usually dinner).

Do not hesitate to ask for this information and confirm the prices when you reserve.

How to choose a B&B

The houses are given by region. Within each region, we have given an alphabetical classification by *département*, then by town and name of the house.

The texts, photos and practical information for each house are intended to guide you in your choice.

You can refer either to the Table of Contents, classified by region and given at the beginning of this Guide; or the alphabetical index at the end.

To locate the house, use the Recta Foldex maps placed at the beginning of the Guide. Each numbered flag corresponds to the number of the B&B given in the text with the photo.

These maps are preceded by an overall map of France which will enable you to locate the region of your choice and also to see the breakdown of the various maps.

To improve the Guide constantly, we are always very pleased to have your reactions and comments on the B&Bs we have selected.

If you would like to have a B&B included in the Guide, we would appreciate your sending us the address of the house and we will be pleased to contact the owners.

We update our Guide every year. For the next edition, letters should be sent as of November 1995 and by January 15, 1996 at the latest, to:

Véronique De Andreis
Editions Payot-Rivages
106, Boulevard Saint-Germain
75006 Paris.

We thank our readers for the new addresses they have been kind enough to propose for inclusion in this Guide.

Photographic Credits:

n° 7 © Daniel Millot - n° 50 © Photo Barbotin - n° 85 © CHANTAL Christian - n° 117 © De Visu - n° 124 © François Quiniou - n° 146 © Jean-Charles Briens - n° 168 © D.R. - n° 136 and n° 229 © François Tissier - n° 267 © Guy Clément - n° 270 © LCI Wallis - n° 272 © D.R. - n° 301 © Hoa Qui - n° 340 © Valentin - n° 363 © Hardouin - n° 371 © Editions du Vieux Chouan (Fromentine) - n° 414 © J-P Rivaux - n° 434 © J.M. Ducroux.

CONTENTS

ALSACE - LORRAINE

AQUITAINE

Pyrénées – Atlantiques (64)

A U V E R G N E - L I M O U S I N

Allier (03)

BOURGOGNE (BURGUNDY)

B R E T A G N E   (B R I T T A N Y)

C E N T R E

Indre (36)

Indre – et – Loire (37)

Loir – et – Cher (41)

CHAMPAGNE - ARDENNES

FRANCHE - COMTE

M I D I - P Y R E N E E S

Gers (32)

Lot (46)

Hautes – Pyrénées (65)

Tarn (81)

NORTH - PAS-DE-CALAIS

NORMANDY

Orne (61)

Seine – Maritime (76)

P A Y S   D E   L A   L O I R E

Loire – Atlantique (44)

Maine – et – Loire (49)

P I C A R D I E

P O I T O U - C H A R E N T E S

P R O V E N C E - R I V I E R A

R H O N E - A L P S

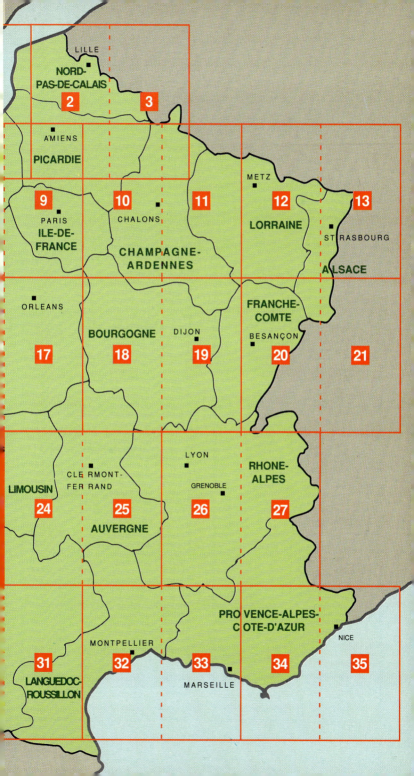

KEY TO THE MAPS

Scale: 1:1,000,000
Maps 30 & 31: scale: 1:1,180,000

MOTORWAYS

❶ Interchange
❷ Half-interchange
❸ Toll-barrier

Kilometre-distance
❶ in total
❷ partial

Motorway
❶ under construction
❷ projected

ROAD CLASSIFICATION

Dual-carriageways

High traffic road

Trunk road

Other road

Road ❶ under construction
       ❷ projected

TOWNS CLASSIFICATION

❶ by the population

– less than 10,000 inhabitants   ○
– from 10.000 to 30.000   ○
– from 30.000 to 50.000   ◉
– from 50.000 to 100.000   ◉
– more than 100.000   ●
– towns with over
  50.000 inh.   ⬠

❷ Administrative
– Chief-town of
  department   **TARBES**
– Main subdivision of
  department   **CARPENTRAS**
– Districts   **Combeaufontaine**
– Commune, hamlet   Andrézieux-Bouthéon

ROAD WIDTH

4 carriageways

3 lane or
2 wide lane
2 lane

Narrow road
Kilometre-distance
❶ in total
❷ partial

BOUNDARIES

National boundary

County boundary

TOURISM

Picturesque locality   Chenonceaux

Very picturesque locality   **Amboise**∗

Interesting site or   Roches de Ham
natural curiosity

Historic castle
Ruins of outstanding beauty

Abbey
National park

DIVERS

Civil Airport
Dam

Canal
Car-ferries

Motorail

Pass

Summit   ▲ 2392

4

côte

Plouguerne

Ploudalmézeau · 17

D 28

D 168

D 27

16

13

25 D 26

18

Ouessant

PARC

Lampaul
Plouarzel

St-Renan

Goues

D 67

D'ARMORIQUE

D 5

Guilers

I. Molène

D 67

15

BREST

le Conquet

Plouzané

D 789

24

P^nte St-Mathieu

Camaret

Pnte de Pen-Hir

D 355

Crozon

Morgat

G

Cap de la Chèvre

P^nte ✳

du Raz

D

I. de Sein

D 784 5

Pont-Croix

Audierne

Ploz

Pe

N.-D.-de

P^nte de Pen

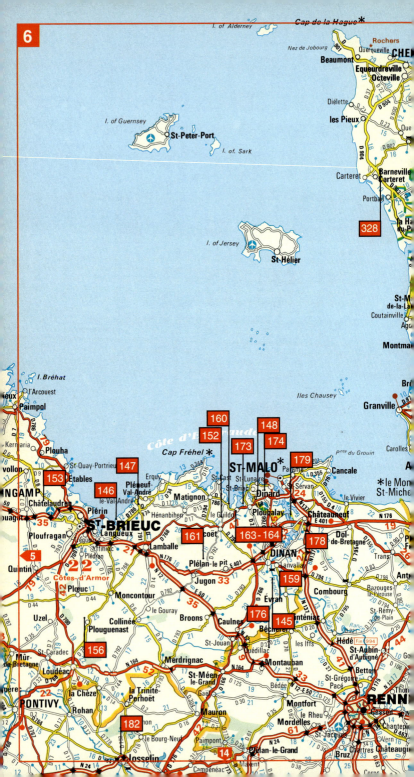

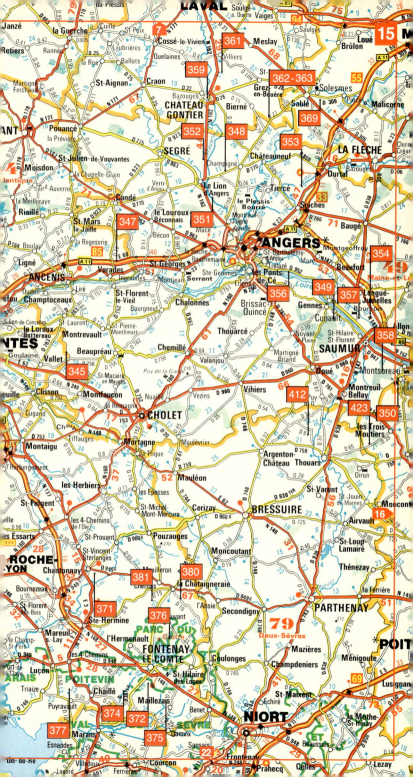

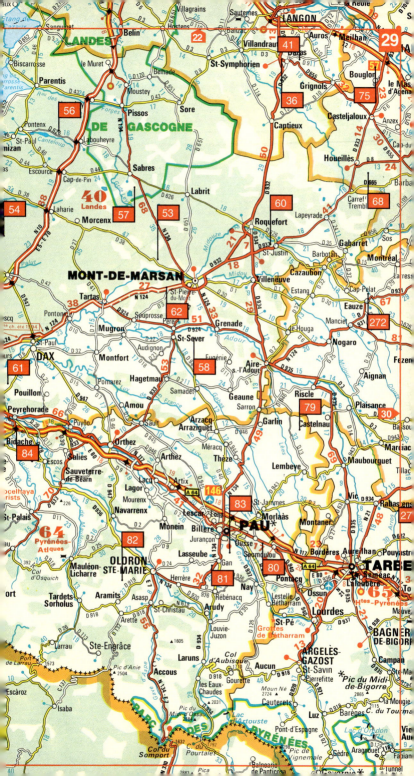

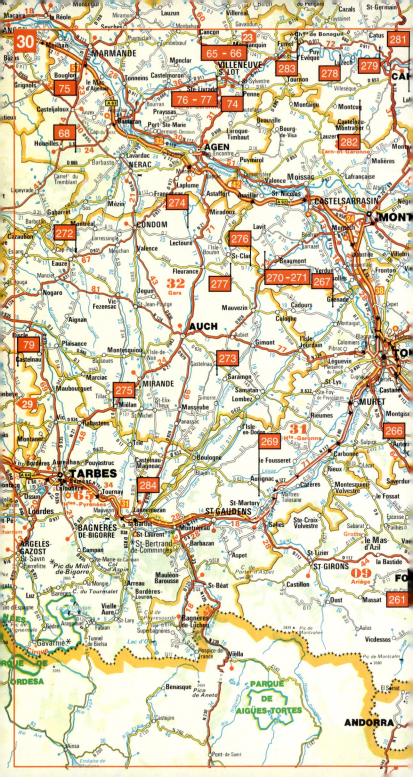

Cap Corse

Ile de la Giraglia

Rogliano
Pino
Sta-Sévera
Luri
D 180
Canari
D 80
Nonza
Brando
Erbalunga
San-Martino-di-Lota

BASTIA

Désert des Agriates
St-Florent
Oletta
Etg de Biguglia

l'Ile-Rousse N 197
Algajola
Santo-Pietro-di-Tenda
Ste-Michèle
la Canonica
St-Antonino
Belgodère
Lama
Murato
Borgo
Casamozza
CALVI
Aregno
Campitello
D 151
Muro
Olmi-Cappella
Calenzana
Castifao
Asco
Ponte
Leccia
Campile
la Porta
Vescovato
Folelli
Pero Casevecchie
D 147
Popolasca
Morosaglia
Piedicroce
San-Nicolao
Francardo
San Lorenzo
Omessa
D 71
Girolata
Calacuccia
Casamaccioli
Valle d'Alesani
Cervione
Pietra-di-Verde
Col de Vergio
CORTE
Sermano
Moita
Porto
Évisa
Piedicorte
N 200
Piana
Soccia
Venaco
Vico
Guagno-les-Bains
Vivario
Vezzani
Cargèse
Sagone
Salice
Mt d'Oro 2391
Ghisoni
Aleria
Vizzavona
N 193
Sari-d'Orcino
Bocognano
Sarrola-Carcopino
Mte Renoso
Bastelica
Prunelli-di-Fiumorbo
la Punta
2A
CORSE-DU-SUD
AJACCIO
Cauro
Frasseto
Zicavo
Iles Sanguinaires
Sta-Maria-Siché
Incudine 2136
Solenzara
Chiavari
Bicchisano
Petreto
Col de Bavella
Acqua Doria
Aullène
Zonza
Filitosa
Serra-di-Scopamène
Levie
San-Gavino-di-Carbini
Porto Pollo
Olmeto
Ste-Lucie-de-Tallano
Propriano
Ospedale
SARTÈNE
Campomoro
Porto-Vecchio
Iles Cerbicale
Cauria
N 196
Figari
Bonifacio
Ile de Cavallo
Ile de Lavezzi

S. Teresa Gallura
C. Testa
Ile Maddalena

RECTA FOLDEX
MAPS
EXPLORE FRANCE
AND THE WHOLE WORD

1

Château de Labessière

55320 Ancemont
(Meuse)
Tel. 29 85 70 21
Fax 29 87 61 60
M. and Mme Eichenauer

Rooms 2 with bath or shower, WC, and 1 suite (5 pers.) with shower and WC. **Price** 200F (1 pers.), 275F (2 pers.), 450F (4 pers.), +60F (extra pers.). **Meals** Breakfast incl. Evening meal 100-125F. **Facilities** Lounge, swimming pool with whirlpool. **Nearby** Golf, riding, fly fishing (4km), Lake La Madine, forest of Argonne, valley of La Saulx. **Credit cards** Not accepted. **Spoken** English, German. **Closed** For Christmas and New Year. **How to get there** (Map 11): Strasbourg Autoroute, Verdun exit, towards Dieue, then right to Ancemont. On Paris Autoroute, exit Voie Sacrée toward Bar-le-Duc to Lemmes, then on left to Senoncourt-Ancemont.

In the village of Ancemont, you will find this small château opposite an ancient wash house, whose interior has been completely refurbished. You will be made very welcome here and sleep in comfortable, well-kept bedrooms with lovely antique wardrobes. The ground-floor furniture is less authentic. Breakfast and dinner are served at separate tables in the pleasant dining room. Before leaving be sure to sit out in the pretty garden, although you'll hear some noise from the road.

2

Château d'Alteville

Tarquimpol
57260 Dieuze
(Moselle)
Tel. 87 86 92 40
Fax 87 86 02 05
M. and Mme L. Barthélemy

Rooms 10 with bath and WC (8 with telephone) and 1 apartment with kitchen and bath. **Price** Room 450-500F (2 pers.), apart. weekly rental 500F/day (2 pers.). **Meals** Breakfast 40F. Evening meals at communal table, by reservation 200F (wine not incl.). **Pets** Small dogs allowed on request (+55F). **Nearby** Restaurants, tennis, riding, fishing. **Credit cards** Not accepted. **Spoken** English, German. **Open** April 1 – Nov 1. **How to get there** (Map 12): 54km east of Nancy via N74 and D38 towards Dieuze, then D999 towards Gelucourt and D199, then D199G.

This is a very lovely country property close to a number of lakes. The public rooms include a billiard room/library, a drawing room with antique furniture, and a dining room festooned with hunting trophies. The bedrooms have been charmingly restored, with up-to-date amenities, and all have views of the park. (Number 11 is somewhat small.) Good *table d'hôtes* meals are served around a beautifully set table, where the hospitality is refined, unaffected and friendly.

3
La Musardière

57340 Lidrezing
(Moselle)
Tel. 87 86 14 05
Fax 87 86 40 16
Cécile and René Mathis

Rooms 3 with bath or shower (incl. 1 with whirlpool, +80F),WC, TV, minibar and 1 with telephone.
Price 295F (2 pers.). **Meals** Breakfast incl. Evening meal at communal table by reservation 110F
(wine not incl.). **Facilities** Lounge, Fragrance garden. **Pets** Dogs not allowed. **Nearby** Tennis,
riding, hiking in Lorraine Regional Park; Vic sur Seille, Marsal. **Credit cards** Not accepted.
Spoken English, German. **Open** Easter – Nov 1. **How to get there** (Map 12): Autoroute A31 20km
south of Metz, Saint-Avold exit. In Han-sur-Nied, D999 southeast past Morhange, then 10km
towards Dieuze; follow signs.

This is a small, simple and unpretentious village house where you will
find a warm and attentive welcome. The bedrooms are quiet and have
many useful and charming object for guests' pleasure. Excellent dinners are
served in a bright room overlooking the garden, where you will find some
thirty aromatic plants and herbs.

4
Chez M. et Mme Krumeich

23, rue des Potiers
67660 Betschdorf
(Bas-Rhin)
Tel. 88 54 40 56
Fax 88 54 47 67
M. and Mme Krumeich

Rooms 3 with shower, WC and TV. **Price** 200-290F (2 pers.), +80F (extra pers.). **Meals** Breakfast
incl. No communal meal. **Restaurant** La Table des Potiers in Betschdorf. **Facilities** Lounge,
sheltered parking, garden lounge; pottery courses. **Pets** No dogs allowed. **Nearby** Swimming
pool, tennis, pottery museum, picturesque villages. **Credit cards** Visa, Eurocard and MasterCard.
Spoken English, German. **Open** All year. **How to get there** (Map 13): 15km north of Haguenau
via D263 towards Wissembourg, then D243.

Betschdorf is a village famous for its potters and here you'll stay in the
house of one of them. The three bedrooms, of different sizes, are
comfortable and well decorated--and quiet as well--since they are away
from the road. Breakfast is served in a pine-paneled room embellished with
pieces of stoneware, and there is a pretty flower garden. The welcome here
is unaffected and friendly.

5
Le Tire-Lyre

2, hameau du Tirelire
67310 Cosswiller
(Bas-Rhin)
Tel. 88 87 22 49
Mme Maud Bochart

Rooms 3, and 1 suite (4 pers./2 rooms) with bath, WC, 3 with telephone. **Price** 285F (1 pers.), 325-350F (2 pers.), 550F (4 pers.); 2 nights min. in high season and national holidays. **Meals** Breakfast incl. (+35F extra pers.). No communal meal. **Restaurant** 3km away and farm/auberge in village (weekends). **Pets** Dogs allowed in kennel. **Facilities** Lounge. **Nearby** Tennis, riding, golf (18 holes, 28km), hiking, châteaux, village of Westhoffen. **Credit cards** Not accepted. **Spoken** Italian. **Closed** July. **How to get there** (Map 12): 25km west of Strasbourg via RN4 towards Saverne. In Wasselonne take the road towards Cosswiller in the direction of the fountain and the chemin du hameau (800m); signposted.

You can't miss the charming Tire-Lyre and its garden which are located in a small hamlet surrounded by pastures and woodland. This is a remarkably well kept hotel, which has been lovingly decorated by Mme Bochard. With several handsome pieces of antique furniture, the owner's passion for beautiful fabrics can be seen in each comfortable bedroom, where the pretty curtains, bed canopies and eiderdowns are beautifully coordinated. The breakfasts, served on beautiful china, are excellent.

6
La Maison Fleurie de Colette Geiger

19, route de Neuve-Eglise
67220 Dieffenbach-au-Val
(Bas-Rhin)
Tel. 88 85 60 48
Mme Geiger

Rooms 3 with shower and WC, and 1 studio (3 pers.) with shower, WC and kitchenette. Rooms cleaned on request. **Price** Room 170F (1 pers.), 210F (2 pers.) +80F (extra pers.); studio 250F (2 pers.). **Meals** Breakfast incl. No communal meal. **Facilities** Lounge. **Pets** Small dogs on request. **Nearby** Restaurants, tennis, swimming pool (4km), cross-country and downhill skiing (15km), Haut-Koenigsbourg, Riquewihr, Wine Route, mont Sainte-Odile, swannery, hawking. **Credit cards** Not accepted. **Spoken** German, English (some). **Open** All year. **How to get there** (Map 12): 15km northwest of Sélestat via D424 to Villé, then D697.

Located on a hillside in a small village, this typically Alsatian house overflows with flowers. Mme Geiger will greet you with a big smile and tell you about the many tourist attractions close at hand. The small bedrooms are simple and well kept and there is a pleasant garden. Good breakfasts are served at a large table in the dining room or outside on the terrace.

7
La Romance

17, route de Neuve-Eglise
67220 Dieffenbach-au-Val
(Bas-Rhin)
Tel. 88 85 67 09
M. and Mme Serge Geiger

Rooms 2 and 2 suites, with small private salon, bath or shower and WC. **Price** Room 260F (2 pers.), suite 290-310F (2 pers.), +50-100F (extra pers.); 2 days min. **Meals** Breakfast incl. No communal meal. **Facilities** Lounge. **Pets** Small dogs allowed on request. **Nearby** Restaurants, cross-country and Alpine skiing; flowery villages. **Credit cards** Not accepted. **Spoken** German, English (some). **Open** All year. **How to get there** (Map 12): 13km northwest of Sélestat. Exit 11 on autoroute at Sélestat, then toward Villé on D424 to Saint-Maurice, then D697; Dieffenbach-au-Val on left. **Non-smokers.**

From the Romance, you will enjoy a panoramic view out over the luxuriant Vosges countryside. Here, the welcome is warm and the hotel is in good taste. The comfortable, well-decorated bedrooms have modern, very well equipped bathrooms. The rooms on the *premier étage* make ideal suites for families, with sitting areas that can easily be made into extra bedrooms. The breakfasts are good and the value is excellent.

8
Neufeldhof

67280 Oberhaslach
(Bas-Rhin)
Tel. 88 50 91 48
M. and Mme André

Rooms 4 with basins (shared shower and WC) and 1 suite (4 pers.) of 2 bedrooms with shower and WC. **Price** 220F-270F (2 pers.), suite 530F (4 pers.). **Meals** Breakfast incl. Evening meals at communal table, lunch on Saturday, Sunday and national holidays: 75F (wine not incl.). **Facilities** Heated swimming pool, equestrian center, lounge. **Pets** Dogs not allowed. **Nearby** Tennis, fishing. **Credit cards** Not accepted. **Spoken** German, English. **Open** All year. **How to get there** (Map 12): 36km west of Strasbourg via A352. At Molsheim, N420 to Urmatt and D218; in the village, D75 towards Wasselonne for 2km; first track on the right.

This big and very old farm has been converted into an equestrian center. The interior is very charming. The bedrooms are comfortable and attractively furnished with antiques, and each has a handsome ceramic stove. The meals are outstanding, the family is very friendly and there are magnificent views over the countryside all around.

9
Le Biblenhof

67120 Soultz-les-Bains
(Bas-Rhin)
Tel. 88 38 21 09
Fax 88 48 81 99
M. and Mme Joseph Schmitt

Rooms We recommend only the rooms in the annexes. 5 and 3 studios (4-5 pers.) with shower and WC, 1 room with shower and shared WC. **Price** 200-260F (2 pers.), 240-380F (4-5 pers.). **Meals** Breakfast incl. Half board possible. Evening meal at communal table 60-80F (wine not incl.). **Facilities** Lounge, billiards, horse stalls. **Pets** Dogs not allowed. **Nearby** Covered swimming pool, tennis, riding, golf course (18 holes, 25km), Wine Route. **Credit cards** Not accepted. **Spoken** German, English. **Closed** Christmas week and 1 week in winter. **How to get there** (Map 12): 20km west of Strasbourg via D45; in the village take D422 towards Irmstett for 500 meters, then follow the signs.

The Biblenhof is a gigantic 18th-century farmhouse with a very welcoming façade covered in geraniums. The large entrance hall has great style, with antique furniture and a beautiful wooden staircase leading to bedrooms, but we recommend only the new rooms in the annexes. The people are very friendly, and you will enjoy excellent dinners and hearty breakfasts.

10
Le Moulin de Huttingue

68480 Oltingue
(Haut-Rhin)
Tel. 89 40 72 91
M. and Mme Thomas

Rooms 4 and 1 studio (2-3 pers.) with shower and WC, 1 duplex (3-4 pers.) in an independent house with bath, lounge and terrace. **Price** 220F (1 pers.), 280F (2 pers.), studio 320F (2 pers.), duplex 1600-1800F per week. **Meals** Breakfast incl. Evening meals (separate tables) 100-200F (wine not incl.). **Facilities** Lounge, horse stalls, fishing. **Nearby** Swimming pool, golf, cross-country skiing, Ferrette. **Credit cards** Not accepted. **Spoken** English, German. **Open** All year. **How to get there** (Map 20): 20km from Bâle (Switzerland) and 6km southeast of Ferrette via D23 towards Kiffis as far as Hippoltskirch, then D21bis towards Oltingue. It's in the hamlet of Huttingue.

The Ill flows a few steps from this large and lovely former mill. On the ground floor there is a welcoming rustic room where breakfast and excellent dinners are served. The bedrooms are comfortable and very attractive (the blue bedroom is especially charming). The hosts treat you with notable kindness.

11
La Maison Bleue

16, rue Saint-Nicolas
68240 Riquewihr
(Haut-Rhin)
Tel. 89 27 53 59
Fax 89 27 33 61
Francine and Clément Klur-Graff

Rooms 4 studios (2 pers.) and 3 apartments (4-5 pers.) with shower, WC and kitchenette. Rooms cleaned on request. **Price** 250F (2 pers.), 1800F per week (4 pers.); 3 nights min. **Meals** Breakfast 30F. No communal meal. **Facilities** Lounge; hiking, gastronomic weekend organized on reserv. **Nearby** Restaurants, village tour, wine and foie gras tasting, Wine Route, Haut-Koenigsbourg, Colmar, golf, swimming pool, tennis. **Credit cards** Visa, Eurocard and MasterCard. **Spoken** English, German. **Open** All year. **Postal address** 105, rue des Trois-Epis, 68230 - Katzenthal. **How to get there** (Map 12): In Riquewihr.

This pretty house stands in a very quiet small street in Riquewihr, a perfect Alsatian village. It has been comfortably furnished in marvelous taste, with cashmeres, pretty colors, and antique furniture. The studios and small apartments have kitchen areas and some have terraces. Every morning, a basket of fresh bread and croissants are left in front of your door. This is a rather individualistic arrangement, but the Maison Bleue is one of our outstanding addresses.

12
Chalet des Ayès

Chemin des Ayès
88160 Le Thillot
(Vosges)
Tel. 29 25 00 09
M. and Mme Marsot

Rooms 2 with bath or shower and WC, and 16 chalets (4-10 pers.). **Price** 340-420F (2 pers.), +80F (extra bed). **Meals** Breakfast 45F, evening meals on reservation, at separate tables, 98-128F (wine not incl.), or at auberge nearby. **Pets** Small dogs allowed on request. **Facilities** Swimming pool, tennis, cross-country skiing. **Nearby** Ski slopes, villages, mountain walks, Wine Route, Ecology Museum. **Credit cards** Not accepted. **Open** All year. **How to get there** (Map 20): 51km west of Mulhouse via N66 to Remiremont, then towards Mulhouse to Le Thillot. In front of "Intermarché" shop, turn left at 200m; follow signs.

This flower-covered mountainside chalet is almost on the border of the Vosges and Alsace. The two comfortable bedrooms are very cozy and elegant. One has a large bay window with a picture-postcard view of the valley. You will enjoy a very friendly welcome; the excellent breakfasts and dinners are served in a beautiful dining room decorated with antiques and family objects. And for those who succumb to the lure of this beautiful place, there is the possibility of renting one of the charming small chalets by the week.

13
Château de Regagnac

Montferrand-du-Périgord
24440 Beaumont
(Dordogne)
Tel. 53 63 27 02
M. and Mme Pardoux

Rooms 5 with bath or shower and WC. **Price** 600F (2 pers.). **Children** Under 13 not allowed. **Meals** Breakfast incl.; champagne dinner by candlelight on reservation 400F. **Facilities** Telephone, tennis, hunting, walks. **Nearby** Golf, equestrian center, Les Eyzies, Trémolat, Domme, Valley of the Dordogne, prehistoric sites. **Credit cards** Not accepted. **Spoken** English, Spanish. **Open** All year. **How to get there** (Map 23): 39km east of Bergerac via D660 to Beaumont, then D2 to Cadouin Regagnac.

The architecture of this old château is elegant and appealing. The bedrooms are very comfortable and all different. The ones in the main building are older, more attractive and bigger. Mme Pardoux is a marvellous cook and her dinners are served in a lovely room with a fireplace. The atmosphere is a bit theatrical but this is in keeping with the château. There is a hearty breakfast with homemade jams.

14
Domaine de la Sabatière

Route d'Agen
24100 Bergerac
(Dordogne)
Tel. 53 24 05 70
Fax 53 61 30 52
Gwenaelle and Bernard Duc

Rooms 7 with bath or shower, WC, telephone and TV. 1 child's room (4 beds) with bath. **Price** 240-260F (1 pers.), 270-290F (2 pers.), child's room 100F, +50F (extra pers.). **Meals** Breakfast 30F. Lunch and dinner at communal table (except Sun. eve and Mon), by reservation day before: 90-180F (wine not incl.). **Facilities** Lounge, swimming pool, 1 pony. **Pets** Dogs not allowed. **Nearby** Golf (18 holes, 20km), parachuting, canoeing, riding; Wine and Tobacco Routes, Circuit des Bastides. **Credit cards** Not accepted. **Spoken** English, Spanish. **Open** All year. **How to get there** (Map 23): 3km south of Bergerac via N21. Go 2km after sign "Sortie Bergerac," then follow signs.

The Domaine de la Sabatière is a charming family house where the hospitality is very friendly. The bedrooms are pleasant, and many are large and prettily decorated. The salons and dining room are warmly welcoming, with antique furniture and personal objects, and as for the communal dinner (sometimes served in the lovely private park), it can be a gourmet meal or quite simple. You have a choice.

15
Chez M. et Mme Trickett

La Rigeardie
24310 Bourdeilles
(Dordogne)
Tel. 53 03 78 90
Fax 53 04 56 95
M. and Mme Trickett

Rooms 4 with shower (2 shared WCs) and 1 suite of 2 bedrooms with shower. Rooms cleaned every 2-3 days. **Price** 160F (1 pers.), 220-240F (2 pers.) +40F (extra pers.), suite 420F (2 pers., + 2 children), family's room 300F. **Meals** Breakfast incl., group meals on request. **Facilities** Language courses (full-board). **Pets** Dogs allowed on request. **Nearby** Restaurants, golf, tennis, kayak, hiking. **Credit cards** Not accepted. **Spoken** English, German, Italian, Spanish. **Open** All year. **How to get there** (Map 23): 27km northwest of Périgueux via D939; at Brantôme take D78 to Bourdeilles, then southwest continue 4km in towards Ribérac.

A cottage gate opens into the pretty garden of this house, which stands on a small road in a hamlet, welcoming you with kindness and discretion. The bedrooms are comfortable and plainly furnished; each contains a charming old school desk and a comfortable bed. The rooms all have a view of the garden. Breakfast with excellent homemade jams is served at a long wooden table in a pretty dining room decorated with exposed stones and pale woodwork.

16
La Bernerie

24320 Bouteilles-Saint-Sébastien
(Dordogne)
Tel. 53 91 51 40
Fax 53 91 08 59
M. and Mme Carruthers

Rooms 2 with shower and WC. Rooms cleaned on request. **Price** 250F (2 pers.); 3 days min. **Meals** Breakfast 25F. **Restaurant** 200 meters away or L'Escalier at Verteillac. **Nearby** Golf, Romanesque churches, Brantôme, Bourdeilles, Saint-Jean-de-Côle. **Credit cards** Not accepted. **Spoken** English. **Closed** Nov. – March. **How to get there** (Map 23): about 50km south of Angoulême via D939; At La Rochebeaucourt take D708 southwest towards Ribérac. In Verteillac turn right before the square towards Bouteilles.

La Bernerie is on the edge of a tiny, well-preserved village which lies in the magnificent green Périgord. Mr and Mrs Carruthers, a friendly Scottish couple, have created two simple guestrooms in their old, (slightly over-restored) house. The bedrooms are light and pleasant and overlook the countryside. This is a lovely place to stay when the weather is good and you can enjoy exploring Brantôme, Bourdeilles, and the small villages and Romanesque churches of this splendid region.

17
Domaine des Farguettes
Paleyrac
24480 Le Buisson-de-Cadouin
(Dordogne)
Tel. and fax 53 23 48 23
Françoise and Claude de Torrenté

Rooms 1, and 2 suites (3-5 pers.) with bath and WC. **Price** 300F (2 pers.), suite 630F (5 pers.). **Meals** Breakfast incl. Half-board: 270F (per pers.). Lunch and dinner at communal or separate table: 120F. **Facilities** Lounge, telephone, swimming pool, bikes, pétanque, badminton. **Nearby** Canoeing (5km), tennis, riding, golf (9 holes, 8km); Les Eyzies, Lascaux, Vallée de la Dordogne, Circuit des Bastides. **Credit cards** Not accepted. **Spoken** English, Spanish, German. **Open** All year. **How to get there** (Map 23): 30km west of Sarlat via D 703 to Siorac, then towards Le Buisson. In 3km, turn left towards Paleyrac, then follow signs.

In a leafy setting with a beautiful woodland at the back stands the charming old Domaine des Farguettes, whose courteous and helpful owners keep it open winter and summer. The two double bedrooms with a large bathroom are ideal for a family, and all the rooms have modern amenities. Those who like quiet surroundings will find many a peaceful spot in the vast garden or the inviting salon. In summer, meals are served outside. The swimming pool is surrounded by trees and overlooks the countryside.

18
Domaine du Pinquet
Cussac
24480 Le Buisson-de-Cadouin
(Dordogne)
Tel. 53 22 97 07
Nicole and Yves Bouant

Rooms 4 and 1 suite (3-4 pers.) with bath or shower and WC. **Price** 320F (2 pers.), +100F (extra pers.); suite 520F. **Meals** Breakfast incl. Meals at communal or separate tables, regional specialties: 120F (wine incl.). Half board 280F (per pers. in double room). **Facilities** Lounge with fireplace and TV, swimming pool. **Pets** Dogs on leash allowed. **Nearby** Tennis, riding, golf, kayak, hiking; valleys of the Vézère and the Dordogne, châteaux, bastides. **Credit cards** Not accepted. **Spoken** English. **Open** All year. **How to get there** (Map 23): 32km east of Bergerac via D660 to Port-de-Couze, then D703 to Lalinde, then D29 for l0km to Cussac; follow signs.

A charming house full of character with carefully tended gardens, the Domaine is located in rolling, wooded countryside. The bedrooms are very comfortable and decorated in simple, pleasant taste. All have lovely modern baths which have been newly redone. Dinners are served in a large dining room with old stone walls and a handsome collection of modern paintings. In good weather, you dine outside. There is a lovely swimming pool.

19
La Bastide du Lion

Le Raysse
24370 Cazoulès
(Dordogne)
Tel. 53 29 84 41
Fax 53 29 17 27
M. and Mme Diemoz–Droyer

Rooms 6, and 1 suite (4-5 pers.) with bath (Royal room) or shower and WC. **Price** 300-600F (2-4 pers.). **Meals** Breakfast incl., meals at communal or separate tables: 65F, 95F; child's menu and picnic baskets on request. **Facilities** Lounge, telephone, swimming pool, basketball net, badminton, mountain bike route and hikes. **Pets** Dogs allowed on request. **Nearby** Tennis and fishing (1/2km), kayak, Vitrac Golf Course (15km); Vallée de la Dordogne, Abbaye de Souillac, Dôme, Rocamadour, Souillac Jazz Festival. **Credit cards** Not accepted. **Spoken** English, German. **Closed** Feb. **How to get there** (Map 23): 35km south of Brive via N20 towards Cahors. Then, in Souillac, at 2nd stop light turn right on D 723 for in 3km towards Cazoulès and follow signs.

This is a big, beautiful house whose gardens are somewhat old-fashioned. The stairway in the tower leads to the bedrooms, which are decorated simply and informally. The Royale room, with a terrace and small lounge, is immense, and the suite on the *deuxième étage* is convenient for families. The Bastide has a large lounge with TV and game tables, and in summer, meals are served outside. The young owners are friendly and hospitable.

20
Château de Laborie

24530 Champagnac-de-Belair
(Dordogne)
Tel. 53 54 22 99
Fax 53 08 53 78
M. and Mme Duseau

Rooms 5 with bath or shower and WC. **Price** 350-400F (2 pers.), +60F (extra pers.); suite 500F. **Meals** Breakfast 20-45F; special rates for long stays; communal dinner: 150F (wine not incl.). **Facilities** Lounge. **Pets** Dogs allowed on request. **Nearby** Restaurants, golf (18 holes, 18km), swimming pool, tennis courts (0.8km), canoeing/kayaks, riding (1.5km); Brantôme, Bourdeilles, Richemont, Mareuil, Villars (caves, châteaux...). **Credit cards** Not accepted. **Closed** Nov. 5 to April 5. **How to get there** (Map 23): 3km north of Brantôme towards Nontron. Before Brantôme exit, just before Avia gas station, follow "La route de chez Ravailles" northeast for 3.2km.

Well located in the country, the Château de Laborie is undergoing progressive restoration, whose magnificent results can already be seen in the bedrooms. They are large, tastefully decorated with antique 19th-century furniture, cheerful fabrics and wallpapers, old engravings and curios. The bathrooms are superb. In contrast, the other rooms, though majestically proportioned, seem old-fashioned. The owners are very natural and helpful.

21
La Commanderie

24570 Condat-sur-Vézère
(Dordogne)
Tel. 53 51 26 49
Fax 53 51 60 39
Mme Roux

Rooms 5 with bath or shower, WC, telephone, TV. **Price** 380F (1 pers.), 420-450F (2 pers.), +50F(extra pers., child). **Meals** Breakfast.:50F; Dinner at separate tables: 90F (wine not incl.). **Facilities** Lounge, swimming pool, tennis court, trout fishing in river and on trout farm on property. **Pets** Dogs allowed on request. **Nearby** Canoes, kayaks in village; châteaux, villages, Périgord caves, Lascaux (10km). **Credit cards** Not accepted. **Closed** July, Aug (Sept on reserv.). **How to get there** (Map 23): 25km north of Sarlat. At Le Lardin, on N 89 between Périgueux and Brive, take the road to Condat-sur-Vézère; house in village.

This beautiful *commanderie*--a residence of the Knights Templars--which dates in part from the 18th century, is in a stunning village that has many vestiges of the Templars. The immaculate private park is traversed by small canals which empty into the Vézère River bordering the property. The Commanderie is elegantly decorated inside, and the handsome stairways, vaulted ceilings, and wall recesses lend touches of character. The bedrooms are pleasant and bright, and are furnished with antiques. This is a lovely place to stay, with the atmosphere of an old family home.

22
Cazenac

24220 Le Coux-et-Bigaroque
(Dordogne)
Tel. 53 31 69 31
Fax 53 28 91 43
Philippe and Armelle Constant

Rooms 4 with bath, WC and telephone. **Price** 650F (2 pers.). **Meals** Breakfast 35F. Lunch and dinner at communal or separate tables: 200F (wine incl.). **Facilities** Lounge, swimming pool, tennis court, horse-drawn carriage, cooking lessons and other courses. **Pets** Dogs allowed on request. **Nearby** Golf courses (18 holes, 25km), eel fishing, hunting, riding, canoeing; Dordogne villages, châteaux, prehistoric sites. **Credit cards** Not accepted. **Spoken** English and Italian. **Open** All year. Rented only weekly in July, Aug. **How to get there** (Map 23): 25km west of Sarlat. From Périgueux, take N 89 towards Brive, then D110 towards Fumel. In Le Bugue, take D 51 south to Le Buisson, then Le Coux-et-Bigaroque. Sign before village on left.

Located on the crest of a hill overlooking the magnificent Dordogne countryside, the Château de Cazenac has just been carefully restored by a very friendly young couple. The interior decoration is truly exceptional. Styles and epochs are brought together beautifully and vividly, spotlighting handsome furniture, paintings and objects. At Cazenac, there are all the modern amenities, excellent food, and a number of interesting things to do.

23
La Daille

Florimont-Gaumiers
24250 Domme
(Dordogne)
Tel. 53 28 40 71
M. and Mme Derek
Vaughan Brown

Rooms 3 with bath, WC and terrace and 1 with shower and WC. **Price** 435F (half board per pers., wine incl.). 3 nights min. **Children** Under 7 not allowed. **Meals** Breakfast incl., restaurant in evening on reservation: 135-150F (1 menu, wine not incl.). **Pets** Dogs not allowed. **Nearby** Golf (9 holes), canoeing, Domme, Sarlat, L'Abbaye-Nouvelle. **Credit cards** Not accepted. **Open** May 1-Nov 2. **How to get there** (Map 23): 25km approx. south of Sarlat via D46 (Cenac/Saint-Martial). 3 km after Saint-Martial go right on D 52, then in 1.5km turn left, towards Gaumiers; after bridge go left, towards Péchembert and La Daille. **No smoking.**

Set in the midst of wild and rolling country, this former farm is surrounded by one of the most beautiful gardens imaginable. The comfortable bedrooms are very well decorated with English furniture. All have large bathrooms and private terraces overlooking the flowers and the hills. The necessity of taking half board is largely made up in the beautyiful small restaurant (with blue table linen, antiques and crystal glasses) with its excellent *cuisine*. This is a very welcoming place and very British.

24
Rouach

Rue Bertrand-de-Borne
24390 Hautefort
(Dordogne)
Tel. 53 50 41 59 (after 6:30 PM)
Mme Marie-Françoise Rouach

Rooms 2 with private bath, shared WC. 1 suite (4 pers.) with bath, WC and kitchen. **Prices** 350F (2 pers.), suite 500F. **Meals** Breakfast: 25F. No communal meal. **Restaurants** Auberge du Parc in Hautefort, Les Rocailles in Les Broussilloux and Les Tilleuls in Badfol d'Ans. **Facilities** Lounge. **Pets** Dogs not allowed. **Nearby** Swimming pool, lake, tennis courts in village; Château de Hautefort, Brantôme, Saint-Jean-de-Côle, Vallée de la Dordogne, concerts in July-Aug. **Credit cards** Not accepted. **Closed** Mid-Oct. – May 1. **How to get there** (Map 23): 50km northeast of Périgueux via N 89 towards Brives, then after Thenon, north on D 704. House in center of village.

Built on the flank of the magnificent village of Hautefort, this beautiful residence enjoys a breathtaking panorama over the countryside. The garden follows the configuration of the hill, with rare species of flowers cascading down the slope. Inside, Rouach is decorated with traditional old furniture and it has all the charm of a family home. The pretty bedrooms have modern amenities and immaculate bathrooms. Breakfasts are served on the terrace and the hospitality is both refined and very warm.

25
Le Petit Pey

Monmarvès
24560 Issigeac
(Dordogne)
Tel. 53 58 70 61
Mme Annie de Bosredon

Rooms 3 with shower and WC, and 3 single beds for teenagers in the dovecote. **Price** 250F (2 pers.), +50F (extra pers.). **Meals** Breakfast 30F. No communal meals. **Facilities** Lounge. **Pets** Dogs allowed (+15F). **Nearby** Golf (18km), sailing, fishing, riding. **Credit cards** Not accepted. **Spoken** English. **Open** Easter – end Oct. **How to get there** (Map 23): 2km south of Issigeac towards Castillonnès, then follow the signs.

This elegant 17th- and 18th-century house has 3 guest rooms. The most attractive and the "youngest" is all in pink and occupies the upper floor, under the eaves. The other two rooms share a bath on the same landing and are recommended for families. Outside, the old converted dovecot has 3 single beds and is suitable for teenagers. A lovely salon is available for guests. The beautiful park is a perfect place for a picnic. The welcome is lively and cordial.

26
Saint-Hubert

24520 Liorac-sur-Louyre
(Dordogne)
Tel. 53 63 07 92
Muriel and Patrice Hennion

Rooms 4 with bath or shower and WC. **Price** 240-290F (2 pers.). **Meals** Breakfast incl. Dinner at communal table: 90F (drinks incl.). **Facilities** Lounge, swimming pool and hiking in forest on property. **Pets** Small dogs only allowed. **Nearby** Golf (9 holes, 5km), riding, tennis; Périgord châteaux, old villages and bastides, Bergerac vineyards. **Credit cards** Not accepted. **Spoken** English. **Open** All year. **How to get there** (Map 23): 14km northeast of Bergerac. In Bergerac, take D 32 towards Sainte-Alvère; 14km on right, 0.8km before Liorac.

You are in the heart of the countryside here, where the immense paths of the forest converge on the private park of this beautiful residence. We were immediately captivated by the charm and friendliness we found at the Saint-Hubert. Inside, there is the refinement of a gentleman-farmer's house, with equestrian lithographs, antique furniture and handsome, deep sofas. The bedrooms are pleasant and comfortable. The communal evening meal is good and the atmosphere is friendly. You should phone your arrival time as the property is guarded by dogs.

27
Le Prieuré

Meyrals-le-Bourg
24220 Meyrals
(Dordogne)
Tel. 53 28 56 60
Mme Eliane Vielle

Rooms 1 with shower and WC, and 1 studio (5 pers.) with shower, WC and kitchen. **Price** 260F (2 pers.), studio 350F (2 pers.), +95F (extra pers.). 2 days min. **Meals** Breakfast incl. Dinner at communal table: 120F (wine incl.). **Facilities** Lounge. **Pets** Dogs not allowed. **Nearby** Free municipal tennis courts (in front), riding in village, hiking paths, boat rides on the Dordogne, Périgord Noir sites. **Credit cards** Not accepted. **Spoken** English and Dutch. **Open** All year, winter on request. **How to get there** (Map 23): 15km west of Sarlat. In Périgueux, go southeast towards Les Eyzies, then take D 20/D 35; before Saint-Cyprien, left towards Meyrals.

The Prieuré is built in the authentic Périgord style of the 16th century, which has been fully respected in interior restoration. The floors are made of bright local stone or of wide boards, and the handsome doors are antique. The pleasant bedrooms are very tastefully decorated and modern amenities have not been forgotten. A delicious evening meal is served around a communal dining table near the old fireplace or on the covered terrace, and the hosts are very welcoming.

28
La Rouquette

24240 Monbazillac
(Dordogne)
Tel. 53 58 30 60/53 58 30 44
M. Eric de Madaillan

Rooms 5 with bath and WC. **Price** 240-300F (2 pers.), +50F (extra pers.). **Meals** Breakfast incl. No communal meals. **Restaurants** Le Château de Monbazillac in the village; in Malfourat (2km) La Tour des Vents and Le Périgord. **Nearby** Tennis, swimming pool, golf (9-hole, 7km), vineyards and château of Monbazillac. **Credit cards** Not accepted. **Spoken** English. **Open** All year (by reservation in winter for the 2 heated rooms). **How to get there** (Map 23): 7km south of Bergerac via D13; 150m from the church at Monbazillac on D14E, take the small road on the right; La Rouquette is 200m further on.

La Rouquette is an elegant 17th-century country house overlooking vineyards and the plain of Bergerac. You will be received with great kindness. The bedrooms are quiet and comfortable and have good views. The largest is beautifully decorated and has a private balcony. The smallest is just as charming, with Venetian painted wood furniture. Breakfast is served in a big room on the ground floor.

29
Fonroque

24230 Montcaret
(Dordogne)
Tel. 53 58 65 83
Brigitte Fried

Rooms 5 with bath or shower and WC. Rooms cleaned twice weekly. **Price** 260F (1 pers.), 300F (2 pers.), 400F (3 pers.); children under 2 free. Child under 12 in parents' room: 1/2 price. **Meals** Breakfast incl. Dinner at communal table: 100F. Half-board 344F (1 pers.), 468F (2 pers.).-20% for 2 days and more from Oct. 1 to April 30. **Facilities** Lounge. **Pets** Dogs allowed on request. **Nearby** Golf (18 holes, 15km), tennis (1km); Tour de Montaigne (3km); Gallo-Roman excavations 1km; Bergerac and Saint Emilion vineyards; Romanesque churches circuit. **Credit cards** Not accepted. **Open** All year. **How to get there** (Map 22): 8km east of Castillon-la-Bataille, on D 936 between Bergerac and Libourne; in Montcaret-Tête-Noire, go to the Gallo-Roman ruins, then follow signs for Fonroque.

We very much enjoyed Brigitte Fried's hospitality at her small winegrowing estate. The bedrooms are very pleasant, with charmingly painted walls, curtains in soft, bright colors, and some antique furniture. There is a beautiful bathroom in each bedroom. The communal evening meal features family recipes and is served in a lovely dining room. Outside, the private park is lush with foliage, and it includes a ravishing swimming pool in the former greenhouse.

30
Le Bastit

Saint-Médard-de-Mussidan
24400 Mussidan
(Dordogne)
Tel. 53 81 32 33
M. and Mme Zuidema

Rooms 5 with bath and WC. **Price** 245-260F (1 pers.), 285-300F (2 pers.). **Meals** Breakfast incl. No communal meals. **Facilities** Lounge, swimming pool, fishing. **Pets** Dogs not allowed. **Nearby** Restaurants, Wine Route, châteaux, prehistoric sites, walled towns, golf (18-hole, 35km), riding (6km), canoeing, kayaking. **Credit cards** Not accepted. **Spoken** English. **Open** Easter – All Saints (by reservation in winter). **How to get there** (Map 23): On the N89 coming from Bordeaux, turn left towards Saint-Médard just before entering Mussidan; phone for directions. Behind the church on the banks of the Isle.

We loved this opulent house standing on the banks of the river. The bedrooms are very comfortable, with pretty English fabrics and some antique furniture. You will be welcomed as friends. Excellent breakfasts are served in an elegant dining room or outside in the flowery garden. This is a very special place to stay between Périgord and the vineyards of Bordeaux.

31
Le Moulin Neuf

Paunat
24510 Sainte-Alvère
(Dordogne)
Tel. 53 63 30 18
Fax (idem)
Robert Chappell and Stuart Shippey

Rooms 6 with bath or shower and WC. **Price** 250F (2 pers.), +50F (extra pers.). **Meals** Breakfast 35-50F. No communal meals. **Facilities** Lounge; fishing in river and swimming in lake on property. **Pets** Dogs allowed. **Nearby** Restaurants, canoes, kayaks (4km), yacht basin (5km), tennis (7km); the Périgord Noir (caves, châteaux, Limeuil, Trémolat, La Rocque Gageac, Bénac, Château des Mirlandes. **Credit cards** Not accepted. **Spoken** English, German. **Open** All year. **How to get there** (Map 23): 8km southwest of Le Bugue via D703, towards Sainte-Alvère, then D 31 towards Limeuil. After the Cingle de Limeuil, on D 31, go downhill, then D2, towards Sainte-Alvère, 2km down on left.

L e Moulin Neuf is actually two houses of bright golden stone surrounded by a park filled with flowers and murmuring streams that tumble into the lakes. Inside, you will find small, comfortable and immaculately kept bedrooms decorated in light colors, with equally pleasant bathrooms. There is a comfortable guest lounge with old English furniture, deep sofas and bright white curtains. Excellent breakfasts are very courteously served here. The "New Mill" is irresistible.

32
Doumarias

24800 Saint-Pierre-de-Côle
(Dordogne)
Tel. 53 62 34 37
Fax (idem)
François and Anita Fargeot

Rooms 6 with bath or shower and WC. Rooms cleaned on request. **Price** 270F (2 pers.) +40F (extra pers.). **Children** under 10 not accepted. **Meals** Breakfast 20F, half board 440F per day (2 pers. in double room, 4 days min.), evening meal at communal table 80F (wine incl.). **Facilities** Swimming pool, fishing in the river. **Pets** Dogs not allowed. **Nearby** Tennis, riding, golf, caves and château at Villars, Brantôme. **Credit cards** Not accepted. **Open** April – mid-Oct. **How to get there** (Map 23): 12km southeast of Brantôme via D78 towards Thiviers; 1.5km after Saint-Pierre-de-Côle.

D oumarias stands beneath an old ruined château not far from the lovely village of Saint-Jean-de-Côle. The bedrooms are charming, with beautiful antique furniture, curios and small paintings. They are comfortable and quiet. Breakfast and dinner are served in a pretty dining room overlooking the garden and the cuisine is excellent. You will receive a very friendly welcome.

33
Château de Puymartin

24200 Sarlat-la-Canéda
(Dordogne)
Tel. 53 59 29 97
Fax 53 29 87 52
Comte and Comtesse
Henri de Montbron

Rooms 2 with bath and WC. **Price** 750F (2 pers.) +150F (child, bed and breakfast). **Meals** Breakfast incl. No communal meals. **Restaurants** La Métairie (4 km) or in Sarlat and in Eyzies (8 km). **Facilities** Lounge, private tours of the château. **Pets** Dogs allowed on request. **Nearby** Swimming pool, tennis, riding. **Credit cards** Not accepted. **Open** April – Nov 1 (by reservation for winter weekends). **How to get there** (Map 23): About 60km southeast of Périgueux via D710 to Le Bugue, then D706 to Les Eyzies and D47 towards Sarlat: it's on the D47 before Sarlat.

The evocative, crenellated silhouette of the Château de Puymartin looms over a landscape of hills and forests. The welcome is simple and kind. One of the bedrooms is furnished in medieval style and has two splendid canopied beds. The other is arranged like a lounge with a collection of mostly Louis XVI marquetry furniture. Both rooms are very large and comfortable and contain some charming objects.

34
Le Chaufourg-en-Périgord

24400 Sourzac-Mussidan
(Dordogne)
Tel. 53 81 01 56
Fax 53 82 94 87
M. Georges Dambier

Rooms 7 and 2 suites (with minibar) with bath or shower, WC, telephone and TV. **Price** 700-1050F (2 pers.); suite 1300F (2 pers.), 150 F (extra pers.). **Meals** Breakfast 65F; other meals by reservation and if possible, in evening (separate tables) from 250F. **Facilities** Lounge, piano, billiards, swimming pool, fishing in river, boat rides on the property. **Pets** Dogs allowed on request. **Nearby** Restaurants, golf courses (18 holes); tennis, horseback riding, main sites of Périgord. **Credit cards** Not accepted. **Spoken** English. **Open** All year in winter by reservation. **How to get there** (Map 23): N 89, Bordeaux-Lyon-Geneva road. 3km after Mussidan SNCF station.

This is one of our most splendid addresses. Georges Dambier has restored his family home with unique taste and demanding standards of comfort . The reception rooms and bedrooms are decorated with beautiful antique furniture, personal objects and bright ivory fabrics. There is an immaculate garden overhanging the Isle River where guests can take a relaxing boat trip. Le Chaufourg has the charm one finds in an elegant house, coupled with gracious, almost professional service.

35
Manoir Pouyols

24140 Villamblard
(Gironde)
Tel. 53 81 92 92
M. and Mme du Puch

Rooms 2 with bath and WC, and 3 spare bedrooms. **Price** 550F (2 pers.); 400F (1 pers.), 450F (2 pers.). **Meals** Breakfast incl. No communal meals. **Restaurants** De la Place and La Devinière, 10km. **Facilities** Lounge, swimming pool for children, visit to Les Cluzeaux, hot-air balloon on property, and 3-day foie gras cooking lessons in Feb. **Pets** Dogs allowed on request. **Nearby** Villages, bastides and châteaux of Périgord; golf (18 holes), and all sports. **Credit cards** Not accepted. **Spoken** English. **Closed** Dec., Jan. **How to get there** (Map 23): East of Mussidan via D38, towards Villamblard, then left on D4; follow sign.

This ancient manor house overlooks a splendid panorama which you can enjoy from the vast flagstone terrace. Madame du Puch will welcome you like a member of the family. The interior decoration of the Manoir de Pouyols combines styles, colors and objects from her travels. The two bedrooms and their baths are truly immense. This is a very pleasant place to stay and you shouldn't leave without first visiting the ancient underground apartments called the *Cluzeaux*.

36
Château d'Arbieu

33430 Bazas
(Gironde)
Tel. 56 25 11 18
Fax 56 25 90 52
Comte and Comtesse
Philippe de Chénerilles

Rooms 4 and 1 suite (4 pers.) with bath or shower, WC and telephone. **Price** 400F (2 pers.); suite 430F (1 pers.), 455F (2 pers.), +80F (extra pers.) Special rates for long stays on request. **Meals** Breakfast incl., evening meal at communal table, by reservation 150F (wine incl.). **Facilities** Lounge, swimming pool. **Credit cards** Amex, Visa, Eurocard and MasterCard. **Spoken** English, German. **Closed** Dec 15 – Jan 15. **How to get there** (Map 29): 60km southeast of Bordeaux via A62, Langon exit, then D932 to Bazas, then take D 655, towards Casteljaloux.

Set in a quiet park overlooking the Bazas countryside, the Château d'Arbieu belongs to a very hospitable family. Its bedrooms are very large and beautifully decorated, notably with lovely traditional furniture, antiques, old objects, paintings and engravings. All but two bathrooms have excellent modern amenities. The salons are ravishing and the lovely dining room beckons with delicious dinners where guests are made to feel at home.

37
Pigou

4, bois de Pigou
Cartelègue
33390 Blaye
(Gironde)
Tel. 57 64 60 68
M. and Mme Heinz Krause

Rooms 1 with shower, WC and TV. **Price** 190F (1 pers.), 250F (2 pers.), 300F (3 pers.). **Meals** Breakfast incl., evening meal at communal table by request 90F (wine incl.). **Facilities** Lounge. **Pets** Dogs allowed on request. **Nearby** Fishing, hiking, riding, tennis, châteaux of Medoc, Blaye, Saint-Emilion. **Credit cards** Not accepted. **Spoken** English, German. **Open** May 1 – Nov 1. **How to get there** (Map 22): About 30 km north of Bordeaux via A10 to Blaye exit, then N137 northwest; it's 1km from N137: opposite D134 E1.

N estling in a pine grove, this one-story house consists of two buildings. The smaller one is reserved for guests and has a spacious bedroom with 2 comfortable beds, pretty green lacquered furniture and a large library. Adjoining it is a bathroom and a terrace where breakfast is served. Pigou is very pleasant, quiet and welcoming.

38
La Monceau

33650 La Brède
(Gironde)
Tel. 56 20 24 76
Fax 56 78 45 43
M. and Mme Baseden

Rooms 2 with bath and WC. No smoking rooms available. **Price** 650F (2 pers.), +150F (extra pers.). **Meals** Breakfast incl. No communal meal. **Facilities** Lounge, swimming pool. **Pets** Dogs not allowed. **Nearby** Restaurants, golf (27 holes, 12km); riding center (500m); Bassin d'Arcachon, Château de la Brède, Graves vineyards. **Credit cards** Not accepted. **Spoken** English, Spanish. **Closed** Aug. **How to get there** (Map 22): 18km south of Bordeaux, via Toulouse autoroute, exit 1 La Brède. In La Brède, take D 220 towards Saint-Morillon for 800m, then follow sign on Chemin de Beney.

T his old winegrowers' house has just been magnificently renovated and the decor down to the tiniest detail could be featured in an interior-decoration magazine. The overall effect is one of bright colors, very sophisticated design and comfortable accommodations. The bedrooms are equally lovely, and although the bathrooms could be bigger, they are nevertheless charming. The breakfasts are as outstanding as La Monceau itself.

39
Château du Foulon

Le Foulon
33480 Castelnau-de-Médoc
(Gironde)
Tel. 56 58 20 18 Fax 56 58 23 43
Vicomte and Vicomtesse
Jean de Baritault du Carpia

Rooms 3, 1 studio (2-3 pers.) and 1 studio (4 pers.) with bath and WC. **Price** 350F (1 pers.), 400F (2 pers.); suite or studio 500F (2 pers.) +150F (extra pers.). **Meals** Breakfast incl. No communal meal. **Restaurants** Le Savoye in Margaux, Le Lion d'Or in Arcins. **Facilities** Lounge, tennis, equestrian center. **Pets** Dogs not allowed. **Nearby** Golf (36-hole), châteaux of Médoc. **Credit cards** Not accepted. **Spoken** English. **Open** All year. **How to get there** (Map 22): 28km northwest of Bordeaux via D1.

Some distance out of the village, the Château du Foulon, built in 1840, is a small paradise where you will feel completely at ease. The comfortable bedrooms are handsomely decorated with beautiful antique furniture, and all have views of the park. A studio and a suite for long stays have been added. Before setting out for the great Médoc vineyards, you will enjoy a delicious breakfast served in a lovely dining room. This is a welcoming, especially elegant place to stay.

40
Domaine de Carrat

Route de Sainte-Hélène
33480 Castelnau-de-Médoc
(Gironde)
Tel. 56 58 24 80
M. and Mme Péry

Rooms 3 with bath and WC. **Price** 220F (1 pers.), 250-300F (2 pers.), suite 450F (4 pers.). **Meals** Breakfast incl. No communal meal. **Facilities** Lounge, equestrian center and swimming in the stream (safe for children). **Pets** Dogs allowed on request. **Nearby** Restaurants, tennis, golf (18 holes), horseback riding, lakes, châteaux of Médoc. **Credit cards** Not accepted. **Spoken** English, German. **Open** All year. **How to get there** (Map 22): 28km northwest of Bordeaux via D1; at the 2nd set of traffic lights in Castelnau, head southwest towards Sainte-Hélène on D 5; turn right 200m after leaving Castelnau.

You will find this lovely house in a park in the midst of a forest. M. and Mme Péry have tastefully transformed the spacious old stables into comfortable guest rooms with family furniture; some can be made into suites, and all look out on the peaceful countryside. (In summer, the ground-floor room is the loveliest.) Good breakfasts are served in the attractive dining room, and the people are very friendly.

41
Cabirol

33430 Gajac-de-Bazas
(Gironde)
Tel. 56 25 15 29
M. and Mme Dionis du Séjour

Rooms 2 and 1 suite (4 pers.) with bath, shower and WC; 1 with shower and WC. **Price** 210-230F (1 pers.), 230-250F (2 pers.), 400F (4 pers.). **Meals** Breakfast incl. No communal meals. **Facilities** Lounge, American billiards, visit to farm (geese, ducks, cows). **Pets** Dogs not allowed. **Nearby** Restaurants, boats, fishing and bird observatory (500m); swimming pool, tennis, riding (4km); lakes; Old Bazas, vineyards. **Credit cards** Not accepted. **Spoken** English. **Open** All year. Winter on reservation only. **How to get there** (Map 29): 4km northeast of Bazas on D9. Follow signs.

Y ou will be received very graciously in this beautiful house, one part is entirely reserved for guests. There you will find pleasant, very comfortable bedrooms, brightened with pretty fabrics; their bathrooms are lovely. On the ground floor, there are a small salon-library and large dining table where delicious breakfasts are served; in summer, they are served outside where you can gaze at the peaceful countryside.

42
Domaine de Guillaumat

33420 Genissac
(Gironde)
Tel. 57 24 49 14 or 57 51 18 99
M. and Mme Fulchi

Rooms 2 with bath or shower, and WC. **Price** 250-300F (2 pers.). **Meals** Breakfast incl. No communal meal. **Restaurants** In Saint-Emilion and in Libourne. **Facilities** Swimming pool and horseback riding on property. **Nearby** Golf (18 holes, 30km), tennis (1km); vineyards, Romanesque churches, Saint-Emilion, Libourne. **Credit cards** Not accepted. **Spoken** English, Spanish. **Open** All year. **How to get there** (Map 22): 10km southwest of Libourne. From N89, east of Bordeaux, take exit Arveyres, then go towards Cadarsac. 50m before sign for village, exit, go straight ahead, then left; then follow sign 100m on right.

L ocated on an estate overlooking the vineyards of Entre-Deux-Mers, the Domaine de Guillaumat houses guests in an inviting small house which is reserved for them. The bedrooms are on the ground floor and seem like real country guest-rooms with their bright white walls, warm terra cotta floors, antique furniture and comfortable beds. Exposed due east, the rooms are flooded with the morning sun, and there is a pleasant bathroom in each. Breakfasts are served in your room or in the pretty garden.

43
La Petite Glaive

33620 Lapouyade
(Gironde)
Tel. 57 49 42 09
Fax 57 49 40 93
Mme Christiane Bonnet

Rooms 2 with bath or shower and WC. Rooms cleaned on request. **Price** 220F (2 pers.) +50-80F (extra pers.). **Meals** Breakfast incl., lunch and evening meals 90F (wine incl.). **Facilities** Lounge. **Pets** Dogs not allowed. **Nearby** Golf, Bordeaux, Saint-Emilion, Wine Route. **Credit cards** Not accepted. **Closed** 1st week Sept. **How to get there** (Map 22): 27km north of Libourne via D910. In Guîtres take D247 west through Bayas; follow signs before Lapouyade.

This farmhouse auberge is located on the fringes of an oak and pine forest. The bedrooms are simple, pleasant and quiet; two rooms have a ground-floor terrace. From the pleasant lounge-library you look out ththrough open-worked timber looks onto a small garden where dinner is served in the summer. The hospitable Christiane Bonnet uses only home-grown farm produce in her cuisine. La Petite Glaive is a lovely country place to stay in good weather.

44
Château de la Bûche

10, avenue de la Porte-des-Tours
33580 Monségur
(Gironde)
Tel. 56 61 80 22
Dominique and Evelyne Ledru

Rooms 4 and 1 suite (4-5 pers.) with shower and WC. **Price** 210F (1 pers.), 270F (2 pers.); suite 330F (3 pers.), +60F (extra pers.). **Meals** Breakfast incl. Communal meal in evening on request 90F (wine incl.). **Facilities** Lounge, piano, parking lot, fishing, park, pétanque on property. **Pets** Housebroken dogs on leash allowed. **Nearby** Golf (18 holes, 35km), swimming pool, tennis, riding, mountain bike rental; bastides, abbeys of Gironde, Route des Moulins du Drot, Château de Duras, vineyards. **Credit cards** Not accepted. **Spoken** English. **Closed** Mid-Dec. – March 1. **How to get there** (Map 22): 45km southeast of Libourne, via D 670. In Sauveterre-de-Guyenne, go left towards Monségur; in La Halle, towards Duras, then turn left in 300m.

The small Château de la Bûche is surrounded by lush foliage on the edge of a tiny village. Guests are greeted graciously and they are comfortably housed in the left wing of the château. The rooms, which have recently been redone, are simply furnished, and good traditional family cuisine is served in the family dining room. This is a good choice for fishing enthusiasts, families or hikers.

45
La Bergerie

Les Trias
33920 Saint-Cristoly-de-Blaye
(Gironde)
Tel. 57 42 50 80
M. and Mme de Poncheville

Rooms 2 houses for 2-6 pers. with lounge, kitchen, bathroom and WC. **Price** 400F (2 pers.) +150F (extra pers.); rooms cleaned periodically. **Meals** Breakfast incl. No communal meals. **Facilities** Lounge, swimming pool, riding on request, boating on the lake. **Pets** Dogs allowed on request **Nearby** Restaurants, wine route, Saint-Emilion (35km), châteaux and places of historic interest, golf, tennis (3km). **Credit cards** Not accepted. **Open** All year. **How to get there** (Map 22): 11km southeast of Blaye via D22 towards Saint-Cristoly-de-Blaye, then Saint-Urbain; follow signs to Les Trias; on left, follow signs.

In the countryside near Blaye with a lovely park and small lake, La Bergerie is made up of three well renovated old houses. Each has a sitting room with fireplace, a kitchen and one or three bedrooms. The handsome terra cotta floors, beautiful antique furniture and elegant fabrics all create a lovely ensemble. You will be offered several breakfast menus. The owners are charming people.

46
Château du Parc

Le Parc
33580 Saint-Ferme
(Gironde)
Tel. 56 61 69 18
Fax 56 61 69 23
M. and Mme Lalande

Rooms 5 and 1 suites (3 pers.) with bath and WC (tel. and TV on request). **Price** 450-560F; suite 800F (3 pers.). **Meals** Breakfasts 40F. Half-board 425-550F (per pers., 3 days min.). Weekend package price 1700-2350F. Communal meal noon and evening in summer 200F (wine incl.). **Facilities** Lounge, billiards, park, poss. bike rentals, swimming pool. **Pets** Dogs allowed on request. **Nearby** Golf (18 holes, 30 min.), tennis, lake; Circuit des Abbayes, vineyards, Saint-Emilion (30 min.), Château de Duras. **Credit cards** Not accepted. **Spoken** English. **Open** All year. **How to get there** (Map 22): 30km southeast of Libourne. Take D670 for 18km, towards Sauveterre; go about 12km more. It's 500m before Saint-Ferme on left.

Surrounded by hillsides covered with vineyards, this traditional Aquitaine château has just been entirely refurbished by its young owners. We were immediately charmed by the spaciousness and beautiful materials used. In the large bedrooms, the furniture and linens have been tastefully chosen. English-style breakfasts are served in the handsome kitchen which opens wide onto the garden. Simple, discreet refinement are the key words here.

47
Manoir de James

33580 Saint-Ferme
(Gironde)
Tel. 56 61 69 75
M. and Mme Dubois

Rooms 3 with bath and WC. Price 230F (1 pers.), 280F (2 pers.), +50F (extra child), +70F (extra pers.). **Meals** Breakfast incl. No communal meal. **Facilities** Lounge, garage on property; swimming pool, ping pong, bike rentals. **Pets** Dogs allowed on request. **Nearby** Restaurants, golf (18 holes, 35km), riding, mountain bikes, lakeside sports, fishing in river; Abbaye de Saint-Ferme, Romanesque churches. **Credit cards** Not accepted. **Spoken** English, German, Spanish. **Closed** Mid-Dec – mid-Jan. **How to get there** (Map 22): From Libourne, take D670 to Sauveterre, then 2km farther follow signs to Saint-Ferme, then go towards Sainte-Colombe; the Manoir is 2km on left.

You will be courteously welcomed to this small manor house located on a hillside among the Entre-Deux-Mers vineyards. The large, quiet bedrooms are furnished with antiques. In summer, the English-style breakfast is served early around the swimming pool. Madame Dubois will be happy to tell you about the many attractions of this beautiful region near Bordeaux.

48
Château de Gourdet

33620 Saint-Mariens
(Gironde)
Tel. 57 58 99 33/57 58 05 37
Yvonne and Daniel Chartier

Rooms 1 with shower and WC, 3 with private hall bathroom and 4 communal WCs. **Price** 155-180F (1 pers.), 180-240F (2 pers.), +75F (extra pers.). **Meals** Breakfast incl., evening meals at communal table (by reservation in summer) 80F (wine incl.). **Facilities** Lounge, riding in summer. **Nearby** Restaurants, walks, rides, citadels of Blaye and Bourg, Saint-Emilion, Bordeaux, Médoc via the Blaye Ferry. **Credit cards** Not accepted. **Spoken** English. **Open** All year. **How to get there** (Map 22): 31km north of Bordeaux via A10, Saint-André-de-Cubzac exit, then N10 approx. 12km towards Montlieu, then D18 northwest towards Saint-Savin. From Paris, via Autoroute 10, exit 28 Blaye. Follow itinerary "Bis" to Saint-Mariens.

This quiet mansion just outside a small village is friendly and relaxed. The *premier étage* bedrooms are large and light, and simply but comfortably furnished. Each has its own bathroom outside the room. There are good evening meals with regional specialties, accompanied by a bottle of Côte de Blaye. The Château is particularly suitable for a family.

49
Gaudart

33910 Saint-Martin-de-Laye
(Gironde)
Tel. 57 49 41 37
M. and Mme Garret

Rooms 3 with bath or shower and WC, independent entrances. **Price** 170-230F (2 pers.). **Meals** Breakfast incl., evening meals by reservation (except Aug) 80F (wine incl.). **Facilities** Lounge, terrace. **Pets** No dogs allowed. **Nearby** Swimming pool, golf (18 holes), Saint-Emilion, abbey at Guîtres, vineyards. **Credit cards** Not accepted. **Closed** End-April – beg-Oct. **How to get there** (Map 22): 9km north of Libourne via D910. In Saint-Denis-de-Pile, left on D22 for 5km, then follow signs for 1km.

A few minutes from the great vineyards of Saint-Emilion, this typical Gironde house is nevertheless set in quiet pastureland. The vast living room, where breakfast and dinner are served, has its original old regional furniture. The bedrooms are quite large and the beds are comfortable. Two have very charming bathrooms. We preferred the one with the *curtained bed*, which is very well furnished. You will receive a very kind welcome.

50
Château Lamothe

33450 Saint-Sulpice-et-Cameyrac
(Gironde)
Tel. 56 30 82 16
Fax 56 30 88 33
Luce and Jacques Bastide

Rooms 2 and 1 suite (2-4 pers.) with TV, bath and WC. No smoking rooms available. **Price** 700-800F (2 pers.), +100F (extra pers.); suite 950F (2 pers.). **Meals** Breakfast incl. No communal meal. **Facilities** Lounge, swimming pool, fishing in moats, boat on property. **Nearby** Restaurants, golf (18 holes, 2km), Bordeaux vineyards, villages of Saint-Emilion, circuit des Abbayes. **Credit cards** Not accepted. **Spoken** English, Spanish. **Open** Easter – Nov 1. **How to get there** (Map 22): 18km east of Bordeaux via N89; exit 5 (Beychac, Cameyrac, Saint-Sulpice), then D13 to Saint-Sulpice. Road to stadium on right as you enter village. Follow signs.

The very old, beautifully restored Château Lamothe is totally surrounded by water. It has superb bedrooms with all the modern amenities, including stunningly beautiful bathrooms. All the rooms are vast, bright and decorated in the same tasteful spirit, with some traditional old furniture, white drapes, pictures of luxuriant landscapes, pretty *faïences* and the family's handsome decorative objects. Delicious breakfasts are served in the beautiful dining room. The owners are helpful and graciously hospitable.

51
Domaine du Ciron

Brouquet
33210 Sauternes
(Gironde)
Tel. 56 76 60 17
Fax 56 76 61 74
M. and Mme Peringuey

Rooms 3 with bath or shower and WC. **Price** 220F (2 pers.) +70F (extra pers.). **Children** under 7 not accepted. **Meals** Breakfast incl. No communal meal. **Restaurants** Auberge des Vignes and Le Saprien in Sauternes. **Facilities** Swimming pool. **Pets** Dogs not allowed. **Nearby** Tennis, golf (18 holes), riding (8km), canoeing (8km), Sauternes Wine Route, châteaux. **Credit cards** Not accepted. **Spoken** English. **Open** All year. **How to get there** (Map 22): 11km west of Langon. Take A62, then D8 in the direction of Villandraut. For 1km after the Sauternes crossroads; at Brousquet turn right by the water tower; follow signs.

Monsieur and Madame Peringuey are winegrowers, as you would expect in famous Sauternes. They are very welcoming and will give you good advice on the regional riches to be discovered. The three bedrooms are very simple but adequately comfortable. The view of the vineyards is everywhere and there is an inviting swimming pool in the garden. Breakfast is served beside it in a pretty dining room.

52
Le Barbé

Place de l'Eglise
40390 Biaudos
(Landes)
Tel. 59 56 73 37
Fax 59 56 75 84
M. and Mme Iriart

Rooms 4 with private shower and WC. Rooms cleaned on request. **Price** 140-150F (1 pers.), 155-195F (2 pers.), +60F (extra pers.). **Meals** Breakfast incl. No communal meal. Use of equipped kitchen. **Restaurant** Chez Pétiole in Saint-Martin-de-Seignanx and small auberges nearby. **Facilities** Lounge, swimming pool. Touristic and restaurant advice given. **Pets** Small dogs allowed. **Nearby** Golf, Adour Valley, walled towns, abbeys, Basque festivals, Basque and Landes Coasts. **Credit cards** Not accepted. **Open** April 1– Nov 11. **How to get there** (Map 28): 16km northeast of Bayonne via N117.

Monsieur and Mme Iriart take great pleasure in welcoming and looking after their guests. In the garden of this large village house they have installed a swimming pool surrounded with small tables where breakfast and dinner are served in good weather. The bedrooms are large, very light, and often decorated with souvenirs of their journeys. Le Barbé is very charming from every point of view.

53
Lamolère

40090 Campet-Lamolère
(Landes)
Tel. 58 06 04 98h
Philippe and Béatrice de Monredon

Rooms 1 with bath and WC, 2 with bath and shared WC. Rooms cleaned every three days or on request. **Price** 160-200F (2 pers.). **Meals** Breakfast incl., evening meal at communal table 75F. **Facilities** Lounge, 12th-century chapel, horse stalls, fishing, bicycles. **Pets** Dogs allowed in the kennel on request. **Nearby** Golf, swimming pool (4km). **Credit cards** Not accepted. **Spoken** English, Spanish. **Open** All year. **How to get there** (Map 29): 5km northwest of Mont-de-Marsan via D38; on the Morcenx road.

A large mansion set in an 18-acre park, Lamolère has bedrooms which combine beauty and modern comfort. Most of the beds are very wide, the colors are tastefully coordinated and there are many charming decorative details. You will find some handsome pieces of antique furniture. The excellent evening meals are usually served outside on a large terrace. You will enjoy beautiful views, a warm welcome and very reasonable prices for the quality.

54
Estounotte

Quartier Naboude
40170 Levignacq
(Landes)
Tel. 58 42 75 97
Mme Lalanne

Rooms 1 with private bathroom, 3 with private shower (2 shared WC). **Price** 240-285F (2 pers.) depending on season, babies up to 2 years +35F extra. **Meals** Breakfast incl. Evening meals at communal table, by reservation (except for one night a week) 90F (wine incl.). **Facilities** Lounge, bicycles. **Pets** Dogs allowed on request (+50F week). **Nearby** Riding, seaside, boat trips, Levignacq church. **Credit cards** Not accepted. **Spoken** Spanish. **Open** All year (by reservation). **How to get there** (Map 29): 30km north of Dax. Leave N10 at Castets, exit 13, and head for Levignacq; follow signs.

N estling among pine trees, this lovely country mansion has been completely redone. Good dinners are served at the large table in the modern, "rustic style" dining room. The decor in the bright, quiet bedrooms is in the same idiom. You will receive a pleasant welcome.

55
La Marie Clairière

Les Bas Lugadets
40170 Lit-et-Mixe
(Landes)
Tel. 58 42 77 24
M. and Mme Utz

Rooms 5 with private shower and communal WCs. **Price** 230F (1 pers.), 250F (2 pers.), +50F (extra children under 6 year), +70F (extra pers.). **Meals** Breakfast incl. No communal meal. **Facilities** Lounges, outdoor games for children, pétanque. **Pets** Dogs allowed on request. **Nearby** Moliets golf course (40km); riding, tennis, canoes, kayaks, ocean (10km), fishing in river and lake (10km). **Credit cards** Not accepted. **Spoken** English, German, Spanish. **Open** All year. **How to get there** (Map 28): 30km northwest of Dax. From N10 take exit 13 at Castet to Saint-Girons, then D652 to Lit-et-Mixe. On leaving village, first on left.

Nestling in the heart of the Landes Forest, La Marie Clairière is a charming house surrounded by a vast, luxuriant garden. On the ground floor, there is a large living room with television. The bedrooms are arranged around another parlor; they are simply decorated and have a view of the beautiful, peaceful countryside. There are full accommodations for children. No meals are served in the house, but in the clearing (*clairière*), the owners have built a small restaurant where they serve salads and grills.

56
L'Oustau

Quartier Baxentes
40210 Lue
(Landes)
Tel. 58 07 11 58
Guy and Patricia Cassagne

Rooms 3 with private bath, shared WC. 2 with bath and WC. **Price** 175F (1 pers.), 190-200F (2 pers.). 220-330F. **Meals** Breakfast incl. No communal meal. **Restaurant** L'Auberge Landaise in Luë. **Pets** Dogs not allowed. **Nearby** Swimming pool, tennis, golf (35km), village of Pontenx-les-Forges, Marquèze Ecomuseum, farm products sold. **Credit cards** Not accepted. **Spoken** English, Spanish. **Open** Easter – Oct. **How to get there** (Map 29): From N10, exit Labouheyre, then D626 west towards Mimizan. Go 8km, through village of Loué, continue for 2km; L'Oustau on left.

The approach to this old country house is through immensely tall pine trees, giving way to oaks. Some 19th-century furniture, pine-paneled ceilings and beautiful paintings give character to the interior. Mme Cassagne is a very hospitable hostess. The pleasant bedrooms overlook the park and are furnished with antiques. Cars on the road about 100m away can disturb the tranquillity.

57
Le Bos de Bise

40630 Luglon
(Landes)
Tel. 58 07 50 90
M. and Mme Congoste

Rooms 2 (1 with lounge), with shower and WC. Rooms cleaned on request. **Price** 200-250F (2 pers.), +100F (extra pers.). **Meals** Breakfast incl. No communal meal. **Facilities** Lounge, bicycles, 2 horse stalls, lake. **Pets** Small dogs allowed. **Nearby** Riding, tennis, golf, canoeing, Napoleon III museum, Marquese museum. **Credit cards** Not accepted. **Open** May – Oct. **How to get there** (Map 29): 25km northwest of Mont-de-Marsan via N134 towards Sabres, then D14 to the left.

Surrounded completely by pine trees, le Bos de Bise is made up of several buildings connected by a carefully tended lawn. The two bedrooms are very comfortable and decorated in traditional style. One has an adjoining lounge and the other is larger with a private terrace. Breakfast is served in a rustic beamed dining room. Outside, a covered kitchen for preparing light meals and a lake with fish are available for your use.

58
Château Robert

40500 Montgaillard
(Landes)
Tel. 58 03 58 09
M. Clain

Rooms 3 with bath and WC. **Price** 300-400F (2 pers.). **Meals** breakfast incl. No communal meal. **Facilities** Lounge, telephone, swimming pool. **Nearby** Restaurant in auberge; riding, golf, walled towns. **Credit cards** Not accepted. **Spoken** English, Italian. **Open** All year. **How to get there** (Map 29): 22km south of Mont-de-Marsan via D933 towards Saint-Sever, then east on D352 towards Larrivière, then D387 towards Montgaillard and 1st turn on left after 1km.

In a lovely park with a swimming pool, Château Robert has two different façades. The one on the garden side is typically 18th-century while the other, overlooking the countryside, is rather Spanish baroque. There are very pleasant bedrooms prettily decorated with antique furniture made of honey-colored English pine. Breakfasts are very hearty and are served in a beautiful circular dining room decorated with plants and Louis XV plasterwork.

59
Au Masson

Route du Port
40300 Port-de-Lanne
(Landes)
Tel. 58 89 14 57
M. and Mme Duret

Rooms 3 suites (2-3 pers.), 2 with bath and WC and 1 with shower and WC. **Price** 200-230F (2 pers.) +75F (extra pers.). **Meals** Breakfast incl. No communal meal. **Restaurants** Excellent small auberge in the port (100m) and other restaurants (4km) on the banks of the Adour. **Pets** Dogs not allowed. **Nearby** Tennis, fishing, water sports, swimming pool, golf in Biarritz, historic landmarks, bullfightis. **Credit cards** Not accepted. **Open** All year. **How to get there** (Map 28): 29km northeast of Bayonne via N117. In the village.

The luxuriant garden of Au Masson with its ornamental lake and exotic trees is lovely for a stroll. Breakfasts are served in a covered garden area in summer. Ask for the duplex bedroom which is charmingly furnished in 1930s style. The others are comfortable but perhaps somewhat less attractive. The Durets are informal and very friendly.

60
Betjean

D 933
40240 Saint-Justin
(Landes)
Tel. 58 44 88 42
Marie-Claire Villenave

Rooms 4 with bath or shower and WC. Rooms cleaned on request. **Price** 220-240F (2 pers.). **Meals** Breakfast incl. No communal meal. **Restaurants** In Saint-Justin and Villeneuve. **Facilities** Lounge, telephone, fishing. **Pets** Small dogs allowed on request. **Nearby** River fishing (1000m), golf, walks, lake, Labastide d'Armagnac. **Credit cards** Not accepted. **Spoken** English, Italian. **Open** April – Sept. or by reservation. **How to get there** (Map 29): 25km northeast of Mont-de-Marsan via D932, then D933, the Périgueux road; 3km after Saint-Justin exit, small road to left. Follow signs.

Lying at the end of a long lane bordered by pines and ferns, this house is as lovely inside as it is out. The bedrooms are very comfortable and well decorated, and some have a well-designed small shower-room. Breakfasts with home-made jams served in a magnificent room with a beamed ceiling and exposed stones, handsome furniture and music in the background. This is a charming place to stay, although somewhat disturbed in the summer by nearby vacationers.

61
Château de Monbet

40300 Saint-Lon-les-Mines
(Landes)
Tel. 58 57 80 68
Fax 58 57 89 29
M. and Mme Hubert de Lataillade

Rooms 3 and 2 suites (4 pers.) with bath or shower and WC. **Price** 250-550F (2 pers.), suite 600-900F (4 pers.). **Meals** Breakfast incl. No communal meal. **Facilities** Lounge. **Pets** Dogs allowed on request (kennel). **Nearby** Restaurants, golf (18 holes), seaside, abbeys. **Credit cards** Not accepted. **Spoken** English. **Open** All year. **How to get there** (Map 29): 13km southwest of Dax via D6.

Monbet is a very pretty small château set on a hill with a wonderful view. The welcome is very pleasant and the bedrooms have an old-fashioned country-house atmosphere. The largest, Les Palombes, is very charming. Not all bathrooms are in the room, but each is private. In good weather, breakfast is served outside on a sheltered patio.

62
Larroque

40090 Saint-Perdon
(Landes)
Tel. 58 75 88 38
Marguerite and Louis Lajus

Rooms 2 and 1 suite (3 pers.) with bath and WC. Rooms cleaned on request. **Price** 220F (1-2 pers.); suite 240F (2 pers.), +80F (extra pers.). **Meals** Breakfast incl.No communal meal. **Facilities** Lounge. **Nearby** Tennis, golf, Saint-Sever, Saint-Girons. **Credit cards** Not accepted. **Spoken** English. **Open** All year. **How to get there** (Map 29): 5.5km southwest of Mont-de-Marsan via N124, then D3 left towards Saint-Perdon-Mugron; follow signs as you enter Saint-Perdon.

This country mansion still has an atmosphere of the past and you will be received as if you are part of the family. The interior is full of family objects and furniture and ancestral portraits. The bedrooms are very large and you'll sleep between superb embroidered sheets. (The soundproofing could be better.) Very good breakfasts are elegantly served in a lovely dining room. There is a pleasant and charmingly old-fashioned lounge.

63
Marchannau

40390 Sainte-Marie-de-Gosse
(Landes)
Tel. 59 56 35 71
M. and Mme Michel Février

Rooms 3 with bath, shared WC. Rooms cleaned on request. **Price** 250F (2 pers.). **Meals** Breakfast incl. No evening meals. **Restaurant** Auberge Piet on the Adour. **Facilities** Lounge, fishing. **Pets** Dogs not allowed. **Nearby** Tennis, golf, Basque and Landes coast, Basque villages. **Credit cards** Not accepted. **Spoken** English, Spanish. **Open** All year. **How to get there** (Map 28): 25km from Bayonne via N117. Before the bridge over the Adour, take the towpath for 2km.

Located in a magnificent countryside, this house is right on banks of the River Adour, which flows gently beneath the windows and makes Marchannau beautifully peaceful. Apart from the tables on the terrace, M. and Mme Février have provided a pleasant breakfast room. The bedrooms are big, comfortable and well renovated. There are no evening meals but there is an excellent restaurant on the Adour.

64
Le Cassouat

Magescq
40140 Soustons
(Landes)
Tel. 58 47 71 55
M. and Mme Gilbert Desbieys

Rooms 2 rooms en suite with shared bath and WC, and 2 with shower and WC. **Price** 210-250F (2 pers.), +70F (extra pers.). **Meals** Breakfast incl. No communal meal. **Facilities** Lounge, lake, bikes **Nearby** Golf in Molietz (9 and 18 holes, 16km), mountain biking, hiking, seaside (16km), lake, Landes regional park, tennis, swimming pool (15km). **Credit cards** Not accepted. **Spoken** Some English and Spanish **Open** All year. **How to get there** (Map 28): 16km northwest of Dax. From N 10, take exit 10 at Majescq, then Herm road (D150).

This very modern house with triangular shapes and long roofs is set in the middle of a beautiful oak forest. The atmosphere is pleasant and the bedrooms very comfortable and decorated in contemporary style. Beyond the big bay windows, there is a lovely sheltered terrace where you can enjoy breakfast and admire the pretty countryside. And, with luck, a deer might just leap in the distance!.

65
Chanteclair

47290 Cancon
(Lot-et-Garonne)
Tel. 53 01 63 34
Fax 53 41 13 44
Mme Larribeau

Rooms 3 and 1 suite (2-4 pers.) with bath or shower and WC. **Price** 270-310F (2 pers.); suite 270-370F. Reduced terms for 4 days +. **Meals** Breakfast 30F, half board 255-275F (per pers.). Evening meal by reservation 90F. **Facilities** Lounge, billiards, piano, swimming pool. **Pets** Small dogs allowed. **Nearby** Châteaux, golf (27 holes, 7km), tennis (800m), lake fishing, river fishing, riding, mountain biking, sailing, canoeing. **Credit cards** Not accepted. **Spoken** English, Spanish. **Open** All year. **How to get there** (Maps 23 and 30): 1km west of Cancon, on D124 towards Marmande.

This large country house lies on the edge of the Périgord region. The interior decoration is elegant, including four beautiful, comfortable guest rooms. They are furnished with prettily colored eiderdowns, lovely wallpaper and many pleasant decorative details. You might wander in the lovely garden, enjoy the swimming pool, or try the billiard table inside. Madame Larribeau is very hospitable and serves excellent regional cuisine.

66
Manoir de Roquegautier

Beaugas
47290 Cancon
(Lot-et-Garonne)
Tel. 53 01 60 75
Christian and Brigitte Vrech

Rooms 2 and 2 suites (3-4 pers.) with bath or shower and WC. Rooms cleaned on request. **Price** 350-370F (2 pers.), suite 570F (3 pers.), 610F (4 pers.). **Meals** Breakfast incl.. Evening meal at communal table 92F (wine not incl.), 62F (children). **Facilities** Lounge, piano, swimming pool. **Pets** No animals allowed. **Nearby** Golf (27 holes, 3km), equestrian center, tennis, lake, châteaux of Bonaguil and Biron, Monpazier, Villeréal, Monflanquin. **Credit cards** Not accepted. **Open** April – Oct. **How to get there** (Maps 23 and 30): 17km north of Villeneuve-sur-Lot via N21 towards Cancon.

Between the Périgord and the Landes, this lovely manor looks out over a gentle landscape of farmland and trees. Brigitte and Christian are especially friendly and hospitable hosts. The recently renovated bedrooms are light and very comfortable, with thick quilts on the beds and pretty pastel-colored curtains. The large bedroom under the eaves has handsome beamed architecture and extends into a round tower. The dinners are excellent.

67
Soubeyrac

47150 Envals
(Lot-et-Garonne)
Tel. 53 36 51 34
M. Rocca

Rooms 4 and 1 suite (4 pers.) with bath (whirlpool and jet-showers cost extra), WC and telephone (TV on request). Rooms cleaned on request. **Price** 350-480F (2 pers.); suite 700F (3-4 pers.), +50F (extra pers.). **Meals** Breakfast 35F. Meals at communal or separate tables 130F. **Facilities** Lounge. Swimming pool, bicycles, ping-pong. **Nearby** Fishing, tennis, hiking, golf (18 holes, 15km); bastides, châteaux of Périgord, music and theatre festivals. **Credit cards** Not accepted. **Spoken** English. **Open** All year. **How to get there** (Map 23): 20km north of Villeneuve-sur-Lot via D676 to Monflanquin then 2km northeast towards Monpazier on D 272; then left towards Envals on C3; then follow signs.

Soubeyrac is a 17th-century country mansion which has been beautifully restored. Located in magnificent countryside, the house offers a vast suite and two lovely bedrooms on the ground floor of the outbuildings; and two other bedrooms in the main building. Each room is equipped with whirlpool bathtubs. Monsieur Rocca will serve you his delicious meals which are made with fresh farm products of the region; he is very warm and hospitable.

68
Cantelause

47420 Houeillès
(Lot-et-Garonne)
Tel. 53 65 92 71
M. and Mme Nicole and François
Thollon Pommerol

Rooms 2 with bath and WC in guest house. No extra beds for children. **Price** 220F (2 pers.). **Meals** Breakfast 25F. Communal evening meal 100-130F. **Facilities** Lounge. **Pets** Dogs not allowed. **Nearby** Casteljaloux golf course (18 holes, 20km); riding, tennis, swimming pool, lake, bikes; Circuits des Bastides et Chapelles. **Credit cards** Not accepted. **Spoken** English, Spanish. **Open** All year. **How to get there** (Maps 29 and 30): 20km south of Casteljaloux, via D933; then turn left on D 156 and D 154 towards Durance; it's 8km east of Houeillès.

Nestling in the midst of pine groves on the edge of the Landes Forest, Cantelause is a lovely house with a rustic but elegant annex. There are two small, prettily decorated bedrooms with very modern bathrooms. Breakfasts and dinners--including homemade *foie gras*, bread and brioches - are served in the main house or, in summer, in the garden. A haven for golfers (package stays are possible), Cantelause is also delightful for those who love peaceful surroundings and fine food.

69
Frémauret

Roumagne
47800 Miramont-de-Guyenne
(Lot-et-Garonne)
Tel. 53 93 24 65
M. and Mme Claude Aurélien

Rooms 1 suite with bath, small lounge and WC. **Price** 230F (1 pers.), 290F (2 pers.), +50F (extra pers.). **Meals** Breakfast incl. Evening meals by reservation at communal table 90F (wine incl.), gastronomic menu 170F. **Nearby** Swimming pool, lake, tennis, golf, walks, Duras, Pujols, Eymet. **Credit cards** Not accepted. **Spoken** Spanish. **Open** All year. **How to get there** (Map 23): 21km northeast of Marmande via D933 to Miramont, then D668 towards Duras.

The converted dovecote of this elegant farmhouse surrounded by corn fields and pastureland is kept for guests. The two-level suite has a pretty, small lounge and upstairs, a very pleasant bedroom with old mahogany furniture and pink fabrics. There is a large modern bathroom. M. and Mme Aurélien will welcome you with great hospitality; excellent seasonal cuisine, made with products from the farm, is served in the evening.

70
Château de Pechgris

Salles
47150 Monflanquin
(Lot-et-Garonne)
Tel. 53 36 53 01
Dr and Mme Xavier Chaussade

Rooms 2 with bath, WC and TV. 1 child's bedroom. **Price** 180-280F (2 pers.) (3 nights stay min. in high season). **Meals** Breakfast 30F. No communal meal; poss. picnic lunch. **Restaurant** Auberge de Vézou (3km). **Facilities** Lounge, swimming pool, tennis, bikes. **Pets** Dogs and cats not allowed. **Nearby** Various sports and cultural activites. **Credit cards** Not accepted. **Spoken** English, German. **Open** April – late Oct. **How to get there** (Map 23): 23km north of Villeneuve-sur-Lot via D676 to Monflanquin, then D150 towards Salles, then right on the road to Libos, and after 1.2km, a drive on the right edged with lime trees. Follow signs from Salles.

The Knights Templar wisely chose this quiet, gently rolling spot on which to build their beautiful *commanderie*. The house forms a square which is dominated by an imposing octagonal tower. The lovely bedrooms are spacious and pleasantly furnished with family furniture and very comfortable beds. Madame Chaussade is a charming hostess.

71
Manoir de Barrayre

Le Laussou
47150 Monflanquin
(Lot-et-Garonne)
Tel. 53 36 46 66
Fax 53 36 55 26
Mme Charles

Rooms 2 and 1 suite (4 pers.) with bath or shower and WC, 2 apartments (2 pers.) and 1 (4 pers.) with lounge, kitchen, bath and WC. **Price** 350-405F (2 pers.); suite 610F (2 pers.); apartments 1 750-2 500F a week (2 pers.), 1 900-3 500F a week (4 pers.). **Meals** Breakfast incl. Evening meals by reservation 90F. **Facilities** Lounge, billiards, swimming pool. **Pets** Small dogs allowed. **Nearby** Fishing, riding, golf, walled towns, châteaux, Sarlat, Monbazillac. **Credit cards** Not accepted. **Spoken** English. **Open** All year (by reservation Oct. – April). **How to get there** (Map 23): 25km north of Villeneuve-sur-Lot via D676 to Monflanquin, then D272 towards Monpazier; turn left after Laurès; signposted.

This converted 12th-century priory, surrounded by beautiful countrysides, has kept its imposing medieval character. The enormous bedrooms are furnished with antiques and handsome paintings, and the thick stone walls lend the manor house great character. The bathrooms vary in size but are always well kept. Delicious breakfasts are served by the fireplace in winter.

72
Moulin de Majoulassis

Gavaudun
47150 Monflanquin
(Lot-et-Garonne)
Tel. 53 36 41 82
M. and Mme Perreau

Rooms 2 and 1 suite (5 pers.) with bath and WC. Rooms cleaned every 3 days. **Price** (2 nights min.) 225F (1 pers.), 250-300F (2 pers.), +125F (extra pers.). **Meals** Breakfast incl. Half board 210-235F (per pers., 3 nights min.). Evening meals at communal table 85F (wine incl.). **Facilities** Lounge, fishing in the lake or river. **Pets** Dogs not allowed. **Nearby** Swimming pools, golf, climbing, fitness center, châteaux. **Credit cards** Not accepted. **Spoken** English. **Open** March – Oct. by reservation. **How to get there** (Map 23): 25km north of Villeneuve-sur-Lot via D676 to Monflanquin, then D150 towards Lacapelle-Biron.

The bedrooms are not in the main building but very close by, on the *premier étage* of a pretty guest house. They are large and light, with practical modern furnishings. Each is decorated in a different color and has a small balcony overlooking the fields. The bathrooms are pleasant. Hearty breakfasts are served in the rustic living/dining room, and the friendly atmosphere is enlivened by two charming young children.

73
L'Ormeraie

47150 Paulhiac
(Lot-et-Garonne)
Tel. 53 36 45 96
Fax (idem)
Minitel: 11 l'ormeraie 47
Michel de L'Ormeraie

Rooms 4 with bath or shower and WC, and 1 suite (2 pers.) with bath, lounge/library and WC.
Price 380-472F (2 pers.), suite 690F (2 pers.), +125F (extra pers.). **Meals** Breakfast incl. No
communal meal. **Facilities** Lounge, swimming pool. **Pets** Dogs allowed on request (+10F/day).
Nearby Golf (25km), riding, tennis. **Credit cards** Visa, Eurocard and MasterCard. **Spoken**
English, Spanish. **Open** April – mid-Nov. **How to get there** (Map 23): 21km north of Villeneuve-
sur-Lot via D676 to Monflanquin, then D272 towards Monpazier; follow the signs.

L'Ormeraie stands on a low hill, with its back to a forest. The house
spreads out with many charming views from its dovecote and its various
architectural angles. Every bedroom is personalized with antique furniture
but the bathrooms are very modern. Breakfast is served in front of the house
facing a beautiful garden with a lovely view down the hill.

74
L'Air du Temps

Mounet
47140 Penne-d'Agenais
(Lot-et-Garonne)
Tel. 53 41 41 34
Geneviève Bovy-Cazottes

Rooms 3 with bath or shower and WC. **Price** 220-240F (2 pers.). **Meals** Breakfast incl., meals at
communal or separate tables 90F (wine not incl.). **Facilities** Lounge. **Nearby** Lake and tennis (500m),
yacht basin on Lot, mountain bikes, horseback riding, hiking; Penne-d'Agenais (500m), Castelnau.
Credit Cards All major. **Spoken** English, Spanish. **Closed** 15 days in Feb. and in Nov. **How to get there**
(Map 30): 30km northeast of Agen, to Villeneuve-sur-Lot, then towards Tournon d'Agenais via D911.

This lovely house is halfway between Port-de-Penne and the charming
medieval village of Penne-d'Agenais. We loved L'Air du Temps
immediately. Three white-walled bedrooms, brightened with pretty fabrics,
colorful objects and a beautiful pale parquet floor open directly onto the
garden. On the other side, you will find a large, light room with a sofa and
dining tables, where Madame Bovy-Cazotte serves delicious regional cuisine,
or spicy exotic dishes like fish *tajine*. Guests gather on a pretty, shaded terrace
that opens onto another garden where meals are served in summer. We look
forward to the pleasure of going back.

75
Château de Cantet

Cantet
47250 Samazan
(Lot-et-Garonne)
Tel. 53 20 60 60
Fax 53 89 63 53
M. and Mme J.-B. de la Raytrie

Rooms 1 with bath and WC and 1 suite (4-5 pers.) with shower and WC. **Price** 280F (1 pers.), 280F (2 pers.); suite 400-420F, +60F (extra pers.). **Meals** Breakfast 25F. Communal meal in evening 80F (wine incl.). Rooms cleaned twice a week on request. **Facilities** Lounge. **Pets** Dogs not allowed. **Facilities** Covered swimming pool, fishing, 3 horse stalls, riding, bicycles. **Nearby** 9- and 18 holes golf courses (15km), lake; Mas d'Agenais, Marmande, Casteljaloux, opera festival in Aug. **Credit cards** Not accepted. **Spoken** English. **Open** All year. **How to get there** (Maps 29 and 30): 10km southwest of Marmande via D933. After bridge above autouroute, take 2nd road on right, 2nd lane after railroad crossing.

This is a solidly built, traditional house, surrounded by tall trees and lovely flowers. The owners will greet you with great enthusiasm and informality. The bright bedrooms are tastefully decorated with antiques and look out over the gentle Gascon countryside. Meals are served around the large dining table or, in summer, in the garden. For a family or a group of friends, this is an ideal place to stay.

76
Domaine de Clavié

Soubirous
47300 Villeneuve-sur-Lot
(Lot-et-Garonne)
Tel. 53 41 74 30
Fax 53 41 77 50
Mme Waridel and M. Diserens

Rooms 4 with bath or shower and WC and 1 guest house with 2 double rooms, 2 baths, living room and kitchen. **Price** 600-800F; 1000F per week. **Meals** Breakfast incl. Communal meal at separate tables 145F (wine not incl.). **Facilities** Lounge, swimming pool. **Pets** Animals allowed only by prior arrangement. **Nearby** Golf (9 and 18 holes, 3km), bastides, Romanesque Aquitaine. **Credit cards** All major. **Spoken** English, Italian. **Closed** Jan. 3 - March 1. **How to get there** (Map 30): 7km north of Villeneuve-sur-Lot via N21; 7km from Soubirous. After going downhill to intersection, go left towards Casseneuil Saint-Livrade, then immediately right, on a small road for 500m. Signs on a pillar on left.

The Domaine de Clavié is an elegant 18th-century mansion in the countryside near Agen. A charming stay awaits you here, where your hosts are attentive and friendly. You will find large bedrooms with pretty antique furniture; luxurious baths, and a patio where meals are served in summer. The delicate cuisine is made with fresh products from this rich farmland; meals are served on a charming table set with lovely china.

77
Les Huguets

47300 Villeneuve-sur-Lot
(Lot-et-Garonne)
Tel. 53 70 49 34
Ward and Gerda
Poppe-Notteboum

Rooms 4 with bath and WC. **Price** 250F (2 pers.). **Meals** Breakfast 30F. Communal meals 60F (noon); 100F (in evening, apéritif and wine included). **Facilities** Lounge, swimming pool, tennis, riding, sauna; concerts around campfire, organized tours of region organized. **Pets** Dogs allowed on request. **Nearby** Water skiing on the Lot, hiking, fishing, canoeing and kayaking, golf (18 holes, 15km). **Credit Cards** Not accepted. **Spoken** English, German and Flemish. **Open** All year. **How to get there** (Map 30): 4km south of Villeneuve-sur-Lot via La Rocade towards Cahors, 2nd road on right, then follow signs.

This large rustic house in the midst of the country has been decorated by a young Belgian couple. Equipped with all the modern amenities, the bedrooms are bright and simple, with views out over the valley or the old village. M. Poppe will be delighted to take you horseback riding or touring the region. In the evening, he occasionally organizes concerts. You can also relax around the swimming pool or in in the garden. Traditional Périgord cuisine, with biologically grown vegetables, is served in the evening. There is a happy family atmosphere at Les Huguets.

78
Moulin de Labique

Saint-Eutrope-de-Born
47210 Villeréal
(Lot-et-Garonne)
Tel. 53 01 63 90
Hélène and François
Boulet-Passebon

Rooms 1 suite (4 pers.) and 4 rooms with bath or shower and WC. **Price** 250F (1 pers.), 380F (2 pers.); suite 540F (3 pers.), 720 F (4 pers.); 130F (children under 18 years). **Meals** Breakfast incl. Meals at communal or separate tables 98F. **Facilities** Lounge, swimming pool, riding, horse-drawn carriage, lake and river fishing on property. **Credit Cards** Diners, Visa, Eurocard and MasterCard. **Pets** Dogs allowed on request. **Nearby** Tennis (800m), hiking, golf (18 holes, 7km); Castelnau, Circuit des Bastides, châteaux of Périgord, Route des Vins. **Spoken** English. **Closed** 2 weeks. in Nov. **How to get there** (Map 23): 45km southeast of Bergerac via N21, to Cancon; then D 124 on left to Beauregard, then to Saint-Vivien. After Saint-Vivien, 2nd road on right, then follow signs.

The blue-grey of the shutters lends a touch of elegance to this beautiful, rustic 17th-century mansion. In the main house, two bedrooms share an immense antique-style bathroom and a cool, flowery terrace: They are ideal for a family. In the outbuildings overlooking the old mill, two bedrooms and a suite combine modern amenities with elegant decor. You can enjoy relaxing in the comfortable salon, the swimming pool, or in the quiet, shady garden.

79
Sauveméa

64350 Arroses
(Pyrénées-Atlantiques)
Tel. 59 68 16 01/59 68 16 08
José and Annie Labat

Rooms 4 and 1 suite (4 pers.) with bath and WC. **Price** 240F (1 pers.), 260F (2 pers.); suite 450F (4 pers.). **Meals** Breakfast incl. Evening meals 60F (wine incl.). **Facilities** Lounge, swimming pool, fishing, horse boxes, riding. **Pets** Dogs not allowed in rooms. **Nearby** Vineyards of Madiran. **Credit cards** Not accepted. **Spoken** English. **Open** All year. **How to get there** (Maps 29 and 30): 44km north of Tarbes via D935 towards Aire-sur-l'Adour, then D248 and D48 to Madiran, and D66 towards Arroses, then D292.

This spacious farm is built around a very beautiful mansion. The bedrooms and bathrooms are all roomy, well renovated, and have attractive furniture in light wood They are comfortable and quiet. Breakfast is served in a large lounge and the dinner menus of this farmhouse-auberge are excellent. You can enjoy a pretty swimming pool with viewsover the countryside and the lake below.

80
Château Saint-Jean

1, rue de l'Eglise
64420 Artigueloutan
(Pyrénées-Atlantiques)
Tel. 59 81 84 30
Fax 59 81 84 20
Christiane and Patrice Nicaise

Rooms 3 and 1 suite (3 pers.) with bath or shower, WC and TV. **Price** 190-280F (1 pers.), 310F (2 pers.); suite 330F (2 pers.), +90F (extra pers.). **Meals** Breakfast incl.; at lunch and dinner auberge on property (closed Sunday evening and Wednesday): menus 105-240F; carte (wine not incl.). **Facilities** Lounge, swimming pool, tennis (+30F), trout fishing on river, horseback riding (60F/h), carriage rides (100F/1-4 pers.) on property. **Pets** Dogs not allowed. **Nearby** Golf (18 holes, 15km), cross-country and Alpine skiing (40km); Château de Pau, caves of Bettarain (10km). **Credit cards** Not accepted. **Spoken** English. **Open** All year. **How to get there** (Map 29): 10km east of Pau via N117. 10km from Lartigueloutan. Follow signs. Ii's in village next to church.

This strange crenelated house towers over the Ossau Valley and a beautiful private park, part of which is reserved for ponies, ducks and miniature goats. The bedrooms are very pleasant, well furnished and decorated with soft pastel wallpapers and elegant fabrics. Freshly renovated, the Château Saint-Jean is impeccably maintained. The breakfasts are copious and the owners are very friendly.

81
Trille

D 934, Route de Rébénacq
64290 Bosdarros-Gan
(Pyrénées-Atlantiques)
Tel. 59 21 79 51
Fax 59 21 66 98
Mme Christiane Bordes

Rooms 5 with bath or shower, WC and TV. **Price** 250F (1 pers.), 310F (2 pers.). **Meals** Breakfast incl. No evening meals. **Restaurant** Auberge le Tucq (100m). **Facilities** Lounge, large terrace and interior courtyard. **Pets** Small dogs allowed. **Nearby** Golf (18 holes), walks, ski slopes. **Credit cards** Visa, Eurocard and MasterCard. **Spoken** English, Spanish. **Open** All year. **How to get there** (Map 29): 10km south of Pau via N134 to Gan; from the 'Cave des Producteurs de Jurançon' in Gan, pass 4 sets of traffic lights, then take D934 towards Rébénacq and Arudy, for about 3.5km. It's on the left.

Trille is a Béarn house which has been completely refurbished. The comfortable, immaculately kept bedrooms look out over a beautiful panorama of high hills. Friendly and energetic, Christiane Bordes welcomes her guests with obvious pleasure. There is an inviting lounge with a fireplace which is reserved for guests. It opens onto the terrace where you can occasionally hear cars on the road. The breakfasts are excellent.

82
Château de Boues

Route d'Arette
La Pierre-Saint-Martin
64570 Féas
(Pyrénées-Atlantiques)
Tel. 59 39 95 49
Mme Monique Domon

Rooms 4 with bath, WC and TV. **Price** 270F (1 pers.), 310F (2 pers.). **Meals** Breakfast incl. No communal meal. **Facilities** Swimming pool. **Pets** Dogs allowed on request. **Nearby** Restaurants, tennis, golf at Pau, ski slopes and cross-country skiing, la Madeleine, Basque country, Pierre-Saint-Martin. **Credit cards** Visa, Eurocard and MasterCard. **Spoken** English. **Open** March 1 – end Oct and by reservation. **How to get there** (Map 29): 42km southwest of Pau via N134 to Gan, then D24 to Oloron-Sainte-Marie; go towards Saragosse to bridge, then towards Bayonne to traffic lights and turn. At left go second traffic light. At right towards Arette for approx. 4km.

Behind this majestic façade you will find a family-style house where Monique Dornon will greet you hospitably. The comfortable bedrooms have been extensively refurbished: We recommend Number 4 (and also 3), which is small but charmingly decorated; they all have double-glazing windows and enjoy a pretty view. The very good breakfasts are served in a beautiful room or in a garden full of flowers.

83
Ferme de Loutarès

64800 Haut-de-Bosdarros
(Pyrénées-Atlantiques)
Tel. 59 71 20 60
Fax 59 71 26 67
Mme Pucheu de Monteverde

Rooms 6 rooms with bath or shower and WC. Rooms cleaned twice a week. **Price** (2 nights min.) 225F (1 pers.), 295F (2 pers.), +70F (extra pers.). **Meals** Breakfast incl. Meals noon and evening at communal or separate tables 80F (wine not incl.). Special rates for half-board and children. **Facilities** Lounge, billiards, swimming pool, riding, fitness facilities (sauna, hot baths) on property. **Pets** Dogs allowed on request. **Nearby** Golf (18 holes, 20km), cross-country and Alpine skiing (45km), rafting. **Credit cards** Not accepted. **Spoken** English, Spanish. **Open** All year. **How to get there** (Map 29): 20km south of Pau, go east towards Nay via Gelos to Arros-Nay, then follow signs.

L ocated at the summit of a small, winding road through the lush mountains of the Béarn, the Ferme de Loutarès comprises a group of beautiful, small rustic houses clustered around a pretty garden with a swimming pool. The bedrooms are small and somewhat austere except for two in an older house. There is a large, informal room for breakfast and reading. This is a good place for hiking and the owners are very friendly and helpful.

84
Le Lanot

64520 Sames
(Pyrénées-Atlantiques)
Tel. 59 56 01 84
Mme Liliane Mickelson

Rooms 3 rooms with shower and WC. Rooms cleaned twice a week. **Price** 250F (1 pers.), 280F (2 pers.), +70F and 140F (extra pers.). **Meals** Breakfast incl. Communal meals in evening on reservation only 150F. Special conditions half-board and children. **Facilities** Lounge open to guests in winter. **Pets** Dogs allowed on request. **Nearby** Restaurants, golf (30km), lake, fishing, riding, ocean, surfing (35km); Saint-Jean-de-Luz, Saint-Jean-Pied-de-Port, visits to Basque, Béarn and south Landes regions. **Credit cards** Not accepted. **Spoken** English. **Open** All year. Reservations desirable. **How to get there** (Map 29): 6km southwest of Peyrehorade exit from A64 autoroute; follow signs beginning at Peyrehorade (on the bridge over river Adour) through Hastingues, Sames-Bourg, and small road for Bidache.

L e Lanot is an 18th-century Basque house not far from the River Adour. Very prettily furnished, it has three comfortable guest rooms which are decorated in an elegant, flowery country style. The bathrooms are beautiful and have thoughtful small touches which say much about the hostess's charming hospitality. Lilian Mickelson knows her region intimately and you might want her to tell you about it over breakfast.

85
Larchoincoborda

64310 Sare
(Pyrénées-Atlantiques)
Tel. 59 54 22 32
M. and Mme Berthon

Rooms 2 with bath and WC. No-smoking rooms available. **Price** 250F (1 pers.), 280-300F (2 pers.), 400F (3 pers.). **Children** Under 6 not accepted. **Meals** Breakfast incl. Communal meal in evening 85F. **Restaurants** In village and in Ventas, Spain. **Pets** Dogs not allowed. **Facilities** Lounge; hiking. **Nearby** Golf (18 holes, 14km), tennis, swimming pool, ocean (14km); visit of Sarre (village and prehistoric caves), Spain, Basque villages, Saint-Jean-de-Luz, La Rhune. **Credit cards** Not accepted. **Spoken** English. **Open** All year. **How to get there** (Map 28): 15km southeast of Saint-Jean-de-Luz to Ascain, then Sare; take, road to Vera (signs); house is 2.5km from village.

You will find this beautiful house in a landmarked site off a long path that slowly ascends the breathtakingly beautiful Rhune Mountains. There are very pleasant, comfortable small bedrooms. Breakfasts are served in a large, inviting, elegantly decorated room, or outside on the terrace. You will enjoy a stunning view out over superb countryside: hills, pastures with low stone walls, beautiful vegetation and scattered Basque houses. The welcome is very friendly.

86
Maison Dominxenea

Quartier Ihalar
64310 Sare
(Pyrénées-Atlantiques)
Tel. 59 54 20 46 (Hôtel Arraya)
Fax 59 54 27 04 (Hôtel Arraya)
M. Jean-Baptiste Fagoaga

Rooms 3 with bath or shower and WC. **Price** 290F (2 pers.). **Meals** Breakfast incl. No communal meals. **Facilities** Lounge. **Pets** Dogs not allowed. **Nearby** Restaurants, swimming pool, tennis, hiking, sports on Basque coast. Golf (18 holes, 13km), Saint-Sébastien, Pamplona, Loyola, Basque villages. **Credit cards** Not accepted. **Spoken** English, Spanish. **Open** All year. **How to get there** (Map 28): 1km north of Sare, go to Hotel Arraya on the main square, and you will be taken to the Maison Dominxenea.

There is not a single house built after the 17th century in this lovely small Basque village where you will find the Maison Dominxenea. The bedrooms are very pleasant with beautiful wallpaper, comfortable beds and large bathrooms. In the morning, an excellent breakfast awaits you; you may enjoy it in your room, the dining room or on the terrace, which looks out on the village and the garden. This is a welcoming place where you can live in total independence.

87
Olhabidea

64310 Sare
(Pyrénées-Atlantiques)
Tel. 59 54 21 85
Mme Jean Fagoaga

Rooms 3 and 1 suite (4 pers.) with bath and WC. **Children** Under 12 not accepted. **Price** 350F
(2 pers.), 3020F (if 2 nights or more). **Meals** Breakfast incl. No communal meal. **Facilities**
Lounge, riding (tel. for info.). **Pets** Dogs not allowed. **Facilities** Lounge, riding. **Nearby**
Restaurants, mountains, seaside, Basque villages, Spain, golf (14km), swimming pool, tennis.
Credit cards Not accepted. **Spoken** English. **Open** March – end-Nov (in winter by reservation).
How to get there (Map 28): 14km southeast of Saint-Jean-de-Luz; from A63 take Saint-Jean-
de-Luz Nord exit, then D918 to Ascain and D4 to Sare. Leave Sare in the direction of Saint-Pée
sur Nivelle and go 2km. Turn right in front of the old chapel; follow signs.

I f you do not know the Basque country here is a marvellous reason for a
visit. The comfort and interior decoration of Olhabidea are as splendid
as the landscape here. You will find lovely embroidered sheets, old
engravings, exposed beams, balustrades and bright terra cotta floors, notably
in the magnificent entrance hall. Mme Fagoaga's friendly welcome lends
further charm to this special place.

88
Ferme Pinodiéta

Route d'Aïnhoa
par le col de Pinodiéta
64250 Souraïde
(Pyrénées-Atlantiques)
Tel. 59 93 87 31
M. and Mme Massonde

Rooms 5 with bath (1 with twin beds) or shower, and WC. Rooms cleaned (except beds). **Price**
190-210F (2 pers.), +50F (extra pers.). **Meals** Breakfast incl. **Restaurant** Run by owner's son
(200m). Meals 70F for guests, wine incl. Other menus and à la carte. **Facilities** Pétanque,
children's games on property. **Pets** Small dogs allowed on request. **Nearby** Golf (3km), tennis,
swimming pool, ocean (20km), biking, Lac de Saint Pée (4km); Spain (4km), Aïnhoa, La Rhune
(cog railway10km). **Credit cards** Not accepted. **Closed** Dec and Jan. **How to get there** (Map 28):
20km south of Bayonne, take D932 to Cambo, D20 southwest through Espelette and towards
Aïnhoa (and border).

L ying at the top of a hill, this small farm enjoys a panoramic view over
the pastures and beautiful mountains in the distance. The bedrooms are
small, simple and rustic, and all have modern amenities. Hiking enthusiasts
can enjoy walking to the charming villages nearby. The restaurant belonging
to the owners' son has a beautiful terrace and serves regional specialties. The
owners are friendly and warm.

89
Château de Boussac

Target
03140 Chantelle-de-Boussac
(Allier)
Tel. 70 40 63 20
Fax 70 40 60 03
Marquis and Marquise de Longueil

Rooms 4 and 2 suite with bath and WC. **Price** 600-800F (1-2 pers.), suite 950-1100F (1-3 pers.). **Meals** Breakfast 50F; half board 1100F per pers. in double room (5 days min.), evening meals at communal table, by reservation, 260-320F (wine incl.). **Facilities** Lounge. **Pets** Dogs allowed on request (+100F per day). **Nearby** Tennis, golf; Romanesque churches. **Credit cards** Amex, Visa, Eurocard and MasterCard. **Spoken** English. **Open** April 1 – Nov 30. **How to get there** (Map 25): 44km east of Montluçon. From A71, exit 11 Montmarault, then D46 and southeast on D42 to Chantelle.

Boussac is a beautifully beautiful château reflecting many architectural styles, from medieval austerity to the grace of the 18th century. The rooms are magnificently furnished in traditional style, and the bedrooms are comfortable and well decorated, with charming family mementoes. The convivial evening meals are much prized by lovers of game in season. This is truly a noble and welcoming place.

90
Château de Fragne

03190 Verneix
(Allier)
Tel. 70 07 88 10
Fax 70 07 83 73
Comtesse Louis de Montaignac

Rooms 4 and 1 suite of 2 bedrooms with bath and WC. **Price** 420F (1 pers.), 600F (2 pers.), suite 600F (3 pers.). **Meals** Breakfast 40F, evening meals at communal table (separate tables available) 250F (wine incl.). **Facilities** Lounge, fishing in lake. **Pets** Dogs allowed on request. **Nearby** Equestrian center, golf. **Credit cards** Not accepted. **Spoken** English. **Open** May 1 – mid-Oct. and by reservation. **How to get there** (Map 17): 10km northeast of Montluçon. From A71 take Montluçon exit, then D94 southeast towards Montluçon for 2km, then right on D39 towards Verneix; sign at the stop sign on the right.

An immense drive leads up to this château and its beautiful park. All the bedrooms have been restored and are decorated in soft colors with antique furniture, while the bathrooms have modern amenities. The lounges and dining room overlook a large terrace where you may have breakfast. The overall effect is lovely, recreating the elegance and simplicity of château life in the past. The owners are very hospitable.

91
Château du Riau

03460 Villeneuve-sur-Allier
(Allier)
Tel. 70 43 34 47
Fax 70 43 30 74
M. and Mme Durye

Rooms 3 with bath or shower and WC and poss. suites (3-5 pers.). **Price** 600-680F (2 pers.), suite 900F (3-4 pers.), 980F (5 pers.). **Meals** Breakfast incl., evening meal at communal table, by reservation 250F (wine incl.). **Facilities** Lounge. **Pets** Dogs not allowed. **Nearby** Swimming pool, tennis, riding, golf, Tronçais forest, Balaine arboretum, châteaux. **Credit cards** Not accepted. **Spoken** English. **Open** All year. **How to get there** (Map 18): 15km northwest of Moulins via N7 to Villeneuve-sur-Allier, then D133

This is an exceptional ensemble of buildings in typically Bourbonnais style. Having crossed the moat and passed through the postern gate you reach the main part of the château. The bedrooms look the same as they must have to guests in past centuries; each is still decorated with beautiful 18th-century or Empire furnishings. Breakfast is served at the big table in the dining room, which, like the lounge, is pleasant and well furnished. The hospitality is familial and elegant.

92
Le Chalet

Les Ferrons
03160 Ygrande
(Allier)
Tel. 70 66 31 67/70 66 30 72
Mme Vrel

Rooms 5 with shower and WC. **Price** 160-170F (1 pers.), 210-220F (2 pers.) +60F (extra pers.). **Meals** Breakfast incl. No evening meals. **Restaurant** Le Pont des Chèvres in Cosne d'Allier (12km). **Facilities** Bicycles. **Pets** Dogs not allowed. **Nearby** Swimming pool, tennis, lake, Tronçais forest, châteaux of the Route Jacques Cœur. **Credit cards** Not accepted. **Open** All year. **How to get there** (Map 17): 33km west of Moulins via D953 through Bourbon-l'Archambault; follow the signs.

You will be very pleasantly received in this small turn-of-the-century house located in beautiful countryside. The good-sized bedrooms are simply and prettily done. We recommend the very charming Room 2; Number 1 and the large bedroom, which is particularly suitable for families. Mme Vrel lives close by and comes every morning to make the hearty breakfasts, which are served in a small lounge.

93
Château de la Vigne

15700 Ally
(Cantal)
Tel. 71 69 00 20
M. and Mme du Fayet de la Tour

Rooms 3 with bath or shower and WC. **Price** 600-700F (2 pers.), suite 700F (4 pers.).
Meals Breakfast 30F, evening meals by request (separate tables) 200F (wine incl.).
Facilities Tennis. **Pets** Small dogs permitted by special request. **Nearby** Fishing, golf (9 holes)
in Mauriac, lake, beach. **Credit cards** Not accepted. **Spoken** English. **Open** Easter – Nov 1.
How to get there (Map 24): 52km north of Aurillac via D922, then west on D680 to Ally and
D681 towards Mauriac.

The very old Château de la Vigne lies in the midst of the country. The
owners will welcome you like old friends and see that your breakfast
is served the minute you get out of bed. Each room is decorated with
beautiful family furnitur, the lounge is superb and the bedrooms are
comfortable; some are elegant, while others are grandiose. Before leaving
ask for a tour of the château.

94
Barathe

15130 Giou-de-Mamou
(Cantal)
Tel. 71 64 61 72
Isabelle, Pierre and Julien Breton

Rooms 5 with shower and WC. **Meals** Evening meal at communal table; half-board 180F per pers.
(wine incl.). **Facilities** Lounge. **Pets** Dogs not admitted. **Nearby** Riding, tennis, swimming pools,
golf (9 holes, 5km), cross-country and alpine skiing; village of Salers, Tournemire, Château d'Anjony,
Route des Crêtes, Puy Mary. **Credit cards** Not accepted. **Open** All year. **How to get there** (Map 24):
8km east of Aurillac via N122, then in 7km turn left towards Giou-de-Mamou; follow sign.

Overlooking a very beautiful countryside lulled by the tinkling of
cowbells, this very old house truly revives the atmosphere of centuries
past. The large dining room is stunningly typical of the region, with its old
Auvergne furniture and its splendid *souillarde*, an old wash tub of the
Auvergne. The bedrooms are basic but comfortable, and they can easily
accommodate children. The evening meal is a joyous occasion, and the
cuisine, often praised in the guest book, is made with fresh products from
the farm. (Nearby Salers is famous for its beef). The owners are very kind
at Barathe, a rustic place ideal for families.

95
Château de Bassignac

Bassignac
15240 Saignes
(Cantal)
Tel. 71 40 82 82
M. and Mme Besson

Rooms 3 with bath and WC, 1 apartment (3-4 pers.) with 2 bedrooms, hall, bathroom and WC. **Price** 410-520F (2 pers.), apartment 650F (4 pers.). **Meals** Breakfast incl., half board 390-415F per pers., evening meal at communal table 250F (wine incl.). **Facilities** Lounge, fishing. **Pets** Dogs allowed on request. **Nearby** Golf, cross country ski ing, villages, Romanesque churches, châteaux. **Credit cards** Not accepted. **Spoken** English. **Open** Easter – Nov 1 (by reservation in winter). **How to get there** (Map 24): 67km north of Aurillac via D922; 12km before Bort-les-Orgues take D312 towards Brousse.

Bassignac is a fortified house of great character set in a rolling, wooded countryside An immediately welcoming impression is given by the two ground-floor rooms. There are lovely bedrooms with 19th-century furniture, curios and charming fabrics. A log fire adds atmosphere to the excellent evening meals. The younger generation of the family runs a farmhouse-auberge at the entrance to the park.

96
Chez M. et Mme Prudent

Rue des Nobles
15410 Salers
(Cantal)
Tel. 71 40 75 36
M. Philippe Prudent

Rooms 6 with bath and WC. **Price** 191F (1 pers.), 212F (2 pers.), 263F (3 pers.). **Meals** Breakfast incl. No evening meals. **Nearby** Restaurants, swimming pool, cross-country and downhill skiing.; mountain climbing with guide; Auvergne Volcano Park. **Credit cards** Visa, Eurocar and MasterCard. **Spoken** English, German. **Open** All year. **How to get there** (Map 24): 47km north of Aurillac. From D922 take D680 east; in center of Salers go to Place Tyssendier d'Escous and take first small street on left.

Entirely built of volcanic basalt, Salers is a small medieval treasure which has been miraculously spared by the passage of time. In this attractive house the bedrooms are small, simple and not all well soundproofed, but they are comfortable and well kept. Choose those overlooking the volcanos. A good breakfast is served with a smile in the bedrooms or in a beautiful garden with a magnificent view. This is an inexpensive and welcoming place to stay.

97
Château d'Arnac

Nonards
19120 Beaulieu-sur-Dordogne
(Corrèze)
Tel. 55 91 54 13
Fax 55 91 52 62
Joe and Jill Webb

Rooms 4 with bath or shower and WC. Rooms cleaned every day, linens changed every 3 days. Price 400F (July – August), 300F (low season), 2 pers. Special rates for long stays. **Meals** English breakfast 40F. Evening meals at communal or separate tables 80F (wine incl.). **Facilities** Lounge, fishing in river and tennis on property. **Pets** Dogs allowed on request. **Nearby** Swimming pool (8km), riding (25km), canoeing, hiking, Coiroux golf course (35km); the Dordogne, Collonges-la-Rouge, Saint-Céré. **Credit Cards** Visa, Eurocard and MasterCard. **Spoken** English. **Closed** Christmas. **How to get there** (Map 24): 50km southeast of Brive via D38. Before Beaulieu, go turn left on D940, 2km, then right in front of cemetery.

The Château d'Arnac, which is located in a magnificent setting, offers vast, bright bedrooms that still have the charm of the past with their beautiful fireplaces. In decorating the château, Mrs. Webb has added refined English amenities, including large bathrooms which are modern and pleasant. The salon is in the large room on the ground floor where English-style breakfasts are served in winter. This is a true English bed and breakfast.

98
Domaine des Tilleuls

La Seiglière
23200 Aubusson
(Creuse)
Tel. 55 83 88 76
Fax 55 66 38 15
M. and Mme Sheridan

Rooms 3 with shower and WC, 1 with basin and WC. **Price** 250F (2 pers.). **Meals** Breakfast incl., evening meal 100F (wine incl.). **Facilities** Lounge. **Pets** Dogs not allowed. **Nearby** Restaurants, tapestry museum in Aubusson, workshops of Lissiers, Vassivière lake, golf (35km), equestrian center. **Credit cards** Not accepted. **Spoken** English. **Open** All year. **How to get there** (Map 24): 2km east of Aubusson, at the entrance to La Seiglière.

Mark Sheridan, an Englishman, has renovated this welcoming country mansion and opened it for guests. The well-proportioned bedrooms have 19th-century furniture and floral wallpapers. They are all comfortable and quiet, though the (invisible) road sometimes can be heard. Looking out on the park, there is an elegant lounge/dining room decorated in English style with beautiful wallpaper, pictures, and deep sofas. The Domaine offers good value for the money.

99
Chez Christiane et Raymond Steï

Chamalières Saint-Eblé
43300 Langeac
(Haute-Loire)
Tel. 71 77 12 26
Christiane and Raymond Sdeï

Rooms 3 with shower, WC and loft. Rooms cleaned on request. Price 150F (1 pers.), 185F (2 pers.), 245F (3 pers.), 305F (4 pers.). **Meals** Breakfast incl. Communal evening meal by reservation 60F (wine incl.). **Facilities** Lounge, trout fishing in river, archery, ping-pong, forest hiking, gold-panning on property. **Nearby** Tennis, swimming pool, riding, mountain bikes, fresh-water sports, golf (9 holes, 20km), cross-country skiing (5km); Romanesque churches, volcanos. **Credit cards** Not accepted. **Spoken** English (understood). **Open** All year. **How to get there** (Map 25): 32km northwest of Le Puy-en-Velay via N102. At intersection for Langeac turn left, then in 200m, left again.

This is a rustic, peaceful place to stay in the heart of the country. At the end of a small, well marked road, you will see the Steïs' pretty stone house surrounded by flowers. The bedrooms, which are located in the adjacent hay barn, have lofts and basic, modern amenities. Christiane and Raymond Sdeï can introduce you to panning for gold (!) or paleontology – or take you hiking. They are simple and charming.

100
Les Bastides du Mézenc

43550 Saint-Front
(Haute-Loire)
Tel. 71 59 51 57
Paul and Nadège Coffy

Rooms 2, 2 suites (3 pers.) with shower and WC. Rooms cleaned on request. **Price** 140F (per pers.), +50F (extra pers.). **Meals** Breakfast 30F, evening meals at communal table 150F (wine incl.). **Facilities** Lounge, piano, billiards, fishing, riding, horse boxes, dog sleds, cross-country and downhill skiing. **Pets** Dogs allowed on request. **Nearby** Lake Saint-Front, Le Puy-en-Velay (30km), golf (25km). **Credit cards** Not accepted. **Spoken** English, Spanish. **Open** All year. **How to get there** (Map 25): about 30km southeast of Le Puy; at Le Puy head east towards Valence, at Les Pandraux take D36, then D500 towards Fay; follow signs.

The small road leading to this isolated house crosses an immense, fantastic plateau of grassland and broom with Mount Mézenc (1754m) soaring in the distance. Inside, a large, magnificent lounge has antique furniture, exotic objects, paintings, and comfortable sitting areas. The bedrooms are equally attractive. The excellent evening meal is served in a friendly atmosphere.

101
Château de la Roche

La Roche-Chaptuzat
63260 Aigueperse
(Puy-de-Dôme)
Tel. 73 63 65 81
(1) 46 37 30 00 (winter)
Comte de Torcy

Rooms 3 and 2 suites (1-3 pers.), bath and WC. **Price** 600-800F (2 pers.), suite 1000F (2 pers.). **Meals** Breakfast incl. No evening meals. **Restaurants** Le Grillon in Chaptuzat (400m) and Le Marché (4km). **Facilities** Lounge, tour of the château. **Nearby** Swimming pool, riding, golf, gorges of La Sioule, Riom, Vichy. **Credit cards** Not accepted. **Spoken** English. **Open** End May – end Oct. **How to get there** (Map 25): 35km north of Clermont-Ferrand. From A71 take Gannat exit (12), then D12 towards Aigueperse, Chaptuzat, La Roche; follow signs.

On your arrival in the village, you will see this imposing medieval château standing on a verdant hillside Many rooms have their original stained glass windows and the furniture is equally antique. The bedrooms are. Copious, elegant breakfasts are served on china hand-painted by the owners. Count de Torcy and his daughter will welcome you with friendly hospitality.

102
Château de Collanges

63340 Collanges
(Puy-de-Dôme)
Tel. 73 96 47 30
M. and Mme Huillet

Rooms 3 with bath or shower, WC and telephone (TV on request). Rooms cleaned every day; linens changed every 3 days. **Price** 340F (1 pers.), 420F (2 pers.), +75F (extra pers.). **Meals** Breakfast incl. Evening meal at separate tables 130F. **Facilities** Lounge, billiards, baby grand piano, pond. **Nearby** Tennis, riding, lake and water sports, gliding, hiking, cross-country and alpine skiing (45km); châteaux of Auvergne, Romanesque abbeys, volcanos. **Credit cards** Not accepted. **Spoken** English. **Open** All year. **How to get there** (Map 25): 10km south of Issoire. From A75, take exit 17 (Saint-Germain-Lembron), and D214 to Ardes, then follow n signs to Collanges and château.

Several years ago, Georges and Michelle Huillet fell in love with this château, which was built in the 12th century and then modified in the 18th. They live there with their children and they offer guests three lovely, large bedrooms with period furniture and ultra-modern bathrooms. The elegant linens, the beautiful red walls of the salons, the orange groves and the music room in the romantic private park all combine to ensure you of an elegant and pleasant stay. You will be welcomed to the Château de Collanges with enthusiasm and warmth.

103
Chez M. Gebrillat

Chemin de Siorac
63500 Perrier – (Puy-de-Dôme)
Tel. 73 89 15 02
Fax 73 55 08 85
Paul Gebrillat and
Mireille de Saint-Aubain

Rooms 4 with bath or shower and WC. **Price** 250-290F (2 pers.) +100F (extra pers.). **Meals** Breakfast incl., evening meals by reservation 100F (wine not incl.). **Facilities** Fishing. **Pets** Dogs not allowed. **Nearby** Restaurants, volcano park, châteaux, forests, golf (40km), swimming and riding center, ski slopes and cross-country skiing, hang-gliding. **Credit cards** Not accepted. **Spoken** English. **Open** All year. **How to get there** (Map 25): 3km west of Issoire towards Champeix (D996); it's in the middle of the village.

This very old village house, situated close to the volcanos, has been tastefully restored and made comfortable. The bedrooms have a good blend of old regional furniture, unusual objects and very pretty fabrics. In the former stables, there is a double bedroom, an immense dormitory for children and a terrace. A large communal room and an equipped kitchen are at your disposal. In summer, breakfast is served outside overlooking the garden. The owners are welcoming and the prices very reasonable.

104
Moulinard

Moulinard-Boisseuil
87220 Boisseuil
(Haute-Vienne)
Tel. 55 06 91 22
M. and Mme Ziegler

Rooms 4 with shower (1 is hall shower), and WC. Rooms cleaned and linens changed every day. **Price** 210F (2 pers.), 280F (3 Pers.). **Meals** Breakfast incl. No evening meals. **Facilities** Lounge. **Pets** Dogs accepted on request. **Nearby** Restaurants, tennis, sports center, sports track, basketball, golf (18 holes, 6km); Romanesque Abbey of Solignac, Château de Chalucet, Limoges. **Credit cards** Not accepted. **Spoken** English. **Open** April - Oct. **How to get there** (Map 35): 12km south of Limoges. From A20, exit Boisseuil. In the commercial center; follow signs from N20 or A20.

Facing the farmhouse, the big white house and its shady garden are reserved for guests. Downstairs, a breakfast/sitting room and a kitchen are at your disposal. Upstairs, there are four bedrooms equipped with modern showers. The white bedrooms still have the atmosphere of the past with their parquet floors and authentic regional furniture. This is a lovely place to stay for relaxation in the heart of the lush Limoges countryside. The welcome is courteous.

105
Les Ourgeaux

Pageas
87230 Châlus
(Haute-Vienne)
Tel. 55 78 50 97
Fax 55 78 54 76
M. and Mme McKeand

Rooms 5 (3 with TV) with bath or shower, WC. **Price** 350-400F (2 pers.), +130F (extra pers.). **Children** under 7 not accepted. **Meals** Breakfast incl. In house-restaurant for lunch and evening meal 145F (wine not incl.) also à la carte. **Facilities** Lounge, bicycles. **Pets** Dogs not allowed. **Nearby** Tennis, golf, lake. **Credit cards** Visa, Eurocard and MasterCard (+2%). **Spoken** English. **Open** All year (Nov. – Easter by reservation). **How to get there** (Map 23): 25km southwest of Limoges via N21. In Châlus, turn right on D901 towards Rochechouart; after 2.5km follow signs. **No smoking.**

This house nestles among fields and woods and is totally quiet. The very friendly British owners have impeccably decorated the bedrooms with light, soft color schemes, pretty quilts, and some pieces of antique furniture.The salon and the small, intimate restaurant are also lovely, and the cuisine is truly gastronomic.

106
Château de Brie

87150 Champagnac-la-Rivière
(Haute-Vienne)
Tel. 55 78 17 52
Fax 55 78 14 02
Comte and Comtesse
du Manoir de Juaye

Rooms 4 with bath and WC. **Price** 500-600F (2 pers.), possible suite 800F (3 pers.). **Meals** Breakfast incl.; evening meals by reservation or at nearby restaurants. **Facilities** Lounge, lake and swimming pool. **Pets** Dogs allowed on request. **Nearby** Riding, sailing, fishing, walks, mountain biking, lake Saint-Mathieu. **Credit cards** Not accepted. **Spoken** English. **Open** April 1 – Nov. 1 (or by reservation). **How to get there** (Map 23): 45km southwest of Limoges via N21 to Châlus, then D42; it's between Châlus and Cussac.

Built in the 15th-century on medieval foundations, the Château de Brie has superb views over the countryside. Each huge bedroom has a style of its own, with antiques and beautiful decor. Decorative styles range from 16th-century to Empire; the small, impeccable bathrooms are resolutely modern. A very elegant lounge is available and breakfasts are served in the library. You will receive a warm and natural welcome in a château which has retained all its traditional style.

107

La Croix de Reh

Rue Amédée-Tarrade
87130 Châteauneuf-la-Forêt
(Haute-Vienne)
Tel. 55 69 75 37
Fax 55 69 75 38
Elizabeth and Patrick Mc Laughlin

Rooms 4 with bath or shower and WC; and 1 room with washbasin and shared WC. Price 150-250F (1 pers.), 200-300F (2 pers.), +80F (extra pers.), +100F (supp. room). **Meals** Breakfast incl. Evening meal at communal or separate tables 110F (wine not incl.). **Facilities** Lounge, tea room in house; weekend or 5-day English courses. **Pets** Dogs accepted on request. **Nearby** 3 tennis courts in village, lake, fishing; Pompadour, Uzerche, Saint-Léonard-de-Noblat. **Credit cards** Not accepted. **Spoken** English. **Open** All year. **How to get there** (Maps 23 and 24): 34km southeast of Limoges. From A20 exit Pierre-Buffière, then to Saint-Hilaire-Bonneval and follow Châteauneuf-la-Forêt.

Lying at the foot of the picturesque Millevaches Plateau, this pretty village house has just been restored by a very friendly Scottish couple. The *Rose, Bleue* and *Familiale* bedrooms are pleasantly decorated and have modern conveniences. The living room also serves as a charming tea room, where excellent Scottish pastries are served. In summer, dining tables are set out amidst the flowers and trees of the private park. ˙

108

Les Hauts de Boscartus

87520 Cieux
(Haute-Vienne)
Tel. 55 03 30 63
M. and Mme Hennebel

Rooms 2 with shower and shared WC. Rooms cleaned, beds made at extra cost. **Price** 200F (1 pers.), 250F (2 pers.). **Meals** Breakfast incl. No evening meals. **Facilities** Lounge. **Pets** Dogs not allowed. **Nearby** Restaurants, tennis, lake, golf, Montemart, Monts de Blond. **Credit cards** Not accepted. **Open** All year. **How to get there** (Map 23): 30km northwest of Limoges via N147 towards Bellac as far as Chamboret, then D711 to Cieux, then D204 and D95. **Non smokers** preferred.

Standing on a hillside, this house is surrounded by fir trees. The pleasant lounge is arranged around a fireplace at one end and a large picture window with a view of the beautiful lake. The attractive and comfortable bedrooms have lovely views and are totally quiet. On the breakfast table you will find croissants, white cheese and excellent home produce (honey, jams, spice bread). You will be warmly welcomed.

109
Moulin de Marsaguet

87500 Coussac-Bonneval
(Haute-Vienne)
Tel. 55 75 28 29
Valérie and Renaud Gizardin

Rooms 3 with bath or shower, and WC. Rooms cleaned every day, linens changed every 5 days. **Price** 200-220F (2 pers.). **Meals** Breakfast incl. Evening meal at communal table 80F (wine incl.). **Facilities** Lounge, 32-acre lake, sports fishing and boat rides, hiking on property. **Pets** Dogs allowed on request. **Nearby** Swimming pool, tennis, hiking paths, mountain bikes; Limoges, Ségur-le-Château, Pompadour Stud Farm, Lascaux (1 hr.). **Credit cards** Not accepted. **Spoken** English. **Open** All year. **How to get there** (Map 23): 40km south of Limoges via A20; exit Pierre-Buffière; take D19 towards Saint-Yrieix to intersection with Croix d'Hervy, then D57 towards Coussac for 5km along lake; it's on the left.

R enaud Girardin and his young wife live on the family duck farm at the charming Moulin de Marsaguet. They both are very friendly and he will be happy to take you fishing on the immense lake at the foot of the house. The bedrooms here are simple, bright and they have modern amenities. There is a large room for reading where evening meals are served in winter. In summer, breakfasts and dinners with homemade products are served beneath a beautiful linden tree.

110
Fougeolles

87120 Eymoutiers
(Haute-Vienne)
Tel. 55 69 11 44/55 69 18 50
Mme Jacques Du Montant

Rooms 3 with bath and WC. **Price** 250-300F (2 pers.) +50F (child). **Meals** Breakfast incl., poss. communal meals by reservation. **Facilities** Lounge, fishing, toy train museum, pedal cars. **Pets** Dogs not allowed. **Nearby** Golf, tennis, swimming pool, marine sports, plateau des Millevaches, lake Vassivière, Aubusson. **Credit cards** Not accepted. **Spoken** English. **Open** All year. **How to get there** (Map 24): 45km southeast of Limoges via D979; follow signs 500m before entering the village, on the left.

I n the heart of a vast farm, this 17th-century residence has pleasant, comfortable bedrooms furnished with antiques and brightened with lovely fabrics. The lounge and dining room have their original furnishings and numerous unusual objects. In good weather breakfast is served outside. This is truly a lovely place, where you will be warmly welcomed by the master of the house or his charming granddaughter.

111
Laucournet

Glanges
87380 Saint-Germain-les-Belles
(Haute-Vienne)
Tel: 55 00 81 27
M. and Mme Desmaison

Rooms 1 suite (up to 5 pers.) with 2 bedrooms, bath, shower and WC. Rooms cleaned at extra cost. **Price** 200F (1 pers.), 240F (2 pers.), 280F (3 pers.), 310F (4 pers.). **Meals** Breakfast incl. No evening meals. **Facilities** Lounge, horse boxes. **Nearby** Restaurants, tennis, rivers, lakes, riding, golf. **Credit cards** Not accepted. **Spoken** English. **Open** May – Sept. **How to get there** (Map 23): 36km southeast of Limoges via A20 to Magnac (exit 41), then D82 for 1km going east, then D120 for 5km towards Saint-Meard road. Follow signs.

Even if there are only two of you, this delightfully typical Limousin house will be reserved for you alone. On the ground floor is a lounge with some regional furniture, a more modern bathroom and a covered terrace for breakfast. On the *premier étage,* two comfortable and pleasantly decorated bedrooms have lovely views over the fields. You will enjoy the quiet privacy and excellent hospitality.

112
Le Repaire

87140 Vaulry
(Haute-Vienne)
Tel. 55 53 33 66
M. and Mme Richard Hartz

Rooms 3 and 1 suite (5 pers.) with shower and 2 shared WC (3 heated in winter). **Price** 130F (1 pers.), 170F (2 pers.), 210F (3 pers.); suite 350F (5 pers.). **Meals** Breakfast incl., half board 1000F per pers. weekly in double room, evening meal at communal or separate table 70F (wine incl.). **Pets** Animals not allowed. **Facilities** Horse stalls, river fishing. **Nearby** Lake, tennis, walks. **Credit cards** Not accepted. **Spoken** English. **Open** All year. **How to get there** (Map 23): 30km northwest of Limoges via N147. At Le Chatain take D72 to Breuilaufa, then Le Repaire.

This is an old renovated farmhouse in the heart of the Blond Mountains near forests and lakes. The bedrooms are very simple, with pine beds, old stone walls and Limousin-style wide-board floors. (Our favorite room has pretty pink curtains). The ambience is half-old, half-modern. There is often local trout or lamb for dinner. You will receive a friendly and discreet welcome.

113
Château de
Chorey-les-Beaune

Rue Jacques Germain
21200 Chorey-les-Beaune
(Côte-d'Or)
Tel. 80 22 06 05 Fax 80 24 03 93
M. and Mme François Germain

Rooms 5 and 1 suite (4 pers.) with bath, WC and telephone. **Price** 550-610F, +100F (extra pers.), suite 810F. **Meals** Breakfast 65F. No evening meals. **Facilities** Lounge, wine tasting in the cellars. **Nearby** Restaurants, golf (18 holes), Hôtel-Dieu in Beaune, wine growing area of Burgundy, Romanesque churches, abbeys. **Credit cards** Visa, Eurocard and MasterCard. **Spoken** English, German. **Open** April 1 – Nov. 3. **How to get there** (Map 19): 3km north of Beaune, at the entrance to the village.

The Château de Chorey-les-Beaune is very close to Beaune, in a wine-growing village. Entirely restored, it has belonged to the Germain family for several generations. The main building is 12th-century, the towers are 13th-century and the garden, encircled by a moat, breathes the Burgundian *art de vivre*. The bedrooms have been tastefully and simply decorated. M. and Mme. Germain are charming hosts and will take you to visit their cellars and taste their wines, which are known throughout the region.

114
Le Relais de Chasse

Chambœuf
21220 Gevrey-Chambertin
(Côte-d'Or)
Tel. 80 51 81 60
Fax 80 34 15 96
Michelle and Hubert Girard

Rooms 4 with bath and WC. **Price** 340-400 (2 pers.), 2 nights min. **Meals** Breakfast incl. No evening meal. **Facilities** Lounge, telephone. **Pets** Dogs not allowed. **Nearby** Restaurants, Beaune, Dijon, Wine Route. **Credit cards** Not accepted. **Spoken** English. **Open** All year. **How to get there** (Map 19): 18km southwest of Dijon via A31 exit Nuits-Saint-Georges, then N74 to Gevrey-Chambertin, then left on D31 towards Chamboeuf; 1st private drive on the left after the church. **No smoking.**

Le Relais de Chasse is a lovely house overlooking a beautiful park. It is in a charming small village close to the greatest vineyards of Burgundy. Most of the bedrooms are large and decorated in regional style with beautiful antique furniture. At a big table in the rustic dining room excellent breakfasts are served, including fruit, spice bread, cheeses and homemade jams. In good weather they are served outside on the terrace facing the garden. You will receive a warm welcome.

115
Château de Longecourt

21110 Longecourt-en-Plaine
(Côte-d'Or)
Tel. 80 39 88 76
Comtesse Bertrand de Saint-Seine

Rooms 3 with bath and WC, 2 with bath and shared WC. **Price** 700F (1-2 pers.), +150F (extra pers.). **Meals** Breakfast incl., evening meal at communal table 250F (wine incl.). **Facilities** Lounge, horse stalls, fishing. **Pets** Dogs allowed. **Nearby** Riding, golf (18 holes), Wine Route. **Credit cards** Not accepted. **Spoken** English. **Open** All year. **How to get there** (Map 19): 18km southeast of Dijon via D996 and D968 towards Saint-Jean-de-Losne; it's on the Place de la Mairie in Longecourt.

L ongecourt is a 17th-century jewel in pink brick surrounded by water, where Comtessse de Saint-Seine will welcome you simply and kindly. Some of the rooms are very sumptuous, while others are more informal. The salon-library and the pink dining room are very refined. All the bedrooms are different, quiet, comfortable and are furnished with antiques. The placid waters of the moat can be seen from the bedroom windows. We preferred the Catherine de Medici room.

116
L'Enclos

Arrans
21500 Montbard
(Côte-d'Or)
Tel. 80 92 16 12
Mireille and Marcel Clerget

Rooms 3 with shower and WC, 1 with bath and shared WC. Rooms cleaned on request. **Price** 250-300F (2 pers.) +100F (extra pers.). **Meals** Breakfast incl. No evening meals. **Facilities** Lounge, telephone. **Nearby** Restaurants, swimming pool, tennis, golf, Fontenay abbey (5km), Burgundy canals, Ancy le Franc. **Credit cards** Not accepted. **Open** March 1 – Nov. 30. **How to get there** (Map 18): 42km southwest of Châtillon-sur-Seine via D980. In Montbard take D5 towards Laignes for 9km.

L 'Enclos is a pretty village house in a flowery garden. It is ideal for families with its two large bedrooms and several beds. One is a very large, split-level room, but its bathroom is rather far away. The other, under the eaves, has three wide beds, a pretty shower room and a lovely view of the countryside; both are decorated in a very rustic style. The owners are very kind and welcoming.

117
Château de Beauregard

21390 Nan-sous-Thil
(Côte-d'Or)
Tel. 80 64 41 08
Fax 80 64 47 28
Nicole and Bernard Bonoron

Rooms 3 with bath and WC, and tel; and I suite (4 pers.), with bath, shower, 2 WC and telephone. **Price** 520-720F (2 pers.), suite 990F (2 pers.) +100F (extra pers.). **Meals** Breakfast incl. No evening meals. **Facilities** Lounge, pond on property. **Pets** Dogs accepted on request (100F suppl.). **Nearby** Restaurants, tennis, riding, bicycles, lakes (water sports), golf (18 holes, 15km); Abbaye de Fontenay, Semus-en-Auxois, Forges de Buffon. **Credit cards** Not accepted. **Spoken** English. **Closed** Nov. – Easter. **How to get there** (Map 18): I8km north of Saulieu. Autoroute A6, exit Bierre-Les-Semur towards Saulieu for 3km, then on left towards Vitteaux for about 3km. At stop sign, turn left towards Vitteaux and immediately on right to Nan-sous-Thil; go through village.

Beauregard, "beautiful view", well deserves its name, for it looks out far over the rich valleys of Burgundy. It has just been magnificently restored by Monsieur and Madame Bonoron, who will greet you with warm hospitality. There are three comfortable, elegant bedrooms decorated with antiques and the ultra-modern bathrooms have the charm of the past. There is also a sumptuous suite. Excellent breakfasts are served in a bright salon; the restaurant we recommend is also a real find.

118
Domaine de Loisy

28, rue Général-de-Gaulle
21700 Nuits-Saint-Georges
(Côte-d'Or)
Tel. 80 61 02 72
Fax 80 61 36 14
Comtesse Michel de Loisy

Rooms 4 with bath and WC, 2 without bath or shower. **Price** 450-850F (2 pers.), 250F. **Meals** Breakfast incl., evening meals at communal table 270F (wine incl.). **Facilities** Lounge, telephone, visit to the wine cellars and wine tasting 300F (2 pers.). **Pets** Dogs allowed on request. **Nearby** Swimming pool, tennis, riding, Dijon, Beaune, château of Clos de Vougeot. **Credit card** Amex. **Credit cards** Not accepted. **Spoken** English, Italian. **Open** All year by reservation. **How to get there** (Map 19): 22km south of Dijon via N74; it's on the edge of town on the Beaune road.

Mme Loisy is an enologist, giving wine lovers a special reason to enjoy this townhouse and its refined ambience. Two rather exotic gardens encircle the building. The bedrooms are very comfortable and furnished in old-fashioned style. Double-glazing insulates them from the busy road on which only one room is located. There is a lovely lounge, and breakfast (and sometimes dinner) are served in the large dining room.

119
Le Château de Flée

Flée
21140 Semur-en-Auxois
(Côte-d'Or)
Tel. 80 97 17 07
Fax 80 97 34 32
M. and Mme Bach

Rooms 1 suite (2 pers.) with bath, WC, telephone; a private house on lakefront with bath, WC, telephone and fax, TV, kitchenette, private parking, pontoon for windsurfing and motorboat, safe, minibar. **Price** Suite 850F (2 pers.); house 400F (2 pers.) +100F (extra pers.). **Meals** Breakfast incl. Meals at communal table 250F (wine incl.). **Facilities** Lounge and music room; swimming pool, pond, riding, bikes, hot-air balloon rides, glider rides, Epoisses cheese tasting on property. **Pets** Dogs accepted on request. **Nearby** Tennis, lake, golf (18 holes, 20km); Vézelay, Alésia, châteaux of Burgundy. **Credit cards** Not accepted. **Spoken** English, German. **Open** All year. **How to get there** (Map 18): 8km southeast of Saumur-en-Auxois. Exit Autoroute A6 Bierre-les-Semur: 2km, signs.

The 18th-century Château de Flée, which is being restored, lies in a peaceful, natural surrounding. It offers a suite which has exceptionally comfortable modern amenities. You can enjoy many different activities here, from horseback riding, taking a ride in a plane or a hot-air balloon (Monsieur Bach is a pilot), to fishing or biking. It is also pleasant to relax in the garden, which has a beautiful view of the lush hillsides nearby. Monsieur and Madame Bach are very open and warm.

120
Bouteuille

58110 Alluy
(Nièvre)
Tel. 86 84 06 65
Fax 86 84 03 41
Colette and André Lejault

Rooms 4 with bath or shower, WC and TV (1 with suppl. room). **Price** 220F (1 pers.), 250-300F (2 pers.). **eals** Breakfast incl. No evening meals. Kitchen for guests, barbecue and flat-stone grill in pigeon loft. **Pets** Dogs not allowed. **Nearby** Restaurants, barge trips on canal, mountain bikes, riding, swimming pool, fishing and hunting on 295-acre preserve; Château de Chatillon, Musée du Septennat et de la Mine. **Credit cards** Not accepted. **Spoken** English. **Open** All year. **How to get there** (Map 18): 40km east of Nevers via D978 towards Château Chinon and Autun: signs beginning at L'Huy-Moreau; 5km after Rouy.

This inviting 17th-century house is part of a beautiful group of farm buildings which look out over fields as far as the eye can see. The house is furnished with a number of lovely antiques and is kept immaculate. The bedrooms are quite large and comfortable and have gleaming, modern bathrooms. Madame Lejault serves delicious breakfasts in a pleasant small room in the kitchen, and the welcome at Bouteille is very friendly.

121
Château de Lesvault

58370 Onlay
(Nièvre)
Tel. 86 84 32 91
Fax 86 84 35 78
Mme Lee and M. Simonds

Rooms 6 with bath or shower and WC, 4 with bath and shared WC. **Price** 250-400F (1 pers.), 350-475F (2 pers.). **Meals** Breakfast incl., poss. evening meals at communal table, 130F (wine not incl.). **Facilities** Telephone, horse stalls, fly fishing. **Pets** Dogs allowed in the kennel on request. **Nearby** Swimming pool, tennis. **Credit cards** Amex, Visa, Eurocard and MasterCard. **Spoken** English. **Open** All year. **How to get there** (Map 18): 5km west of Château-Chinon via D978, then D37 to Moulins-Engilbert, then 5km towards Onlay on D18.

From its lovely sloping park, le Château de Lesvault overlooks a green landscape. The hospitality is charming; the atmosphere artistic. Painters and sculptors from all over the world come here and their work is scattered about the rooms. All the bedrooms are quiet, comfortable and well decorated. Breakfast is served at separate tables in a small dining room, and candlelight dinners, which are delicious and elegant, are served in a bright vaulted room.

122
La Rêverie

6, rue Joyeuse
58150 Pouilly-sur-Loire
(Nièvre)
Tel. 86 39 07 87
M. and Mme Lapeyrade

Rooms 5 with bath and WC, telephone and TV, 1 with whirlpool bath. **Price** 250-420F (2 pers.). **Meals** Breakfast 35F. No evening meals. **Facilities** Lounge, art gallery. **Pets** No animals allowed. **Nearby** Restaurants, tennis, golf, Sancerre. **Credit cards** Not accepted. **Spoken** English. **Open** All year (on request in winter). **How to get there** (Map 17): 40km from Nevers and Bourges; 15km south of Cosne-sur-Loire via N7.

Set in the peace of the charming village of Pouilly-sur-Loire, La Rêverie (the dream) well deserves its name. The care and kindness of M. and Mme Lapeyrade are worthy of special mention. All the comfortable bedrooms have been lovingly decorated with well-matched fabrics, wallpapers and carpets. The bathrooms are luxurious. The sitting-room decoration is in 19th-century style, and the excellent, refined breakfasts are served in the art gallery to musical accompaniment.

123
Château du Vieil Azy

Le Vieil Azy
58270 Saint-Benin-d'Azy
(Nièvre)
Tel. 86 58 47 93
Vicomtesse Benoist d'Azy le Noan

Rooms 5 and 1 suite with bath, WC and telephone. **Price** 300-400F (1-2 pers.), suite 600F (1-4 pers.). **Meals** Breakfast 30F, evening meals by reservation 120F (wine incl.), 90F (child). **Restaurants** Auberge de Sauvigny and Moulin de L'Etang (15km). **Facilities** Lounge, riding, fishing. **Nearby** Golf (18 holes), swimming pool, tennis, château d'Azy, château of the dukes of Nevers, Apremont. **Credit cards** Not accepted. **Open** Easter – Nov 1. **How to get there** (Map 18): 16km east of Nevers via N81 towards Decize, then D978 to St-Benin-d'Azy, then D9 after the municipal swimming pool.

This château stands in the middle of a park with ancient trees, close to a large lake. There is a beautiful wooden staircase in the entrance hall and the large lounge has a library and an impressive fireplace. The lovely bedrooms are somewhat dark and have an atmosphere of the past. The château is a good departure point for various excursions.

124
La Ferme

71460 Bissy-sous-Uxelles
(Saône-et-Loire)
Tel. 85 50 15 03
M. and Mme de La Bussière

Rooms 2 with shower and WC, 2 with shower and shared WC, 2 with basin sharing 1 shower and 2 WCs. **Price** 100-200F (1 pers.), 160-290F (2 pers.). **Meals** Breakfast incl. No evening meals. **Facilities** Horse stalls. **Nearby** Restaurants, lake, fishing, golf, Cluny, Cormatin. **Credit cards** Not accepted. **Spoken** English, German. **Open** All year. **How to get there** (Map 19): 17km west of Tournus via D215 towards Mancey. Go through Mancey then, on left, towards Bussy. In Bissy beside the church.

In this delightful small village close to the church, you will find the courtyard of this charming farmhouse. The hospitality here is very friendly and lively. The bedrooms have been well restored and furnished with regional furniture; two have a kitchenette. (The one with the parquet floor is more inviting; we do not recommend those with only a wash room.) Excellent and generous breakfasts are served at a large table.

125
Château de Sassangy

Sassangy
71390 Buxy
(Saône-et-Loire)
Tel. 85 96 12 40
Fax 85 96 11 44
M. and Mme Marceau

Rooms 6 with bath or shower, WC and telephone, and 1 suite (4-6 pers.) with 2 bedrooms, lounge, bath and WC. **Price** 430-480F (1 pers.), 540-680F (2 pers.), 640-940F (3-6 pers.). **Meals** Breakfast incl., evening meals by reservation 180F (wine incl.). **Facilities** Lounge. **Pets** Dogs not allowed. **Nearby** Golf, cellar visits, châteaux, Romanesque churches, Beaune, Cluny. **Credit cards** Visa, Eurocard and MasterCard. **Spoken** English. **Open** March – Nov. **How to get there** (Map 19): 6km west of Buxy via A6 Châlon Sud exit, then towards Monchanin on N80, exit Sassangy after 15km.

This elegant 18th-century château has been artistically and tastefully restored. Standing on a small hill, it enjoys panoramic views over a lovely park, an ornamental lake, and pastures. The bedrooms are large and very comfortable. You will dine in a huge, bright, vaulted kitchen, which is well equipped and tastefully decorated. Mme Marceau does the cooking and will welcome you warmly.

126
Ferme-Auberge de Lavaux

Chatenay
71800 La Clayette
(Saône-et-Loire)
Tel. 85 28 08 48
M. Paul Gélin

Rooms 5 with bath or shower and WC. **Price** 260-300F (2 pers.). **Meals** Breakfast incl., meals at the farm restaurant 80-100F (wine not incl.). **Facilities** Fishing. **Pets** Dogs not allowed. **Nearby** Romanesque churches, Cluny, Paray-le-Monial. **Credit cards** Not accepted. **Open** Easter - Nov. 11. **How to get there** (Map 18): about 40km southeast of Paray-le-Monial via N79 towards Charolles, then D985 towards La Clayette and D987 towards Mâcon for 5km, then left on D300 towards Chatenay.

In this green, hilly part of Burgundy, this lovely farmhouse inn stands on a hillside surrounded by well tended gardens. The bedrooms (somewhat expensive this year) open onto an outside wooden gallery. They are simple, quite large, and decorated in rustic style; however, they are somewhat dark. The former stables have been converted into a pleasant inn, with beams and exposed stonework. You will enjoy tempting local cuisine at very good prices; the owner is very hospitable.

127
Les Buissonnets

102, Grande-Rue
71150 Fontaines
(Saône-et-Loire)
Tel. 85 91 48 49
Jacotte and Michel Chignac

Rooms 3 with bath and WC. **Price** 270-380F (1-2 pers.). **Meals** Breakfast incl. Meals at separate tables 150F (wine incl.). **Facilities** Lounge. **Nearby** Golf (18 holes, 8km), tennis in village, jogging track, swimming pool, riding, hot-air ballon; Beaune, Tournus, Cluny, Route des Vins. **Credit cards** Not accepted. **Spoken** English, Italian. **Open** All year. **How to get there** (Map 19): 12km northwest of Châlon-sur-Saône. Autoroute exit Châlon Nord, then N6 towards Chagny. 3km after Champforgeuil, go towards Fontaines on left. At 10km from autoroute exit. (Access possible via TGV train.)

Les Buissonnets is an elegant Burgundian house surrounded by a private park and located in a charming village. The interior decoration is especially lovely. There are beautiful fabrics coordinated with pretty English wallpaper, antique furniture and, in the beautiful bedrooms, soft eiderdowns and patchwork quilts. A salon/library is reserved for guests. In the adjacent dining room, you will be served excellent family cuisine. The Chignacs are very friendly and welcoming.

128
Château de la Fredière

Céron
71110 Marcigny
(Saône-et-Loire)
Tel. 85 25 19 67
Fax 85 25 35 01
Mme Edith Charlier

Rooms 9 and 2 suites with bath or shower, WC and telephone. **Price** 290-620F (1-2 pers.), suite 750F. **Meals** Breakfast 55F, evening meals by reservation (except Wednesday) 100-150F (wine not incl.). **Facilities** Lounge, swimming pool, 18-hole golf course. **Pets** Dogs allowed on request. **Nearby** Romanesque churches. **Credit cards** Not accepted. **Spoken** English. **Open** Jan 10 – Dec 20. **How to get there** (Map 25): 40km north of Roanne via D482 and D982 to Marcigny, then D990 towards Le Donjon-Lapalisse; signposted golf.

Château de la Fredière is surrounded by a lovely golf course. Mme Charlier will welcome you with warm hospitality. The pleasant *premier étage* bedrooms are well decorated and furnished. (Avoid the Rose room, which is too small.) Those on the *second étage*, which have just been added, are truly luxurious, perfectly soundproofed and brightened with beautiful fabrics. There is a beautiful, charming lounge. Near the lake, you will find the prettily decorated new restaurant.

129
Chez M. et Mme Lamy

Anzy-le-Duc
71110 Marcigny
(Saône-et-Loire)
Tel. 85 25 17 21
M. and Mme Christian Lamy

Rooms 2 with private bath and shared WC. **Price** 220F (1 pers.), 250F (2 pers.) +100F (extra pers.). **Meals** Breakfast incl. Rooms cleaned every 5 days. No meals (kitchenette and washing machine available). **Restaurants** L'Auberge du Prieuré 10km, and others. **Facilities** Lounge. **Pets** Dogs allowed on request. **Nearby** Golf (18 holes, 15km), tennis in village, swimming in river (500m), riding (10km), barge trips on Canal de Bourgogne, canoeing, kayaks, Romanesque church circuit, Faïence Museum in Marcigny, Paray-le-Monial. **Credit cards** Not accepted. **Closed** Nov. 1 – April 1. **How to get there** (Map 25): 25km southeast of Paray-le-Monial via D362 towards Roanne. In Montceaux, L'Etoile, towards Anzy-le-Duc. In village near church.

Monsieur and Madame Lamy have a small independent guest house— once a schoolhouse —which is located in the beautiful village of Ancy-le-Duc, a veritable haven of tranquillity. The modern, comfortable bedrooms are decorated in pretty, bright colors and each has its own bath; the toilets, however, are shared. The large living room is warm and welcoming with music, games, or television. You can enjoy two lovely gardens, as well as warm hospitality in this friendly family house.

130
Les Récollets

Place du Champ-de-Foire
71110 Marcigny
(Saône-et-Loire)
Tel. 85 25 03 34
Fax 85 25 06 91
Mme Badin

Rooms 7 with bath and WC, 2 suites (4-6 pers.) with 2 bedrooms, bath and WC. **Price** 320F (1 pers.), 420-450F (2 pers.) +120F (extra pers.). **Meals** Breakfast incl., evening meals by reservation (separate tables) 200F (wine incl.). **Facilities** Lounge. **Credit cards** Amex, Visa, Eurocard and MasterCard. **Nearby** Golf, Roman tour. **Credit cards** Not accepted. **Open** All year. **How to get there** (Map 25): 30km north of Roanne via D482 and D982 in the Digoin direction to Marcigny.

Marcigny was once a charming village and Les Récollets was a beautiful house, with bedrooms elegantly decorated with antique furniture and floral fabrics. The house is still pleasant but we were horrified by what has become of the view. The beautiful garden today is spoiled by two sheds which have been subsidized by the village and built at its edge. Fortunately, Madame Badin's devotion and kindness have not changed and Les Récollets has not lost its personality. It is a good place for an overnight stay.

131
Château de Poujux

Saint-Aubin-en-Charollais
71430 Palinges
(Saône-et-Loire)
Tel. 85 70 43 64
M. and Mme Céali

Rooms 7 with bath or shower and WC. **Price** 350-500F (2 pers.) +50F (extra pers.); children under 6 free. **Meals** Breakfast 30F. No evening meals. **Facilities** Lounge. **Nearby** Cluny abbey, Romanesque churches, villages of Berzé-le-Châtel and Martailly-les-Briançon. **Credit cards** Not accepted. **Spoken** English, German. **Open** End May – Sept 30. **How to get there** (Map 18): 14km north of Paray-le-Monial via Paris-Châlon autoroute, then N80 to Le Creusot, then 'route express' towards Paray-le-Monial, exit Charolles; it's before Saint-Aubin.

A part from looking after their guests, the owners of this château breed racing thoroughbreds. The bedrooms are large, pleasant, but rather simply furnished, with some 19th-century pieces and comfortable beds. There is a lounge and a dining room where generous breakfasts are served. The château is a very quiet place where you will be well received, but the prices are still high.

132
Château de Martigny

Poisson
71600 Paray-le-Monial
(Saône-et-Loire)
Tel. 85 81 53 21
Mme Edith Dor

Rooms 3 with bath and WC, 1 with bath and shared WC, 2 with shared bath and WC, 1 studio (4 pers.) and 1 suite (3 pers.) with bath and WC. **Price** 350-600F (1-2 pers.), suite 500-700F (3 pers.), 600-750F (4 pers.). **Meals** Breakfast incl., lunch and evening meal at communal table, or not as preferred, 160F (wine not incl.). **Facilities** Lounge, swimming pool, bicycles, drama courses, painting (introduction to artists). **Pets** Dogs allowed on request. **Nearby** Riding, tennis, fishing, golf (25km), Romanesque churches. **Credit cards** Not accepted. **Spoken** English. **Open** Easter – Nov 1. **How to get there** (Map 18): 8km south of Paray-le-Monial via D34.

L ying in the midst of the countryside, the Château de Martigny has been extrremely tastefully furnished and has a superb view. The beautiful, comfortable bedrooms are furnished with antiques. (Those beneath the eaves are less classic and are handsomely arranged, but the view is less beautiful.) The cuisine is excellent and artists occasionally come here for dinner or to work. Edith Dor is a charming hostess.

133
La Chaumière

Le Bourg
71370 Baudrières
(Saône-et-Loire)
Tel. 85 47 32 18
Fax 85 47 41 42
Mme Vachet

Rooms 2 with bath or shower and WC (TV on request). Rooms cleaned on request. **Price** 260F (1 pers.), 320F (2 pers.) +80F (extra pers.). **Meals** Breakfast incl. No evening meals. **Facilities** Lounge, tennis (+supl.). **Nearby** Riding, swimming pool, lake, fishing, golf (18 holes), wine cellar visits, Romanesque churches. **Credit cards** Not accepted. **Spoken** English, Italian. **Open** March - Nov. (on request out of season). **How to get there** (Map 19): From north, exit Chalon-Sud on A6, towards Chalon. Itineraire Lyon bis for 15km via D978 to Auroux-sur-Saône, then D933 to Nassey, and on right, signs Baudrières via D160. From south, via RN6. In Sennecy-le-Grand, D18 to Gigny-sur-Saône. Go across Saône. Follow signs.

This very pretty house covered in Virginia creeper is located in a peaceful small village. The bedrooms, tastefully arranged, are comfortable and welcoming. The decor is equally tasteful in the lounge, which has old regional furniture. Excellent breakfasts are served outside under a wooden canopy in good weather. You will be received with friendly hospitality.

134
Château de Beaufer

Route d'Ozenay
71700 Tournus
(Saône-et-Loire)
Tel. 85 51 18 24
Fax 85 51 25 04
M. and Mme Roggen

Rooms 6 with bath and WC, including 1 single with shower. **Price** 400F (1 pers.), 550-680F (2 pers.), 710F (3 pers.). **Meals** Breakfast incl. No evening meal. **Restaurants** In Tournus. **Facilities** Lounge, swimming pool. **Pets** Dogs allowed on request (+40F). **Nearby** Golf, polo. **Credit cards** Visa, Eurocard and MasterCard. **Spoken** English, Italian, German. **Open** Mid-March – Nov 1 (by reservation out of season, 3 days min.). **How to get there** (Map 19): 25km south of Chalon-sur-Saône via N6 and A6 to Tournus, then D14 towards Ozenay; signposted 3km from Tournus.

This small château backs onto a hill and faces a rural, wooded landscape. Beautifully arranged for the comfort and pleasure of its guests, it has a handsome, high-beamed lounge that opens onto a swimming pool. The bedrooms, located in several buildings, are large, well kept, and decorated with prints and pretty furniture; the beds are huge and the bathrooms superb.

135
Château de Prunoy

Prunoy
89120 Charny
(Yonne)
Tel. 86 63 66 91
Fax 86 63 77 79
Mme Roumilhac

Rooms 13 with bath, WC and telephone, 6 suites (4-5 pers.) with 2 bedrooms, bath, WC and telephone. **Price** 650F (2 pers.), suite 850F (4 pers.). **Meals** Breakfast 50F, half board 420F per pers. in double room, (3 days min.), lunch and dinner 180F (wine not incl.). **Facilities** Lounge, swimming pool, tennis, whirlpool bath, boating on the lake. **Nearby** Riding, golf, Wine Route. **Credit cards** All major. **Closed** 3 Jan. – 15 Feb. **How to get there** (Map 18): 23km west of Joigny via A6, exit Joigny towards Montargis, Charny (D943 and D16).

Standing in a superb park with two lakes, this château is full of surprises. The extremely comfortable bedrooms contain an amazing accumulation of old furniture, objects, and ceramics. Even the beautiful bathrooms are unusual. Generous breakfasts can be served the minute you awake; and there is an excellent restaurant in the château, with simple but refined cuisine. Mme Roumilhac's warm hospitality completes the picture.

136
La Borde

89130 Leugny
(Yonne)
Tel. 86 47 64 28
Fax 86 47 60 28
Christine and François-Jean Duclos

Rooms 4 with bath and shower, WC and telephone. Sheets changed every 2-3 days, towels every day. **Price** 580, 680F (2 pers.). **Meals** Breakfast incl. Special weekend full-board price 1150-1250F (wine incl.). Meals noon and evening at communal or separate tables 150, 180F (wine incl.). **Facilties** Lounge. Fishing on pond, bikes and riding (suppl.). **Pets** Dogs allowed on request. **Nearby** Swimming pool, tennis (4km), golf (18 holes, 20km); Route des Vins, Château de Saint-Fargeau, Moutier fresco, Saint-Sauveur-en-Puisaye. **Credit cards** Not accepted. **Spoken** English. **Open** All year. **How to get there** (Map 18): 20km southwest of Auxerre. A6 exit Toussy. In Toussy, D950 towards Avallon and in Lugny, sign.

These 16th-century houses have been marvelously restored by an enthusiastic, welcoming young couple. The decor includes antique-style plaster on the walls, handsome old floor tiles, doors and beams of pale oak, and superb bathrooms. The bedrooms are delightfully elegant and comfortable. The same tasteful details can be admired in the salon, the library/TV room and the kitchen, which is bright and beautiful with its gleaming copper pots. We are told the meals are delicious!

137
Les Morillons

89250 Mont-Saint-Sulpice
(Yonne)
Tel. 86 56 18 87
Fax 86 43 05 07
Françoise and Didier Brunot

Rooms 3 rooms with bath or shower. Rooms cleaned every day. **Price** 350F (2 pers.). **Meals** Breakfast incl. Meals at communal table 160F (wine incl.). **Facilities** Lounge, fishing, horse-drawn carriage, mountain bikes. **Nearby** Tennis, Golf (18 holes, 26km); Route des Vins (Chablis), Auxerre, Canal de Bourgogne. **Credit cards** Not accepted. **Spoken** English. **Open** All year. **How to get there** (Map 18): 22km north of Auxerre. Autoroute A6, exit Auxerre Nord towards Moneteau (D84), go through Seignelay, Hauterive, on right Mont-Saint-Sulpice: 2km road in front of "Mairie". **No smoking.**

Surrounded by fields, the Morillons estate is made up of several buildings built around a vast courtyard, with a terrace overlooking the peaceful Serein River. The interior is tastefully decorated and very well kept. Didier and Françoise Brunot adore their region and, on request, they will organize numerous sports, cultural and wine-tasting activities. Hospitable and friendly, they attach great importance to the quality and atmosphere of their dinners.

138
La Coudre

La Coudre
89120 Perreux
(Yonne)
Tel 86 91 61 42/86 91 62 91
M. and Mme Lusardi

Rooms 3 with bath and WC. **Price** 470-560F (2 pers.). **Meals** Breakfast incl., evening meals at communal table, by reservation 180F (wine incl.). **Restaurant** Le Cheval Blanc in Charny. **Facilities** Lounge, telephone, potter's studio on the property. **Pets** Dogs not allowed. **Nearby** Golf (18 holes), tennis, riding, château de Saint-Fargeau. **Credit cards** Not accepted. **Spoken** English, Italian. **Open** All year. **How to get there** (Map 18): From Paris (otherwise phone for itinerary): 15km from A6 Joigny exit. Head towards Montargis, then D3 towards Toucy to Sommecaise and D57 towards Perreux; 1km before the village.

This large, well-restored house, with a pretty garden beside a small country road, has spacious rooms furnished with beautiful antiques. The large bedrooms, plush, comfortable, and handsomely decorated, feature superb bathrooms. Breakfast is served at a long wooden table, dinners are made with the best regional produce, and the wines are excellent.

139
Le Moulin
de Poilly-sur-Serein

89310 Poilly-sur-Serein
(Yonne)
Tel. 86 75 92 46
Fax 86 75 95 21
Hester and Pascal Moreau

Rooms 5 with bath or shower and WC. **Price** 230F (1 pers.), 300-360F (2 pers.). **Meals** Breakfast incl. or 60F (extra pers.). No evening meals. **Facilities** Lounge; fishing and swimming in river on property. **Pets** Dogs allowed on request. **Nearby** Restaurants, riding, visit of village of Noyers, Route des Vins (Chablis). **Credit cards** Not accepted. **Spoken** German, English, Dutch and Swedish. **Closed** Nov 1 – Easter. **How to get there** (Map 18): 12km southeast of Chablis. Autoroute A6, exit Auxerre Sud, then D965 towards Tonnerre. In Chablis, D45 towards Chiché, Chemilly. 3km after Chemilly: Moulin at entrance to Poilly.

This majestic mill, restored by a friendly couple (Mme is a potter and M. is a winegrower), spans the Serein River at the entrance to the village. The spaciousness and the dominant colors – the natural wood tones of the beams and pillars, white and beige – confer a beautiful harmony to the interior decoration, including that in the comfortable bedrooms. Beautiful antique furniture and decorative objects further enhance the decor. The Moulin is a refined place to stay, and... is as serene as the river of that name.

140
La Chasseuserie

Lavau
89170 Saint-Fargeau
(Yonne)
Tel 86 74 16 09
Mme Anne-Marie Marty

Rooms 1 with bath and WC, 1 suite of 2 bedrooms with bath and WC. Rooms cleaned, if required, on payment of supplement. **Price** 250F (2 pers., 1st night), 210F (2 pers., 2nd and 3rd nights), suite 430F (4 pers.,1st night), 350F (4 pers., 2nd and 3rd nights). **Meals** Breakfast incl. No evening meal. **Facilities** Lounge, tennis, bicycles. **Pets** Small dogs allowed on request. **Nearby** Restaurants, canals, shooting, fishing, Saint-Fargeau, Ratilly. **Credit cards** Not accepted. **Spoken** English. **Open** All year, by written reservation. **How to get there** (Map 17): 52km southwest of Auxerre via D965 to Lavau, then D74 towards Bléneau for 3km; signposted.

Standing in a countryside covered with forest, this house is surrounded by flowers. The two guest rooms, including a suite for families, are comfortable and prettily decorated. There are also a pleasant lounge and a charming dining room where breakfasts are served. (In good weather, they are served in the garden.) Madame Marty is a friendly hostess and her prices are very reasonable.

141
Chez Mme Defrance

4, place de la Liberté
89710 Senan
(Yonne)
Tel. 86 91 59 89
Mme Defrance

Rooms 1 with shower and WC, 2 sharing bath and WC (possible suite). **Price** 180-260F (1 pers.), 250-350F (2 pers.). **Meals** Breakfast incl., evening meals at communal table, by reservation 90F (wine incl.). **Facilities** Lounge. **Pets** Dogs not allowed. **Nearby** Restaurants, tennis, golf. **Credit cards** Not accepted. **Spoken** English. **Open** All year. **How to get there** (Map 18): 26km northwest of Auxerre via A6 exit Auxerre Nord, then N6 towards Joigny and D14. In Bassou turn left for Neuilly and D153 to Senan. From Paris, A6 exit Joigny, then D89.

This is a charming house in a village, set back somewhat from a grass-covered walk planted with lime trees. It is very quiet. The interior is simple and well kept with some antique furniture. We recommend the large bedroom, which is very pleasant with floral wallpaper, waxed wood floor and a superb shower room. Mme Defrance, who is very friendly, will ask you to choose where you would like to have breakfast: in your bedroom, the garden or the dining room.

142
Les Lammes

89210 Venizy
(Yonne)
Tel. 86 43 44 42
Mme Antoinette Puissant

Rooms 8 suites (2-4 pers.) with kitchen, lounge, bath and WC; and 2 family suites (5-8 pers.) **Price** 420F (2 pers.) +120F (extra pers.). **Meals** Breakfast incl. No evening meals. **Facilities** Swimming pool, fishing. **Nearby** Restaurants, tennis, Wine Route, Fontenay abbey. **Credit cards** Not accepted. **Spoken** English, German, Italian. **Closed** End Oct. – Easter (poss. weekly or weekend rental of apartment). **How to get there** (Map 18): 30km northeast of Auxerre via N77. Go through Saint-Florentin and take D30 towards Venizy; 300m after l'Auberge de Pommerats on the left.

This large farm is made up of several buildings. The bedrooms are all suites with a living area and a kitchen area. Patchwork bedcovers and antique furniture make for a pleasant atmosphere, and many rooms have a view of the large swimming pool. Breakfast is served in a huge well-decorated room or outside under a canopy. You will receive anthusiastic welcome.

143
Domaine de Montpierreux

Route de Chablis
89290 Venoy - (Yonne)
Tel. 86 40 20 91
Fax 86 40 28 00
Francoise and François Choné

Rooms 5 with bath or shower, WC, and telephone. Sheets changed every 2-3 days, towels every day. **Price** 250-300F (2 pers.), +60F extra pers.). **Meals** Breakfast incl. No evening meals. **Facilities** Hiking on property. **Pets** Dogs allowed in kennel only. **Nearby** Restaurants, tennis in village, Chablis and Auxerre Route des Vins, Cistercian Abbey of Pontigny, village of Noyers-sur-Serein. **Credit cards** Not accepted. **Spoken** English. **Open** All year. **How to get there** (Map 18): 10km east of Auxerre. A6 exit Auxerre Sud, then D965 towards Chablis, then signs: house in 3km on right.

L ying in the midst of the country, this large farm produces wine and truffles. You will enjoy very pleasant bedrooms which are located on the *second étage* (third floor); they are comfortable, personalized and each has a small bathroom which is kept immaculate. Breakfasts are served in a room reserved for guests or in the garden in good weather. The Chonés are very friendly and helpful.

144
Cochepie

Chochepie
89500 Villeneuve-sur-Yonne
(Yonne)
Tel. 86 87 39 76
Fax 86 87 39 77
Mme Claire Strulik

Rooms 1 and 2 suites (4 pers.) with bath or shower and WC; and 3 rooms which share 1 bath and WC. Price 350F (1 pers.), 400F (2 pers.); suite 650-750F; +200F (extra pers.). **Meals** Breakfast incl. No evening meals. **Restaurant** La Lucarne aux Chouettes (1.5km). **Facilities** Lounge, swimming pool and tennis court on the property. **Pets** Dogs not allowed. **Nearby** Golf (18 holes, 25 km). **Credit cards** Not accepted. **Spoken** English, Spanish and German. **Open** All year. **How to get there** (Maps 10 and 18): Autoroute A 6, exit Courtenay, then Villeneuve-sur-Yonne. From the church, on left, go under Sens portal, then towards Dixmont, 1st on right for 1km, go under bridge; then 2nd lane on left and house.

T his is an old farm which has been converted into a superb residence in the heart of the countryside. The bedrooms have very comfortable accommodations and are decorated in faultless taste. Each can be combined with another to form a suite, which is ideal for a family or a group of friends. Copious breakfasts are served in a beautiful salon reserved exclusively for guests that opens onto the garden. This is a magnificent place to stay, with a swimming pool, tennis court and friendly people.

145
La Tarais

22100 Calorguen
(Côtes d'Armor)
Tel. 96 83 50 59
Deborah and Bernard Kerkhof

Rooms 4 with shower and WC. **Price** 250F (2 pers.) +75F (extra pers.). **Meals** Breakfast incl. (English breakfast poss. +15F); meals at separate tables from July 1 – Sept. 30 75-100F (wine incl.). **Facilities** Lounge. **Pets** Dogs not admitted. **Nearby** Restaurants, swimming pool, tennis court in village, hiking along the Rance, golf (20km); sea (20km), Saint-Malo, Château Bourbansais, Combourg, Vieux Dinan, villages of Bécherel and Léhon. **Credit cards** Not accepted. **Spoken** English, German, Dutch. **Open** All year. **How to get there** (Map 6): 7km south of Dinan via D12 towards Léhon. In Léhon, take road to Calorguen, then signs.

A friendly young Anglo-Dutch couple have just finished decorating four small guest bedrooms in this old farm located in a tiny Breton hamlet. The rooms are sober but have been brightened with pretty eiderdowns and handsome English furniture. They are kept in excellent condition. Breakfasts are served at separate tables in a pleasant dining room (which also serves as a tea room) or outdoors when the weather permits. La Tarais is well worth the reasonable price.

146
Château de Bonabry

22120 Hillion
(Côtes d'Armor)
Tel. 96 32 21 06
Vicomte and Vicomtesse Louis du Fou de Kerdaniel

Rooms 2 suites (room and salon, 4-6 pers.) with bath or shower and WC (1 with whirlpool; TV on request in suite. **Price** 500-600F (2 pers.) +100F (extra pers.). **Meals** Breakfast incl., meals at communal table twice/week 150F (wine incl.). **Facilities** Lounge, fishing on rocks, horse stalls (poss. riding), paddocks and quarry on property. **Pets** Dogs allowed in kennel only. **Nearby** Restaurant, sea (300m); Cap Fréhel ornithological preserve (Saint-Brieuc), Château de Bienaisis. **Credit cards** Not accepted. **Spoken** English. **Open** June 1 – Sept 30. **How to get there** (Map 6): 12km northeast of Saint-Brieuc. On N 12, exit Yffiniac/Hillion. In Hillion, towards La Granville. 30m from Hillion on left, entrance to property (cross).

B onabry spreads out over fields, woods, and cliffs, with the lanes of the château leading to an immense beach. The façade as well as the stables, the pigeon loft and the chapel have been left in their original state, while the interior of the château has just been very tastefully refurbished. The two suites, each with an immense private salon, are superb. The decor essentially includes antique furniture, family paintings and hunting tropies. You will enjoy authentic château life at Bonabry, and very friendly hospitality.

147
Ferme de Malido

Saint-Alban
22400 Lamballe
(Côtes d'Armor)
Tel. 96 32 94 74
Fax 96 32 92 67
M. and Mme Robert Legrand

Rooms 6 with shower and WC. **Price** 180F (1 pers.), 200-300F (2 pers.) +70F (extra pers.). **Meals** Breakfast incl. No evening meals; barbecue in the garden. **Facilities** Lounge, telephone. **Pets** Dogs allowed on request (+20F). **Nearby** Restaurants, swimming pool, tennis, fishing, riding, sailing, golf, walks. **Credit cards** Not accepted. **Spoken** English, German. **Open** All year. **How to get there** (Map 6): 21km northeast of Saint-Brieuc. Take N12 to Lamballe, then D791 north from Lamballe towards Le Val André. At Saint-Alban, take the Saint-Brieuc road for 2km.

In the heartland of France near many farms, Malido looks out on a pretty, flowery courtyard where you will be warmly received. The house has been extensively renovated. The bedrooms are simple, pleasant, and well kept. Our favorite is the very pretty Euphonie room, and we also like the Hortensias room. The lounge and dining room are reserved for guests. Many tourist attractions are nearby and the seaside is only 4km away.

148
Les Hortensias

Villeneuve
40, rue du Moulin
22770 Lancieux
(Côtes d'Armor)
Tel. 96 86 31 15
Jacqueline and Eric Cosson

Rooms 3 with bath or shower and WC. Sheets changed every 4 days, towels every 2 days. Price 280F (2 pers., 1 night), 250F (2 pers., 2-5 nights), 230F (2 pers., more 5 nights); +80F (extra pers.). **Meals** Breakfast incl. No evening meals. **Nearby** Restaurants, riding (3km), sea (100m); Saint-Malo, Cancale, Dinan and Côte d'Emeraude. **Credit cards** Not accepted. **Spoken** English, Italian. **Open** All year. **How to get there** (Map 6): 8km from Dinard via D786 towards Ploubalay. House 1km after Lancieux.

If you don't mind the road in front, you will discover a very pleasant house at Les Hortensias. The comfortable bedrooms are very tastefully decorated and well kept. A warm atmosphere is created by the many books, seascapes and the few pieces of handsome antique furniture. Jacqueline Cosson is very friendly and open, and her breakfasts are always a special moment of the day.

149
Manoir de Kerguéréon

Ploubezre
22300 Lannion
(Côtes d'Armor)
Tel. 96 38 91 46
M. and Mme de Bellefon

Rooms 2 with bath and WC. **Price** 500F (2 pers.) + 100F (extra pers.). **Meals** Breakfast incl. No evening meal. **Restaurants** 8km away, and Les Côtes d'Armor in Plestin-les-Grèves (10km). **Facilities** Lounge. **Pets** Dogs allowed on request. **Nearby** Water sports, tennis, riding, golf, châteaux of Rosanbo, Kergrist and Tonquedec, chapels, Lannion, Tréguier, Morlaix, pink granite coast, concerts and folklore festivals. **Credit cards** Not accepted. **Spoken** English. **Open** Easter – Nov 1. **How to get there** (Map 5): 10km south of Lannion via D11, then at Kerauzern D30 towards Ploumillau; 4th road on the left after the railway line.

Standing in the middle of the countryside beside a small stud farm, this is the archetypal Breton manor, with a tower and Gothic arched doorways. The superb interior contains beautiful furniture and pottery and has kept its old character. The lounge, dining room, and the two very beautiful bedrooms are charming. You will enjoy excellent breakfasts (hot pancakes and home-made jams), and a very warm welcome.

150
Le Colombier

Coat Gourhant
22700 Louannec
(Côtes d'Armor)
Tel. 96 23 29 30
M. and Mme Fajolles

Rooms 4 with shower and WC. **Price** 220-280F (2 pers.). **Meals** Breakfast incl. No evening meals. Numerous restaurants nearby. **Facilities** Lounge, library. **Pets** Dogs allowed on request. **Nearby** Seaside, golf, tennis, riding, sea fishing, road of golden gorse, Port Blanc, Tonquedec. **Credit cards** Not accepted. **Spoken** English. **Open** All year. **How to get there** (Map 5): Coming from Lannion, at the large traffic circle in Perros-Guirec, turn right towards Louannec for 20m, then 1st small road on right; signs. (Colombier in 2km.)

This old, well-renovated farmhouse is in the middle of the countryside, yet only a few minutes from the sea. You will be warmly greeted and will like the bedrooms with their mansard ceilings; they are light, comfortable and pretty, each with its own color scheme. In the small sitting room there is a mass of tourist information. Excellent breakfasts are served in a large rustic room with elegant, inviting decor. Le Colombier is a good, economical place to stay.

151
Rosmapamon

Louannec
22700 Perros-Guirec
(Côtes-d'Armor)
Tel. 96 23 00 87
Mme Annick Sillard

Rooms 3 with bath or shower and WC. **Price** 260-315F (1 pers.), 310-365F (2 pers.) +100F (extra pers.); 1 child's room 250F. **Meals** Breakfast incl. No evening meals. **Facilities** Lounge, telephone. **Pets** Dogs allowed on request. **Nearby** Golf (18 holes), seaside, water sports, seawater therapy, bird watching, pink granite coast. **Credit cards** Not accepted. **Spoken** English. **Open** April 1 – end Sept. **How to get there** (Map 5): 2km east of Perros-Guirec on D6.

A few hundred meters from the sea and the port of Perros-Guirec, Rosmapamon stands on a hillside in a beautiful wooded park. The house once belonging to Ernest Renan and is simple and elegant. You will be very pleasantly greeted. The peaceful *premier étage* bedrooms are charming and overlook the garden. When you awake, a good breakfast with fresh orange juice and homemade pastries will be served at the large table in the dining room, where there is often a cheerful fire in the fireplace. The adjacent lounge is decorated with antiques.

152
La Pastourelle

Saint-Lormel
22130 Plancoët
(Côtes-d'Armor)
Tel. 96 84 03 77
Mme Ledé

Rooms 5 with bath or shower and WC. **Price** 230F (2 pers.) +80F (extra pers.). **Meals** Breakfast incl., half board175F per pers. in double room (5 nights min.), evening meals at separate tables, by reservation 75F (wine not incl.). **Facilities** Lounge. **Pets** Small dogs allowed on request. **Nearby** Tennis, sailing, Saint-Cast golf course (10km), Dinan. **Credit cards** Not accepted. **Spoken** English. **Open** All year. **How to get there** (Map 6): 4km north of Plancoët via D768 towards Dinard and Saint-Lormel; 1st road on the left leaving Plancoët.

La Pastourelle lies deep in the country, bordered by a pretty garden. It is a cheerful, bright place, and the interior is full of charm. The bedrooms are cozy and well kept and overlook the garden. Excellent dinners are served at separate tables in a large dining room prettily decorated in local style.

153
Le Char à Bancs

22170 Plélo
(Côtes d'Armor)
Tel. 96 74 13 63
Famille Jean-Paul Lamour

Rooms 4 with bath or shower and WC. **Price** 350-500F (2 pers.), 450-550F (3 pers.), 650-680F (4 pers.). **Meals** Breakfast incl. No evening meal. Auberge, 400m (light meals only). **Facilities** Lounge, farm museum, paddle boats on the river, ponies. **Nearby** Seaside, Chatelaudren, Paimpol, golf (10km), tennis. **Credit cards** Not accepted. **Open** All year (on request out of season). **How to get there** (Map 6): Between Saint-Brieuc (20km to the west) and Guingamp. 4km north of the Paris-Brest highway, exit Plélo; signposted.

Le Char à Bancs is a charming mill–auberge with a waterway and, nearby, La Ferme des Aïeux, which is surrounded by vegetation. The bedrooms are all very pleasant, comfortable and well kept; beamed ceilings, pretty floral eiderdowns and retro furniture give each a personal touch. Excellent, generous breakfasts are served in a room reserved for guests. The owners are very pleasant.

154
Le Presbytère

Tregrom
22420 Plouaret
(Côtes d'Armor)
Tel. 96 47 94 15
Nicole de Morchoven

Rooms 3 with bath or shower and WC. **Price** 280-320F (2 pers.), suite 320-430F; poss. weekly rental in west wing (4-5 pers.) 2900-3400F. **Meals** Breakfast incl., evening meals on request. **Restaurants** 7km away in Belle-Isle-en-Terre and Plouaret. **Facilities** Lounge. **Pets** Dogs allowed on request (suppl.). **Nearby** Fishing, riding, tennis, golf, walks, seaside (20km), Paimpol, Tréguier, Lannion, Morlaix. **Credit cards** Not accepted. **Spoken** English. **Open** All year. **How to get there** (Map 5): 20km south of Lannion. On N12 between Saint-Brieuc and Morlaix turn off at Louargat; in Lourgat, take D33 to left of church, then go 7km to Tregrom.

This beautiful rectory opposite the church has a very charming interior. Each room is a perfect blend of beautiful wallpapers, lovely fabrics and antique furniture. The bedrooms and bathrooms are very comfortable and the breakfast room is thoroughly enchanting. You will feel quite at home here.

155
Manoir de Kergrec'h

22820 Plougrescant
(Côtes d'Armor)
Tel. 96 92 59 13/96 92 56 06
Fax 96 92 51 27
Vicomte and Vicomtesse
de Roquefeuil

Rooms 5 and 2 suites with bath and WC. **Price** 420-550F (2 pers.), suite 700F (3 pers.), 800F (4 pers.). **Meals** Breakfast incl. No evening meal. **Restaurants** In Tréguier. **Facilities** Telephone, coastal walks. **Pets** Dogs allowed on request. **Nearby** Beach, windsurfing, sea fishing, tennis, golf, Ile de Bréhat, pink Granite Coast, road of golden gorse. **Credit cards** Not accepted. **Spoken** English. **Open** All year. **How to get there** (Map 5): Between Perros-Guirec and Paimpol; 7km north of Tréguier. From Guingamp take D8, signposted.

With a park stretching along the pink Granite Coast, the Manoir de Kergrec'h is charming and the hosts are very friendly. The bedrooms have recently been tastefully renovated; each has antique furniture and a character of its own. Breakfast, served around the dining room table or in the bedrooms, consists of crêpes, *far breton* (a flan with prunes), fruit and homemade jams. This is a very beautiful place.

156
Château de Pontgamp

22150 Plouguenast
(Côtes d'Armor)
Tel. 96 28 72 32
M. Pourdieu Le Coz

Rooms 2 suites of one bedroom and sitting room (2 pers.) with bath and WC. **Price** 250-300F (2 pers.) +120F (extra room). **Meals** Breakfast incl. No evening meals. **Restaurant** L'Auberge du Cheval Blanc in Loudéac. **Facilities** Lounge, Breton crêpe cookery courses. **Pets** Dogs not allowed. **Nearby** Beaches (30km); Fishing, seaside, tennis, châteaux and manor houses, village of Moncontour, guided or unaccompanied tours of the area, guided tours of antiques shops. **Credit cards** Not accepted. **Spoken** English. **Open** All year. **How to get there** (Map 6): 12km north of Loudéac via D768; it's in the village.

Located in the village of Plouguenast, Pontgamp is a very quiet place, surrounded by greenery. The bedrooms are large, comfortable and nicely furnished. A very large room on the ground floor acts as both lounge and dining room and has exceptional 1950s furniture designed by Le Corbusier. You will be received as friends. The breakfasts are hearty and there is good value for the money.

157
Mogerwen

Lann Kerallig
22300 Ploumilliau
(Côtes d'Armor)
Tel. 96 35 26 92
Colette Cardinal

Rooms 2 with bath or shower and WC. **Price** 220-280F (2 pers.) +50F (extra pers.). **Meals** Breakfast incl., no evening meals. **Facilities** Lounge, sea, beach, paths on property. **Pets** Dogs allowed on request. **Nearby** Restaurants, sailing school and tennis (2km), golf (18 holes, 20km); path on cliffs, Château de Coal Frédrez, villages of Trédrez, Ploulec'h, Séhar and Dourven Points. **Credit cards** Not accepted. **Spoken** English. **Open** All year. **How to get there** (Map 5): 10km west of Lannion via D786 towards Morlaix for 4km. At village La Croix Rouge, turn right towards Locquérmeau via Christ. In Locquérmeau, 1st on right after signs in village.

It is true that this small house has been extensively renovated, but we loved it for its extraordinary location. Nestling in the heart of a protected site of pines, broom and rocks, Morgerwen has a panoramic view over the magnificent Bay of Lannion, whose blue waters crash onto the shore some 300 feet away. The house is comfortable, decorated with several pieces of handsome old Breton furniture, and it is very well kept. The bedroom named *Les Balises* is especially beautiful. Over a delicious breakfast, you will enjoy a view of the sea, and Colette Cardinal's welcome is most pleasant.

158
Château de Kermezen

22450 Pommerit-Jaudy
(Côtes d'Armor)
Tel. 96 91 35 75
Compte and Comtesse de Kermel

Rooms 4 bedrooms and 1 suite (4 pers.) with bath and WC. **Price** 420-520F (2 pers.) +130F (extra pers.), suite 780F (4 pers.). **Meals** Breakfast incl. No evening meals. **Restaurants** Nearby. **Facilities** Lounge, fishing and Kermezen path. **Nearby** Riding, tennis, golf, seaside, isle of Bréhat, pink Granite Coast. **Credit cards** Visa, Eurocard and MasterCrad. **Spoken** English. **Open** All year. **How to get there** (Map 5): 10km south of Tréguier via D8 to La Roche-Derrien and Pommerit-Jaudy; signposted.

Kermezen stands in beautiful green, rolling Breton countryside. You will receive a marvelous welcome from the owners, whose family has lived here for 500 years. Inside there is a large, light lounge which is very well furnished. The bedrooms are also elegant. (The Aux Coqs room is a small masterpiece.) Breakfast can be served in the bedrooms but it would be a shame not to use the lovely 17th-century dining room. The château is a very beautiful place.

159
Le Presbytère

Les Hautes Mares
22630 Saint-André-des-Eaux
(Côtes d'Armor)
Tel. 96 27 48 18
M. and Mme Mousquey-Piel

Rooms 2 with bath or shower, WC. Rooms cleaned on request; sheets changed every 4 days, towels every 2 days. **Price** 220F (2 pers.), +50F (extra pers.). **Meals** Breakfast incl.; no evening meal. **Restaurants** Within 5-10km and in Dinan (10km). **Facilities** Lounge. **Nearby** Fishing (500m); riding (3km); sailing, surfboarding, canoeing, kayaking (Bettineuc Lake, 500m), golf (18 holes, 30km); Dinan, Valley of the Rance, Saint-Malo, the Emerald Coast, Paimpont (40km). **Credit cards** Not accepted. **Spoken** English. **Open** All year. **How to get there** (Map 6): 10km south of Dinan via Lehon, Saint-André-des-Eaux. Or via Rennes, Bécherel, Evran and Saint-André-des-Eaux.

When a family of artists decides to open their home to guests, it has got to be something special. And so it is. At Le Presbytère, the garden is like an Impressionist painting, and the colored woodwork in the dining room and salon highlight the pastel pictures and sculptures which are on permanent display. The bedrooms have been freshly refurbished and yet have retained their charm of the past. The view over the flower garden is marvelous. This is a lovely, tranquil place, and the owners are charming.

160
Château du Val d'Arguenon

Notre-Dame-du-Guildo
22380 Saint-Cast
(Côtes-d'Armor)
Tel. 96 41 07 03 – Fax 96 41 02 67
M. and Mme de La Blanchardière

Rooms 2 with bath and WC, 2 with shower and WC, 1 suite (2 pers. + 1 child) with bath and WC. **Price** 420-600F (2 pers.), suite 660F (2 pers.) +100F (child). **Meals** Breakfast incl. No evening meals. **Restaurants** 3 within 400 meters. **Facilities** Lounge, tennis, fishing, horse boxes, beach. **Pets** Small dogs allowed on request. **Nearby** Golf courses, riding, sailing club, Mont-Saint-Michel, Saint-Malo, Dinan, Cape Fréhel, Emerald Coast, Channel Islands. **Spoken** English. **Open** All year (on request in winter). **How to get there** (Map 6): 16km west of Dinard via D786; just after Guildo bridge.

The château is by the sea and offers very beautiful coastal walks. The rooms are decorated with antiques and the bedrooms, regularly renovated by Armelle and Olivier, are pleasant, comfortable and prettily decorated. They are very quiet and all have a view of the park and sometimes you can glimpse the ocean. Good breakfasts are served in the large dining room. The hosts are young and friendly.

161
La Corbinais

22980 Saint-Michel-de-Plelan
(Côtes-d'Armor)
Tel. 96 27 64 81
Fax 96 27 68 45
M. Beaupère

Rooms 4 with bath or shower and WC (of which 1 has external WC). **Price** 200F (1-2 pers.) +50F (extra pers.). **Meals** Breakfast 20F, evening meals at communal table, by reservation 70F (wine not incl.). **Facilities** Lounge, horse boxes, golf (9 holes) and practice green. **Nearby** Riding, golf. **Credit cards** Not accepted. **Spoken** English. **Open** All year. **How to get there** (Map 6): 17km west of Dinan via N176 towards Plélan, then right onto D19 for 3km towards Plancoët through Plélan-le-Petit.

This is a small Breton granite house with a flower garden is surrounded by wooded groves. There is a warm, country-style room with a tall fireplace, antique furniture and objects and a long wooden table where very good dinners are served. The five charming bedrooms upstairs have pretty pale fabrics and pleasant, small bathrooms. You can practice your golf here (even without your own clubs) and you will enjoy a particularly kind welcome.

162
Le Queffiou

Route du Château
22140 Tonquédec
(Côtes-d'Armor)
Tel. 96 35 84 50
Mme Sadoc

Rooms 4 with bath or shower and WC. **Price** 300-350F (2 pers.) +100F (extra pers.). **Meals** Breakfast incl. No evening meals. **Facilities** Lounge. **Pets** No dogs allowed. **Nearby** Tennis, riding, fishing, golf, pink Granite Coast. **Credit cards** Not accepted. **Spoken** English. **Closed** Oct 1 – April 1. **How to get there** (Map 5): 10km southeast of Lannion via D767 towards Guingamp to Cavan, then right towards Tonquédec. Once in the village, it's 500m on the road to the château.

Surrounded by a large, carefully tended garden and lawn, this is a very welcoming house a few hundred meters from the fortress of Tonquédec. The bedrooms are large, light, and very comfortable. Each has a style of its own--from modern and 1970s style to antique--and all have beautiful bathrooms. Breakfasts are served in a bright dining room. There is no restaurant but Madame Sadoc will suggest the best ones in the region.

163
Château de la
Ville-Guérif

22650 Trégon
(Côtes d'Armor)
Tel. 96 27 24 93
Fax 96 27 32 50
Vicomte S. de Pontbriand

Rooms 5 with bath or shower and WC. **Price** 350-400F +100F (extra pers.). **Meals** Breakfast incl. No evening meals. **Facilities** Lounge. **Pets** Dogs allowed on request. **Nearby** Swimming pool, tennis, fishing, riding center, golf, Mont-Saint-Michel, Saint-Malo, Dinan, Dinard, Cap Fréhel. **Credit cards** Not accepted. **Spoken** English, German. **Open** June – Sept. **How to get there** (Map 6): 10km west of Dinard towards Saint-Brieuc (2.5km after Ploubalay); turn towards Plessix-Balisson; in Trégon head for the beaches.

This astonishing small 19th-century château has the aura of a pretty Italian villa. The interior is very authentic, with antique furniture, paneling, paintings and ornaments. The walls are newly and tastefully papered or painted. An incredible double staircase leads to vast bedrooms which are light, full of charm and well equipped, as are the bathrooms. And finally, the staff are energetic and full of fun. And the park will make you forget the road near this very lovely place.

164
La Ferme du Breil

22650 Trégon
(Côtes d'Armor)
Tel. 96 27 30 55
Comtesse de Blacas

Rooms 4 with bath and WC. **Price** 360-410F (2 pers.) +110F (extra pers.) +60F (child). If you stay 7 days, 1 day is free. **Meals** Breakfast incl. No evening meals. **Facilities** Lounge. **Pets** Dogs allowed on request. **Nearby** Restaurants, golf, riding (10km), tennis, seaside, sailing school, Mont-Saint-Michel, Saint-Malo, Dinan, pink Granite Coast, Cap Fréhel. **Credit cards** Not accepted. **Spoken** English, Spanish. **Closed** June 1 – 15, Dec 1 – 15. **How to get there** (Map 6): 13km west of Dinard towards Saint-Brieuc through Ploubalay; after 2km turn left towards Plessix-Balisson.

This charming farmhouse with its well-kept garden is very close to the sea and to the road, but this does not disturb the peace of the bedrooms under the sloping roof. These lovely rooms are very cozy with their floral fabrics, engravings and antique furniture. All have pleasant, modern bathrooms. There is an elegant lounge with deep, green leather chairs for the use of guests, and breakfast is served there at separate tables. This is a pleasant, comfortable place to stay.

165
Manoir de Kervezec

Kervezec
29660 Carantec
(Finistère)
Tel. 98 67 00 26
Mme Bohic

Rooms 6 with bath and WC. Sheets changed every 4 days, rooms cleaned every day. **Price** 220-270F (1 pers.), 260-340F (2 pers.), +80F (extra pers.). **Meals** Breakfast incl. No evening meals. **Restaurants** Le Cabestan, Les Iles in Carantec (1.5 km). **Facilities** Lounge, pay telephone. **Nearby** Sailing, golf (9 holes), surfboarding, diving in 1km from village; Armorique Park, tumulus, museums, churchyards, picturesque villages. **Credit cards** Not accepted. **Open** All year. **How to get there** (Map 5): 12km north of Morlaix via D58 towards Roscoff, then turn right towards Carantec. Sign on left at entrance to village.

Surrounded by truck farms, the handsome 19th-century Manoir de Kervezec enjoys an outstanding location and a splendid panoramic view from the terrace looking due south over the Breton coast and the Atlantic. There are small and large bedrooms, all of which are quiet, simple and bright. Good breakfasts are served on the terrace or in a room decorated with furniture typical of the Finistère region.

166
Kerfornedic

29450 Commana
(Finistère)
Tel. 98 78 06 26
M. and Mme Le Signor

Rooms 2 with shower and WC. **Price** 220F (1 pers.), 250F (2 pers.); 2 nights min. in May, June, Sept and 3 nights min. in July and Aug. **Meals** Breakfast incl. No evening meal. **Pets** No dogs allowed. **Nearby** Restaurants, riding, tennis, mountain biking, golf, walks, lake, bathing, windsurfing, fishing (200m), Crêtes d'Arrée hiking path, local history museums. **Credit cards** Not accepted. **Open** All year. **How to get there** (Map 5): 41km southwest of Morlaix via N12 to Landivisiau, then D30 and D764 to Sizun, then D30 after Sizun to Saint-Cadou, then towards Commana; it's on the right after 2km.

This very old rambling house, surrounded by flowers, is set in the superb landscape of the Arrée hills. Once over the threshold, you will be captivated by the beauty of the simple interior with its whitewashed walls, beams, dried flowers and well-chosen decorative objects. The bedrooms are just as lovely. The hosts are friendly and Kerfornedic is a charming place.

167
Manoir de Kervent

29100 Douarnenez
(Finistère)
Tel. 98 92 04 90
Mme Lefloch

Rooms 2 with shower and WC, 1 suite (4 pers.) with shower and WC. **Price** 240F (2 pers.), suite 350-400F (4 pers.). Weekend rates (Friday and Saturday incl. evening meals) 700F for 2 pers.; applies from mid-Sept. – mid-June. **Meals** Breakfast incl. No evening meals. **Facilities** Lounge. **Pets** Dogs allowed on request. **Nearby** Restaurants, beach, tennis, golf, Pointe du Raz, Locronan, Port-Museum in Douarnenez, Quimper (20km). **Credit cards** Not accepted. **Open** All year. **How to get there** (Map 5): 2km southwest of Douarnenez via D765 towards Audierne; it's on the right 500m after the traffic lights.

Kervent is on the outskirts of Douarnenez but in the countryside. With flowers both inside and out, this house will charm you at first sight. The spacious bedrooms are well furnished and very pleasant. Breakfast is served at a big table in the light, elegant dining room. Madame Lefloch is amusing and kind and has prepared a veritable itinerary to help you enjoy her region.

168
Pen Ker Dagorn

Chemin des Vieux-Fours
29920 Kerdruc
(Finistère)
Tel. 98 06 85 01
Mme Brossier-Publier

Rooms 3 with bath or shower and WC. **Price** 240F (2 pers.); 2 days min. **Meals** Breakfast 30F. No evening meal. **Restaurants** In Port-Manech, Pont-Aven, Riec and Nevez. **Facilities** Lounge. **Pets** Dogs not allowed. **Nearby** Beaches, bicycle and boat rentals, tennis, riding, golf, Belon, Pont-Aven. **Credit cards** Not accepted. **Open** Easter – Oct 30 (on request in winter). **How to get there** (Map 5): 5km south of Pont-Aven, via 783 towards Trégunc; in Croaz Hent Kergez, D77. In Nevez-Kerleun, turn left (C8) towards Port-de-Kerdruc. At entrance to Kerdruc, on the small square, Chemin des Vieux Fours; signs.

A very attractive country house set amid lush greenery, Pen Ker Dagorn is 200 meters from the port of Kerdruc. It has been charmingly decorated. Each bedroom has a style of its own; all are large, comfortable and light, and some of the amusing bathrooms are hidden in deep closets. Excellent breakfasts are served and M. and Mme Publier are charmingly attentive.

169
Château du Guilguiffin

29710 Landudec
(Finistère)
Tel. 98 91 52 11
M. Philippe Davy

Rooms 4 and 2 suites (3-4 pers.) with bath, WC and TV; and 1 spare room. **Price** 350-750F (2 pers.), suite 750-1200F (3-4 pers.) +150F (extra pers.). **Meals** Breakfast incl. Evening meal at communal table. **Facilties** Lounge, pay telephone. **Pets** Dogs allowed only in kennel or on ground floor. **Nearby** All sports and activities within 10km, bike and boat rentals, golf courses (18 holes, 20km and 30km); Pointe du Raz, Port- Museum in Douarnenez. **Credit cards** Not accepted. **Closed** Nov. 1 – April 1 (open in winter on request). **How to get there** (Map 5): 13km west of Quimper via D784 towards Audierne; property 3km before Landudec.

The Château du Guilguiffin is an architectural masterpiece with its concentric colonnaded enclosures, its splendid gardens and a façade in the purest 18th-century tradition. Philippe Davy has a passion for his château and receives his guests like old friends. The splendid bedrooms have been impeccably refurbished and the bathrooms are beautiful. The drawing rooms with their original 18th-century wood paneling are magnificent; there is a warm dining room where simple dinners are served, or you can request more elaborate meals. The château is a very distinguished place to stay.

170
La Grange de Coatélan

29640 Plougonven
(Finistère)
Tel. 98 72 60 16
Charlick and Yolande de Ternay

Rooms 2 with bath and WC. **Price** 170F (1 pers.), 230F (2 pers.) + 80F (extra pers.); 2 days min. **Meals** Breakfast incl., crêperie in the evenings (not Wed.) 120F. **Pets** No dogs allowed. **Nearby** Riding, seaside, Arrée hills, wayside cross of Plougonven. **Credit cards** Not accepted. **Spoken** English. **Open** Easter – Nov 1. **How to get there** (Map 5): 7km south of Morlaix via D109 towards Plourin-lès-Morlaix, then Plougonven; signposted.

Lying close to the Arrée hills, La Grange was once a weaver's farm. On the ground floor there is a bright small auberge in pale wood with an open fireplace, and a bar area in the shape of a boat's hull. The cuisine is excellent and the atmosphere is delightful. The two bedrooms are tastefully decorated and have unusual bathrooms. La Grange de Coatélan is a magic place.

171
La Clarté

25, La Clarté
29310 Querrien
(Finistère)
Tel. 98 71 31 61
Jean and Lucie Guillou

Rooms 2 with bath and WC, 2 with shower and WC, one of which is a family room (3 pers.). Rooms cleaned on request. **Price** 240F (2 pers.), 70F (extra pers.); 2 nights min. **Meals** Breakfast incl., no evening meals. **Restaurants** Auberge on the farm and farmhouse-auberges 4km and 10km away. **Facilities** Lounge, telephone. **Pets** No dogs allowed. **Nearby** Beaches, footpaths, tennis, river fishing, hacking, golf (25km), chapels of Sainte-Barbe, Saint-Fiacre La Clarté, bread oven, Kerasquet. **Credit cards** Not accepted. **Open** All year. **How to get there** (Map 5): 15km northeast of Quimperlé via D970 towards Le Faouët; signposted from Querrien. **No smoking.**

Near a charming Breton village, La Clarté stands in the middle of a superb garden full of flowers and different varieties of trees. Inside it is comfortable and pleasant with its both modern and quaint decor. The bedrooms are bright and cheerful, with a lovely view. Hearty breakfasts include pancakes, honey, wholegrain organic bread and other homemade products. The hosts are extremely hospitable.

172
Le Chatel

29124 Riec-sur-Belon
(Finistère)
Tel. 98 06 00 04
M. Roger Gourlaouen

Rooms 2 with bath and WC, 3 with shower and WC. Rooms cleaned on request. **Price** 250F (2 pers.) +50F (extra pers.). **Meals** Breakfast incl., no evening meals, restaurants within 500m **Pets** Dogs allowed on request. **Facilities** Deer farm, bicycles. **Nearby** Tennis, riding, golf (18 holes), beaches, Pont-Aven. **Credit cards** Not accepted. **Spoken** English. **Open** All year. **How to get there** (Map 5): 1km east of Pont-Aven via D783 towards Riec-sur-Belon for 800m, then signs on the right.

A few minutes from Pont-Aven, this lovely farm is made up of a number of buildings which are all very charming. There are flowers everywhere. The bedrooms are pleasant, comfortable and pretty, with white walls and country-style decorations. The owner is very kind. Excellent breakfasts are served in an attractive room containing antique Breton country furniture, *faïences*, and a connoisseur's tasteful collection of Pont-Aven paintings. Before leaving, ask to see the deer farm.

173
The Laurel Tree

41, boulevard de la Houle
Saint-Briac-sur-Mer
35800 Dinard
(Ille-et-Vilaine)
Tel. 99 88 01 93
M. and Mme Martin

Rooms 3 (incl. 2 with mezzanine for 2-4 pers.) with bath or shower and WC. **Price** 225-310F (2 pers.), 325-385F (3 pers.), 400-460F (4 pers.). **Meals** Breakfast incl., meals at communal or separate tables, by reservation day before. **Facilities** Lounge, portable telephone, ocean fishing, barbecue, beach (150m) on property. **Pets** Dogs not allowed. **Nearby** Riding, sailing, hiking, tennis, sea, bike rentals, golf (18 holes, 100m); the Coast, Saint-Briac, Dinan, Saint-Malo, Cape Fréhel, Fort Calatte. **Spoken** English, German. **Open** All year. **How to get there** (Map 6): 1km north of Saint-Briac-sur-Mer towards of golf course.

This charming house, which was immortalized by Signac, has a lovely warm living room–dining room with a beautiful fireplace. The comfortable, beautiful bedrooms are decorated with tasteful English fabrics and are impeccably maintained. The breakfasts are good and often served on the sunny side of the garden. Monsieur and Madame Martin are very hospitable. Note that the Laurel Tree is on a street which is busy during the day but quiet at night; the proximity of the sea and the golf course also help to diminish the noise.

174
Manoir de la Duchée

La Duchée
Saint-Briac-sur-Mer
35800 Dinard
(Ille-et-Vilaine)
Tel. 99 88 00 02
Jean-François Stenou

Rooms 5 with bath, WC and TV, of which 1 is a duplex. **Price** 300F (1 pers.), 350F (2 pers.), 500F (3-4 pers.) +80F (extra pers.). **Meals** Breakfast incl., no evening meals. **Restaurants** Nearby. **Facilities** Lounges, riding, mountain bikes on the property. **Pets** No dogs allowed. **Nearby** Sea, sailing, tennis, swimming pool, golf (3km), Mont-Saint-Michel, Saint-Malo, Dinan, Dinard, Cap Fréhel. **Open** March 1 – Nov. 30 and during school holidays (by reservation). **How to get there** (Map 6): In Saint-Malo, go towards Saint-Brieuc via D168, then D603 towards Saint Brieuc; then first road to left on entering town; signs. Coming from Dinard, via D786 towards Camping Municipal. Signs.

This small manor house lies deep in the countryside. The very comfortable bedrooms for the most part have late 19th-century furniture painted with floral motifs. On the ground floor, a beautiful room with beams and exposed stonework serves as a slightly theatrical background for good breakfasts: The atmosphere is created by a cheerful log fire, a large chandelier, antique furniture and objects, and music. Breakfast is also served in the winter garden. Note that the staircase to some bedrooms is steep, to say the least.

175
La Forêt

5, chemin du Pâtis
35300 Fougères
(Ille-et-Vilaine)
Tel. 99 99 00 52
M. and Mme Juban

Rooms 1 with shower and WC, 2 with washbasin and shared bath and WC. **Price** 230-250F (2 pers.). **Meals** Breakfast incl., evening meals at communal table, by reservation 100F (wine incl.) **Facilities** Lounge, forest trail, jogging course, bicycles. **Pets** Dogs allowed on request. **Nearby** Swimming pool, tennis, riding, lake fishing, golf, Mont-Saint-Michel, old Fougères, Saint-Malo, Cancale. **Credit cards** Not accepted. **Spoken** English. **Open** All year. **How to get there** (Map 7): In Fougères on the Flers road in the direction of the forest of Fougères.

Sheltered by a beautiful flower-filled garden, this modern house is on the edge of Fougères, not far from a superb forest. It is very peaceful and the owners are spontaneous and warm. The arrangement of the house and the bedrooms is very pleasant and full of thoughtful details-- antiques, pretty fabrics, books and objects. You will feel quite at home and there is an exceptionally good breakfast. The prices are very reasonable.

176
Château de Léauville

35369 Landujan
(Ille-et-Vilaine)
Tel. 99 07 21 14
Fax 99 07 21 80
Marie-Pierre and Patrick
Gicquiaux

Rooms 7 with bath, WC and telephone (of which 6 have fireplace and sitting area) and 1 small bedroom with shower, WC and telephone. **Price** 270-720F (2 pers.) +100F (extra pers.). **Meals** Breakfast 56F, half board 476-600F (per pers.), evening meal by reservation (separate tables) 185F (wine not incl.). **Facilities** Lounge, heated swimming pool, equestrian center. **Pets** Dogs allowed on request. **Nearby** Golf. **Credit cards** Not accepted. **Spoken** English. **Open** Mid-March – mid-Nov. **How to get there** (Map 6): In the Brest direction on RN12; 30km after Rennes take exit Bécherel Landujan; signposted.

The Château de Leauville is a mixture of 16th- and 17th-century architecture. Set a beautiful park with a swimming pool, it is quiet and very charming The comfortable bedrooms are well decorated and have large bathrooms (often in the towers). Breakfast and evening meals are served in a rustic, pleasant dining room. You will be warmly welcomed. The prices are somewhat high for certain bedrooms.

177
Château des Blosses

35406 Saint-Ouen-de-la-Rouërie
(Ille-et-Vilaine)
Tel. 99 98 36 16
Fax 99 98 39 32
M. and Mme Jacques Barbier

Rooms 7 with bath and WC. **Price** 520-800F (2 pers.). **Meals** Breakfast incl., half board 480-580F per pers. in double room (3 nights min.), evening meals by reservation (separate tables) 225F (wine incl.). **Facilities** Lounge, golf range. **Pets** No dogs allowed. **Nearby** Golf, swimming pool, Mont-Saint-Michel. **Credit cards** Amex, Visa, Eurocard and MasterCard. **Spoken** English. **Open** Mid-Feb. – mid-Nov. **How to get there** (Map 7): 28km northwest of Fougères via D155 to Antrain, then D296 for 4km; signs. Coming from Pontorson-Mont-Saint-Michel, take N175 towards Rennes for 9km, then D97; signposted.

Built in the 19th-century, this château stands in a very large wooded park. The interior is authentically rural, with hunting trophies and old furniture. The comfortable bedrooms are very charmingly arranged. There are excellent evening meals, at which M. and Mme Barbier are sometimes present.

178
Le Petit Moulin du Rouvre

35720 Sainte-Pierre-de-Plesguen
(Ille-et-Vilaine)
Tel. 99 73 85 84
Fax 99 73 71 06
Mme Annie Michel-Québriac

Rooms 4 with bath and WC. **Price** 250F (1 pers.), 300F (2 pers.) +110F (extra pers.). **Meals** Breakfast incl., half board 245F per pers. in double room, evening meals at communal table by reservation from 95F (wine not incl.). **Facilities** Lounge, fishing. **Pets** Small dogs allowed on request (+50F). **Nearby** Golf, Mont-Saint-Michel, old Dinan. **Credit cards** Not accepted. **Spoken** English. **Open** All year. **How to get there** (Map 6): 13km east of Dinan via D794, then N137 and D10; follow signs in the village.

It would be hard not to be attracted by this small mill standing alone on the edge of the millpond. If you arrive at the end of a beautiful afternoon you will see the sunlight glittering on the water and dappling the pretty furniture in the lounge. The bedrooms are small but pleasant. The east wall of one of them is all glass. Do not miss the evening meals of Breton specialties. Your hostess is charming .

179
Les Mouettes

Grande-Rue
35430 Saint-Suliac
(Ille-et-Vilaine)
Tel. 99 58 30 41
Fax 59 58 39 41
Isabelle Rouvrais

Rooms 5 with bath or shower and WC. **Price** 220-260F (1 pers.), 250-290F (2 pers.). **Meals** Breakfast incl., no evening meals. **Restaurants** In 150m and in village. **Facilities** Lounge. **Pets** Dogs not allowed. **Nearby** Beach (200m) with water-sports facilities, tennis in village, mountain bikes, hiking; village of Saint-Suliac, Saint-Malo, Cancale, Dinan. **Spoken** English, Spanish. **Open** All year. **How to get there** (Map 6): 3km north of Châteauneuf (near Saint-Malo). On highway Rennes/Saint-Malo, exit Châteauneuf, go into village then follow signs for Saint-Suliac.

Located just off the port in a charming village, Les Mouettes has been decorated with beautiful taste. In the bedrooms, the blond wood of the furniture and the parquet floors blends handsomely with the pastel shades of the walls, curtains and lampshades. The overall arrangement is comfortable, sober and very relaxing. The young owner greets you with genuine hospitality; her house is immaculate and her breakfasts alone (fresh fruit juice, yogurt, pastries...) are worth a detour. "The Sea Gulls" is a true find.

180
Ty Horses

Route de Locmaria
Le Rouho
56520 Guidel
(Morbihan)
Tel. 97 65 97 37/98 96 11 45
M. and Mme Hamon

Rooms 4 with shower and WC (poss. TV). **Price** 200F (1 pers.), 250F (2 pers° +70F (extra pers.). **Meals** Breakfast incl., no evening meals. **Restaurants** At Guidel Beach (2km), Guidel (4km) and nearby. **Facilities** Salmon fishing in river on property. **Nearby** Queven golf course (6km); Pont Aven (20km), Lorient, Carnac. **Credit cards** Not accepted. **Spoken** English. **Open** All year. **How to get there** (Map 5): 4km north of Guidel. Autoroute Nantes-Brest exit Guidel, go around church towards Centre Commercial, then Route de Locmaria for 4km: lane on left indicated.

This is a charming small house with flowers growing everywhere and a few horses grazing in the fields. The four quiet, comfortable bedrooms --each with its own name and color--look out on the pretty garden in the front, or the fields in the back. Breakfasts are served in a small salon with large bay windows adjacent to the house, or, in good weather, in the garden.

181
Le Clos

Rue Neuve
Le Bourg
56780 L'Ile-aux-Moines
(Morbihan)
Tel. 97 26 34 29
Mme Michèle Béven

Rooms 1 independent suite (2-3 pers.) with bath, WC, kitchen and 1 spare bedroom. Rooms cleaned by guests for stays of more than 2 days. **Price** 300F (2 pers.), +75F (extra pers.). **Meals** Breakfast incl., no evening meal. **Restaurants** San Francisco, La Désirade and Les Embruns (200-400m). **Pets** Dogs allowed on request. **Nearby** Tour of island on foot or on bicycles, beach in 400m, surfboarding, Fée-des-Iles excursions, tour of the island and the Gulf by boat, dolmens and menhirs. **Open** All year. **How to get there** (Map 14): Boat (tel. 97 26 31 45) for L'Ile aux Moines in Port-Blanc. Departure every 30 mins. from 7 AM to 7:30 PM in winter and from 7 AM to 10 PM in July, Aug. In the village.

L e Clos is a very old Breton fishermen's house surrounded by a charming garden and is located on a pretty small island of the Morbihan Gulf. The bedroom is vast, decorated in rustic Breton style, and somewhat austere, but it is brightened with pretty curtains. Next to it is a kitchen and a bathroom decorated in 1960s style. Ideal for a family or a group of friends, Le Clos is just off the seashore. Madame Béven is a charming hostess.

182
La Carrière

8, rue de la Carrière
56120 Josselin
(Morbihan)
Tel. 97 22 22 62
M. and Mme Bignon

Rooms 4 with bath and WC, 2 with shower and WC, and 2 for children without bath or shower. **Price** 290-340F (2 pers.) +90F (extra pers.), childrens room 180F. **Meals** Breakfast incl. no, evening meal. **Restaurants** Within 500m. **Facilities** Lounge. **Pets** Dogs allowed on request. **Credit Cards** Visa, Eurocard and MasterCard . **Nearby** Sailing on Lac aux Ducs, Ploermel golf course (9 holes), riding Josselin, Rochefort-en-Terre. **Credit cards** Not accepted. **Spoken** English, German. **Open** All year. **How to get there** (Map 6): 54km north of Vannes via N166 to Roc-Saint-André, then D4; it's behind the château.

L a Carrière and its beautiful garden stand on a hill just outside the small town of Josselin, with its famous medieval château. It is a vast, very refined house. The beautiful reception rooms are bright and furnished with antiques, and they open onto a magnificent hall with 18th-century gilt paneling. The bedrooms are charming, classic and pleasant (five have twin beds.) The owners are very welcoming.

183
Chaumière de Kérizac

56390 Locqueltas
(Morbihan)
Tel. 97 66 60 13
Fax 97 66 66 73
M. and Mme Cheilletz-Maignan

Rooms 1 with shower and WC, 2 with bath and shared WC. **Price** 250F (1 pers.), 330-360F (2 pers.). **Meals** Breakfast incl., no evening meal. **Restaurants** In Locqueltas and Vannes. **Facilities** Lounge, pond, jogging course. **Pets** No dogs allowed. **Nearby** Swimming pool, tennis, riding, golf, Gulf of Morbihan. **Credit cards** Not accepted. **Spoken** English. **Open** All year. **How to get there** (Map 14): Via D767 towards Pontivy-Saint-Brieuc, express highway, exit Locqueltas. First intersection after going through village, on left. Signs.

In this Breton hamlet, you will come to several farms and then, somewhat further on, these two charming thatched cottages. We recommend the two vast bedrooms (which are somewhat expensive this year) under the expansive beamed ceiling. The lovely decoration is enhanced with antique furniture, lace, small pictures, souvenirs from all over the world and pretty colors. Excellent breakfasts are served inside or in the garden, depending on the weather. The hosts are warm and hospitable.

184
Le Cosquer–Trélécan

56330 Pluvigner
(Morbihan)
Tel. 97 24 72 69
Bernard and Françoise Menut

Rooms 1 suite (4 pers.) with bath and WC (+ washbasin in each bedroom). **Price** 200F (1 pers.), 250F (2 pers.), 300F (3 pers.), 350F (4 pers.). **Meals** Breakfast incl., no evening meal. **Restaurants** Close by. **Facilities** Lounge. **Pets** No dogs allowed. **Nearby** Seaside, riding, Camors forest, Gulf of Morbihan, Saint-Goustan. **Credit cards** Not accepted. **Spoken** English. **Open** All year. **How to get there** (Map 5): 32km northwest of Vannes via N165 to Auray and D768 towards Pontivy. At Pluvigner take D102 towards Languidic, then signs for "Brocante".

Madame Menut, an antiques dealer, and Monsieur Menut, a beekeeper, are the owners of this charming thatched cottage set in peaceful green countryside. The pretty, small suite is perfect for a family (for children, it has an authentic Breton enclosed bed). Breakfast is a treat served in a very beautiful living room decorated with lovely antiques; there is an open fire in winter, and music. The Menuts are very friendly.

185
Les Hortensias

Saint-Trémeur
56330 Pluvigner
(Morbihan)
Tel. 97 24 96 10
Mme Simone Le Boudouil

Rooms 2, and 1 studio with kitchenette (3 pers.) shower and WC. Small house on property for rent (2-5 pers.) with 2 bedrooms, kitchenette, shower, WC and private garden. Rooms cleaned every day or on request. **Price** 200F (1 pers.), 250F (2 pers.), +50-70F (extra pers.). **Meals** Breakfast incl., no evening meals. **Restaurants** La Croix Blanche in Pluvigner, and La Cahumière in 7km. **Facilities** Swimming pool on property. **Pets** Small dogs only. **Nearby** Horseback riding center, tennis, golf (18 holes, 13km); village museum, national forest, galleries, museums. **Open** All year. **How to get there** (Map 5): 3km south of Pluvigner towards Sainte Anne d'Auray via D102. Go 2km and on right go towards Brech for 800m: Saint-Trémur on your right; sign for house.

Les Hortensias was bought from a nursery owner and is so surrounded with flowers and trees that it is well deserving of its name, "The Hydrangeas." Designed especially for long stays, the three bedrooms are simple, well appointed and decorated with handsome period furniture. It is very peaceful here, and as soon as it's sunny weather, breakfasts are served outdoors. The hostess is pleasant.

186
Manoir de Kerlebert

56530 Quéven
(Morbihan)
Tel. 97 05 06 80/97 05 24 18
Pol and Cathy Chenailler

Rooms 2 with bath and WC, 2 with shower and WC. Rooms cleaned every 5-6 days. **Price** 195F (1 pers.), 210F (2 pers.). **Meals** Breakfast incl., no evening meal. **Restaurants** In Lorient. **Facilities** Lounge, equestrian center, horse boxes. **Pets** Dogs allowed on request. **Nearby** Sea, golf. **Credit cards** Not accepted. **Open** All year. **How to get there** (Map 5): 3km northwest of Lorient via N165, exit Quéven; signposted from Quéven; 1km from the village.

The manor house of Kerlebert is outside the small town of Quéven and is surrounded by large trees. It is a peaceful, unspoiled place. The bedrooms are simple, and the Art Déco room is our favorite. It is a shame that the salon and dining have not been decorated with the same care. (Fortunately, the very reasonable prices compensate for this drawback.) Your hosts are young and informal.

187
Château de Talhouët

56220 Rochefort-en-Terre
(Morbihan)
Tel. 97 43 34 72
M. Jean-Pol Soulaine

Rooms 8 with bath and WC, 1 with shower, telephone and TV. **Price** 550-950F (2 pers.). **Meals** Breakfast incl., half board 505-705F per pers. in double room, evening meal (separate tables) 230F (wine not incl.). **Facilities** Lounge. **Credit cards** Visa, Amex. **Pets** Dogs allowed (+30F). **Nearby** Tennis, fishing, golf. **Credit cards** Not accepted. **Spoken** English. **Open** All year. **How to get there** (Map 14): 33km northwest of Redon via D775 towards Vannes, then D774; turn right towards Rochefort-en-Terre. Go through Rochefort and take D774 towards Malestroit for 4km, then left to Château de Talhoüet.

O verlooking a beautiful countryside, Talhouët is a château in true Breton style. The interior is absolutely splendid and has been been restored in excellent taste. There is a magnificent series of rooms on the ground floor, including a salon, billiards room, and dining room. Some of the bedrooms are vast and extraordinarily comfortable, and there are antiques throughout; the bathrooms are luxurious. The host is very charming.

188
Ferme–Auberge du
Château de Castellan

56200 Saint-Martin-sur-Oust
(Morbihan)
Tel. 99 91 51 69
Fax 99 91 57 41
M. and Mme Cossé

Rooms 4 and 1 suite with 2 rooms (4 pers.), with bath or shower and WC. **Price** 350-400F (2 pers.), +80F (extra pers.). **Meals** Breakfast incl., evening meals at separate tables 100-150F (wine not incl.). **Facilities** Pay telephone. **Pets** Dogs not allowed. **Nearby** Tennis, ocean 45km, boat rides on Morbihan Gulf (special rates), Rochefort-en-Terre, Josselin, La Gacilly (artisans' village), Saint-Marcel Museum. **Spoken** English. **Open** All year. **How to get there** (Map 14): 20km northwest of Redon via D764 towards Malestroit, then in Peillac, turn right towards Les Fougerêts; then, before the village, towards Saint-Martin. On leaving village, D149 for 1.5km, then road on right; signs.

S urrounded by the splendid Breton countryside of the Morbihan, Castellan is a typically 18th-century château whose outbuildings serve as a farm-auberge. You will be greeted by very pleasant, friendly hosts. Recently renovated, the bedrooms are bright, well furnished and very prettily decorated in delicate and cheerful colors. (The *Médaillon, Rose* and *Verte* rooms are our favorites.) Good meals are served in an immense dining room whose rustic austerity may not be to everyone's taste.

189
Lann Kermané

56470 Saint-Philibert
(Morbihan)
Tel. 97 55 03 75
Fax 97 30 02 79
M. and Mme Cuzon du Rest

Rooms 2 with bath or shower and WC. **Price** 350F (2 pers.), +80-100F (extyra pers.). **Meals** Breakfast incl., no evening meals. **Restaurants** L'Azimuth and L'Ostréa (2km) and crêperies (300m). **Facilities** Lounge, fishing, terrace on water **Pets** Dogs not allowed. **Nearby** Beach 1.5km, tennis 1.5 km, water sports, golf (27 holes, 10km); cruises on Morbihan Gulf, Carnac stones, Belle-Ile, many historic sites. **Credit cards** Not accepted. **Spoken** English. **Open** All year. **How to get there** (Map 5): 10km S of Auray. Coming from Vannes, D165 exit Carnac-Locmariaquer, then D28 to Rond-Point du Chat Noir; then D781 for 50m and road on left for 300m. Route des Palladiers on left for 300m left then on Rue des Peupliers: house on right at end of dead-end.

This welcoming Breton house is located in a small hamlet near one of the numerous lovely inlets dotting the Gulf of Morbihan. The interior decoration, which includes beautiful antique furniture and a few handsome objects, gives the house a warm atmosphere, heightened in winter by a beautiful fireplace. The small bedrooms are pleasant, elegant, comfortable, quiet and well maintained. The hospitality is very friendly.

190
La Maison du Latz

56470 La Trinité-sur-Mer
(Morbihan)
Tel. 97 55 80 91
Nicole Le Rouzic

Rooms 3 and 1 suite (4 pers.) with bath and WC. **Price** 270-320F (2 pers.), suite 470F (4 pers.). **Meals** Breakfast incl., evening meals at communal or separate tables (reservation the evening before) 80-120F (wine not incl.). **Facilities** Lounge, telephone, fishing. **Nearby** Golf, tennis, riding, sailing, sea fishing, Quiberon, Belle-Ile, Carnac, Gulf of Morbihan. **Credit cards** Not accepted. **Spoken** English. **Open** All year. **How to get there** (Map 5): 11km south of Auray via D28 and D781 towards La Trinité-sur-Mer until the bridge, then towards Le Latz.

The maritime view from this house is typical of the Gulf of Morbihan. with its many small islands and white boats. To make the most of this view there is a veranda overlooking the bay and breakfast is served there from daybreak onwards. The bedrooms are quiet, comfortable and simple; all overlook the sea, but the Verte room has the best view. Mme Le Rouzic makes you feel very much at home.

191
Château de la Verrerie

Oizon
18700 Aubigny-sur-Nère
(Cher)
Tel. 48 58 06 91
Fax 48 58 21 25
Comte and Comtesse A. de Vogüé

Rooms 10 with bath, WC and telephone (of which 1 with shower and WC) and 1 suite (2 pers.) with bath and WC. **Price** 880-1100F (2 pers.) +250F (extra pers.), suite 1300F (2 pers.). **Meals** Breakfast 55F, evening meals at communal table, by reservation (15 days in advance) 450F (wine incl.), or restaurant in the park. **Facilities** Lounge, tennis, riding, fishing, horse boxes, lake. **Credit cards** Visa, Eurocard and MasterCard. **Pets** Small dogs allowed on request. **Nearby** 18-hole golf, village of La Borne (pottery), route Jacques-Coeur (châteaux). **Spoken** English, German. **Open** 1 March – 1 Nov. **How to get there** (Map 17): 40km south of Gien via D940 to Aubigny-sur-Nère; then D89 to La Verrerie.

Standing on the edge of the water and the forest, this ducal château was built just after the Hundred Years' War. The interior is absolute perfection: vast, sumptuous, comfortable, authentic. You can have dinner either with the owners or in the small, 17th-century farmhouse restaurant in the park.

192
Domaine de Vilotte

Ardenais
18170 Le Châtelet-en-Berry
(Cher)
Tel. 48 96 04 96
Fax The same
M. and Mme Jacques de Champenier

Rooms 5 with bath and WC. **Price** 390F(2 pers.) +80F (extra pers.). **Meals** Breakfast incl., meals at communal table 90-120F. **Facilities** Lounge, tel.; pond, fishing, woods and park on property. **Nearby** Golf (18 holes, 60km), water sports center, tennis, riding; châteaux, Noirlac Abbey, Nonant House, Tronçais Forest. **Credit cards** Not accepted. **Spoken** English. **Closed** Sept. 30 to April 3. **How to get there** (Map 17): 21km southwest of Saint-Amand Montrond (exit A71 Autoroute Clermont-Ferrand), towards Orval, then La Châtre-Culan, then Fosse Nouvelle. Go towards Le Châtelet. In village of Ardenais, turn left towards Culan on D38 and follow signs.

Nestling in the gentle, peaceful Berry countryside not far from the Loire Valley, the Domaine de Vilotte is an ancient Roman site. Monsieur and Madame Cheval, who are friends of the owners, offer beautiful, elegant guest rooms which are tastefully furnished and look out over a vast garden. (The *Marguerite* room is the one we like least). The decoration of the house itself is quite attractive and includes numerous collections of objects found in antique shops nearby. The hospitality is very friendly and the location is very quiet.

193
Manoir d'Estiveaux

Estiveaux
18170 Le Châtelet-en-Berry
(Cher)
Tel. 48 56 22 64
Mme de Faverges

Rooms 2 with bath, WC and TV, 2 with shower, WC and TV, and 1 suite of 2 bedrooms with bath and WC. **Price** 300-500F (1-2 pers.) +80F (extra pers.), suite 550F. **Meals** Breakfast incl., evening meals at communal or separate table from 150F (wine incl.). **Facilities** Large non-smoking lounge and small smoking lounge, game room, telephone, fishing. **Pets** Dogs allowed on request. **Nearby** Swimming pool, golf (18 holes), tennis, riding, Romanesque churches, châteaux. **Credit cards** Not accepted. **Open** All year. **How to get there** (Map 17): 46km north of Montluçon via D943 to Culan, then D65 to Le Châtelet; then D951 for 1.5km, towards La Châtre.

This country mansion stands in a park with a lake and lies close to the Route Jacques-Cœur and its many châteaux. The house is beautifully preserved and the huge bedrooms are perfectly decorated. Mme de Faverges' hospitality is warm and unaffected. Ask her advice on touring the area; she participates in numerous cultural activities and knows the region well. Dinners are served in the large dining room or in the small private salon.

194
La Rongère

18110 Saint-Eloy-de-Gy
(Cher)
Tel. 48 25 41 53
Fax 48 25 47 31
Florence and Philippe
Atger-Rochefort

Rooms 1 with bath and WC, 2 with shower and WC, 1 suite of 2 bedrooms with bath and WC. **Price** 240F (1/2 pers.) +65F (extra pers.), suite 400F (4 pers.). **Meals** Breakfast incl.; no evening meal; poss. picnic lunch on request. Restaurant in Saint-Eloy. **Facilities** Lounge. **Nearby** Tennis, riding, Bourges. **Spoken** English, German. **Open** All year. **How to get there** (Map 17): 8km northwest of Bourges via N76 towards Mehun-sur-Yèvre, then right on D104 towards Vouzeron.

This pleasant, turn-of-the-century house is set in a large, quiet park. The façade may be in need of refurbishing but the interior is charming. The small dining room is pretty and has interesting stained-glass windows; the large bedrooms are furnished with antiques and have pleasant bathrooms. There is an attractive restaurant in the adjoining building. The owners are young and informal.

195
Château de Quantilly

Quantilly
18110 Saint-Martin-d'Auxigny
(Cher)
Tel. 48 64 51 21
M. de Botmiliau

Rooms 3 with shower and WC (poss. suite), TV on request. **Price** 300F (2 pers.), 2 nights min.
Meals Breakfast incl., no evening meals. **Pets** No dogs allowed. **Facilities** Horse boxes. **Nearby**
Restaurants, golf (18 holes), bathing lake, châteaux, village of La Borne (pottery), Bourges,
Menetou vineyards. **Credit cards** Not accepted. **Spoken** English. **Open** May 1 – end Oct. **How
to get there** (Map 17): 15km north of Bourges via D940 towards Gien, then D59 towards Quantilly;
signposted.

The Château de Quantilly has the atmosphere of an old country house.
The entrance hall is somewhat "bohemian"; the lovely old furniture in
the three large bedrooms seems as if it has always been there. It is a shame
that the shower rooms are rather cramped (they are in the turrets). Hearty
breakfasts are served in the beautiful dining room overlooking the park.
The hospitality is as natural as the place itself.

196
Ferme du Château

Levéville
28300 Bailleau-L'Evêque
(Eure-et-Loir)
Tel. 37 22 97 02
Bruno and Nathalie Vasseur

Rooms 2 with bath or shower and WC. **Price** 190-200F (1 pers.), 230-250F (2 pers.), +70F (extra
pers.). **Meals** Breakfast incl.; meals at communal or separate tables 65-100F (wine incl.).
Facilities Tel. **Pets** Dogs not allowed. **Nearby** Golf (18 holes, 15km); Chartres cathedral,
museums, Old Town. **Credit cards** Not accepted. **Spoken** English. **Open** All year. **How to get
there** (Map): 8km NW of Chartres. Towards Dreux via RN154 at Pont de Poisvilliers, exit towards
Bailleau-L'Evêque via D134.

The quadrangular enclosure of this beautiful farm is adjacent to a
magnificent château and from the fields all around, you can see the
solitary spire of Chartres cathedral rising up to the sky. The hospitality here
is very friendly and refined, and the comfortable bedrooms are tastefully
decorated with cheerful colors. Dinners are served in the living room or in
the beautiful dining room, depending on whether you wish your meals at
a communal table or not. This is a beautiful place to stay and the price is
reasonable.

197
Château de Maillebois

28170 Maillebois
(Eure-et-Loir)
Tel. 37 48 17 01
M. Armand-Delille

Rooms 1 with bath and WC, 1 with bath and WC not in room. **Price** 700F. **Meals** Breakfast incl., no evening meals. **Facilities** Tennis. **Pets** Dogs allowed in the kennels. **Nearby** Swimming pool, riding, Chartres cathedral, Verneuil-sur-Avre, Senonches forest. **Credit cards** Not accepted. **Open** Mid-April – mid-Oct. **How to get there** (Map 8): 34km northwest of Chartres via D939 towards Verneuil-sur-Avre; it's 9.5km after Châteauneuf-en-Thymerais at the crossroads with D20 (the Dreux-Senonches road).

This magnificent 17th-century château towers over a 750-acre park. M. Armand-Delille will greet you unaffectedly and leave you to your own activities. The interior is very charming; a majestic corridor hung with old tapestries leads to the bedrooms, all of which have antique furniture, functional bathrooms and a superb view. Breakfast is served in a room furnished in Directoire style.

198
Château de Blanville

28190 Saint-Luperce
(Eure-et-Loir)
Tel. 37 26 77 36
Fax 37 26 78 02
Emmanuel and Lisa
de Cossé Brissac

Rooms 5 and 1 suite (2 pers.) with bath or shower and WC. **Price** 600-700F (1-2 pers.) +100F (extra pers.); suite 800F (2 pers.). **Meals** Breakfast 50F; evening meals by reservation 24 hrs. ahead 150F (lunch), 250F (dinner (Wine incl.). **Facilities** Lounge; swimming pool, pond, bikes. **Pets** Dogs allowed on request. **Nearby** Tennis 1km, riding, golf (18 holes, 30km); Chartres Cathedral, Château de Maintenon. Spoken English. **Credit Card** Amex. **Closed** Feb. **How to get there** (Map 8): 12km southwest of Chartres. Autoroute A10, exit Chartres, then N123, then N23 towards Nogent-le-Rotrou, then exit Saint-Luperce. In village, D114 towards Courville, and signs.

The splendid 17th-century Château de Blanville dominates an immense private park and is extremely elegant inside. The salons, library and dining room are entirely at your disposal. The decor includes handsome 17th- and 18th-century furniture, along with antique objects and ancestral portraits. The rooms are comfortably furnished and still have all the charm of the past. The dinners are sumptuous and the owners are young and friendly. The château is an exceptional place to stay in every respect.

199
Château de Boisrenault

36500 Buzançais
(Indre)
Tel. 54 84 03 01
M. and Mme Y. du Manoir

Rooms 4 with bath and WC, 2 with shower and WC, 2 sharing shower and WC, 1 suite (4 pers.) with bath and WC. **Price** 330-430F (1 pers.), 370-475F (2 pers.), suite 790F (4 pers.). **Meals** Breakfast incl., evening meals at communal table 140F (wine not incl.). **Facilities** Lounge, swimming pool. **Credit cards** Amex, Visa, Eurocard and MasterCard. **Nearby** Golf, Brenne (lake), châteaux of the Loire. **Spoken** English. **Closed** January. **How to get there** (Map 16): 25km northwest of Châteauroux via N143 towards Buzançais, then D926 towards Levroux; turn right 3km from the village.

A neo-Gothic château set in a lovely park, Boisrenault has huge bedrooms which are luxuriously classical, like the Aux Faisans room; the others are more unusual but still beautiful. The studied elegance of the decor includes details such as the motifs painted on the bathroom tiles, which harmonize with the fabrics in each bedroom. The library/TV room is at the guests' disposal, as is an enormous salon. You will receive a very pleasant welcome at this château not far from the Thousand Lakes of La Brenne.

200
La Maison des Moines

1, route de Neuillay
36500 Méobecq
(Indre)
Tel. 54 39 44 36 (before 9:00 and about 19:00)
Mme Cécile Benhamou

Rooms 2 with private bath or shower, communal WC. **Price** 260F (2 pers.), +100F (extra pers.). **Meals** Breakfast incl.; no evening meals. **Restaurant** Le Boeuf Couronné in Mézières-en-Brenne (18km). **Facilities** Lounge. **Nearby** Golf (10km), swimming in Bellebranche Lake, swimming pools, tennis, hiking paths; La Brenne (lakes and forests), villages. **Credit cards** Not accepted. **Spoken** English. **Open** All year. **How to get there** (Map 16): 30km W of Châteauroux via D925 towards Châtellerault. After 18km, on left D27 towards Neuillay-Les-Bois, then continue on D27, towards Méobecq; house behind church.

L ocated behind a small church, the "Monks' House" is a pleasant departure point for discovering the splendid Parc des Mille Etangs-- Thousand Lakes Park--of the Brenne region. The two guest rooms are bright, decorated with provincial furniture and pretty, colorful fabrics, and they are very well kept. In the large room, the bathroom has not been partitioned in order to respect the proportions of the room. The breakfasts are pleasant and cheerfully served in charming rooms or near a lovely garden.

201
Moulin de Chézeaux

Rivarennes
36800 Saint-Gaultier
(Indre)
Tel. 54 47 01 84
Fax 54 47 10 93
Ren Rijpstra

Rooms 2 with bath and WC, 1 with shower and WC. **Children** Under 10 not admitted. **Price** 350-450F (1 pers.). **Meals** Breakfast incl., evening meals 160F. **Facilities** Lounge, fishing, winter garden . **Pets** No animals allowed. **Nearby** Golf (18 holes), swimming pool, tennis, canoeing, riding, La Brenne (lake). **Spoken** English, German, Dutch. **Open** All year. **How to get there** (Map 16): 10km west of Argenton-sur-Creuse; D927 and N151 towards Le Blanc; 2km after Saint-Gaultier turn left; signposted. **No smoking.**

This small white mill with blue shutters is surrounded by masses of geraniums and overlooks a lake. It has been restored by Ren Rijsptra, an interior decorator. The lounge is furnished in English style with a fireplace. The bedrooms are enchanting, with antique furniture, lovely curtains, embroidered sheets, and pretty flower arrangements. Breakfasts and dinners are served outside or in a beautiful conservatory on the lake. The hospitality is discreetly attentive.

202
Château du Gerfaut

37190 Azay-le-Rideau
(Indre-et-Loire)
Tel. 47 45 40 16/47 45 26 07
Fax 47 45 20 15
Marquis de Chenerilles
Madame Salles (born Chénerilles)

Rooms 4 with bath and WC, 1 with bath and external WC, 2 with shower and WC. **Price** 295-480F (1 pers.), 395-580F (2 pers.) Poss. weekly rental of apt. **Meals** Breakfast incl., evening meals at communal table, by reservation 200F (all incl.). **Facilities** Lounge, tennis, lake, telephone. **Credit cards** All major. **Pets** No dogs allowed. **Nearby** Golf, châteaux, wine cellars. **Credit cards** Not accepted. **Spoken** English. **Open** All year (in winter on request). **How to get there** (Map 16): 18km northeast of Chinon via D751 towards Tours, then leaving Azay-le-Rideau take the Villandry road; signposted.

Louis XI's falcons were bred here but the château itself was built in the last century. A majestic staircase leads to the huge bedrooms. Breakfast is served in a large room with exceptional Empire furniture which once belonged to Jérôme Bonaparte. The château stands in lands and forests extending to Villandry and Azay-le-Rideau. Guests receive a courteous welcome.

203
Le Château du Coteau

37270 Azay-sur-Cher
(Indre-et-Loire)
Tel. 47 50 47 47/47 50 43 50
Fax 47 50 49 60
M. and Mme Pierre Lemoine-Tassi

Rooms 5 with bath or shower, and WC, TV and Canal Plus private TV; 1 suite (6 pers.) with bath, WC, kitchen, corner lounge, TV and Canal Plus. **Price** 350F (1 pers.), 490FG (2 pers.), suite 650F (2 pers.) +150F (extra pers.). **Meals** Breakfast incl. (except in suite suppl.); no evenings meals. **Restaurants** La Planchette and Les Chandelles Gourmandes 5km. **Facilities** Lounge; fishing on pond, bikes, overland bikes on property. **Nearby** Fishing on Cher, horseback riding, swimming pool, tennis; visits of châteaux in hot-air balloon. **Credit cards** Not accepted. **Spoken** English, Spanish. **Open** All year. **How to get there** (Map 16): 15km E of Tours via N76 towards Vierzon. Or Autoroute exit Saint-Avertin-Vierzon, then N76.

Chopin loved to stay at the Château du Coteau and the beautiful romantic park seems as if it is still waiting for him. The very hospitable owners share the pavilion in the outbuildings with their guests. The superbly decorated bedrooms have all the modern amenities, as do the bathrooms. The salon/dining room is vast, bright and elegantly furnished, and there is an amusing 19th-century veranda where breakfasts are served in summer.

204
Manoir de Montour

37420 Beaumont-en-Véron
(Indre-et-Loire)
Tel. 47 58 43 76
Mme M. Krebs

Rooms 3 (of which 1 for 4 pers.) with bath and WC. **Price** 360F (2 pers.), 460F (4 pers.). **Meals** Breakfast incl., no evening meals. **Facilities** Lounge, telephone. **Pets** Small dogs allowed. **Nearby** Swimming pool, tennis, riding, fishing, golf, Azay-le-Rideau, Fontevraud, Giseux, Langeais, Vilandry, Saumur, Rigny-Ussé. **Open** Easter – Nov 1. **How to get there** (Map 16): 5km northwest of Chinon via D749 towards Avoine and Bourgueil until Coulaine, then towards Savigny en Véron.

It is rare to find so much character even in a very old house. The Manoir de Montour owes its charm to an extensive use of wood, terracotta, old fireplaces. Time has stood still here, except in the bathrooms, which are modern. The bedrooms are very large and quiet and the pleasant lounge has pale blue paneling. Breakfast is served in the dining room, in the bedrooms or in the very pretty garden. Marion Krebs will greet you as if you were old friends.

205
La Garenne

37350 La Celle-Guénand
(Indre-et-Loire)
Tel. 47 94 93 02
M. and Mme Devaulx
de Chambord

Rooms 3 and 1 suite (3 pers.) with bath or shower, and WC. Sheets changed every 3 days. **Price** 325F (1 pers.), 350F (2 pers.); suite 500F (2 pers.) +100F (extra pers.). **Meals** Breakfast incl.; no evening meals. **Facilities** Trout fishing in river on property. **Pets** Dogs allowed in kennel only. **Nearby** Restaurants, tennis (10km), horseback riding (10km), golf (18 holes, 24km); Prehistoric Museum of Le Grand Préssigny, Angle-sur-Anglin, Parc de la Haute Touche. **Spoken** English. **Open** All year. **How to get there** (Map 16): 24km southeast of Loches. Autoroute A10 towards Loches, then Ligueil D59, then D50 towards Preuilly for 12km. House as you leave La Celle-Guénand, on the left towards Preuilly.

La Garenne is a 19th-century family mansion, very typical in this region of the Loire. The mansion is superbly decorated with beautiful antique furniture, family portraits and hunting trophies. (The Loire has been a favorite hunting region for centuries). The bedrooms are beautiful, warm and cheerful, with beautifully coordinated carpets and fabrics. This is a beautiful mansion and the owners are very friendly.

206
Domaine de Pallus

Cravant-les-Côteaux
37500 Chinon
(Indre-et-Loire)
Tel. 47 93 08 94
Fax 47 98 43 00
M. and Mme B. Chauveau

Rooms 2 rooms and 1 suite with bath and WC. **Price** 450-500F (2 pers.), suite +150F (extra pers.). **Meals** Breakfast incl., no evening meals. **Restaurants** L'Océanic in Chinon and Château de Marçay. **Facilities** Lounge, telephone, swimming pool. **Pets** No dogs allowed. **Nearby** Fishing, golf, riding, châteaux of the Loire. **Spoken** English, German. **Open** All year. **How to get there** (Map 16): 8km east of Chinon on D21 to Cravant-les-Côteaux; leaving the village, Pallus is on the right after 1.5km.

Located 2km from Cravant, this gorgeous Touraine house has lovely rooms, where antique furniture of different eras blend happily together. Each bedroom has a style of its own, with many good decorative details. The bathrooms are superb and guests may enjoy the lounges as well as the garden. The hospitality is pleasant and breakfast is excellent.

207
La Butte de L'Epine

37340 Continvoir
(Indre-et-Loire)
Tel. 47 96 62 25
M. Michel Bodet

Rooms 2 with bath and WC. **Price** 260-275F (1 pers.), 280-295F (2 pers.) +80F (extra pers.).
Meals Breakfast incl., no evening meals. **Restaurants** 6km. **Facilities** Lounge, bicycles. **Pets**
Not allowed. **Nearby** Golf (18 holes), riding (3km), lake, tennis, walks, vineyards, châteaux,
museums. **Credit cards** Not accepted. **Spoken** English. **Closed** Chrismast. **How to get there**
(Map 16): 13km north of Bourgeuil via D749 towards Château-la-Vallière, then right on D15 to
Continvoir. In Continvoir take D64.

L a Butte de l'Epine is the realization of the owners' dream, which was to
build a 17th-century-style house using materials of the period. In the
center is a large and prettily decorated beamed room which serves as both
lounge and dining room. The two comfortable bedrooms are simple and
charming, and are decorated with pretty floral wallpaper. Breakfast is served
at a communal table inside or outside depending on the weather. The Bodets
are friendly hosts.

208
Manoir du Grand Martigny

Vallières, 37230 Fondettes
(Indre-et-Loire)
Tel. 47 42 29 87
Fax 47 42 24 44
Henri and Monique Desmarais

Rooms 5 and 2 suites (3-4 pers.) with bath and WC. **Price** 450-690F (2 pers.) +150F (extra
pers.), suite 950F (3-4 pers.). **Meals** Breakfast incl., no evening meals. **Restaurants** Pont de la
Motte in Fondette, La Poële d'Or in Saint-Cyr-sur-Loire. **Facilities** Lounge, horse boxes, park.
Pets No dogs allowed. **Nearby** Riding, tennis, golf, Loire châteaux. **Credit cards** Not accepted.
Spoken English. **Open** End March – mid-Nov. **How to get there** (Map 16): 5km west of Tours
via N152 towards Luynes. Stay on Right Bank of Loire to Chambre d'Hôtes sign. From Tours,
600m after BP gas station. From Langeais, 1km after Total gas station in Vallières.

T his elegant building stands on the banks of the Loire in a peaceful well-
kept park. Inside, the unaffected luxury of the lounge is found in all
the comfortable bedrooms and bathrooms. We particularly liked the lovely
Jouy bedroom. The proximity of Tours compensates for the lack of evening
meals at the Manoir. The owners are efficient and discreet.

209
Domaine de Beauséjours

37220 Panzoult
(Indre-et-Loire)
Tel. 47 58 64 64
Mme Marie-Claude Chauveau

Rooms 1 with bath and WC, 2 with shower and WC, 2 suites of 2 bedrooms with bath and WC. Rooms cleaned on request. **Price** 420F (2 pers.), suite 580-620F (3-4 pers.). **Meals** Breakfast incl., no evening meals. **Facilities** Lounge, swimming pool. **Pets** Dogs allowed on request. **Nearby** Restaurants, tennis, golf, fishing, Loire châteaux. **Credit cards** Not accepted. **Spoken** English. **Open** All year. **How to get there** (Map 16): 12km east of Chinon via D21 to Panzoult; on the left before the village.

B eauséjours is a charming vineyard property. The simple bedrooms are comfortable, with beautiful views over vineyards and the plain below. The pleasant lounge, terrace and swimming pool are at your disposal. If you are interested in wine, a member of the family will invite you to a tasting, affording you a pleasant and sure means of becoming acquainted with the regional wines.

210
Le Clos Saint-Clair

Départementale 18
37800 Pussigny
(Indre-et-Loire)
Tel. 47 65 01 27
Fax 47 65 04 21
Mme Anne-Marie Liné

Rooms 4 with shower and WC (2-4 pers.); independent entrances. Room cleaned on request. **Price** 200F (1 pers.), 250F (2 pers.) +60F (extra pers.). **Meals** Breakfast incl., evening meals at communal table, on reservation (except national holidaysand Sunday) 90F (wine incl.). **Facilities** Lounge, tennis, fishing, bicycle rentals. **Pets** No dogs allowed. **Nearby** Golf, swimming pool, Romanesque churches, châteaux, wine cellars. **Credit cards** Not accepted. **Open** All year. **How to get there** (Map 16): 50km south of Tours via A10, exit Sainte-Maure, then right on RN10 to Port-de-Piles, then right on D5 towards Pussigny for 2km, then left for 1km; in front of Mairie.

A t the entrance to a pretty Touraine village you will find these two old houses in a flowery and well-tended garden. The charming bedrooms are rustic and elegant, with some antique pieces of furniture, colorful fabrics and many charming details. Excellent breakfasts are served on a bright veranda which opens onto the garden in good weather. Madame Liné is delightfully hospitable.

211
Les Religeuses

24, place des Religieuses
37120 Richelieu
(Indre-et-Loire)
Tel. 47 58 10 42
Mme Marie-Josèphe Le Platre-
Arnould

Rooms 1 with bath and WC, 3 with shower and WC, 1 suite (3 pers.) with washroom and WC.
Price 210F (1 pers.), 250-330F (2 pers.), suite 430F (3 pers.). **Meals** Breakfast incl., no evening
meals. **Facilities** Lounge. **Pets** Small dogs sometimes allowed. **Nearby** Restaurants, swimming
pool, tennis, golf, châteaux of the Loire, Chinon, Azay-le-Rideau. **Credit cards** Not accepted.
Closed Mid-Dec. – mid-Jan. **How to get there** (Map 16): 29km northwest of Châtellerault via
A10 then D749; signposted in Richelieu.

Within the ramparts of Richelieu, this mansion is truly delightful. Mme
Le Platre-Arnould is charming and will take pleasure in showing you
around the house, which is full of antiques and curios. Everything is clean
and shiny and smells of fresh polish, and the comfortable bedrooms are well
kept. The house is reasonably quiet for a small town. In summer, breakfast
is served in the sunlit garden.

212
Château de Montgouverne

37210 Rochecorbon
(Indre-et-Loire)
Tel. 47 52 84 59
Fax 47 52 84 61
Christine and Jacques Desvignes

Rooms 4 and 2 suites (3 pers.) with bath, WC, TV, and tel. **Price** 500-650F (2 pers.), suite 750-
990F (2 pers.) +150F (extra pers.). **Meals** Breakfast incl.; half-board (2 days min.) 425-625F.
Evening meals at communal or separate tables 200F (wine incl.). **Facilities** Lounge; heated
swimming pool, riding, overland bikes, hiking on property. **Pets** No dogs. **Nearby** Golf 18 holes
16km, tennis (500m); châteaux of the Loire. **Credit cards** Not accepted. **Spoken** English,
Spanish. **Closed** Nov. 16 – Feb. 28. **How to get there** (Map 16): 7km E of Tours. Autoroute A10,
exit Tours - Sainte-Radegonde, towards Vouvray via N152. In 600m on left, signs.

The private park of the Château de Montgouverne is laid out like a
paintings, telling you at once that this is an exceptional place. The
interior is just as stunning, with a beautiful decor of antique furniture,
charming objects, still-life paintings of fruits and flowers, and handsome
fabrics. The salons and bedrooms are all very beautiful and comfortably
appointed. The young owners of this near-perfect place to stay are truly
dedicated to pleasing their guests.

213
Manoir du Port Guyet

37140 Saint-Nicolas-de-Bourgueil
(Indre-et-Loire)
Tel. 47 97 82 20
Fax 47 97 98 98
Mme Valluet Deholin

Rooms 3 (double bed or twin beds) with bath and WC. 10% reduction after 3 days. **Price** 550-750F (2 pers.). **Meals** Breakfast incl. Dinner at Manoir on reservation at communal table. **Facilities** Lounges. **Pets** Dogs allowed on request. **Nearby** Tennis, lake, Loire, Vienne, riding, golf courses (18 holes, 17km), swimming pools; châteaux of Loire, Chinon, Cadre Noir Riding School, Saumur. **Spoken** English, Spanish, some Italian. **Closed** Nov. 1 to March 31. **How to get there** (Map 16): Autoroute Paris-Tours, exit Tours-Nord towards Langeais-Saumur. After Langeais, D35 to Saint-Nicolas-de-Bourgeuil. Before Saint-Nicolas, Monument Historique signs indicating the Manoir.

It was in this 15th-century manor house that Ronsard lived and wrote beautiful love sonnets to Marie. Today admirably restored after centuries of gradual decline, the Manoir du Port Guyet offers guests the pleasures of tasteful interior decoration along with modern accommodations. The light tones of the stone and fabrics complement the patina of the handsome old furniture, making the overall effect quite beautiful. It is a captivating and lovely reflection of the gentle way of life in the "Garden of France".

214
Le Prieuré des Granges

37510 Savonnières
(Indre-et-Loire)
Tel. 47 50 09 67
Fax 47 50 06 43
M. Philippe Dufresne

Rooms 5 with bath or shower, WC and tel. **Price** 420-470F (1 pers.), 450-500F (2 pers.), +120F (extra pers.). **Meals** Breakfast incl.; no evening meals. **Facilities** Lounge. Swimming pool, tennis and antiques on property. **Nearby** Restaurants, fishing, riding, golf (18 holes, 2km); Château de Villandry and other châteaux of Loire. **Spoken** English. **Closed** Jan. 1 to March 30. **How to get there** (Map 16): 11km from Tours. In Tours, go towards Tours Sud/Villandry to Savonnières.

High in the hills of Savennières (known for its lovely white wine), this charming house dating from the 17th, 18th and 19th-centuries is a lovely place to stay. The bedrooms are outstanding for their comfort as well as their beautiful decoration in which Philippe Dufresne, an antiques dealer, has tastefully combined antique furniture with handsome old decorative objects. The bathrooms are very pleasant. There is an elegant 18th-century dining room decorated in shades of blue to match the colorful Chinese porcelains, and the salon is warm and inviting. The Prieuré looks out onto a flowery private park. Monsieur Dufresne is very hospitable.

215
Le Prieuré Sainte Anne

10, rue Chaude
37510 Savonnières
(Indre-et-Loire)
Tel. 47 50 03 26
Mme Caré

Rooms 1 suite (2 pers.) with shower and WC. **Price** 220F (1 pers.), 290F (2 pers.) +85F (extra pers.). **Meals** Breakfast incl., no evening meals. **Facilities** Lounge. **Pets** Dogs allowed on request. **Nearby** Restaurants, golf (18 holes), châteaux. **Credit cards** Not accepted. **Open** March – Nov. **How to get there** (Map 16): 13km west of Tours via D7 towards Villandry; in the village, on the Druye road, take Rue du Paradis before the Mairie, then turn right.

This 15th-century house is somewhat set back from a quiet village street and is furnished in lovely rustic style with old polished furniture, antique plates on the wall, immense fireplaces, and comfortable wool mattresses in the bedrooms. It is a simple, quite well kept place which transports the visitor to another era. Friendly Madame Caré serves good breakfasts next to the fireplace or outside in the lovely flower garden which is protected from the wind by old stone walls.

216
La Ferme des Berthiers

37800 Sepmes
(Indre-et-Loire)
Tel. 47 65 50 61
Mme Ane-Marie Vergnaud

Rooms 1 with bath and WC, 2 with shower and WC and 1 child's room. Room cleaned every 3 days. **Price** 180F (1 pers.), 220-250F (2 pers.), 280-300F (3 pers.), suite 340F (3 pers.). **Meals** Breakfast incl., evening meals at communal or separate tables 90F (wine incl.). **Facilities** Lounge. **Pets** Dogs allowed on request. **Nearby** Fishing and bathing in a lake, golf, Loire châteaux, wine cellars. **Credit cards** Not accepted. **Spoken** English, Dutch, German. **Open** All year. **How to get there** (Map 16): 40km south of Tours via A10 exit Sainte-Maure-de-Touraine, then D59 towards Ligueil; signposted as you leave the village.

You will be warmly welcomed at this beautiful farm. The comfortable bedrooms are prettily decorated and have superb bathrooms; our favorites are the Blue and the Yellow bedrooms. There is a magnificent terracotta floor. Anne-Marie Vergnaud prepares excellent evening meals and hearty breakfasts. Children are welcome in this country-style way of life.

217
Manoir de Foncher

37510 Villandry
(Indre-et-Loire)
Tel. 47 50 02 40
M. and Mme Salles

Rooms 1 with bath and WC, possibility of a suite. **Price** 600F (2 pers.), suite 850F (3-4 pers.).
Meals Breakfast incl., no evening meals. **Facilities** Lounge. **Nearby** Restaurants, riding, golf.
Credit cards Not accepted. **Spoken** English. **Open** April to Sept. **How to get there** (Map 16):
15km west of Tours via D7 towards Villandry. At Savennières, cross the bridge and turn left
along the right bank of the Cher for 3km.

At the tip of a spit of land between the Loire and the Cher, this manor
house surely looks the same as it did in the 16th-century, with its
mullioned windows, exterior gallery and an exceptional spiral staircase.
Breakfast is served on an immense convent table in a room with a a huge
fireplace. The very comfortable bedrooms and the suite are beautiful and
authentic. The bathrooms are charming. This is a magic place for visiting
the châteaux of the Loire.

218
Château de Jallanges

Vernou-sur-Brenne
37210 Vouvray
(Indre-et-Loire)
Tel. 47 52 01 71
Fax 47 52 11 18
Mme Danièle Ferry-Balin

Rooms 4 with bath and WC, 2 suites (2/5 pers.) with lounge, dressing room, bath and WC. **Price**
680F (2 pers.), 830F (3 pers.); suite 730-880F (2 pers.) +150F (extra pers.). **Meals** Breakfast
incl., evening meals at communal table, on reservation 260F (wine incl.). **Facilities** Lounge,
telephone, billiards, bicycles, carriage trips, hot-air balloon, antique shop; events and exhibits.
Pets Dogs allowed on request (+50F). **Nearby** Golf, fishing, riding. **Credit cards** Not accepted.
Spoken English, German. **Open** All year. **How to get there** (Map 16): 15km east of Tours via
N152 towards Amboise, then at Vouvray take D46 towards Vernou-sur-Brenne (or TGV 55 mins
from Paris).

With its brick-and-stone Renaissance façade and grand courtyard, this
château is a beautiful sight. It is being lovingly restored by the family,
who will welcome you with kind hospitality. The bedrooms and suites are
prettily decorated, with views over the park or the small formal garden.
Special mention should made of the rooms on the *premier étage*, which are
large, beautiful and comfortable. The evening meals are excellent.

219
La Farge

41600 Chaumont-sur-Tharonne
(Loir-et-Cher)
Tel. 54 88 52 06
M. and Mme de Grangeneuve

Rooms 3, 1 suite (2 - 4 pers.); 1 studio 3 pers.; and 1 studio 3-4 pers. (with living room, fireplace, TV, kitchen) with bath and WC. Special rates for more than 3 days. **Price** 325F (2 pers.), suite 325-450F (2 pers.); studio 450-550F. **Meals** Breakfast incl.; no evening meals, poss. kitchen in evening. **Restaurant** La Grenouillère (5km). Living room with fireplace and TV. **Facilities** Swimming pool, riding center. Footpaths. **Pets** Dogs only. **Nearby** Golf (18 holes, 10km), tennis, fishing on lake, bike rentals; pretty villages, châteaux of Loire. **Credit cards** Not accepted. **Spoken** English. **Open** All year. **How to get there** (Map): 5km E of Chaumont-sur-Taronne, take C2 towards Vouzon. La Farge 4km on right. (35km S of Orléans via N 20).

Set in the midst of a forest, this is a beautiful group of 17th-century buildings. The comfortable bedrooms are pleasantly furnished and the bathrooms are beautiful. The apartment is outstanding with its beautiful small salon, fireplace and kitchen. Breakfasts are served in a beautiful, spacious room. Copper pots, hunting trophies and handsome old furniture create a warm atmosphere in this welcoming place.

220
La Rabouillère

Chemin de Marçon
41700 Contres
(Loir-et-Cher)
Tel. 54 79 05 14
Fax 54 79 59 39
Mme Thimonnier

Rooms 5 with bath, WC and TV. **Price** 300F (1 pers.), 380-550F (2 pers.), 650F (3 pers.), 700F (4 pers.). **Meals** Breakfast incl., no evening meals. **Restaurants** In Court-Cheverny and Contres. **Facilities** lounge, telephone. **Pets** No dogs allowed. **Nearby** Tennis, riding, fishing, golf (18 holes), Loire châteaux. **Spoken** English. **Open** 1 March – 30 Nov. **How to get there** (Map 16): 19km south of Blois via D765. At Cheverny take D102 towards Contres for 6km; signposted Chambres d'hôtes.

Recently built with old materials, this traditional Sologne "long house" is surrounded by 12 1/2 acres of woods and meadows, which are made into a beautiful garden near the house. The bedrooms are named after flowers. They are pleasant and comfortable and the bathrooms are very attractive. The upstairs room is especially beautiful. Mme Thimonnier loves her house and enjoys opening it to guests. When the weather is cold an open fire burns in the living room, which opens wide onto the garden.

221
La Borde

41160 Danzé
(Loir-et-Cher)
Tel. 54 80 68 42
M. and Mme Kamette

Rooms 3 with shower and WC, 1 suite of 2 bedrooms with bath and WC, 1 suite with shower and WC. **Price** 150-200F (1 pers.), 200-250F (2 pers.), suite 350-400 (3 pers.), 400-450F (4 pers.) – reduction after the 2nd night. **Meals** Breakfast incl., no evening meals. **Restaurants** Le Marmiton in Danzé (2km) and in La Ville-aux-Clercs (3km). **Facilities** Lounge, telephone, fishing. **Pets** Dogs allowed on request. **Nearby** Swimming pools, tennis, riding, golf, Loire châteaux, Loir valley. **Credit cards** Not accepted. **Spoken** English, Spanish. **Open** All year. **How to get there** (Map 16): 15km north of Vendôme via D36 to Danzé, then D24 towards La Ville-aux-Clercs.

La Borde is a beautiful 1930s mansion in a large park. All the bedrooms overlook the park; they are large, comfortable, and are furnished with beautiful 1950s light oak furniture. One room serves as both TV–lounge and dining room, where generous breakfasts are served. La Borde offers good value for the money, and the hospitality is very pleasant.

222
Manoir de Clénord

Route de Clénord
41250 Mont-près-Chambord
(Loir-et-Cher)
Tel. 54 70 41 62
Fax 54 70 33 99
Mme Renauld

Rooms 4 with bath and WC and 2 suites (2/4 pers.). **Price** 380-700F (2 pers.), suites 800-1100F. **Meals** Breakfast incl., evening meals at communal table, by reservation 140-190F (wine incl.). **Facilities** Lounge, swimming pool, tennis, bicycles, canoes, French language course. **Pets** No dogs allowed. **Nearby** 18-hole golf, forest, Loire châteaux, wine cellars. **Credit cards** Visa, Eurocard and MasterCard. **Credit cards** Not accepted. **Spoken** English, Spanish. **Open** All year. **How to get there** (Map 16): From Paris, A10 exit Blois, towards Vierzon via D765. In village of Clénord, turn left on Mont-Près Chambord; entrance 200m.

You drive through lovely woods to reach this small 18th-century manor house. Mme. Renauld will greet you very warmly and show you the bedrooms, which have pretty antique furniture and a view of the formal gardens. Breakfast is served in a rustic dining room or on the terrace, weather permitting. You will find a very pleasant and restful atmosphere.

223
Château de Colliers

41500 Muides-sur-Loire
(Loir-et-Cher)
Tel. 54 87 50 75
Fax 54 87 03 64
M. and Mme de Gélis

Rooms 4 with bath and WC, 1 suite (4 pers.) of 2 bedrooms with bath and WC. **Price** 550-700F (2 pers.), suite 800F. **Meals** Breakfast incl., evening meals at communal table, by reservation 200F. **Restaurants** Le Relais de B. Robin in Bracieux (18km) and Les Calanques in Mer (5km). **Facilities** Lounge, telephone, swimming pool. **Nearby** Kayak, hot-air balloon, helicopter, golf (18 holes), equestrian center, watersports, Loire châteaux. **Credit cards** Not accepted. **Spoken** English, Spanish. **Open** All year (by reservation in winter). **How to get there** (Map 16): A10, exit Mer, follow towards Chambord to Muides-Loire, then D951 towards Blois. Colliers on right, on bank of Loire, 300m after last house.

This fanciful 18th-century house enjoys an outstanding location on the banks of the Loire. The interior is truly elegant: the salons are superbly furnished, the dining room is covered with original frescos and the pretty bedrooms have cheerful fireplaces. Almost all have a splendid view over the Loire. (One has an amusing private terrace on the roof.) The owners are pleasant and discreet.

224
En Val de Loire

46, rue de Meuves
41150 Onzain
(Loir-et-Cher)
Tel. 54 20 78 82
Fax 54 20 78 82
Mme Langlais

Rooms 2 with bath and WC, 3 with shower and WC. **Price** 330F (2 pers.). **Meals** Breakfast incl., evening meals (some days) at communal or separate table 100-250F. **Facilities** Lounge. **Pets** Dogs not allowed. **Nearby** Swimming pool, tennis, riding, golf, châteaux of the Loire. **Credit cards** Not accepted. **Spoken** English. **Open** All year (by reservation in low season). **How to get there** (Map 16): 15km southwest of Blois via N152 towards Amboise, then right on D58 at Chouzy towards Monteaux as far as Onzain.

A long garden leads up to this pretty house surrounded by flowers. It is small and welcoming and has been decorated by M. and Mme Langlais themselves, who have created a model of good rustic taste and comfort. The bedrooms are furnished with antiques and some have upholstered walls with matching lampshades. There is an inviting lounge-dining room with deep armchairs in front of the fire. Breakfast includes 21 different types of preserves. This is a very beautiful place.

225
La Villa Médicis

Macé
41000 Saint-Denis-sur-Loire
(Loir-et-Cher)
Tel. 54 74 46 38 Fax 54 78 20 27
Baronne Baxin de Caix
de Rembures

Rooms 1 with bath and WC, 4 with shower and WC, 1 suite (2 pers.). **Price** 300F (1 pers.), 350F (2 pers.), suite 450F. **Meals** Breakfast incl., evening meals, by reservation, at communal or separate tables 200F. **Facilities** Lounges. **Pets** Dogs not allowed. **Nearby** Riding, canoeing, rowing, windsurfing, fishing, Loire châteaux. **Spoken** English, German, Italian, Spanish. **Open** All year. **How to get there** (Map 16): 3km north of Blois via N152 towards Orléans, then Macé; 500m on the right before the church.

Marie de Medicis loved to bathe in the three springs in this park which borders the Loire. If the bathrooms are rather small (except the one on the ground floor), the bedrooms, dining room and lounge are large, light, welcoming rooms, that are prettily arranged. Madame de Caix's care and kindness make the Villa a very friendly place to stay.

226
Château de la Voûte

41800 Troo
(Loir-et-Cher)
Tel. 54 72 52 52
MM. Clays and Venon

Rooms 2 with bath and WC, 1 with shower and WC, 2 suites with bath and WC. **Price** 370-470F (2 pers.), suite 550F (2 pers.). **Meals** Breakfast incl., no evening meals. **Restaurants** Le Cheval Blanc, La Grotte, La Paix (200m). **Facilities** Fishing. **Pets** Dogs not allowed. **Nearby** Riding, tennis, golf, Loir valley, Ronsard's birthplace. **Credit cards** Not accepted. **Spoken** English. **Open** All year. **How to get there** (Map 16): 25km west of Vendôme via D917 and 5km from Montoire; signposted in the village.

The gardens of the Château de la Voûte are laid out on two terraces. The bedrooms reflect the hospitable owners' taste for antique decoration; each has its own style of pictures, furniture and carpets, ranging from Pompadour to Empire and Louis XIII; they are all comfortable and quiet. Breakfast is served in the bedrooms or on the terrace.

227
Château de la Giraudière

41220 Villeny
(Loir-et-Cher)
Tel. 54 83 72 38
Mme Anne Giordano-Orsini

Rooms 2 with bath and WC, 3 with bath and shared WC. **Price** 350F (2 pers.). **Meals** Breakfast incl., no evening meal; light meals poss.; restaurants nearby. **Facilities** Lounge, tennis. **Pets** No dogs allowed. **Nearby** Fishing, riding, golf. **Credit cards** Not accepted. **Spoken** English. **Open** Easter – Nov 1. **How to get there** (Map 17): 39km east of Blois via D951 to Muides-sur-Loire, then D103. At La Ferté-Saint-Cyr take D925 towards La Marolle-en-Sologne; it's 800m from the road.

This attractive Louis XIII château has beautifully kept grounds and lies in mid-forest off a small lane. The interior is lovely, with light streaming in through the large living room windows and illuminating the elegant furniture. The bedrooms are very refined and have a lovely view over the gardens. The château is an excellent place to stay while visiting the Sologne. You will be made very welcome.

228
Sainte Barbe

Route de Lorris
Nevoy
45500 Gien
(Loiret)
Tel. 38 67 59 53
Mme Annie Le Lay

Rooms 1 with bath and WC, and 1 studio (5 pers.) in annex with shower room and 2 WC. **Price** 270F (1 pers.), 320F (2 pers.) +50F (extra pers.), studio 800F (2 pers.), 1000F (5 pers. per weekend) 1 small house (5 pers.) in outbuilding with washroom and 2: WCs; on weekend: **Meals** Breakfast incl., evening meals (separate tables) 75F (wine not incl.). **Pets** Dogs allowed in kennels. **Facilities** Lounge, tennis, horse stalls, fishing. **Nearby** Riding, hunting, golf. **Credit cards** Not accepted. **Spoken** English. **Open** All year on request. **How to get there** (Map 17): 5km northwest of Gien via D44.

Surrounded by woods and fields, this old house has a superb guest-bedroom, decorated in exceptionally good taste, behind its deceptively simple appearance. You will be made very welcome and can enjoy a lounge for guests' use. The furniture, much of it *Haute Epoque*, a Chesterfield sofa, and numerous objects connected with hunting and riding lend special charm to Sainte-Barbe. Note also the "little house", which is ideal for a stay in a country setting. This is a lovely place.

229
La Giberie

La Giberie
10500 Petit-Mesnil - (Aube)
Tel. 25 92 22 00
Fax 25 92 26 86
Baron and Baronne
Bertrand de Taisne

Rooms 1 and 1 suite (2-4 pers.) with bath and WC, and 1 spare room. **Price** 300-450F; suite 700F (4 pers.) +100F (extra pers.). **Meals** Breakfast incl.; no evening meals, poss. cold plate 100F. **Restaurant** Auberge de la Plaine (4km). **Facilities** Lounges. Biking in forest on property. **Nearby** Tennis, water skiing, swimming, sailing (15km); Old towns of Troyes and Bar-sur-Aube; Château de Cirey-sur-Blaise, Cristalleries Royales de Bayel, Colombey-les-Deux-Eglises. **Spoken** English, German. **Open** All year. **How to get there** (Map 11): 38km E of Troyes towards Nancy. In Breyenne-le-C. go towards Bar-sur-Aube. In La Routhière, take left towards Petit-Mesnil and Giberie. Go through Petit Minimes, continue in La Giberie for 1km: house on left (white grill).

Nestling in a small hamlet, this is an elegant, prettily decorated large house which was built in the early 19th-century. There are beautiful rooms with Directoire wood paneling and a view over the lovely park. The bedrooms are vast, comfortable and decorated with charming English fabrics; two rooms have an immense private terrace with a superb view. The owners are young and very friendly, and the château is a perfect place from which to discover this beautiful, yet little-known, region.

230
Château d'Etoges

51270 Etoges par Montmort
(Marne)
Tel. 26 59 30 08
Fax 26 59 35 57
Mme Anne Filliette-Neuville

Rooms 17 rooms and 3 suites (3 pers.) with bath, WC and telephone (TV on request). **Price** 480-620F (2 pers.) +80F (extra pers.), suite 950F (3 pers.). **Meals** Breakfast 55F, evening meals (separate tables) 160-180F (wine not incl.). **Facilities** Lounges, fishing, billiards, piano, croquet, 2 bikes. **Credit cards** Visa. **Pets** Dogs allowed on request (+40F). **Nearby** Riding, tennis, golf, vineyards and wine cellars. **Spoken** English. **Closed** End Jan. – mid-Feb. **How to get there** (Map 10): 22km south of Epernay via D51 to Montmort, then D18: signposted.

It would be difficult not to fall in love with this gorgeous 17th-century château. After crossing the main courtyard you will find an interior with a bright east-west exposure. The view from the bedrooms is unique, and their decor is traditional and cheerful – a model of good taste. There are beautiful bathrooms with lovely tiles, while antique furniture and delicate colors lend charm throughout. You will be warmly welcomed to this sublime château which is a hotel and guest house combined.

231
Château du Ru Jacquier

51700 Igny-Comblizy
(Marne)
Tel. 26 57 10 84
Fax 26 57 11 85
M. Granger

Rooms 5 with bath and WC, 1 with shower and WC. **Price** 380-410F (2 pers.) +100F (extra pers.). **Meals** Breakfast incl., evening meals 150F (wine not incl.). **Facilities** Lounge, trout fishing, horse-drawn carriage. **Pets** Dogs allowed (+30F). **Nearby** Mountain bikes, golf (18 holes, 6km), champagne route, cellar visits, château de Montmort, Condé en Brie. **Credit cards** Not accepted. **Open** All year. **How to get there** (Map 10): 20km southwest of Epernay via N3 towards Château-Thierry, then left on D18 towards Dormans for 7km.

The turrets of this welcoming and well renovated château rise above a park where horses and deer graze. A beautiful wooden staircase leads to the quite large bedrooms, which are comfortable and prettily decorated with antique furniture. Good dinners are served in a lovely dining room with beautifully set tables. In good weather breakfast is served outside. The château is a lovely place to stay.

232
Domaine des Oiseaux

12, Grande Rue
51390 Rosnay
(Marne)
Tel. 26 03 63 07
Mme Legros

Rooms 2 with bath and WC, 2 sharing bath and WC. **Price** 200-220F (1 pers.), 265-285F (2 pers.). **Meals** Breakfast incl., no evening meals. **Restaurants** 5 and 7km. **Facilities** Lounge, swimming pool, hunting, fishing. **Pets** Dogs allowed on request. **Nearby** Tennis, golf (3km), Champagne vineyards and cellars, Reims Cathedral. **Credit cards** Not accepted. **Open** All year. **How to get there** (Map 10): 12km west of Rheims via N31; autoroute exit Reims-Tinqueux; then N31 towards Soissons, then after Thillois D27 left towards Rosnay; in the village.

This is a very pretty village house with a pleasant garden and a swimming pool. The comfortable, prettily furnished bedrooms under the eaves are tastefully decorated with lovely fabrics on the walls. Breakfast is served at a large table in the dining room, next to the lounge with an open fire. A very friendly welcome awaits you.

233
Domaine de Boulancourt

Boulancourt
52220 Montier-en-Der
(Haute-Marne)
Tel. 25 04 60 18
M. and Mme Viel-Cazal

Rooms 5 with bath or shower and WC, and 1 appart.(4-6 pers.) with bath or shower and WC. **Price 185F** (1 pers.), 220F (2 pers.), +50F (extra pers.); appart. 2500F weekly, +200F (extra pers.). **Meals** Breakfast 25F, evening meals, by reservation, at communal or separate table 110F (aperitif and wine incl.). **Facilities** Lounge, telephone. **Pets** Dogs not allowed. **Nearby** Tennis (2km), churches, Der Chantecoq Lake. **Open** All year. **How to get there** (Map 11): 48km southwest of Saint-Dizier via D384. At Montier-en-Der head for Troyes; at Ceffonds right on D174 Longueville/Laines. Pass through Longeville/Laines; 1km after village, first intersection on the left.

Once called the Ferme du Désert, this guest house is set in quiet surroundings, with a very pleasant garden and a lake and river below. It has been beautifully decorated with cheerful, bright colors. The refurbished bedrooms are charming and comfortable. Excellent evening meals often include local game. The fish comes from the nearby lake and boars are raised on the property. You will receive a very warm welcome.

234
Le Crêt l'Agneau

25650 La Longeville
(Doubs)
Tel. 81 38 12 51
Yves and Liliane Jacquet-Pierroulet

Rooms 7 with bath or shower, and WC (2 with communal WC). Rooms cleaned every 2 days.
Price 500F, 2500-300F weekly. **Meals** Noon and evening at communal table. **Pets** Dogs not
allowed. **Facilities** Theme weekends and organization of activities: cross-country skiing, ice
skating, mountain bikes, picnics (grills). **Credit cards** Not accepted. **Spoken** English, Spanish.
Closed April. Weekend in spring and autumn or week of Dec. I5- March 31. **How to get there**
(Map 20): 15km northeast of Pontarlier (60km southeast of Besançon via N57) via D437 towards
Morteau. In Montbenoît, towards Gilley; signs in village Les Auberges (or TGV train Frasne).

This is a 17th-century farm tucked away in the heart of splendid countryside.
Yves will happily take you on cross-country skiing trips or mushroom-
hunting, while Liliane is in charge of preparing delicious meals made with
homemade products (bread, pastries, ham and sausages, preserves...). Meals
around the large dining table are very friendly occasions. The comfortable
bedrooms are tastefully decorated with bright wood paneling. Sports, relaxation
and gastronomy are the key words at Le Crêt l'Agneau.

235
Château de l'Hermitage

25120 Mancenans-Lizerne
(Doubs)
Tel. 81 64 09 24
Sylvia and André Tanner

Rooms 2 with bath or shower, and private WCs, but outside rooms; and 2 spare rooms. **Price** 250F
(1 pers.), 300F (2 pers.), +100F (extra pers.). **Meals** Breakfast incl. Special rates out of season.
Evening meals at communal or separate tables 60-90F (wine incl.). **Facilities** Lounge. Visit of
château, forest, Waroly Caves on property. **Nearby** Riding, swimming in river; Château de Belvoir,
Monastère de Consolation. **Credit cards** Not accepted. **Spoken** English, Spanish. **Closed** Nov. 1
– Easter. **How to get there** (Map 19): 5km NW of Maîche. A36, exit Montbéliard, then road to
Pontarlier. In Maîche, D464 towards Grottes de Waroly. The château: 100m after Grottes.

On the slope of a beautiful hillside surrounded by vegetation , the Château
de l'Hermitage is a former monastery which was converted into a residence
by Joseph Auber, a famous painter of the Saint Sulpice religious order. The Château
has been kept in its original state; its interior a perfect example of late 19th-century
style. Flamboyant Gothic architecture, frescos, paintings, sculptures and rugs
throughout combine to form a unique ensemble. The large bedrooms are as they
were, old-fashioned but comfortable. The owners are friendly and informal, the
breakfasts are copious, and there is a fabulous panoramic view over the valley.

236
Rue du Puits

3, rue du Puits
39100 Gévry
(Jura)
Tel. 84 71 05 93
Fax 84 71 08 08
M. and Mme Picard

Rooms 3 with bath and WC, 3 with shower and WC. **Price** 170F (1 pers.), 200F (2 pers.) +30F (extra pers.). **Meals** Breakfast incl., evening meals at communal table 100F (wine incl.) **Facilities** Lounge. **Nearby** Tennis, riding, golf, Jura and Burgundy vineyards, forest of Chaux. **Credit cards** Not accepted. **Spoken** English, German. **Open** All year. **How to get there** (Map 19): 8km south of Dole via N73 towards Chalon-Beaune, then left on N5 towards Genève; right in the first village.

Formerly a village farm, this large house still has its original beams and pillars. The lounge is pleasant and bright, and the beautiful bedrooms have been redone, comfortably furnished, and decorated with prettily colored fabrics. With the first nice weather, the excellent, copious evening meal is served in the. garden. The Picards are cheerful, humorous, and welcoming.

237
Ferme–Auberge de la Bergerie

Crenans
39260 Moirans-en-Montagne
(Jura)
Tel. 84 42 00 50 – Fax 84 42 08 60
M. and Mme Baron

Rooms 4 with shower and WC. **Price** Half board 220F per pers., full board 280F per pers. in double room, +50F (1 pers.). **Meals** Auberge on the spot, menus: 65-170F. **Facilities** Lounge, equestrian center, theme tours. **Pets** Dogs allowed on request. **Nearby** Tennis, lake, Gallo-Roman sites, Château du Pin. **Credit cards** Not accepted. **Spoken** English, Spanish. **Closed** First few days of Sept. Half board or full board only. **How to get there** (Map 19): 38km southeast of Lons-le-Saunier via N78 and D470 towards Saint-Claude-Genève via Moirans; 3km before Moirans, left on D296 towards Crenans; it's in the village.

Behind a beautifully austere stone façade lies this very welcoming house. You will find the works of several talented sculptors, pale wooden regional furniture, beams, stone walls--and much human warmth. The bedrooms are pleasant and quiet, the cuisine wholesome and delicious. Off the beaten track, this is an ideal place for enthusiastic walkers.

238
Château Gréa

39190 Rotalier
(Jura)
Tel. 84 25 05 07
Bénédicte and Pierre de Boissieu

Rooms 1 and 1 suite (4 pers.) with bath or shower, and WC. Rooms cleaned on request; sheets changed every 2 days. Price 360F (2 pers.) +90F (extra pers.). **Meals** Breakfast incl.; 5% reduction for 8 days, 10% 15 days. Light meal on arrival 60F (wine incl.). Kitchen at disposal. **Facilities** Lounge, tel.: Teleservice. **Facilities** Hiking GR59, bikes. **Nearby** Restaurants (3km), tennis (3km), lakes, golf (18 holes, 9km); Beaume-les-M., Wine Route, Château d'Arlay (birds of prey). **Credit cards** Not accepted. **Spoken** English, Spanish. **Open** All year. **How to get there** (Map 19): 12km S of Lons-le-Saulnier via N83, towards Bourg-en-Bresse and Lyon for 10km. At railway crossing of Paisia, turn left towards Rotalier, just before the village on left.

The bedrooms at Château Gréa have been very prettily renovated, making them cheerful, elegant and comfortable. The parquet floors are as shining as the bathrooms. There is beautiful antique furniture throughout, and a beautiful salon and dining room. The breakfasts are hearty and are served outside in good weather. Children are welcome and the owners are very hospitable. This is an excellent place to stay on the lovely Jura Wine Route, overlooking the hillsides covered with woodland and vineyards.

239
Château d'Epenoux

Route de Saint-Loup
Epenoux
70000 Vesoul
(Haute-Saône)
Tel. 84 75 19 60
Mme Germaine Gauthier

Rooms 4 with bath, telephone, WC and TV, 1 with shower, WC and TV. **Price** 300-360F (1-2 pers.). **Meals** Breakfast incl., half board 650-750F (2 pers.) evening meals at communal table 200F (wine incl.). **Facilities** Lounge. **Nearby** Swimming pool, tennis, riding, golf (18 holes), Luxeuil, villages of Montigny and Charriez, Vesoul, Ronchamp Chapel. **Credit cards** Travellers Cheques, Eurocheque. **Spoken** English, German. **Open** All year. **How to get there** (Map 20): 4km north of Vesoul via D10 towards Saint-Loup; at the entrance to the village, left opposite the sign.

The small Château d'Epenoux backs onto a 12-1/2-acre park and is owned by a very charming woman who will welcome you as if you were part of her family. The interior is furnished in 19th-century style and is comfortable and colorful. The large bedrooms are charmingly decorated. In the evening, guests sit at an elegant table to share an excellent meal.

240
La Ferme de Vosves

Vosves
77190 Dammarie-les-Lys
(Seine-et-Marne)
Tel. (1) 64 39 22 28/
(1) 64 39 02 26
Mme Lemarchand

Rooms 1 with bath and WC, 1 with shower and WC, and 1 auxiliary room. **Price** 200F (1 pers.), 250F (2 pers.) +220F (extra room). **Meals** Breakfast incl., no evening meals. **Restaurants** L'Ile aux Truites in Vulaine. **Pets** Dogs allowed on request. **Nearby** Château de Vaux-le-Vicomte, Forest of Fontainebleau, Barbizon. **Credit cards** Not accepted. **Spoken** English, Italian. **Open** All year. **How to get there** (Map 9): 15km northwest of Fontainebleau (A6 Exit 12). N7 towards Fontainebleau. After Ponthierry, left on N472 for 3km, then right to Vosves.

Mme Lemarchand will receive you with great hospitality at this working farm located on the edge of the small village of Vosves. She is an artist and has decorated her house with excellent taste. For families, the small suite is very pleasant and is decorated in an elegant country style. Otherwise choose the atelier with its high beams and large roof window. You will enjoy the excellent breakfasts.

241
Vivescence

9, place Greffulhe
77810 Thomery
(Seine-et-Marne)
Tel. (1) 60 96 43 96
Fax (1) 60 96 41 13
Mme Brigitte Stacke

Rooms 8 with bath, WC and telephone, 1 with shower, WC and telephone. Room cleaned every day, except weekends. **Price** 320F (1 pers.), 400F (2 pers.) +130F (extra pers.). **Meals** Breakfast incl., evening meals at communal or separate table 140F (wine and coffee incl.), light lunch in the garden in summer. **Pets** Dogs allowed (+30F). **Facilities** Lounge, covered and heated swimming pool, sauna, massage, yoga, fitness training, bicycle rentals (50F per day), horse stalls. **Nearby** Golf, riding (3km), fishing, windsurfing, rock climbing, Château of Fontainebleau, Moret-sur-Loing, Rosa Bonheur museum in Thomery. **Credit cards** Not accepted. **Spoken** English. **Open** All year (except Christmas – New Year's Day). **How to get there** (Map 9): 7km east of Fontainebleau via A6 then N7. At the obelisk in Fontainebleau, N6 towards Sens, then left on D301 towards Thomery; it's on the church square.

At this unusual place many kinds of fitness facilities are available; or you can simply enjoy the very well kept park and the pretty bedrooms (named after spices). The bathrooms are comfortable and the atmosphere is restful.

242
Mont au Vent

2, route de Maule
Herbeville
78580 Maule
(Yvelines)
Tel. (1) 30 90 65 22
Mme Turmel

Rooms 5 (1 with Tel. and TV) and 1 suite, with bath and WC. **Price** 350-400F (2 pers.), suite 650F (4 pers.). **Meals** Breakfast incl. Evening meals on request 100F (wine not incl.). **Facilities** Lounge; tennis, swimming pool, pond, 2 horse stalls, forest on property. **Nearby** Versailles, Saint-Germain-en-Laye, Monet's house, Thoiry, Saint-Nom-la-Bretèche Golf Club. **Credit cards** Not accepted. **Closed** Dec. 24-25; Dec. 31-Jan. 1; 2 wks in summer dep. on reservations. **How to get there** (Map 9): 7km E of Orgeval, Autoroute exit Poissy, then towards Orgeval. In Orgeval (N13), turn left towards Maule. After village Les Alluets Le Roi, first on left towards Herbeville; house at entrance to village.

Despite its proximity to Paris, this country house and its private park overlook a still unspoiled countryside. The bedrooms are comfortable, with beautiful autumn-colored fabrics and carpets, lacquered furniture, and superb bathrooms. In summer, breakfasts are served on a terrace overlooking the lovely countryside, and in a beautiful dining room in winter. There is a magnificent living room with 19th-century blond-oak paneling, and Madame Turmel's welcome is warm and friendly.

243
Château de Villepreux

78450 Villepreux
(Yvelines)
Tel. (1) 30 80 50 00/30 81 78 00
Fax (1) 30 80 50 01
Comtesse de Sainte Seine

Rooms 2 with bath and WC (telephone on request), 5 with bath and shared WCs. **Price** 900-1200F (2 pers.). **Meals** Breakfast incl., no evening meals. **Facilities** tennis, park. **Pets** Dogs allowed on request. **Nearby** Restaurants (500m), golf on weekdays, Versailles, Dompierre, Fontainebleau. **Credit cards** Not accepted. **Open** All year (by reservation). **How to get there** (Map 9): 20km west of Paris via A12 exit Versailles-Ouest, then N307 towards Bailly and Villepreux.

On the edge of a beautiful 500-acre park close to Paris, Villepreux has a magnificent 18th-century façade. You will find a unique ensemble of superb rooms. The Empire furnishings throughout beautifully recreate the elegant 18th-century interior. Decorated in the same style, many of the bedrooms have their original antique wallpaper, and the bathrooms have just been redone. This is a lovely place, especially for history buffs, where you will be greeted with distinguished, warm hospitality.

244
Le Rocher Pointu

Plan-de-Dève
30390 Aramon
(Gard)
Tel. 66 57 41 87
Fax 66 57 01 77
Annie and André Malek

Rooms 1 with bath and WC, 3 with shower and WC. **Price** 330F (1 pers.), 350-400F (2 pers.) +90F (extra pers.), studio and appart. 430-550F (2-4 pers.). **Meals** Breakfast incl., no evening meals. **Restaurants** In Aramon. **Facilities** Lounge, telephone, swimming pool with barbecue. **Pets** Dogs not allowed. **Nearby** Riding, golf, fishing, shooting, Avignon, Les Baux, Séguret, Uzès, Tarascon, Saint-Rémy, Pont du Gard. **Credit cards** Not accepted. **Spoken** English. **Open** All year. **How to get there** (Map 33): 12km west of Avignon; from Avignon head for Nîmes, then D2 towards Aramon and D126 towards Saze; signposted.

Not far from Avignon, this Provençal house is surrounded by vegetation in beautiful hilly countryside. There is a swimming pool, a large reception room with living areas, and very pleasant small bedrooms, along with prettily decorated studios and apartments. The decor is natural: wood, stone, and pretty fabrics. Breakfast is a mini-brunch served outside at green-laquered tables, where is also a barbecue. You will receive a pleasant welcome.

245
Mas de la Ville

Rue Basse
30430 Barjac
(Gard)
Tel. 66 24 59 63
M. and Mme Ciaramella

Rooms 3 with bath or shower, and WC. **Price** 230F (1-2 pers.), 330F (room with 3 beds). **Meals** Breakfast 25F. No evening meals. **Restaurants** Esplanade and Auberge Ribeshautes, 2-3km. **Facilities** Lounge, swimming pool. **Pets** Dogs allowed on request. **Nearby** Golf course, compact green; riding, hiking, speoleology, canoeing, Uzès, Nîmes, Avignon, Orange, small villages and Romanesque art circuit. **Credit cards** Not accepted. **Spoken** English, German. **Open** All year (winter on reserv. only). **How to get there** (Map 32): 40km from Bollène, A7 exit Bollène, then towards Pont Saint-Esprit, then Barjac.

The Mas de la Ville looks austere from the street but on closer inspection, we discovered a large flower garden and a pretty swimming pool. The façade on the garden is charming with its small stairways, numerous balconies, and nooks and crannies everywhere. The bedrooms are all pleasant but our favorite has a small balcony and direct access to the garden. The two others overlook the Rue Basse, which is not noisy, and the room on the top floor has the advantage of a larger bathroom. The owners' welcome to the "Village House" is very friendly.

246
Beth

Hameau de Beth
30580 Lussan
(Gard)
Tel. 66 72 94 80
M. and Mme Schuh

Rooms 1 suite (2-5 pers.) with 3 bedrooms, bath and WC. Room cleaning responsibility of guests. **Price** 300F (2 pers.) +100F (extra pers.), 3 nights min. **Meals** Breakfast incl., no evening meals. **Restaurant** In Vallerargues (5km) and in Méjannes (8km). **Facilities** Lounge, swimming pool. **Pets** Dogs not allowed. **Nearby** Golf (25km), tennis, riding (8km), Gorges of the Ardèche, Uzès, Pont du Gard. **Credit cards** Not accepted. **Spoken** English, German. **Open** All year. **How to get there** (Map 32): 20km north of Uzès via D979. After Lussan take the Malataverne road; in the village, turn right, then in the hamlet of Beth take the road to the menhir; left after 200m.

All that remains of this old shepherds' house are its charming stone walls and roof. The interior has been completely redesigned by an architect, who has created a lovely contemporary place. The beautiful suite is on several levels and opens onto a small terrace. The people are very hospitable and the view is magnificent.

247
Château de Ribaute

30720 Ribaute-les-Tavernes
(Gard)
Tel. 66 83 01 66
Fax 66 83 86 93
Comte and Comtesse Chamski-Mandajors

Rooms 3 with bath and WC, 1 with shower and WC, 1 suite (3 pers.) with bath and WC, 1 studio (2 pers.) with bath, WC and kitchenette. **Price** 350-500F (2 pers.), suite 600F (3 pers.), studio 500F (2 pers.). **Meals** Breakfast 40F, evening meals at communal table 150-200F (wine incl.). **Facilities** Lounge, swimming pool, equestrian center. **Pets** Dogs allowed on request (+50F). **Nearby** Fishing, tennis, golf, skiing on Mont Aigoual, Anduze, Nîmes, Camargue, Cévennes park. **Credit cards** All major (except Amex). **Spoken** English, German. **Open** All year. **How to get there** (Map 32): 27km northwest of Nîmes via N106. At Pont-de-Ners, take D982 towards Anduze for 5km. It's on the right after crossing N110.

Surrounded by a garden with a swimming pool, this 17th-century château is classically beautiful and very quiet. The entrance hall is magnificent and the elegant double staircase is a masterpiece. The comfortable bedrooms are enormous and superbly furnished. Evening meals are excellent and there is a happy, family atmosphere.

248
Mas de Casty

Boisson
Allègre
30500 Saint-Ambroix
(Gard)
Tel. 66 24 82 33
M. and Mme Mesnage

Rooms 4 and 1 studio (with kitchenette) with shower and WC, and 1 suite (2/4 pers.) with bath, WC, bedroom, lounge and kitchen. **Price** 170-350F (2 pers.), suite 350-500F, studio 280-320F (according to season), 2 nights min. **Meals** Breakfast 25F, no evening meals. **Restaurant** In Allègre. **Facilities** Lounge, swimming pool. **Pets** Dogs allowed on request (+20F). **Nearby** Golf, canoeing, Pont du Gard. **Credit cards** Not accepted. **Spoken** English. **Open** All year. **How to get there** (Map 32): 48km northwest of Pont-du-Gard via D981 towards Uzès, then D979 through Lussan and D37. In Pont d'Auzon, right on D16 towards Rivières.

For twenty years, Michèle and Alain Mesnage have been restoring this small paradise in the midst of the country. Located in two houses, the comfortable bedrooms are pretty and have some antique furniture. Breakfast is served on one of the terraces or in the summer dining room surrounded by a rock garden. You will receive a very friendly welcome.

249
Mas du Platane

Place du Platane
Collorgues
30190 Saint-Chaptes
(Gard)
Tel. 66 81 29 04
Claude and Claudine Vieillot

Rooms 1 with shower and WC, 1 studio (2 pers.) with shower, WC and kitchenette (only 1 room heated). **Price** 320F (2 pers.), weekly terms available, 3 nights min. **Meals** Breakfast incl., evening meals at communal or separate table 100F (wine not incl.), menus 120-150F. **Facilities** Swimming pool. **Pets** Dogs not allowed. **Nearby** Golf (18 holes), tennis, seaside (60km), Cévennes park, Nîmes, the Camargue, Anduze. **Credit cards** Not accepted. **Spoken** English. **Open** Mid-June - mid-Sept. **How to get there** (Map 32): 11 km west of Uzès via D982 towards Moussac. After Garrigues right on D114; it's in Collorgues, behind the château.

Le Mas du Platane is tucked away in an enchanting garden filled with the aromas of Provence. There are two very attractive bedrooms, with exposed stonework and lovely modern bathrooms. The bedrooms open directly onto the garden near the swimming pool. The breakfasts are excellent and the people are charming.

250
Hôtel de l'Orange

7, rue des Baumes
30250 Sommières
(Gard)
Tel. 66 77 79 94
M. and Mme Engström

Rooms 4 with bath or shower, WC and TV. **Price** 280-300F (1 pers.), 330-350F (2 pers.). **Meals** Breakfast 35F; no evening meals. **Restaurants** L'Auberge du Pont Romain and L'Evasion in Sommières. **Facilities** Lounge, swimming pool. **Pets** Dogs allowed (+20F). **Nearby** Golf (18 holes, 30km), tennis; Château de Sommières, villages nearby, Nîmes (30km). **Credit cards** Not accepted. **Spoken** English, German. **Open** All year. **How to get there** (Map 32): In village of Sommières on leaving Nîmes via D40.

Although it is located in the village center, the Hôtel de l'Orange has a charming view of the picturesque old houses of this unspoiled medieval village. Apart from the large ground-floor rooms, the rest of this beautiful 17th-century *hôtel particulier* (town house) is centered around a handsome central stairway. The bedrooms, which are upstairs, are very pleasant, and the swimming pool on the roof is conveniently located for a residence in a village. The friendly, cosmopolitan owners are Irish and Swedish.

251
Cruviers

Route de Saint-Ambroix
Cruviers-Larnac
30700 Uzès
(Gard)
Tel. 66 22 10 89
Thérèse Delbos

Rooms 4 with shower and WC. **Price** 280F (1-2 pers.), 330F (3 pers.), 380F (4 pers.). **Meals** breakfast incl., half board +80F per pers., lunch and evening meals (separate tables). **Facilities** lounge. **Pets** dogs allowed on request. **Nearby** 9-hole golf course, swimming pool, tennis, riding (4km), Uzès, Pont du Gard, Gardon gorges, Nîmes, Anduze, Avignon. **Credit cards** Visa, MasterCard, Eurocard. **Open** All year. **How to get there** (Map 33): 5km north of Uzès towards Lussan (autoroute: Remoulins-Pont-du-Gard exit).

There are four guestrooms facing due-south in this old, well renovated inn. They are comfortable and have mezzanines, making them ideal for families. Delightful Provençal fabrics decorate the charming small restaurant, where good, traditional cuisine is served. The young owner is very pleasant.

252
Le Grand Logis

Place de la Madone
30210 Vers-Pont-du-Gard
(Gard)
Tel. 66 22 92 12
M. Maurice Chabrat

Rooms 3 with bath and WC. Rooms cleaned on request. Linens changed every 3 days. **Price** 250F (1 pers.), 300F (2 pers.). **Meals** Breakfast incl.; no evening meals. **Facilities** Lounge. **Pets** Small dogs allowed. **Nearby** Restaurants, swimming in La Gardon, tennis in village; Pont du Gard, Uzès, Avignon, Nîmes. **Credit cards** Not accepted. **Spoken** English, Spanish. **Closed** Nov. 15 – Feb. 15 (except on reserv.). **How to get there** (Map 33): Autoroute 9, Remoulins exit, then towards Uzès-Pont du Gard Rive Gauche, D981, then 1st road on right after La Bégude-de-Vers.

Tastefully renovated by a former antiques dealer, this very pretty house has a beautiful façade with a superb balcony and wrought-iron railing. The shutters are closed during the day to keep the inside cool. A stairway (with worn-out steps) leads to the bedrooms which are furnished in a very simple, traditional style. The embroidered bed linens, the beautifully patinated walls and the small decorative friezes are lovely. There is a delightful garden and a terrace on the last floor, where you can sunbathe. Note that Le Grand Logis is indicated with a copper sign reading *Chambres d'Hôtes* (guest rooms).

253
Domaine de la Redonde

Montels
34310 Capestang
(Hérault)
Tel. 67 93 31 82
M. and Mme Hughes de Rodez
Bénavent

Rooms 1 studio (4 pers.) and 1 suite (2 pers.) with bath and WC. Room cleaning on request. **Price** suite 400F- 500F, studio 430F-500F (according to season). **Meals** Breakfast incl., no evening meals. **Restaurants** Nearby. **Facilities** Lounge, swimming pool. **Pets** Small dogs allowed on request. **Nearby** Tennis, riding, golf, barge trips on the Midi Canal, Narbonne, Carcassonne, Fontfroide Abbey, Minerve. **Credit cards** Not accepted. **Spoken** English, Spanish. **Open** All year. **How to get there** (Maps 31 and 32): 21km southwest of Beziers. Take D11 towards Capestang. South of Capestang on D16.

This small château, surrounded by vineyards, has a new guest suite and studio. The rooms are large, the furniture is tasteful and the overall effect is lovely. A shady path leads to the swimming pool where you can enjoy the classic elegance of the château. You will be independent and comfortable at this charming place, whose young owners are very hospitable.

254
Aux 3 Cèdres

166, avenue des Deux–Ponts
34190 Cazilhac-Ganges
(Hérault)
Tel. 67 73 50 77
Mme Isnard

Rooms 1 room with TV and 1 suite (3 pers.) and 2 rooms with bath or shower, and WC. **Children** Under 12 not allowed. **Price** 250-280F (1 pers.), 300-320F (2 pers.), +100F (extra pers.). **Meals** Breakfast incl. No evening meals. **Restaurants** Jocelyne-Mélodie (800m) and Ferme Auberge Blancardy (8km). **Facilities** Lounge, access to swimming, fishing on property. **Nearby** Tennis, riding, hiking, overland bikes, canoeing, kayaks in village, Golf course 18-holes (18km). Sea (50km), Demoiselles Caves (7km), Eco Silk Museum, Cevennes Museum. **Credit cards** Not accepted. **Open** All year by resevation only. **How to get there** (Map 32): 45km NE of Montpellier. From Montpellier, D986 to Ganges, 45km. In Ganges, D25, towards Cazhillac for 500m.

Aux 3 Cèdres is a former silk factory which Madame Isnard has converted into a warm and very comfortable home. It is decorated with many flowers and pretty colors, which relieve the austere look of the house from the street. Hikers and sports enthusiasts will particularly appreciate the hearty breakfasts which have been thoughtfully prepared for the numerous guests engaging in the many outdoor activities nearby. Note: Slippers have also been provided for guests who return with muddy shoes!

255
Les Prunus

9, rue des Prunus
34230 Plaissan
(Hérault)
Tel. 67 96 81 16
M. and Mme Colin

Rooms 3 with shower and WC, 1 suite (2-3 pers.) with lounge, bath and WC. **Price** 210-260F (2 pers.) +60F (extra pers.), suite 300F. **Meals** Breakfast incl., no evening meals. **Restaurant** Le Beaulieu in Plaissan. **Facilities** Lounge. **Pets** Dogs allowed on request. **Nearby** Golf, seaside, tennis, riding, canoeing, swimming pool, Salagou Lake, Saint-Guilhem-le-Désert, the Midi Canal. **Credit cards** Not accepted. **Spoken** A little English. **Open** All year. **How to get there** (Map 32): 32km southeast of Montpellier (autoroute: Sète exit); take D2 to Poussan, then Villeveyrac: signposted.

This former vineyard owners' house in a small village has a large, pretty garden. The bedrooms are decorated with 1930s objects, furniture and extraordinary frescoes. Modern amenities have not been overlooked, notably in the beautiful, small bathrooms. The hospitality, good breakfasts (served outside in good weather), and the very reasonable prices make Les Prunus an excellent place to stay.

256
Domaine de Fon de Rey

Route de Pézenas
34810 Pomérols
(Hérault)
Tel. 67 77 08 56
M. and Mme Poisson

Rooms 6 (incl. 3 for 3 pers.) with bath or shower, and WC. 3 nights min. in high season. **Price** 230F (1 pers.), 250-300F (2 pers.), 350F (3 pers.) +50F (extra pers.). **Meals** Breakfast incl. Half-board 205-230F (per pers.); meals at communal or separate tables 70-80F. **Facilities** Lounge, telephone, swimming pool, billiards, ping-pong, hiking, biking, poss. stained-glass workshop on property. **Pets** Dogs allowed on request. **Nearby** Sea (10km), golf (18 holes, 10km), tennis, canoeing, kayaks, Pézenas, Canal du Midi, Voie Domintia, Thau Lake. **Credit cards** Not accepted. **Spoken** English, Spanish. **Closed** Jan. – Feb. **How to get there** (Map 33): 44km SW of Montpellier, A9 exit Agde, then towards Saint-Thibéry/Florensac, then Pomérols. Take road to Pézenas.

The Domaine de Fon de Rey is a beautiful, thick-walled mansion which a family of winegrowers had left abandoned. The bedrooms are functional and pleasant, and the owners will be pleased to show you around their property. Their daughter presides over the kitchen, where she turns out delicious regional specialties. Located in the Languedoc vineyards near the seashore, the Domaine is a friendly place to stay, even if (in the low season) you might run into a few business executives attending a seminar!

257
Mas Cammas

66300 Caixas
(Pyrénées-Orientales)
Tel. 68 38 82 27
Fax The same
M. Vissenaeken-Vaes

Rooms 2 and 3 suites (4-5 pers.) with shower and WC. **Price** 440F (2 pers.), suites 660F (4 pers.). **Meals** Breakfast incl., half board (2 days min.) 330F per pers. Lunch and evening meals at separate tables in the auberge 140F (wine not incl.). **Facilities** Lounge, telephone, swimming pool. **Pets** Dogs not allowed. **Nearby** Sea, Castelnou mountains, medieval village of Collioure. **Credit cards** Not accepted. **Spoken** English, German, Dutch. **Open** Easter – end Sept. **How to get there** (Map 31): about 25km southwest of Perpignan via D612A and D615. At Fourques, right on D2 towards Caixas through Montauriol.

Clinging to the hillside 400 meters up, Cammas dominates the Roussillon plain with the sea in the distance. The small, charming bedrooms overlook the valley. Light lunches and excellent evening meals are served in the dark, beautiful dining room. You can stroll on the hills, or relax by the swimming pool and on the terrace with its panoramic views. The people are friendly but the Mas has become somewhat expensive.

258
Château de Camon

Camon
09500 Mirepoix
(Ariège)
Tel. 61 68 14 05
Fax 61 68 81 56
M. du Pont

Rooms 7 with bath or shower and WC. **Price** 500-1000F (2 pers.). **Meals** Breakfast incl., evening meals at communal table, by reservation 300F (wine incl.). **Facilities** Swimming pool, fishing. **Pets** Dogs not allowed. **Nearby** Tennis, riding, prehistoric caves. **Credit cards** All major. **Spoken** English. **Open** March – end Nov. **How to get there** (Map 31): 36km southeast of Pamiers via D119. At Mirepoix take D7 towards Chalabre.

This 12th-century château and its park are in the middle of one of the most beautiful villages of this region. Inside, a large stone staircase leads to a wide gallery off the bedrooms; they are all comfortable and different, with beautiful antiques and shimmering fabrics. The dining room and lounge have an attractive atmosphere. The breakfasts and dinners are elegant, and there is a swimming pool in the park.

259
Saint-Genès

Le Carlaret
09100 Pamiers
(Ariège)
Tel. 61 67 16 31
Fax The same
Szigeti-Dagniaux Family

Rooms 2 with bath and WC; and 3 rooms (incl. 2 with washbasin), which share shower and WC on landing. Rooms cleaned on request. **Price** 170-350F (2 pers.) +50F (extra pers.). **Meals** Breakfast incl. Half-board 150-250F (per pers.); meals noon and evening at communal table by reservation 80F (wine incl.). **Facilities** Lounge, swimming pool and bikes on property. **Pets** Dogs allowed on request (+20F). **Nearby** Golf (18 holes), skiing in Olmes Mountains; canoeing, rafting; Romanesque churches, Cathar châteaux. **Credit cards** Not accepted. **Spoken** English, Spanish. **Open** All year. **How to get there** (Map 31): 5km E of Pamiers via D11, towards Belpech; then towards Lycée Agricole, 1.5km after George on right.

This is a simple but light and spacious house which is run by cousins. There are two large bedrooms with bathrooms and washrooms located in the attics; three other bedrooms with pretty showers and washrooms are convenient for a family to share. You will find everything to make your stay pleasant here, including a warm welcome, a library full of good books and a television room. The meals, which are served in the garden in summer, are prepared with fresh produce from the farm and the vegetable garden.

260
Domaine de Montagnac

09500 Saint-Félix-de-Tournegat
(Ariège)
Tel. 61 68 72 75
Fax 61 67 44 84
Mme Jean Bertolino

Rooms 4 with bath and WC, 4 with shower and WC, 2 spare rooms. **Price** 270-320F (2 pers.). **Meals** Breakfast incl.; half board 225-250F per pers. in double room, lunch and evening meals at communal or separate table 90F (wine incl.). Children under 12, 1/2 price **Facilities** Lounge, telephone, swimming pool, equestrian center, billiards, mountain bike rental. **Pets** Dogs allowed on request. **Nearby** Tennis, golf, skiing. **Credit cards** Not accepted. **Spoken** English, Italian. **Open** All year. **How to get there** (Map 31): 66km southeast of Toulouse via N20. At Pamiers head for Mirepoix; at Pujols turn left for Saint-Amadou, then right for Saint-Félix-de-Tournegat.

This is a house of character surrounded by flowers and overlooking a magnificent landscape typical of the Ariège. The bedrooms are pleasant with a very beautiful view and pretty bathrooms. The decor is simple and rustic with wooden floors and antique furniture. There are excellent breakfasts and evening meals and there is a friendly lounge with billiard table.

261
Le Poulsieu

Cautirac
09000 Serres–sur–Arget
(Ariège)
Tel. 61 02 77 72
Jenny and Bob Brogneaux

Rooms 2 with shower and WC, 2 with basin sharing shower and WC. **Price** 170F (1 pers.), 200F (2 pers.) +50F (extra pers.). **Meals** Breakfast incl., half board (4 days min.) 170F per pers. in double room, evening meals at communal table 70F (wine incl.) At lunchtime there is a kitchenette for guests' use. **Facilities** Lounge, riding, mountain biking. **Pets** Dogs allowed. **Nearby** Golf (18km), swimming pool, tennis, caves. **Credit cards** Not accepted. **Spoken** Dutch, English, German, Spanish. **Open** All year. **How to get there** (Map 30): 12km west of Foix; in Foix head for Saint-Girons, then D17 towards Col de Marrons to La Mouline; left opposite the bar; signposted.

Having traveled the world, Jenny and Bob Brogneaux now welcome other travelerss to their home in this old, isolated mountain village. The white bedrooms are fresh and simple, evening meals are informal, and the hospitality is friendly.

262
Baudeigne

La Rives
09120 Varilhes
(Ariège)
Tel. 61 60 73 42
Fax 61 60 78 76
M. and Mme Jean Baudeigne

Rooms 4 with shower, WC and telephone, and 1 with shower, telephone and shared WC. Room cleaning on request. **Price** 200F (1 pers.), 260F (2 pers.) +40F (extra pers.). **Meals** Breakfast incl., no evening meals. **Facilities** Swimming pool, tennis, fishing, children's games. **Pets** Dogs allowed in kennel. **Nearby** Golf, ski slopes (50km), Romanesque churches, caves. **Credit cards** Not accepted. **Spoken** English and Spanish. **Open** All year. **How to get there** (Map 31): At Foix take N20 towards Toulouse until Varilhes; signposted.

Baudeigne is a beautiful country house very close to the Pyrenees, with a carefully tended park, a tennis court, a swimming pool, and fishing on the property. The bedrooms, decorated with floral wallpaper and antique furniture, all have views over the park. Breakfast is served on the terrace or in a handsome dining room; the guests' lounge is pleasant. The hosts are friendly and discreet.

263
Ferme–Auberge de Quiers

Compeyre
12520 Aguessac
(Aveyron)
Tel. 65 59 85 10
M. and Mme Lombard Pratmarty

Rooms 2 with bath and WC, 4 with shower and WC (of which 1 for 4-6 pers. with mezzanine). Room cleaning once a week. **Price** 200F (2 pers.), mezzanine bedroom 300F (4 pers.) +30F (extra pers.). **Meals** Breakfast 25F, Half-board except when Ferme-Auberge is closed 195F. Evening meals in the Ferme-Auberge (except Mon. all year, and Wed. in low season), by reservation only (separate tables) 80-95F (wine not incl.). **Nearby** Riding, fishing. **Credit cards** Visa, Eurocard and MasterCard. **Open** Easter – Nov 1 (by reservation). **How to get there** (Maps 31 and 32): At Millau take N9 towards Severac. At Aguessac, take D907 to Compeyre; signposted.

Not far from the medieval village of Compeyre, the Ferme-Auberge de Quiers overlooks a hilly countryside. The bedrooms, in a converted barn, open directly onto the outside; they are pleasant and charming with white walls, natural wood furniture and a few touches of pink or blue. Breakfast and good evening meals with regional specialties are served in the two rustic dining rooms of the farm.

264
Château de Saint-Léons

12780 Saint-Léons
(Aveyron)
Tel. 65 61 84 85
Fax 65 61 82 30
Odile and Marc Chodkiewicz

Rooms 2 with bath and WC, and 1 spare room with washbasin and WC. **Price** 330F (1 pers.), 400F (2 pers.), +90F (extra pers.). **Meals** Breakfast incl.; evening meals only 130F (wine incl.), 65F (children under 12). **Facilities** Lounge; garden and park on property. **Pets** Dogs allowed on request. **Nearby** Hiking (marked paths, botanical paths), tennis (8km), mountain bikes; Musée Henri Fabre, Gorges du Tarn and Roquefort. **Spoken** English, German, Italian, Swedish. **Open** All year. **How to get there** (Map 31): 20km north of Millau, towards Rodez (D911). Exit at Le Bois du Four and go 4km to Saint-Léon, château indicated at entrance to village.

The Château de Saint-Léons was built in the 15th century to provide fortification for the village, which explains its hilltop location. The terraced garden looks out over the roofs of the old houses built on the hillsides of the gentle Muze Valley. The rooms are beautifully spacious, with only three on each floor. The communal rooms for guests and the château owners are on the gound floor. The bedrooms are on the *deuxième étage*; two are immense and have bathrooms in the towers; the third room has no bath and is used as an extra bedroom. The sparsely elegant decor lends them all a special charm.

265
Château de Croisillat

31460 Caraman
(Haute-Garonne)
Tel. 61 83 10 09
M. Guérin

Rooms 1 with bath and WC, 4 with bath or shower and shared WCs. **Price** 350-500F (1 pers.), 450-600F (2 pers.). **Meals** Breakfast incl., no evening meals. **Restaurant** La Ferme d'En Bouyssou (10km). **Facilities** Lounge, swimming pool, horse boxes, fishing. **Pets** Dogs allowed on request. **Nearby** Golf, Albi, Castres. **Credit cards** Not accepted. **Spoken** English, German. **Open** Mid-March – mid-Nov. **How to get there** (Map 31): 23km east of Toulouse via N126. At Montauriol take D1. Leaving Caraman follow D1 towards Revel; after 2.5km turn right at avenue of plane trees; signposted.

You will be warmly welcomed at ahis very old house covered in Virginia creeper and surrounded by terraces and a beautiful park. The reception rooms and bedrooms are filled with a diversified mixture of antiques, curios and Spanish-style furniture, creating a charming, old-fashioned yet comfortable decor. The bathrooms are being renovated. We recommend the Empire or Louis XV bedrooms.

266
Serres d'en Bas

Route de Nailloux
31550 Cintegabelle
(Haute-Garonne)
Tel. 61 08 41 11
M. and Mme Deschamps

Rooms 2 and 1 suite (4 pers.) with bath or shower and WC. **Price** 195F (1 pers.), 220-250F (2 pers.), +60F (extra pers.). **Meals** Breakfast incl.; meals noon and evening at communal table 85F (wine incl.). 10% discount after 5 days. Gourmet weekend (1 night, 2 meals and breakfast). **Facilities** Lounge, telephone, laundry room, swimming pool, volley ball, croquet, badminton. **Pets** Dogs allowed on request. **Nearby** Riding (18km), fishing (3.5km), water sports, Nailloux Lake, Cintegabelle, Wissous Dovecote, Monglard. **Credit cards** Not accepted. **Spoken** English, Spanish. **Open** All year. **How to get there** (Map 30): 40km south of Toulouse. Exit N20 in Toulouse, go past Auterive for 7km, go left towards Cintegabelle, then towards Nailloux for 3.5km.

Perched on a hillock in gently rolling countryside, this inviting rustic house, named "The Greenhouses Down Below", opens out onto a luxuriant carpet of grass and shrubs. The bedrooms and the suite are comfortably equipped with modern bathroom facilities. With the first sunny weather, guests enjoy relaxing outdoors and admiring the splendid view over the hillsides. The owners are very welcoming and helpful.

267
Château de Larra

Larra
31330 Grenade-sur-Garonne
(Haute-Garonne)
Tel. 61 82 62 51
Baronne de Carrière

Rooms 2 with shower and WC, and 2 suites with bath and WC. **Price** 350-400F (2 pers.), suite 500F (4 pers.). **Meals** Breakfast incl., evening meals at communal table 100-120F (wine not incl.). **Facilities** Lounge. **Pets** Dogs allowed on request. **Nearby** Riding, golf, Belleperche Abbey, Caumont, Pibrac, Montauban, Toulouse. **Credit cards** Not accepted. **Open** Easter – Nov 1. **How to get there** (Map 30): 30km northwest of Toulouse. On A62 exit 10, then N20 towards Grisolles, Ondes, Grenade. At Grenade, signposted. It's on D87.

The 18th-century ambience of the Château de Larra remains intact, with Louis XVth furniture and painted fabrics in the salon, plasterwork in the dining room, and an impressive staircase with unusual wrought-iron bannisters. The bedrooms and the suites are large and pleasant, old fashioned, but charming. You will enjoy excellent breakfasts and dinners, and Mme de Carrière is a vivacious hostess.

268
Stoupignan

31380 Montpitol
(Haute-Garonne)
Tel. 61 84 22 02
Mme Claudette Fieux

Rooms 4 with bath or shower, and WC. Price 240F (1 pers.), 320F (2 pers.), +80F (extra pers.). **Meals** Breakfast incl.; evening meals at communal table 120F (wine incl.) or restaurants 5km. **Facilities** Lounge, tennis, lake on property. **Pets** Dogs allowed on request. **Nearby** Riding 18km, swimming pool 4.5km, Palmola golf (7km); Verfeil village, Lavaur Cathedral. **Credit cards** Not accepted. **Spoken** English, Spanish. **Open** All year. **How to get there** (Map 31): 20km north of Toulouse via N88, towards Albi; or via A68, exit Troyes, to Montastruc. 500m after the stop light, D30 towards Lavaur-Montpitol, then turn right to Stoupignan.

Madame Fieux will receive you with extremely warm hospitality in this beautiful Louis XIII house. The four bedrooms are spacious, decorated with antiques and very elegant, as are the bathrooms. Beautiful linens and silverware add a further refined touch to the communal dining table where, on request, a delicious regional meal is served. There is a lovely private park with trees and a beautiful view over the valleys nearby. Stoupignan is truly a charming place to stay.

269
Domaine de Menaut

Auzas
31360 Saint-Martory
(Haute-Garonne)
Tel. 61 90 21 51
(at meal times)
Mme Jander

Rooms 2 with bath and WC, and 1 suite (4 pers.) with bath and WC. **Price** 350F (2 pers.), suite (3-4 pers.) 600F. **Meals** Breakfast incl., lunch and evening meals at communal or separate tables from 70F (wine incl.). **Facilities** Lounge, garage ,lakes, fishing, swimming. **Pets** No animals allowed. **Nearby** Tennis, skiing, museums, safari photos. **Credit cards** Not accepted. **Spoken** English, German. **Open** All year. Children under 10 not accepted. **How to get there** (Map 30): About 20km east of Saint-Gaudens, Toulouse N117. In Boussens towards Mancioux, then D33; 5km before D52 (Saint-Martory/Aurignac) go right and follow the fence.

This 225-acre estate lies in the midst of a lovely, unspoiled forest with three small lakes. The interior is tastefully decorated and immaculate, with elegant antique-style furniture in the dining room and lounge. The comfortable bedrooms have beautiful bathrooms and there is a sunny terrace for summer breakfasts. Nature lovers particularly will love the Domaine.

270
La Chavinière

32120 Avensac
(Gers)
Tel. 62 65 03 43
Fax 62 65 03 23
Yveline and Thierry Morel

Rooms 4 with bath and WC. **Price** 350-420F (2 pers.). **Meals** Breakfast 40F; evening meals at communal table on reservation only 200F (wine incl.). **Facilities** Lounge, swimming pool, fishing on pond, bikes, Antiques Tour on property. **Pets** Dogs allowed on request. **Nearby** Golf (9 holes, 30km), tennis; villas and châteaux, Armagnac caves. **Credit cards** Not accepted. **Spoken** English and Spanish. **Open** All year. **How to get there** (Map 30): 40km southwest of Montauban, A62 to Toulouse, exit 9 Castelsarrazin, then D928, towards Auch. After Beaumont-de-Lomagne, go 10km, then small road on right towards La Chavinière.

This is a vast family mansion surrounded by a private park in the midst of the countryside. The interior is simply beautiful, with its floors of terra cotta or blond wood, handsome family furniture, pretty fabrics and decorative touches, all beautifully coordinated. The impeccable bedrooms are decorated with the same care and taste, and the bathrooms are superb (some are quite original). The delicious communal dinner is another plus, as is the friendly atmosphere created by Monsieur and Madame Morel.

271
Le Petit Robin

32120 Avensac
(Gers)
Tel. 62 66 45 06
Mme Sylviane Hantzperg

Rooms 1 room with bath and WC; and 2 rooms which share 1 bath and 2 WC. **Price** 220F (2 pers.), +110F (extra pers.). **Meals** Breakfast incl.; no evening meals. Ferme-Auberge (6km) and restaurants (8km). **Facilities** Lounge, bikes on property. **Pets** Dogs not allowed. **Nearby** Swimming pool, tennis, lake, riding, fishing, archery, golf (9 holes, 30km). **Credit cards** Not accepted. **Spoken** English, some Italian and German. **Open** All year. **How to get there** (Map 30): 45km southwest of Montauban, towards Auch via Beaumont-de-Lomagne, then via D928. 8km after Beaumont, turn right on D556 to Avensac, then towards Pessoulens: 3rd house on right. **No smoking.**

Nestling in the countryside, this small, pretty house has a brand-new wing for guests. It includes one comfortable bedroom with a beautiful bathroom, and two others (ideal for families) which have a communal bathroom (shower) and toilet. The hearty breakfasts include homemade bread and preserves and are served in the lovely main room of the house or in the garden. Madame Hantzperg will welcome you courteously to Le Petit Robin, which is an ideal place to stay if you enjoy a peaceful, relaxing setting.

272
Ferme de Mounet

Avenue de Parleboscq
32800 Eauze
(Gers)
Tel. 62 09 82 85
Fax 62 09 77 45
M. and Mme Molas

Rooms 3 with bath or shower and WC. **Price** 250-350F (2 pers.). **Meals** Breakfast incl., half board 220F per pers. in double room (200F for more than 3 days)., evening meals at communal table 90F, gourmet menu 170F (wine incl.). **Facilities** Lounge, bicycles. **Pets** Dogs not allowed in the bedrooms. **Nearby** Swimming pool, tennis, riding, golf (18 holes). **Credit cards** Visa, Eurocard and MasterCard. **Spoken** English. **Open** Easter – Nov 1. **How to get there** (Map 29 and 30): 39km northeast of Aire-sur-l'Adour via N124 towards Nogaro. At Manciet, left on D931 to Eauze; signposted "Foie Gras."

A mid the Armagnac vineyards, Mounet is the center for another local speciality: *foie gras*. (You will be greeted by the geese.) In this handsome house the bedrooms are comfortable and well renovated, and the largest has a canopied bed. The rooms, unfortunately, overlook a farm building. Excellent evening meals are served in the large, rustic dining room. The owners are very friendly.

273
Le Moulin de Mazères

32450 Lartigue
(Gers)
Tel. 62 65 98 68
Régine and Raymond Bertheau

Rooms 4 with bath or shower, and WC. Rooms cleaned on request. **Price** 250F. **Meals** Breakfast 25F, half-board 250F (per pers.). Evening meals at communal table. **Facilities** Lounge, swimming pool, fishing, riding, quarry, and horse boxes. **Nearby** Tennis, squash, riding, golf in Auch (18 holes, 20km), Auch Cathedral, Castelnau, Barbarens, fortified churches. **Credit cards** Not accepted. **Spoken** English. **Open** All year. **How to get there** (Map 30): 17km southeast of Auch, towards Toulouse, in Aubiet take D40, go past Castelnau dir. Héréchou and go 3.5km on D40.

L ocated on the edge of a small road, this very pretty old mill, which has been tastefully restored, is surrounded by cool, lush vegetation. From the four spacious bedrooms you will hear the soft, reposing sound of the water tumbling through the mill; from the large bay window of one room, you can see the water flowing below. Riders with their horses are welcome to the Moulin de Mazères. The swimming pool and the rich breakfasts prepared by Madame Bertheau complete the feeling of relaxation and pleasure to be enjoyed here.

274
Le Vieux Pradoulin

32700 Lectoure
(Gers)
Tel. 62 68 71 24
Mme Martine Vetter

Rooms 3 sharing 1 bath and WC. **Price** 210-230F (2 pers.). **Meals** Breakfast incl., no evening meals. **Restaurant** Le Bastard (1km). **Facilities** Lounge, telephone. **Pets** Dogs not allowed. **Nearby** Swimming pool, tennis, fishing, riding, golf, Cistercian abbey, cloisters, châteaux. **Credit cards** Not accepted. **Spoken** A little English. **Open** All year. **How to get there** (Map 30): North of Auch via N21 towards Agen. Just before Lectoure, crossroads; take the road to Condom, turn left after 500m.

A very quiet house despite the road, Le Vieux Pradoulin is built on a Gallo-Roman site and on display are ancient oil lamps, terra cotta fragments and other treasures. The lovingly arranged bedrooms overlook the garden and have comfortable, antique beds. The bathroom is shared, but this is a small drawback at this charming, informal place where you will be welcomed like friends.

275
La Tannerie

32170 Miélan
(Gers)
Tel. 62 67 62 62
Fax 62 09 77 45
M. and Mme Bryson

Rooms 3 with bath and WC. **Price** 290F (2 pers.). **Meals** Breakfast incl.; half-board 225F (per pers.); evening meals at separate tables 90F (wine not incl.). **Facilities** Lounge, pétanque on property. **Nearby** Tennis in village, riding (1km), Masseube Golf (18 holes, 25km); water sports (14km), swimming in Loupiac (20km), fishing; Cirque de Gavarny, villas and churches. **Credit cards** Not accepted. **Spoken** English and Spanish. **Open** All year. **How to get there** (Map 30): 40km southwest of Auch, N21 towards Tarbes; in Miélan, before the church, turn right on small street.

We were totally charmed by this beautiful house, its handsome balustraded terrace, and above all, by its delightful owner, Madame Bryson. In the three spacious bedrooms, there is a kettle for making coffee or tea, and the reading/television room and dining room are warm and inviting. With the first sunny days, breakfasts and dinners are served outside at tables with parasols. La Tannerie is delightful for its hospitality, tranquility and the charming view of the hillsides nearby.

276
Le Pigeonnier

32380 Pessoulens
(Gers)
Tel. 62 66 49 25
M. and Mme Jeangrand

Rooms 1 with bath and WC, and 1 for children. **Price** 240F (2 pers.). **Meals** Breakfast incl. **Restaurant** Auberge Jouars (1km). **Facilities** Lounge, telephone. **Nearby** Swimming pool, tennis, lake fishing, Solomiac Sports Center. **Credit cards** Not accepted. **Spoken** Italian, Spanish, some English. **Open** All year. **How to get there** (Map 30): Northeast of Toulouse via D2 and D3. At Beaumont-de-Lomagne take D928 towards Auch, then D18 towards Saint-Clar; it's in the village.

You will immediately feel as if you have been adopted by M. and Mme Jeangrand, two former teachers who have opened their pretty village home to guests. There is only one bedroom, which is very comfortable and delicately decorated in pale pink and white. The lounge–dining room opens onto a pretty garden. Breakfast is a feast and includes cakes, jams and baked apples.

277
En Bigorre

32380 Tournecoupe
(Gers)
Tel. 62 66 42 47
Jean and Jacqueline Marqué

Rooms 5 with shower and WC. Rooms cleaned on request. **Price** 190F (2 pers.). **Meals** Breakfast 25F, half board 190F per pers. (for a couple), evening meals at communal table 70F (all incl.) **Facilities** Lounge, telephone, swimming pool, horse boxes, fishing. **Nearby** Tennis, golf, Saint-Clar, Cologne, Avezan, Solomiac. **Credit cards** Not accepted. **Open** All year. **How to get there** (Map 30): 40km south of Agen via N21 towards Lectoure, then left on D27. Before Lectoure follow signs for Saint-Clar and Tournecoupe.

This is a renovated village house surrounded by a spacious garden. The bedrooms are pleasantly decorated. Breakfast and dinner are served in a pretty dining room or under a canopy (equipped with a barbecue) beside the swimming pool. You will enjoy good regional cuisine at very reasonable prices. The hosts are charming.

278
Château de Cousserans

46140 Belaye
(Lot)
Tel. 65 36 25 77
Fax 65 36 29 48
M. and Mme Georges Mougin

Rooms 4 with bath and WC. **Price** 700-800F. **Meals** Breakfast incl., no evening meals. **Restaurants** In Lascabanes and Saint-Médaud-Catus. **Facilities** Lounge, fishing, music room (organ and 2 pianos). **Nearby** Lauzerte, Montcuq, prehistoric sites. **Credit cards** Not accepted. **Spoken** English, Spanish. **Open** June – Oct. **How to get there** (Map 30): 30km from Cahors via D911. At Castelfranc, left towards Anglars, then D45 towards Montcuq.

This château, set off a small road, is surrounded by beautiful trees. Its medieval appearance is austere and contrasts with the comfortable interior. An elevator takes you to the bedrooms, which are vast, completely renovated, very comfortable and are furnished with antique mahogany furniture. There is a very inviting music room. Breakfast served in a light, vaulted dining room, or on the terrace in summer.

279
Domaine de Labarthe

46090 Espère
(Lot)
Tel. 65 30 92 34
Fax 65 23 97 10
M. and Mme Claude Bardin

Rooms 3, (1 with TV) and 1 suite (3 pers., with kitchenette and telephone), with bath or shower, and WC. Rooms cleaned every day, linens changed every 3 days. **Price** 350-500F (2 pers.). **Meals** Breakfast incl.; no evening meals. **Restaurants** Le Relais des Champs (3km), or Le Gindreau (10km). **Facilities** Lounge, swimming pool open to guests until 1 PM or on request. **Pets** Dogs allowed on request. **Nearby** Tennis (500m), golf (9 holes, 40km), caving, hiking, Castelnau, Montratier, very historic region. **Credit cards** Not accepted. **Spoken** English. **Open** All year. **How to get there** (Map 30): 10km west of Cahors via D911, towards Villeneuve-sur-Lot; on the Place d'Espère turn left at telephone booth. Entrance in 10km.

You will be courteously greeted at this beautiful, vast mansion of white stone. The classic bedrooms are restful and have a lovely view of the park. The breakfasts are generous and refined, and they are served in a room reserved for guests. The pigeon loft has a suite, including a kitchen, and a small private garden. In good weather, you can relax around the beautiful swimming pool which is surrounded by trees and shrubs.

280
Moulin de Fresquet

46500 Gramat
(Lot)
Tel. 65 38 70 60
M. and Mme Ramelot

Rooms 5 with shower and WC (TV on request). **Price** 230-340F (2 pers.) +75F (extra pers.). **Meals** Breakfast incl., evening meals at communal table 100F (wine incl.). **Facilities** Lounge, fishing, boating, footpath. **Pets** Dogs not allowed. **Nearby** Riding, swimming pool, tennis, mountain biking, Rocamadour, Padirac, Loubressac. **Credit cards** Not accepted. **Spoken** English, German. **Open** Mid-March - Nov 1. **How to get there** (Map 24): 800m southwest of Gramat; in Gramat take N140 towards Figeac and turn left after 500m and go 300m to entrance. **No smoking**.

This old mill is in a peaceful setting close to Gramat, with greenery all around. It has been beautifully restored throughout. The bedrooms are beautifully decorated and two overlook the water. There is a charming lounge-library and Claude and Gérard will greet you warmly. The evening meal is remarkably good and so is the *aperitif-foie gras,* which is served on request.

281
L'Ermitage

46230 Lalbenque
(Lot)
Tel. 65 31 75 91
M. Daniel Pasquier

Rooms 2 independent studios with shower, WC and kitchenette. Room cleaning guests' responsibility. **Children** Under 2 not accepted. **Price** 180F (2 pers.). **Meals** No evening meals. **Restaurant** Chez Bertier in the village. **Nearby** Tennis, riding, Saint-Cirq-Lapopie, Gallic ruins. **Credit cards** Not accepted. **Spoken** German. **Open** All year. **How to get there** (Map 30): 16km south of Cahors via D6; turn left at sign at the entrance to Lalbenque.

In a forest of truffle oaks, L'Ermitage consists of three small houses where you can live like a veritable hermit. Completely circular, they are spotlessly clean, cool in summer and warm in winter. They have a kitchenette where you can prepare your meals, a shower room and a comfortable (though somewhat narrow) bed. This an unusual place to stay and the price is very reasonable.

282
La Petite Auberge

Domaine de Saint Géry
Lascabanes
46800 Montcuq
(Lot)
Tel. 65 31 82 51
M. Patrick Duler

Rooms 4 and 1 suite (4-6 pers.) with bath and WC. Rooms cleaned every 2 days. **Price** 220-380F (1-2 pers.), suite 580-630F (4 pers.). **Meals** Breakfast 60F, half board 280-440F per pers. in double room, lunch and evening meals (separate tables) 100-350F (wine not incl.). **Pets** Dogs allowed on request. **Facilities** Swimming pool. **Nearby** Tennis, golf (8km), walks, mountain biking, boating on the Lot. **Credit cards** Not accepted. **Closed** Jan – Feb. **How to get there** (Map 30): 18km southwest of Cahors via N20 towards Toulouse, then right on D653 towards Montcuq and left on D7 to Lascabanes.

In this wild limestone area of Le Quercy there are some lovely houses, and this is one of them. The bedrooms are in various buildings and are delightful, with white plastered or barrel vaulted walls, pretty antique furniture and terra cotta floors. Add to that pleasant bathrooms, excellent regional specialties, and young and cheerful hosts.

283
Domaine du Barry
Barran

"Le Barry", Duravel
46700 Puy-l'Evêque
(Lot)
Tel. 65 24 63 24
M. and Mme Jean François Nioloux

Rooms 5 with bath and WC, 1 with shower and WC. **Price** 250-400F (1-3 pers.) **Meals** breakfast incl., evening meals at communal table, on reservation 105F (wine incl.) **Restaurants** La Roseraie in Duravel (3km) and Bellevue in Puy-l'Evêque (3km). **Facilities** Lounge, telephone. **Pets** Small dogs allowed on request (+10F). **Nearby** Riding, swimming pool, tennis, châteaux. **Credit cards** Not accepted. **Open** Easter – All Saints. **How to get there** (Maps 23 and 30): D911 between Cahors and Villeneuve-sur-Lot; signposted from the hamlet of Girard between Puy-l'Evêque and Duravel.

Perched on the edge of a small valley, this beautiful stone house is a good example of the local architecture. The pleasant bedrooms are bright, simple and comfortable. Each one has a view of the landscape of meadows and hills. The beds are big, the bathrooms impeccable. The large bedroom has a superb covered terrace. The regional cuisine is excellent and the atmosphere is informal.

284
Domaine de Jean-Pierre

20, route de Villeneuve
65300 Pinas
(Hautes-Pyrénées)
Tel. 62 98 15 08
Fax (the same)
Mme Marie Colombier

Rooms 3 with bath and WC, 2 without bath (poss. suite). **Price** 200F (1 pers.), 240F (2 pers.) +60F (extra pers.). **Meals** Breakfast incl., no evening meals. **Restaurants** Chez Maurette and Le Relais du Castera (5 and 7km). **Facilities** Lounge, horse boxes. **Nearby** Swimming pool, tennis, golf, Lourdes, Saint-Bertrand-de-Comminges. **Credit cards** Not accepted. **Spoken** English. **Open** All year. **How to get there** (Map 30): 30km east of Tarbes via N117 towards Toulouse. At Lannemezan head for Pinas and follow the signs.

In a peaceful setting on the edge of the village, this beautiful house is covered with Virginia creeper and surrounded by a very well kept garden. The quiet bedrooms look out over the garden; each has antique furniture and a color scheme of its own, with huge modern bathrooms and very tasteful decor throughout. Mme Colombier is very welcoming and prepares excellent breakfasts, which are served on the terrace in good weather.

285
Chez Mme Salvador

Place des Arcades
81140 Castelnau-de-Montmiral
(Tarn)
Tel. 63 33 17 44
M. and Mme Salvador

Rooms 5 with bath and WC, 1 with bath and shared WC, and 2 suites (2-4 pers., 4 days min.) with lounge, kitchen, bath or shower and WC. Rooms cleaned every 2-3 days or on request. **Price** 150-170F (2 pers.) +30F (extra pers.), suite 300F (2-3 pers.). **Meals** Breakfast 20F, no evening meals. **Restaurants** In the village. **Facilities** Lounge. **Pets** Small dogs allowed. **Nearby** Swimming pool, fishing, tennis, riding, golf, walled towns. **Credit cards** Not accepted. **Open** All year. **How to get there** (Map 31): 30km west of Albi towards Gaillac; once in Gaillac take the Caussade road.

This house is located on the main square of Castelnau, a small medieval masterpiece, and is easily recognizable by its two large mullioned windows. The comfortable bedrooms are simply furnished in country style. The lounge has an extraordinary Louis XIII fireplace. Breakfast is served either in the dining room-lounge or outside under the arcades. The owners are very pleasant.

286
Château de Garrevaques

81700 Garrevaques
(Tarn)
Tel. 63 75 04 54/61 52 01 47
Fax 63 70 26 44
Mme Barande and Mme Combes

Rooms 7 (2-3 pers.) and 2 suites with bath and WC. **Price** 650F (2 pers.), suite 1100F (4-6 pers.). **Meals** Breakfast incl., half board 450F per pers. in double room (3 days min.), evening meal at communal table by reservation 150F (wine incl.). **Facilities** Lounge, telephone, swimming pool, tennis, billiards. **Credit cards** Amex, Visa, Eurocard and MasterCard. **Pets** Small dogs allowed on request. **Nearby** Golf, excursions, antiques. **Spoken** English, Spanish. **Open** All year by reservation only. **How to get there** (Map 31): 50 km southeast of Toulouse via D1. At Revel turn onto D79 (opposite the police station) for 5km.

B urned down during the Revolution and restored at the beginning of the 19th-century, Garrevaques stands in a large park with a swimming pool and a tennis court. The beautiful reception rooms are furnished with Empire and Napoleon III pieces. We recommend the *premier étage* bedrooms and suites, which are large, well furnished and comfortable. The traditional cuisine is good and the owners are very welcoming.

287
Meilhouret

81140 Larroque
(Tarn)
Tel. 63 33 11 18
Minouche and Christian Jouard

Rooms 2 with bath or shower and WC. Rooms cleaned and linens changed every 3 days. **Price** 230F (1 pers.), 250F (2 pers.). **Meals** Breakfast incl. Evening meals at communal or separate tables on request 90F (wine incl.). **Facilities** Lounge, swimming pool. **Nearby** Fishing in lake and water sports in Monclar, tennis, riding, Circuit des Bastides, concerts in summer. **Spoken** English. **Credit cards** Not accepted. **Open** All year (Oct.-April on request). **How to get there** (Map 31): 25 northwest of Gaillac via D 964, towards Caussade. 4km before Larroque, left on D1 towards Monclar (15km) for 3km, then turn right at Chambres d'Hôtes sign, and go 2km in the woods, 2nd house, tar road.

A t the end of a small path through the woods, Meilhouret is a beautiful mansion of pale-gold regional stone where you will be greeted with courteous and discreet hospitality. The bedrooms are comfortable, tastefully furnished and they have a magnificent view of the countryside. In summer, breakfast is served beneath the trees. Meilhouret is a lovely spot for guests who enjoy a peaceful country setting.

288
Château de Montcuquet

81440 Lautrec
(Tarn)
Tel. 63 75 90 07
M. and Mme Vene

Rooms 2 with bath and WC, and 1 spare room without bath or shower. Rooms cleaned on request. **Price** 270F (1 pers.), 300F (2 pers.), +100F (extra pers.). **Meals** Breakfast incl. Evening meals at communal table 80F (wine incl.). **Facilities** TV lounge, reading room; fishing in river and lake on property. **Nearby** Golf (19 holes, 15km); Sidobre, châteaux, Cordes. **Credit cards** Not accepted. **Open** All year. **How to get there** (Map 31): 15km from Castres. Go towards Lautrec. Château is 4km from Lautrec on the road to Roquecourbe.

A beautiful avenue of chestnut trees leads up to this handsome château. Its 14th-century tower stands somewhat apart from the U-shaped wings built around a pleasant courtyard. The largest bedroom, which is impressively proportioned, looks out over Madame Vene's garden just below, as well as the countryside in the far distance. The other bedroom has its own charm, with its attractive small bathroom and a beautiful view over the shady terrace, where breakfasts are served in summer. The owners' good nature and simplicity help make the Château de Montcuquet a lovely place to stay.

289
Taverne de la Dame du Plô

5, rue Père-Colin
81500 Lavaur
(Tarn)
Tel. 63 41 38 77
M. Fèvre

Rooms 4 with shower and shared WC. **Price** 180F (1 pers.), 230F (2 pers.). **Meals** Breakfast incl. **Facilities** Lounge, Catalonian art gallery. **Nearby** Restaurants, golf, river, old town of Lavaur. **Credit cards** Not accepted. **Spoken** English, Italian, Spanish. **Open** All year. **How to get there** (Map 31): 37km east of Toulouse via D112.

Lavaur is a Cathar holy city whose heroine is La Dame du Plô. Bernard Fèvre will tell you the history. Entirely renovated, his ancient house has regular art exhibits. There are four small bedrooms which are pretty and comfortable. Every morning breakfast is set out in the lounge and all you have to do is heat the coffee, tea or hot chocolate.

290
Montpeyroux

81700 Lempaut
(Tarn)
Tel. 63 75 51 17
M. and Mme Adolphe Sallier

Rooms 1 with bath and WC, 2 with shower and WC, 2 sharing bath and WC. Rooms cleaned twice a week, or on request. **Price** 250-300F (1-2 pers.). **Meals** Breakfast incl., evening meals at communal table 100-120F (wine not incl.), or a simple lunch 60F. **Facilities** Lounge, swimming pool, tennis. **Pets** Dogs not allowed. **Nearby** Riding, golf, Saint-Féréol lake, Albi, Toulouse, Carcassonne. **Credit cards** Not accepted. **Open** April 1 – Nov 1. **How to get there** (Map 31): 12km northeast of Revel via D622 towards Castres for 9km, then left on D12. At Lempaut left, on D46 towards Blan, then turn left before cemetery.

Montpeyroux is a very quiet, old residence in a luxuriant setting. Beautiful antique furniture – 18th- and early 19th-century – enhances the decor of the lounge as well as the comfortable bedrooms. The dinners are excellent and, in good weather, breakfasts are served outside under the shade of the porch roof. The owners are informal and very friendly.

291
Villa Les Pins

81700 Lempaut
(Tarn)
Tel. 63 75 51 01
Mme Delbreil

Rooms 5 with bath and WC and 2 small rooms sharing shower and WC. Rooms cleaned twice weekly. **Price** 180-400F (1-2 pers.). **Meals** Breakfast incl., evening meals at communal table on request, 100F (wine incl.). **Facilities** Lounge, fishing. **Pets** Dogs not allowed. **Nearby** Golf (18 holes, 30km), tennis, riding, lake (12km), Montagne Noire, Castres. **Credit cards** Not accepted. **Spoken** English. **Open** April 1 – end Nov. **How to get there** (Map 31): 12km northeast of Revel via D622 towards Castres for 9km, then left on D12. At Lempaut, left on D46 towards Blan, then take 2nd turn left.

This lovely Italian-style villa was built at the beginning of the last century and has been completely renovated with excellent taste and attention to detail. The bedrooms are charming and bright, with flowered wallpaper, and have beautiful family furniture; the largest has a pleasant semi-circular balcony. The park has a view of the Montagne Noire. The hosts are friendly and welcoming

292
Domaine équestre des Juliannes

Les Juliannes
81250 Paulinet
(Tarn)
Tel. 63 55 94 38
M. and Mme Choucavy

Rooms 3 and 3 suites (4-5 pers.) with bath and WC. **Price** 310F (2 pers.), suite 465F (2 pers.) +70F (extra pers.). **Meals** Breakfast incl., half board from 258F per pers. in double room, lunch (cold buffet) and evening meal (67-103F) at communal table, by reservation (wine not incl.). **Facilities** Lounge, swimming pool, equestrian center, fishing. **Credit cards** Visa, Eurocard and MasterCard. **Pets** Dogs allowed on request. **Spoken** English. **Open** March – Dec. weekly bookings for July/August and school vacations. **How to get there** (Map 31): 37km southeast of Albi via D999 towards Millau. Before Alban right on D86 towards Réalmont, then 2nd road on the left; signposted.

This old farm, which has been well restored, is extremely quiet and has a beautiful view. The bedrooms are large and comfortable, and they are decorated with an elegant simplicity that emphasizes the pale wood floors, stone walls and pretty quilts on the beds. The evening meals are delicious, and there is a pleasant lounge. The horseback riding facilities are excellent.

293
Château d'En-Haut

59144 Jenlain
(Nord)
Tel. 27 49 71 80
M. and Mme Demarcq

Rooms 2 with bath and WC, 4 with shower and WC (poss. suite). **Price** 240-340F (2 pers.) +100F (extra pers.). **Meals** Breakfast incl., no evening meals. **Facilities** Lounge. **Pets** Dogs not allowed. **Nearby** Restaurants, golf, Mormal forest. **Credit cards** Not accepted. **Spoken** English. **Open** All year. **How to get there** (Map 3): 8km southeast of Valenciennes via N49 towards Maubeuge.

Jenlain, with its rows of red brick houses, is not a particularly attractive place, which makes it a lovely surprise to discover this delightful château, set far from the road in a beautiful park. Inside, it is extremely comfortable, with handsome carpets, rugs, and antique furniture, all enhanced by lovely color schemes. There are very pleasant bedrooms, and breakfast is served in one of three dining rooms. You will enjoy a friendly welcome and very good value for the money.

294
La Maison de la Houve

62179 Audinghen
(Pas-de-Calais)
Tel. 21 32 97 06/21 83 29 95
Mme Danel

Rooms 3 with bath and WC, 2 with shower and WC, 2 with washbasin. **Price** 100-150F (1 pers.) 125-170F (2 pers.). **Meals** Breakfast incl., no evening meals. **Facilities** Lounge, telephone, botanical garden, rose garden. **Credit cards** Visa, Eurocard and MasterCard. **Nearby** Tennis, riding, golf, seaside, fishing, château and museum in Boulogne-sur-Mer, Museum of the Sea. **Spoken** English. **Open** All year. **How to get there** (Map 1): Between Calais and Boulogne, 5.5km from Cap Gris-Nez on D191 towards Marquise; at Onglevert.

This unusual, pleasant house has a beautiful location with unobstructed views of the Opal Coast. It is comfortable and fabulously decorated and furnished. Excellent breakfasts are served on china in a pretty room with a panoramic view of the countryside and the cliffs of Cape Gris-Nez. Mme Danel is exceptionally kind, and we found it difficult to leave.

295
La Gacogne

La Gacogne
62310 Azincourt
(Pas-de-Calais)
Tel. 21 04 45 61
Marie-José and Patrick Fenet

Rooms 3 with shower and WC, 1 with washbasin and WC. **Price** 220F (2 pers.). **Meals** Breakfast incl., no evening meals. **Restaurants** In Azincourt, Hesdin and Fruges. **Facilities** Lounge, water-color and oil painting courses, carriage rides. **Pets** Dogs not allowed. **Nearby** Seaside, tennis, riding, fishing. **Credit cards** Not accepted. **Spoken** English. **Open** All year. **How to get there** (Map 2): 41km northeast of Abbeville via D928 towards Fruges. Before Ruisseauville, right on D71 towards Azincourt, then towards Tramecourt; signposted.

This welcoming house is on the historical site of Agincourt, on the spot where the English camp once stood. The bedrooms are in a small separate building which has a lounge, kitchen and fireplace. They are all charming and unusual. Breakfast is served at a communal table in an attractively decorated room, and the atmosphere here is convivial.

296
Le Clos Grincourt

18, rue du Château
62161 Duisans
(Pas-de-Calais)
Tel. 21 48 68 33
Annie Senlis

Rooms 1 and 1 suite (4 pers.) with bath or shower and WC. **Price** 170F (1 pers.), 220F (2 pers.) +50F (extra pers.), children under 5 (free); suite 390F (4 pers.). **Meals** Breakfast incl. No evening meals; many restaurants in Arras. **Facilities** Lounge, hiking on property. **Nearby** Tennis in village, golf (18 holes, 4km), riding, old Arras, Route du Camp du Drap d'Or, Flower Route, Air-sur-la-Lys, Saint-Omer Marsh. **Credit cards** Not accepted. **Spoken** English. **Open** All year. **How to get there** (Map 2): 8km W of Arras via N39, then D56 towards Duisans, then follow signs.

Le Clos Grincourt is a beautiful family house surrounded by a private park filled with flowers. The hospitality, the interior decoration and the family photos make you feel immediately at home. We especially recommend the *Chambre d'Amis*, the Friends' Room, which is deliciously retro, large and very comfortable. One room is reserved for guests, where breakfast is served and where you can gather tourist information, including a videotape on the region.

297

La Grand'Maison

62179 Escalles
(Pas-de-Calais)
Tel. 21 85 27 75
Fax The same
Jacqueline and Marc Boutroy

Rooms 4 and 2 studios (2 pers.) with bath or shower and WC. Rooms cleaned on request. **Price** 200-250F (2 pers.) +60-100F (extra pers.). **Meals** Breakfast incl. Evening meals at communal table 80F. **Facilities** Lounge, mountain biking on large hiking trail on property. **Pets** Dogs not admitted. **Nearby** Tennis in village, riding, sea (1.4km), golf (18 holes, 15km), coastline paths, Cap Blanc-Nez, Cap Gris-Nez. **Credit cards** Not accepted. **Spoken** English. **Open** All year. **How to get there** (Map 1): 15km southwest of Calais via D940 (by sea); access to Escalles via highway (A16), exit Cap Blanc-Nez (11 or 10), Peuplingues, then D243. Village of La Haute Escalles.

A stone's throw from the splendid coastline of Cape Blanc-Nez, you will find La Grand'Maison, a vast farm laid out in a rectangle, with beautiful flower beds and a melodic pigeon house in the center. You will be greeted with warm hospitality. The bedrooms are large, beautiful, very comfortable and are furnished with handsome, tall wardrobes, Voltaire-style chairs, engravings and pretty carpets. (The two studios on the ground floor are less attractive.) Good breakfasts are served in a warm, pretty room.

298
Château d'Asnières-en-Bessin

14710 Asnières-en-Bessin
(Calvados)
Tel. 31 22 41 16
M. and Mme Heldt

Rooms 1 with bath and WC. **Price** 450F (2 pers.). **Children** Under 11 not accepted.
Meals Breakfast incl. No communal meal. **Restaurants** Beside the sea. **Pets** Dogs not allowed.
Nearby Tennis, riding, seaside, Normandy landing beaches, Bayeux, Château de Bessin, Balleroy
forest. **Credit cards** Not accepted. **Spoken** English and a little German. **Open** All year.
How to get there (Map 7): 20km northwest of Bayeux via N13 towards Isigny-sur-Mer. In
Normaville, before Deux Jumeaux, right on D198 towards Asnières.

Asnières is charmingly reflected in the round ornamental pond in front of the beautiful château. Inside the decor is tasteful and authentic. The bedroom is very large, comfortable, and furnished with antiques. There is a beautiful parquet floor and pleasant bathroom. Breakfast is served at a large table in the Louis XV dining room. The owners are sophisticated and discreet and the prices are are very reasonable.

299
Le Castel

7, rue de la Cambette
14400 Bayeux
(Calvados)
Tel. 31 92 05 86
Fax 31 92 55 64
Baronne A. de Ville d'Avray

Rooms 2 and 1 suite (4-5 pers.) with bath or shower and WC. **Price** 490-550 (2 pers.) +80F
(extra pers.), suite 910F (4-5 pers.). **Meals** Breakfast incl. No communal meal. **Restaurants** In
Bayeux. **Facilities** Lounge, telephone. **Nearby** Swimming pool, riding, golf, seaside, Bayeux
Tapestry, cathedrals, Suisse Normande. **Credit cards** Not accepted. **Spoken** English. **Open** Mid-
March – Nov 1 (by reservation in high season). **How to get there** (Map 7): On the circular road
south of Bayeux, opposite the Saint-Lô crossroads.

It is a surprise to find a garden hidden behind the small courtyard of this beautiful old house where you'll feel at home. The dining room is at garden level and the 18th-century lounge is very well furnished. The bedrooms are quiet and elegant. Each has its own color scheme and overlooks the gardens, where breakfast can be served. This is a good place to stay in Bayeux.

300
Château de Vaulaville

Tour-en-Bessin
14400 Bayeux
(Calvados)
Tel. 31 92 52 62
Mme Corblet de Fallerans

Rooms 1 with bath and WC, 1 suite (3 pers. and 2 children) with 3 bedrooms, bath and WC. **Price** 350F (1 pers.), 480F (2 pers.), suite 700F (3 pers.). **Meals** Breakfast incl., evening meals by reservation (separate tables) 150-200F (wine incl.). **Facilities** Lounge. **Pets** Dogs allowed on request. **Nearby** Golf, seaside, Bayeux, Memorial museum, Normandy landing beaches. **Credit cards** Not accepted. **Spoken** English. **Open** Easter – Nov 1. **How to get there** (Map 7): 7km west of Bayeux via N13 towards Tour-en-Bessin; signposted.

This small, perfectly proportioned 18th-century château is surrounded by graceful moats. The bedrooms are superb: In one you will enjoy *la vie en rose* because of the dominant pink in the decor, which blends subtly with the antique furniture. Breakfasts and excellent dinners are served in a magnificent circular room, a veritable masterpiece furnished with signed antiques.

301
Chez M. and Mme Rogoff

Le Bourg
Ranchy
14400 Bayeux (Calvados)
Tel. 31 92 36 42
Monique and Guy Rogoff

Rooms 2 with bath or shower and WC. **Price** 150F (1 pers.), 200F (2 pers.) +100F (extra pers.) +120F (2 extra pers.). **Meals** Breakfast incl. No communal meals. **Restaurants** In Bayeux. **Facilities** Lounge. **Pets** Dogs not allowed. **Nearby** Swimming pool, tennis, riding, golf (9 and 18 holes), châteaux, manors, fortified farms. **Credit cards** Not accepted. **Open** April 1 – Nov 1. **How to get there** (Map 7): 3km southwest of Bayeux via D5 towards Le Molay-Littry, then D169; turn left before the church.

A few minutes from Bayeux, this house is set in a pleasant and peaceful garden. Guests may choose between two spacious bedrooms, simply decorated but charming. Each has its own bathroom. (The ground-floor bathroom is next door to the room). Breakfast is served in the large kitchen, or on the terrace in nice weather. Mme Rogoff's friendliness makes you feel very much at home.

302
Château des Riffets

14680 Bretteville-sur-Laize
(Calvados)
Tel. 31 23 53 21
Fax 31 23 75 14
Alain and Anne-Marie Cantel

Rooms 2 with bath and WC, and 2 suites (2-3 pers.) of which 1 with whirlpool and WC and 1 with multi-jet shower and WC. **Price** 460F (2 pers.) +150F (extra pers.); free for children under 13. **Meals** Breakfast incl., evening meals at communal or separate tables 200F (wine incl.); 100F (children). **Facilities** Lounge, swimming pool, boxes horse, sauna. **Pets** Dogs not allowed. **Nearby** Golf (18 holes, 5km), Beauvron-en-Auge, Beaumont, Deauville, Cabourg, Houlgate. **Credit cards** Not accepted. **Spoken** English, German. **Open** All year. **How to get there** (Map 7): 10km south of Caen via N158 towards Falaise. At La Jalousie, D23 and D235 before the village; signposted.

After a long, flat stretch, the road enters rolling countryside where you will find this château surrounded by a beautiful park and swimming pool. The bedrooms, large, comfortable, are decorated differently. We preferred the *Rose* suite and the *Baldaquin* (canopy) bedroom. In the other suite, there is a sophisticated shower room. The decor on the ground floor is stylish but less authentic. The owners are extremely friendly.

303
Manoir des Tourpes

Chemin de l'Eglise
14670 Bures-sur-Dives
(Calvados)
Tel. 31 23 63 47
Fax 31 23 86 10
Mme Landon and M. Cassady

Rooms 4 with bath or shower and WC. **Price** 280-350F (2 pers.) +50F (extra pers.). **Meals** Breakfast incl. No communal meal. **Facilities** Lounge. **Pets** Dogs not allowed. **Nearby** Golf (18 holes, 10km), tennis, swimming pool, riding, sailing, Caen, the Auge region, marshes. **Credit cards** Not accepted. **Spoken** English. **Open** All year. **How to get there** (Map 7): 15km east of Caen via N175; in Troarn, D95 towards Bures-sur-Dives; beside the church.

Next to a church, this elegant manor house overlooks meadows and a small river. The beautiful bedrooms are well-kept and comfortable, with coordinating wallpaper and curtains which complements the antique furniture. There is a beautiful lounge-dining room for fireside breakfasts, and an attractive garden. The Manoir des Tourpes is a very charming, welcoming place.

304
Domaine de la Piquoterie

14320 La Cambe
(Calvados)
Tel. 31 92 09 82
Fax 31 51 80 91
Jean-Gabriel Laloy

Rooms 2 with bath and WC, 1 (1 pers.) with shower and WC; no smoking in guest rooms. **Price** 350-450F (1-2 pers.), cottage 400F (2 pers.) per night or weekly rates, 700F (4 pers.). **Meals** Breakfast 45F. No communal meal. **Facilities** Lounge. **Pets** Dogs not allowed. **Nearby** Restaurants, golf, tennis, seaside. **Credit cards** Diners, Visa, Eurocard and Mastercard. **Spoken** English, German, Italian. **Open** April – Oct. (or by reservation). **How to get there** (Map 7): 21km west of Bayeux via N13. Exit La Cambe, (or Autoroute Paris-Cherbourd, exit La Cambe), in main street of village, 1st road on right; then in 200m, turn left; signposted.

This old house comes as a pleasant surprise. Jean-Gabriel Laloy, an artist, has created a resolutely contemporary but warm style. The Domaine could be featured in an interior-decorationmagazine, with its sober, pure lines, and beautiful objects, paintings and sculptures. The bedrooms are large and comfortable and the bathrooms are a dream. The staff is young and friendly, and there is a delightful garden full of rare plants.

305
Ferme Savigny

14230 La Cambe
(Calvados)
Tel. 31 22 70 06
M. and Mme Maurice Le Devin

Rooms 3 with bath and WC. **Price** 200F (1 pers.), 250F (2 pers.). **Meals** Breakfast incl. No communal meal. **Restaurants** La Marée and La Belle Marinière (3km). **Pets** Dogs not allowed. **Nearby** Tennis, riding, golf (27 holes), seaside, Normandy landing beaches, Bayeux (Tapestry, museum, cathedral), marshland park of Cotentin. **Credit cards** Not accepted. **Open** All year. **How to get there** (Map 7): 25km west of Bayeux via N13 to La Cambe; then at the roadside cross take D113 to the right, towards Grandcamp-Maisy; signposted.

In the Bessin region of Normandy, this farmhouse is covered with a graceful Virginia creeper, a prelude to the charming interior decoration. A stone staircase leads to beautiful, tastefully furnished bedrooms and their very pleasant bathrooms. Breakfast is served downstairs in a large room with stone walls, decorated with red and white patterned curtains and tablecloths. The Ferme Savigny is simple and charming, and the owners are very friendly.

306
Le Relais

19, rue Thiers
14240 Caumont-l'Eventé
(Calvados)
Tel. 31 77 47 85
M. and Mme Boullot

Rooms 4 and 1 suite (2-3 pers.) with bath or shower and WC, and 2 extra bedrooms. Rooms cleaned twice weekly. **Price** 270F (2 pers.); suite 340F (2 pers.), 420F (3 pers.). **Children** Under 3 not allowed. **Meals** Breakfast incl., evening meals at communal table 130F (wine incl.). **Facilities** Lounge, swimming pool, pony, riding (+70F), miniature golf. **Pets** Small dogs allowed on request (+20F). **Nearby** Tennis, golf, Mont-Saint-Michel, Château de Balleroy. **Credit cards** Not accepted. **Spoken** English. **Open** All year. **How to get there** (Map 7): 35km southeast of Caen via D9. At Caumont-l'Éventé, left on D28 towards Balleroy; follow signs, house in 200m.

You will be delighted with Le Relais and its flower-filled setting. The interior is pleasingly rustic and the bedrooms are pretty, with antique furniture and many charming personal touches. Breakfast and excellent dinners are served in a lovely room with a fireplace and corner bar. There is a beautiful lounge overlooking the swimming pool. You will receive a cheerful and lively welcome and Le Relais offers very good value.

307
La Ferme du Vey

Le Vey
14570 Clecy le Vey
(Calvados)
Tel. 31 69 71 02
M. and Mme Leboucher-Brisset

Rooms 3 with shower and WC. A small house for rent (price on request). **Price** 190F (2 pers.), 250F (3 pers.), 280F (4 pers.). **Meals** Breakfast incl. No communal meal. **Facilities** Fishing. **Pets** Small dogs allowed on request. **Nearby** Swimming pool, tennis, riding, canoeing, hang-gliding, golf (18 holes), rock climbing, park of Château du Thury, Château de Pontécoulan. **Credit cards** Not accepted. **Spoken** English. **Open** All year. **How to get there** (Map 7): 37km south of Caen via D562 towards Flers. At Clecy go left towards Le Vey for 1.5km.

This old farmhouse is in the heart of the Suisse Normande, not far from a cliff popular with devotees of rock climbing and hang gliding. The three bedrooms are charming, comfortable, and decorated in country style. Two of them overlook a pretty orchard bordered by a river. This is a very simple place where you will enjoy the hospitable young hosts.

308
Chez Mme Hamelin

Le Bourg
Beuvron-en-Auge
14430 Dozulé
(Calvados)
Tel. 31 39 00 62
Mme Hamelin

Rooms 2 with bath or shower and WC. **Price** 200F (2 pers.), 270F (3 pers.), 340F (4 pers.). Possibility of one extra room for 2 pers. **Meals** Breakfast incl. No evening meals. **Restaurants** La Boule d'Or, Le Pavé d'Auge in Beauvron-en-Auge and the Crêperie La Galère. **Pets** Small dogs allowed. **Nearby** Golf (18 holes), pretty villages. **Credit cards** Not accepted. **Spoken** English. **Open** Easter – Nov 1. **How to get there** (Map 7): 27km east of Caen via N175, then D49; in front of La Boule d'Or at the entrance to village.

This pretty house is located in a splendid Norman village with flower-filled balconies and half-timbered houses. The house is built around a small pretty flower garden with a path to the pastures beyond. There is a charming small bedroom at garden level and another elegant room upstairs with an attractive bathroom. Breakfast is served in a pretty dining room and the owners are friendly and informal.

309
Château des Parcs-Fontaine

Les Parcs-Fontaine
14130 Fierville-les-Parcs (Calvados)
Tel. 31 64 02 02
Fax 31 64 30 90
Morgane Weyenbergh

Rooms 4 with bath and shower, WC; 1 spare room with washbasin and bidet. **Price** 400 F (2 pers.), spare room: 250 F (2 pers.). **Meals** Breakfast incl. No communal meal, restaurants (3km). **Facilities** Lounge, horse stalls on property. **Pets** Dogs not allowed. **Nearby** Golf (18 holes, 5km), fishing, riding, tennis, yacht basin Stud Farm Route, Route des Douets, old Norman manor houses, Beuvron, Beaumont-en-Auge, sea. **Credit cards** Not accepted. **Spoken** English and German. **Open** All year (by written reservation in winter). **How to get there** (Map 8): Autoroute de Normandie, exit Pont-l'Evêque; then D579 towards Lisieux; 300m on left after Blangy-le-Château intersection.

This beautiful 19th-century house, bordering a lovely garden and forest, looks out on a pleasant countryside. The interior is comfortable and well appointed. The living room, decorated in cool colors, extends onto a romantic veranda. The bedrooms, where breakfast is served, are vast and the bathrooms are well equipped. (Two bedrooms with double windows can be noisy because of the road below). The Château des Parcs-Fontaine is particularly attractive to those who like their independence.

310
L'Hermerel

14230 Géfosse-Fontenay
(Calvados)
Tel. 31 22 64 12
M. and Mme François and
Agnès Lemarié

Rooms 4 with shower and WC. **Price** 160-200F (1 pers.), 190-250F (2 pers.) +60-70F (extra pers.). **Meals** Breakfast incl. No communal meal. **Facilities** Lounge. **Pets** Dogs not allowed. **Nearby** Tennis, golf, sailing, fishing, Bayeux, châteaux, manors. **Credit cards** Not accepted. **Spoken** English. **Open** All year. **How to get there** (Map 7): 7km north of Isigny-sur-Mer via RN13. In Osmanville, D514 towards Grandcamp-Maisy then left on D199; 2nd road on the right.

This 17th-century farmhouse, with its beautiful architecture and façade, could pass for a château. The pleasant bedrooms have high ceilings and combine comfortable amenities with rustic charm. The room under the eaves with a mezzanine is extraordinary, while the small ground-floor bedroom is less inviting. Breakfast is served in a large, attractive room. The historic chapel has been converted into the lounge. Mme Lemarié is very welcoming and will advise you on tourist activities.

311
Château de Vouilly

Vouilly
14230 Isigny-sur-Mer
(Calvados)
Tel. 31 22 08 59
M. and Mme James Hamel

Rooms 5 with bath and WC. **Price** 250F (1 pers.), 290F (2 pers.) +70F (extra pers.). **Meals** Breakfast incl. No communal meal. **Restaurants** Auberges de la Rivière and La Piquenotiére, and seaside restaurants. **Facilities** Lounge, fishing, ponies. **Pets** Dogs allowed on request. **Nearby** Tennis, golf, regional marshland park of Contentin and Bessin, Bayeux (Tapestry, cathedral). **Credit cards** Not accepted. **Spoken** English. **Open** March – Nov. **How to get there** (Map 7): 8km southeast of Isigny-sur-Mer via D5 towards Vouilly; signposted.

Close to the village yet very quiet, Vouilly is a charming small château surrounded by a moat. The bedrooms are large and comfortable with beautiful furniture and superb parquet floors. Breakfast is served in a dining room which once was the American press room during the Normandy landings. The owners are very pleasant and you'll get good value for your money.

312
Ferme de la Rivière

Saint-Germain-du-Pert
14230 Isigny-sur-Mer
(Calvados)
Tel. 31 22 72 92
Paulette and Hervé Marie

Rooms 2 with shower and WC, 2 with washbasin sharing bath and WC. Rooms cleaned every 3 days. **Price** 150F (1 pers.), 200F (2 pers.). **Meals** Breakfast incl., evening meals 85F (cidre incl.). **Facilities** Lounge, river fishing. **Pets** Dogs not allowed. **Nearby** Golf, tennis, riding, seaside, marshland paths, Bayeux. **Credit cards** Not accepted. **Open** Easter – Nov 1. **How to get there** (Map 7): 6km northeast of Isigny-sur-Mer; leave N13 at La Cambe, take D113 for 1km and D124 towards Saint-Germain-du-Pert for 1.5km.

This beautiful fortified farm is set in an unspoiled part of Normandy. The bedrooms, decorated in beautiful rustic style, are pleasant and well kept; three of them overlook the marshes. The owners are friendly and the prices are very reasonable. Make reservations in advance.

313
La Varinière

La Vallée
14310 Monts-en-Bessin
(Calvados)
Tel. 31 77 44 73
David and Pippa Edney

Rooms 5 rooms with bath or shower and WC; no smoking. **Price** 150F (1 pers.), 240 F (2 pers.), +40 F (extra pers.). **Meals** Breakfast incl.; evening meal at communal table 85F. **Facilities** Lounge. **Pets** Dogs allowed on request. **Nearby** Tennis, riding, covered swimming pool, lake and fishing, sea (30km); golf courses (9, 18 and 27 holes, 28km); Stud Farm Route, Bayeux, Château de Balleroy, l'Arc-en-Terre, Caen War Memorial, Route des Traditions. **Credit cards** Not accepted. **Spoken** English. **Open** All year. **How to get there** (Map 7): From Caen, take N175 towards Rennes. Exit Villers-Bocage, then take D6 towards Bayeux for 6km. After Fains, follow signs on right.

Surrounded by typically Norman hedgerows, La Varinière is a traditional house which has recently been redecorated by a friendly young British couple. Prettily coordinated wallpapers and cotton fabrics create a color scheme in each room: yellow for the dining room, and blue or rose for the bedrooms. Throughout, the house is bright, extremely well kept and elegantly furnished. The quiet, comfortable bedrooms are conducive to sleeping deliciously late. This is a beautiful place to stay at reasonable prices.

314
Cour l'Epée

14340 Saint-Aubin-Lebizay
(Calvados)
Tel. 31 65 09 45
Bernard and Bernardine Bataille

Rooms 3 with shower and 1 with bath or shower and WC. Rooms cleaned every 2 days. **Price** 260-320F (2 pers.) +70F (extra pers.); 2 nights min. **Meals** Breakfast incl. No communal meal. **Facilities** Tennis. **Pets** Dogs not allowed. **Nearby** Golf, Beuvron-en-Auge, Honfleur Deauville, Cabourg. **Credit cards** Not accepted. **Spoken** English. **Open** All year. **How to get there** (Map 8): 18km east of Cabourg; A13 exit Pont-l'Evêque, then N175 towards Caen. At Dozulé, left on D85 towards Cambremer. 1.8km after Forges-de-Clermont sign, turn left.

Cour L'Epée is like a small private hamlet. From its elevated position there is a superb view of the countryside. The bedrooms are idyllic, with simple and beautiful furniture and fabrics. A beautiful small suite has just been added. Good taste is to be found throughout and the house is very quiet. Excellent breakfasts are served indoors or out. This is an inviting place which is truly close to perfection.

315
La Ferme
des Poiriers Roses

14130 Saint-Philbert-des-Champs
(Calvados)
Tel. 31 64 72 14
Fax 31 64 19 55
M. and Mme Lecorneur

Rooms 6 (of which 2 for 4 pers.) and 1 suite with lounge, all with bath and WC. **Children** Not allowed. **Price** 300-500F (2 pers.). **Meals** Gourmand breakfast 52F. No communal meal. **Restaurant** La Paquine in Ouilly-du-Hauley. **Facilities** Lounge, bicycles. **Pets** Dogs not allowed. **Nearby** Golf (27 holes), tennis, riding, man-made lake, tour of manors. **Credit cards** Not accepted. **Spoken** English. **Open** All year. **How to get there** (Map 8): A13 exit Pont l'Evêque, then D579 towards Lisieux. In Ouilly, left on D98 through Norolles, then D264; 700m before the village.

The Ferme des Poiriers Roses is filled with flowers both outside and inside. The rooms are charming with low beamed ceilings and pretty objects. The superb bedrooms are decorated with a mixture of lovely, shimmering fabrics and wood. All have comfortable amenities and beautiful bathrooms. Breakfasts are a feast and the owners are warm and hospitable.

316
Château de Colombières

Colombières
14710 Trévières
(Calvados)
Tel. 31 22 51 65
Fax 31 92 24 92
Comtesse E. de Maupeou

Rooms 1 with bath and 2 suites (2-4 pers.) with bath and WC. **Price** 800F (1-2 pers.) +200F (extra pers.). **Meals** Breakfast 40F. No communal meal. **Restaurants** Nearby. **Facilities** Lounge, fishing, loose boxes. **Pets** Small dogs allowed on request. **Nearby** Golf (27 holes), Bayeux Tapestry, marshland park. **Spoken** English, Spanish. **Open** June – Sep. **How to get there** (Map 7): 20km west of Bayeux via N13 towards Mosles, signposted 'Monument historique'.

Chiefly built in the 14th and 15th centuries, this superb château is surrounded by a lovely flower-bordered moat. The owners are refined and informal. The bedrooms, which are veritable suites, are large, quiet and very comfortable. Each has a style of its own, from the 15th-century (this room is reached by a rare, wooden spiral staircase), to the splendors of the 18th-century. (This room was our favorite). Breakfast is served in a magnificent dining room. You can enjoy several coastal or marshland walks.

317
Ferme de l'Abbaye

Ecrammeville
14710 Trévières
(Calvados)
Tel. 31 22 52 32
M. and Mme Louis Fauvel

Rooms 2 suite (3-4 pers.) with bath or shower and WC. **Price** 150F (1 pers.), 200F (2 pers.), 260F (3 pers.), 320-340F (4 pers.). **Meals** Breakfast incl., evening meals at communal table 80F (cidre incl.). **Facilities** Telephone. **Pets** Dogs not allowed. **Nearby** Swimming pool, tennis, golf (27 holes), seaside, Normandy landing beaches, Bayeux. **Credit cards** Not accepted. **Open** All year. **How to get there** (Map 7): 19km west of Bayeux via N13, leave the 4-lane highway at the signs to Ecrammeville on the left, then take D30 on the right.

This large farm, set in a pretty village, is surrounded by lovely grounds. The rooms are ideal for families. Those in the farmhouse are prettily decorated with antique furniture; the other occupies a small house of its own and is more soberly decorated. We recommend it particularly for the summer. Monsieur and Madame Fauvel are very friendly hosts.

318
Manoir de L'Hormette

Aignerville – 14710 Trévières
(Calvados)
Tel. 31 22 51 79
Fax 31 22 75 99
M. and Mme Yves Corpet
and M. and Mme Denis Corpet

Rooms 3 with bath or shower and WC, 1 studio (2 pers.) with kitchen, shower and WC, and 2 suites (4-5 pers.) of 2 bedrooms with kitchen, bath or shower and WC; TV and small lounge in each bedroom. **Price** 475-500F (2 pers.), studio 550-600F (2 pers.), suite 800-1000F (4 pers.). **Meals** Breakfast 50F. No communal meal. **Restaurants** L'Omaha in Saint-Laurent-sur-Mer (5km). **Facilities** Telephone. **Pets** Small dogs allowed on request. **Nearby** Golf, riding. **Credit cards** Amex, Visa, Eurocard and MasterCard. **Spoken** English, Italian. **Open** April 1 – end-Dec. **How to get there** (Map 7): 18km west of Bayeux via N13 (4-lane highway) exit Aignerville. Telephone for directions.

Set in rolling countryside, this beautiful manor house is very pleasantly and comfortably decorated. The bedrooms look out on a lovely flower garden. Breakfasts, which are elegantly served, include homemade preserves, honey, soft–boiled eggs, fruit and three different kinds of bread. There is no evening meal, but the restaurant nearby, which belongs to members of the family, serves fish and grills.

319
Chez Régine Bultey

Les Coutances
27210 Beuzeville
(Eure)
Tel. 32 57 75 54
Mme Régine Bultey

Rooms 3 with bath or shower, shared WCs. **Price** 170F (1 pers.), 200F (2 pers.) +50F (extra pers.). **Meals** Breakfast incl. No communal meal. **Pets** Dogs not allowed. **Nearby** Honfleur, le Bec Hellouin, the Vernier marshland. **Credit cards** Not accepted. **Spoken** Some English. **Open** All year. **How to get there** (Map 8): 1km from Beuzeville towards Saint-Pierre-du-Va; sign in the Place de la République in Beuzeville.

This house is surrounded by a delightful garden with a large crimson rose bush. The inside is also flower–filled and tastefully decorated. The bedrooms are simple, quiet and comfortable, and they have a lovely view over the countryside and the small Norman houses nearby. Young Madame Bultey is friendly and very jovial.

320
Le Vieux Pressoir

Le Clos Potier
Conteville
27210 Beuzeville
(Eure)
Tel. 32 57 60 79
Mme Anfray

Rooms 3 and 1 suite (4 pers.) with bath or shower and WC. **Price** 240F (2 pers.) +100F (extra pers.), suite 420F (4 pers.). **Meals** Breakfast incl., evening meals at communal table, by reservation 120F (cider incl.). **Facilities** Lounge, visit to the 17th-century cider press, bicycle rentals. **Pets** Small dogs allowed on request. **Nearby** Swimming pool, tennis, golf, seaside (12km), Honfleur, abbeys. **Credit cards** Not accepted. **Spoken** English. **Open** All year. **How to get there** (Map 8): 12km east of Honfleur via D180 towards Pont-Audemer, then left on D312 at Fiquefleur to Conteville; signposted.

This is an adorable, small Norman farm. In the lounge, the dining room and bedrooms, there is a charming retro decor of dried flowers, pretty lace and thick quilts on the beds. Madame Anfray is a kind hostess and there is an excellent evening meal.

321
Château de Saint-Gervais

Asnières
27260 Cormeilles - (Eure)
Tel. 32 45 37 87
Fax 32 46 49 76
M. and Mme Noirot-Nérin

Rooms 8 with bath or shower and WC, 1 room with washbasin and WC, 1 spare room. **Price** 250-450 F(1-2 pers.). **Meals** Continental breakfast 40 F; noon and evening meals at separate tables by reservation. **Facilities** Lounge, billiards. **Nearby** Restaurants, tennis, riding, fishing, golf (18 holes, 18km); châteaux and manor houses, Honfleur (30km), Lisieux pilgrimage, stud farms. **Credit cards** Not accepted. **Spoken** English, Italian. **Open** All year. **How to get there** (Map 8): 18km northeast of Lisieux, on N13 between L'Hôtellerie and Duranville. At Thiberville, go left on D22 towards Cormeilles for 7.4km; château on left. From Paris via A13: exit Beuzeville, towards Cormeilles, then D22 towards Thiberville 4.5km; château on right.

There are several small, half-timbered outbuildings of the original old Château de Saint-Gervais which still remain; the present structure dates from the 19th-century. Entirely renovated, the interior is decorated in tastefully cheerful colors. The bedrooms are bright, comfortable and soberly decorated with handsome old furniture and engravings. All the rooms have a beautiful view. There is a lovely small salon, a cheerful dining room, and the château is surrounded by a 175-acre private park: Peace and quiet are guaranteed.

322
Les Ombelles

4, rue du Gué
27720 Dangu
(Eure)
Tel. 32 55 04 95
Fax 32 55 59 87
Mme de Saint-Père

Rooms 2 with shower or bath and WC. **Price** 270F (2 pers.) +80F (extra pers.). **Children** Under 3 not accepted. **Meals** Breakfast incl., half board 230F per pers. in double room (wine incl.), 2 days min.; evening meals at communal table (except Saturday) 130F (wine incl.) "Grandmother's dinner" without alcohol 80F. **Facilities** lounge. **Pets** Dogs not allowed. **Nearby** Golf, Giverny, Bray region, Gisors, Giverny. **Credit cards** Not accepted. **Spoken** English. **Open** March 1 – mid-Dec. **How to get there** (Map 7): 8km west of Gisors on D181.

Located in the village, this simple house has a sheltered terrace and a garden on a pretty river. The decoration is elegant. The bedroom on the street is small but charming with its bed in an alcove; double windows keep out noise from the street. The other bedroom is very lovely and overlooks the garden. You will feel at home here.

323
Château du Landin

Le Landin
27350 Routot
(Eure)
Tel. 32 42 15 09
M. Patrice Favreau

Rooms 6 with bath and WC. **Price** 450F (2 pers.). **Meals** Breakfast 40F, evening meals by reservation (separate tables) 180F (wine incl.). **Facilities** Lounge, boxes horse. **Pets** Dogs allowed on request (50F). **Nearby** Golf, stud farms, abbeys. **Credit cards** Not accepted. **Spoken** English. **Open** Easter – end-Dec. **How to get there** (Map 8): 4km north of Bourg-Achard on D313; signposted.

This red-brick château lies at the end of a large park with splendid trees. From the colonnaded entrance hall you will see the Seine below and its verdant riverbanks. All the comfortable bedrooms and their large bathrooms (except one) enjoy this view. The overall decoration is beautiful, but the rotunda bedroom deserves extra praise. Breakfast is served on the terrace in good weather.

324
Château du Hannoy

Le Hanoy
27250 Rugles
(Eure)
Tel. 32 24 70 50
M. and Mme Delaplace

Rooms 6 with bath or shower and shared WC. **Price** 250F (1-2 pers.), 300F (2 pers.) +120F (extra pers.). **Meals** Breakfast incl., half board 430F (2 pers. in double room), full board 610F (2 pers. in double room). Reduced weekly terms. **Facilities** Lounge. **Pets** Dogs allowed on a leash. **Nearby** Golf (18 holes, 20km), fishing, equestrian center, l'Aigle market. **Credit cards** All major. **Open** Feb 14 – Jan 2. **How to get there** (Map 8): 7km southwest of Rugles towards l'Aigle.

This small, typically Norman 19th-century château is sheltered from the road by its 7 1/2-acre flower-filled park. The bedrooms are light, with retro furniture and some have a balcony. Elegant period furniture decorates the lounge and dining rooms (which also serves as a small restaurant). The rooms open onto the garden and meals can be enjoyed outside. You will be welcomed by friendly and attentive hosts.

325
Le Four à Pain

8, rue des Gruchets
27140 Saint-Denis-Le-Ferment
(Eure)
Tel. 32 55 14 45
Madeleine Rousseau

Rooms 2 with shower and WC (1 with bath outside the room). **Price** 170F (1 pers.), 220F (2 pers.), 270F (3 pers.). **Meals** Breakfast incl. No evening meals. **Restaurant** L'Auberge de l'Atelier (500m). **Facilities** Lounge. **Pets** Dogs allowed on request. **Nearby** Riding, tennis, forest, fishing, 2 golf courses (18 holes, 15km); Lyons-la-Forêt, Gisors dungeon. **Credit cards** Not accepted. **Spoken** English. **Open** All year (in winter by reservation only). **How to get there** (Map 9): 6km northwest of Gisors via D14bis towards Bézu and Rouen; then D17 towards Saint-Denis-le-Fervent. In the village, turn left at 2nd Chambres d'Hôtes sign, then Rue des Gruchets.

This charming Norman house offers guests two lovely bedrooms. One, decorated in autumnal shades, is located beneath the high, beamed-ceilings of the roof. The other is installed in the old bread oven *(four à pain)* in the garden. With its terra cotta floors, its charming floral fabrics and a kitchenette, it is ideal particularly for long stays. Several pieces of antique furniture and a large fireplace lend charm to the living/dining room. Good breakfasts are served with courtesy and charm.

326
La Michaumière

72, rue des Canadiens
27370 Tourville-la-Campagne
(Eure)
Tel. 32 35 31 28
Mme Paris

Rooms 2 with bath or shower and WC, 1 with bath and 2 without bath sharing WC. Rooms cleaned on request. **Price** 170F (1 pers.), 200F (2 pers.). **Meals** Breakfast incl. No communal meal. **Facilities** Lounge, bicycle rentals. **Pets** Dogs allowed on request. **Nearby** Restaurants, golf, Harcourt, Giverny. **Spoken** English. **Open** All year. **How to get there** (Map 8): 33km south of Rouen via N138. At Elbeuf, D840 towards Le Neubourg and D26; signposted.

Nestled in a pretty garden, this thatched-roof house is very quiet. It has three comfortable, charming bedrooms which overlook the garden. In winter, excellent breakfasts are served beside the fire in a small lounge decorated with curios, pottery and bright copper; in summer, they are served very bright dining room and include fresh orange juice, yoghurt, *brioches*, and homemade preserves.

327
Manoir d'Arville

Sainte-Geneviève
50760 Barfleur
(Manche)
Tel. 33 54 32 51
Mme Jean Le Bunetel

Rooms Rental of apartment occupying the wing of the manor: 2 bedrooms (2-3 pers.), each with bath and WC, a large paneled lounge/living room, equipped kitchen (dishwasher, washing machine), garden lounge, TV. **Price** 2400-3500 F the week. **Nearby** 2 golf courses (9 holes), tennis, riding, sea (diving, sailing); Barfleur, Tatihan Island, Valogne, Cap de la Hague, D-Day landing beaches. **Credit cards** Not accepted. **Open** May 1 – Oct 1. By written reservation. **How to get there** (Map 7): 2km from Barfleur via D901 towards Cherbourg, then first on left. D10 towards Sainte-Geneviève: signs.

Madame Le Bunetel rents out an independent apartment on a weekly basis. This is a charming 16th- and 17th-century manor house which is located in a beautiful countryside dotted with fields and farms. The interior reflects Madame Le Bunetel's passion for beautiful fabrics, particularly silks, and there are also lovely antique furnishings and objects. The salon is very well furnished and is paneled with 18th-century natural-colored wood. Madame Le Bunetel's hospitality is charming, like the Manoir d'Arville itself.

328
Manoir de Caillemont

Sainte-Georges-de-la-Rivière
50270 Barneville-Carteret
(Manche)
Tel. 33 53 81 16
Mme Eliane Coupechoux

Rooms 1 studio (2 pers.) with kitchenette, shower and WC, and 1 suite (2-4 pers.) with shower and WC. **Price** 330-500F; +100F (extra pers. in room), +250F (2 extra pers. in suite). **Meals** Breakfast 35F. No evening meals. **Restaurant** La Marine in Carteret (5km). **Facilities** Swimming pool, bicycles. **Pets** Dogs allowed on request. **Nearby** Golf, Mont-Saint-Michel, Channel Islands, tennis, riding. **Credit cards** Not accepted. **Spoken** English. **Open** May – Oct. (by reservation out of season). **How to get there** (Map 6): 35km south of Cherbourg via D903. At Barneville-Carteret head for Coutances. Phone for directions.

This old Norman manor has a studio and two suites consisting of a bedroom and a lounge which are very comfortable, quiet and well kept. The studio and one suite are decorated in country style; the other suite is more classic, with dark Louis XV paneling. Breakfast is served in the dining room. There is a heated swimming pool hidden by a terrace. Madame Coupechoux is a very friendly hostess.

329
Le Bel Enault

Sainte-Côme-du-Mont
50500 Carentan
(Manche)
Tel. 33 42 43 27
M. and Mme Gérard Grandin

Rooms 5 with bath and WC. **Price** 230F (1 pers.), 260F (2 pers.) +60F (extra pers.). **Meals** Breakfast 30F. No communal meal. **Facilities** Lounge, tennis, lakes, boating. **Pets** Dogs not allowed. **Nearby** Marshes, footpaths, Normandy landing beaches, museums. **Credit cards** Not accepted. **Spoken** English. **Open** All year. **How to get there** (Map 7): 4km north of Carentan via N13 towards Cherbourg, then D913 towards Sainte-Marie-Du-Mont for 1km; signposted.

Behind this small château, rebuilt in the 19th century, there is an extraordinary garden with exotic plants growing around ponds, grottoes and rock gardens. The interior is simpler: the bedrooms are very well kept, quiet, and prettily arranged. Breakfast is served beside a large fireplace or in the bedrooms. The owners are friendly and informal.

330
Château de Coigny

50250 Coigny
(Manche)
Tel 33 42 10 79
Mme Ionckheere

Rooms 2 (of which 1 has an extra bed) with bath and WC. **Price** 450F (1 pers.), 500F (2 pers.), 600F (3 pers.). **Meals** Breakfast incl., evening meals by reservation 150F (wine incl.). **Facilities** Lounge. **Pets** Dogs not allowed. **Nearby** Riding, golf, museums, Mont-Saint-Michel, Carentan. **Credit cards** Not accepted. **Open** Easter – Nov 1 (by reservation out of season). **How to get there** (Map 7): 11k west of Carentan via D903 towards Barneville, then D223; after the sign for Coigny take the first entrance on the left.

Built by the ancestor of one of Louis XV's marshals, Coigny is a beautiful 16th-century château. Inside, the antique furniture has been replaced by reproductions, but the decor is lovely. The bedrooms are comfortable, quiet and have a pretty view onto the courtyard or the moat. Breakfast and dinner are served in a large room with a fabulous Renaissance fireplace, in front of which is a living area.

331
Le Homme

Le Bourg
Bourg de Poilley
50220 Ducey (Manche)
Tel. 33 48 44 41
Victor and Jeanine Vaugrente

Rooms 1 (2-4 pers.) with bath and WC, 2 (1 with shower) sharing bathroom and WC. **Price** 250-270F (2 pers.) +100F (extra pers.). **Meals** Breakfast 25F No communal meal. **Facilities** Lounge. **Pets** Dogs allowed on request. **Nearby** Restaurants, golf (30km), tennis, canoeing, seaside, Mont-Saint-Michel, Château de Fougères. **Credit cards** Not accepted. **Spoken** English, German. **Open** All year. **How to get there** (Map 7): 10km southeast of Avranches (exit Alençon RN176 towards Ducey);or on the way out of Ducey towards Mont-Saint-Michel for 1km, then turn left towards Poilley.

Near Mont-Saint-Michel, Le Homme is a small village house with a delightful garden. The interior is quiet, light, very comfortable, and pleasantly decorated. On the *premier étage,* two superb bedrooms (very light, with antique furniture and bouquets of dried flowers) share an equally pleasant bathroom. The room on the *deuxième étage* is equally attractive and has a private bathroom. You will enjoy excellent breakfasts and a very warm welcome.

332
Château de la Roque

50180 Hébécrevon
(Manche)
Tel. 33 57 33 20
Fax 33 57 51 20
Mireille and Raymond Delisle

Rooms 15 with bath or shower, WC, telephone and TV. **Price** 210F (1 pers.), 270-330F (2 pers.), 360F (3 pers.). **Meals** Breakfast 20F, half board 500F (2 pers. in double room), evening meals at communal table 95F (wine incl.). **Facilities** Lounge, tennis, bicycle rentals. **Pets** Dogs allowed on request. **Nearby** Riding, fishing, golf, Bayeux, Mont-Saint-Michel. **Credit cards** Not accepted. **Spoken** English, German. **Open** All year. **How to get there** (Map 7): 6km northwest of Saint-Lô via D972 towards Coutances. At Saint-Gilles take D77 towards Pont-Hébert for 3km, then right.

This elegant 18th-century château is built around a lovely central garden. The bedrooms are very prettily decorated, comfortable, and are equipped with telephone and TV. The lounge and dining room may be used by guests on request. The Château de la Roque is so professional it could be a hotel, but the hospitality and the evening meals lend it special personality.

333
Le Cottage de la Voisinière

Route de Sourdeval
50410 Percy
(Manche)
Tel. 33 61 18 47
Daniel and Maryclaude Duchemin

Rooms 5 with shower and WC (1 with kitchenette). **Price** 200F (2 pers.), studio 240F +60F (extra pers.). **Meals** Breakfast incl. No communal meal. **Restaurants** Les Gourmets (1.5km) and others (10km). **Facilities** Lounge. **Pets** Dogs allowed (+20F). **Nearby** Golf (9 holes, 30km), tennis, sea (30km), Mont-Saint-Michel, Ambye abbey, Normandy landing beaches. **Credit cards** Not accepted. **Open** All year. **How to get there** (Map 7): 30km north of Avranches via N175. At Percy, take the Sourdeval road, then signposted, 1.5km from Percy on the right.

Le Cottage is composed of two small, simple, welcoming houses. The bedrooms are well kept and decorated in a pleasantly countrified fashion. We recommend those in the separate wing (the Cyclamen room is very special), where there is also a large room and kitchenette reserved for guests here. Breakfast is served in the charming dining room or outside in a beautiful garden which regularly win prizes at local flower shows.

334
La Fèvrerie

50760 Sainte-Geneviève
(Manche)
Tel. 33 54 33 53
Marie-France Caillet

Rooms 3 with bath and WC (1 with bath outside room). **Price** 200-320 F (2 pers.) +80 F (extra pers.). **Meals** Breakfast incl., 1 meal per week at communal table 60-100F (cider incl.), 130F (shellfish menu); or restaurants and crêperies (3km). **Facilities** Lounge; bikes, horse stalls on the property. **Pets** Dogs allowed on request. **Nearby** Tennis in village, water sports (sea 2km), riding, golf courses (15km); Barfleur, Pointe de la Hague, Hôtel de Beaumont mansion in Valognes. **Credit cards** Not accepted. **Spoken** English, Spanish. **Open** All year (winter by reservation). **How to get there** (Map 7): 3km west of Barfleur via D25 towards Quettehou, then 2nd road on right; signs.

La Févrerie, a beautiful farm/manor house dating from the 16th and 17th centuries, is set in the heart of the countryside not far from the splendid Pointe de Barfleur. The interior is both warm and refined. The delightfully charming bedrooms are comfortable, prettily furnished with antiques and brightened with beautiful fabrics. Breakfasts and dinners are served in front of a large fireplace in the pleasant living room. This is a remarkable place to stay where you will be greeted with warm hospitality.

335
Château de la Brisette

50760 Sainte-Germain-de-
Tournebut
(Manche)
Tel. 33 41 11 78
Fax 33 41 22 32
Gentien and Inès de la Hautière

Rooms 3 with bath and WC, telephone, TV. Linens changed every day. **Price** 450-550 (2 pers.) + 100 F (extra pers.); free for children under 5. **Meals** Breakfast incl.; meals at separate tables 175F (wine incl.), or restaurants nearby. **Facilities** Lounge, pond fishing on property. **Pets** Dogs not allowed. **Nearby** Tennis, riding (6km), golf (18 holes, 6km); sea (10km), animal park (4km); Hôtel de Beaumont mansion in Valognes, Old Barfleur, Nez de Jobourg, Sainte-Marie-l'Eglise. **Credit Cards** All major. **Spoken** English. **Open** All year (by reservation in winter). **How to get there** (Map 7): 8km east of Valognes via D902, road to Quettehou for 6km, then signs at intersection.

The Château de la Brisette, which is splendidly isolated, is a beautiful example of classic 18th-century architecture. The rooms are nobly proportioned, particularly the large salon with its beautiful gilt-wood paneling and its tall French doors. Looking out on the lovely lake and the countryside, the pleasant bedrooms are furnished with antiques, which vary from austere Haute Epoque to elegant Empire styles.

336
La Maurandière

50150 Sourdeval-la-Barre
(Manche)
Tel. 33 59 65 44
Mme Evelyne Dupart

Rooms 4 (of which 1 is in a small building in the garden) with bath or shower and WC. **Price** 180F (1 pers.), 200F (2 pers.), 250F (3 pers.). **Meals** Breakfast incl. No communal meal. Snack avalaible. **Restaurant** La Table de Paulinc (3km). **Facilities** Lounge, fishing (with permit). **Pets** Dogs allowed on request. **Nearby** Riding, climbing, windsurfing, Mont-Saint-Michel, pottery museum, granite museum. **Credit Cards** Not accepted. **Open** All year. **How to get there** (Map 7): 13km south of Vire via D977 towards Mortain; signposted 3km after the village.

In rolling countryside, La Maurandière is a lovely house with a beautiful garden. You will find the same attention to detail in the handsome decoration of the lounge, dining room and bedrooms, which are very prettily furnished. If the weather permits, breakfast is served outside on the terrace. Madame Dupart is very hospitable and the prices are more than reasonable.

337
Le Prieuré Saint-Michel

61120 Crouttes
(Orne)
Tel. 33 39 15 15
Fax 33 36 15 16
M. and Mme Pierre Chahine

Rooms 3 with shower and WC, 2 suites (2 pers.) with bath or shower and WC. **Price** 450-600F (2 pers.), suite 700F (2 pers.) +50F (extra pers.). **Meals** Breakfast incl., evening meals (from June) at communal or separate tables 200F (wine incl.). **Facilities** Lounge, art center, concerts and theatre (Sept). **Pets** Dogs not allowed. **Nearby** Golf, Honfleur, Deauville, Bagnoles-de-l'Orne. **Credit Cards** Visa, Eurocard and MasterCard. **Spoken** English, German, Spanish. **Closed** Feb. **How to get there** (Map 8): 34km south of Lisieux via D579. In Vimoutiers take D916 towards Argentan; signposted "Monuments Historiques".

Once part of Jumièges Abbey, this priory looks out over lovely Norman countryside. It is quiet and you will be quite independent. The half-timbered buildings house very beautiful, comfortable and tastefully decorated bedrooms, and are set in a magnificently landscaped park. In the summer the monumental old cider press is used as a lounge-dining room. Be sure to see the chapel and the 12th-century barn.

338
La Grande Noé

61290 Moulicent
(Orne)
Tel. 33 73 63 30
Fax 33 83 62 92
Pascale and Jacques de Longchamp

Rooms 3 with bath and WC. **Price** 450-620 F (2 pers.), + 120 F (extra pers.), + 80 F (children). **Meals** Breakfast incl., evening meals at communal table 220F (wine incl.), 80F (children). **Facilities** Lounge, horse stalls, horse carriage. **Pets** Dogs allowed in kennel. **Nearby** Tennis, swimming, golf (18 holes, 25km); Trappe Abbey, manor houses, Old Mortagne. **Credit Cards** Not accepted. **Spoken** English, Spanish. **Closed** Nov 30 – April 1 (by reservation in winter). **How to get there** (Map 8): 30km southwesyt of Verneuil-sur-Avre via N12 towards Alençon. At the Sainte Anne intersection, towards Longny via D918, then left for 4km towards Moulicent; house 800m on right.

The Grande Noé is a family mansion built in the 15th and 17th centuries and set in the heart of the countryside. The bedrooms are gorgeous with their lovely old furniture and elegant fabrics; the bathrooms have modern amenities. There is a splendid stairwell with beautiful *trompe-l'œil* marble and early 19th-century stucco, and a vast, handsomely decorated salon with a fireplace. The dining room, with 18th-century natural-oak paneling, is lovely, and the hospitality is very charming.

339
Le Château

Place de l'église
76750 Bosc-Roger-sur-Buchy
(Seine-Maritime)
Tel. 35 34 29 70
M. and Mme Preterre Rieux

Rooms 4 with bath or shower and WC. **Price** 240F (1 pers.), 360F (2 pers.), 420F (3 pers.), 470F (4 pers.). **Meals** Breakfast incl. No communal meal. **Restaurants** In Buchy (1km). **Facilities** Lounges, boxes horse, bicycles, theme weekends (gardens, hiking, golf). **Pets** Dogs allowed on request. **Nearby** Tennis, swimming pool, golf (18 holes), Mortemer Abbey, park of Forges-les-Eaux. **Credit Cards** Not accepted. **Spoken** English. **Closed** In Fev. **How to get there** (Map 1 and 8): 27km northeast of Rouen via N28 towards Neufchâtel, right on D919 towards Buchy, then right towards Bosc-Roger.

Opposite the church in a tiny village, this small château charms immediately with its restful atmosphere. The reception rooms are prettily decorated, comfortable and fresh. The bedrooms are very pleasant and colorful, with cane or pale wood furniture, and they overlook the park (our favorites are the rotunda rooms). The bathrooms are large and also overlook the park. The owners are lively and welcoming, and you will enjoy excellent breakfasts.

340
Domaine de Champdieu

76590 Gonneville-sur-Scie
(Seine-Maritime)
Tel. 35 32 66 82
Messrs Buquet, Maudit and
Vacheron

Rooms 3 with shower and WC. Poss. suite with bedroom and lounge. **Price** 400F (1 pers.), 450F (2 pers.), suite 800F (2 pers.) +150F (extra pers.). **Children** Under 14 not accepted. **Meals** Breakfast 50F, evening meal at communal table (poss. separate table) 400F (fisch dinner), 550F (foie gras), 800F (champagne or game dinner). **Facilities** Lounge. **Pets** Dogs not allowed. **Nearby** Golf, tennis, beaches, château de Miromesnil, gardens of Princess Sturdza and Mme Mallet. **Credit Cards** Not accepted. **Spoken** English, Spanish. **Open** All year. **How to get there** (Map 1 and 8): 14km south of Dieppe via N27. After Tôtes, D50 on right, then D 203, signs for "Chambres d'Hôtes".

This charming house lies deep in the countryside and has a magnificent interior: antique furniture, paintings and curios abound. Denis Buquet is an excellent host and his table settings are a work of art. He is an excellent cook, and dinner by candlelight is a feast to remember.

341
La Marette

76260 Melleville
(Seine-Maritime)
Tel. 35 50 81 65
M. and Mme Etienne Garçonnet

Rooms 1 with bath and WC, 1 with washbasin and WC (poss. suite). Rooms cleaned once a week. **Price** 200-250F (2 pers.) +70F (extra pers.). **Meals** Breakfast incl.. No evening meals. **Facilities** Game room. **Restaurant** Le Moulin de Becquirel (9km). **Pets** Dogs not allowed. **Nearby** Swimming pool, tennis, river fishing, forest of Eu, seaside. **Credit Cards** Not accepted. **Spoken** English, German. **Open** All year. **How to get there** (Map 1): 12km south of Eu via D1314, then left on D78; signposted.

This red brick farmhouse on the edge of the forest is restful and very well kept. The bedrooms can be arranged into a suite for families. They are attractively old-fashioned. We recommend the one with its own bathroom. Breakfast is served in a dining room at separate tables. Children will enjoy a game room which has been set up in a large barn, which includes a ping-pong table and basketball net. This is a simple, charming place and the owners are very hospitable.

342
Le Val de la Mer

76400 Senneville-sur-Fécamp
(Seine-Maritime)
Tel. 35 28 41 93
Mme Lethuillier

Rooms 3 with bath or shower and WC. **Price** 230F (1 pers.), 270F (2 pers.), 350F (3 pers.).
Meals Breakfast incl. No communal meal. **Restaurants** Le Maritime (3km), Le Relais des Dalles
(7km). **Pets** Dogs not allowed. **Nearby** Golf in Etretat (18 holes, 18km). **Closed** August.
How to get there (Map 8): At Fécamp take D925 towards Dieppe; in the village close to the
church.

This pretty house is set on the edge of a village a few hundred meters from the sea and the chalk cliffs. You will be made very welcome and advised on the local tourist attractions. The small bedrooms are quiet, comfortable and pretty. The ground-floor room opens onto a lovely flower garden. In the morning breakfast is served at a large table in the lounge-dining room.

343
Le Clos du Vivier

Chemin du Vivier
76540 Valmont
(Seine-Maritime)
Tel. 35 29 95 05/35 29 90 95
Fax 35 27 44 49
Mme Dominique Cachera

Rooms 2 with bath and WC, TV. Sheets changed evey 3 days, towels every day. **Price** 250F (1 pers.),
310F (2 pers.), 390F (3 pers.); free for children under 6. **Meals** Breakfast incl., meals at communal
or separate tables by reservation 90F (cidre incl.), or restaurants (1km). **Facilities** Lounge, tel. (with
Carte Pastel). **Pets** Small dogs allowed on request. **Nearby** Hiking, tennis, golf (18 holes, 30km), bike
rentals and fishing (1km); sea (10km), Château de Valmont, Benedictine and Terres-Neuves Museums.
Credit Cards Not accepted. **Spoken** English, Spanish. **Open** All year. **How to get there** (Map 1 and
8): 10km east of Fécamp towards Yvetot, then Valmont via D150. Place de la Mairie, towards Ourville
for 1km. At indication for 1st crossroad, Chemin du Vivier on right, 2nd house on right.

This lovely Norman thatched-roof cottage with its pretty garden lies at the edge of the small historic village of Valmont. The Clos du Vivier has just been beautifully and comfortably renovated. The bedrooms have antique furnishings and are brightened with a charming assortment of colors. On the ground floor, the half-timbering and its openwork add brightness to the rooms, the salon and the very lovely dining room. The brunches are excellent and the staff is very friendly.

344
Château du Housseau

Le Housseau
44470 Carquefou
(Loire-Atlantique)
Tel. 40 30 21 95
Fax 40 25 14 05
Jean-Luc Audonnet

Rooms 5 with bath or shower, WC, direct telephone and TV. Rooms Cleaned every day, sheets changed every 2 days. **Price** 390-440 F (1 pers.), 450-495 F (2 pers.). **Meals** Breakfast 40-65 F. Meals at separate tables 200 F (wine incl.). **Facilities** Swimming pool. **Nearby** Tennis (50m, +10F), golf (18 holes, 3km); banks of Erdre, Old Nantes, Route des Vins, La Baule (45 min.). **Credit Cards** Not accepted. **Spoken** English, Spanish. **Open** All year. **How to get there** (Map 14): 3km northeast of Nantes. Autoroute, Paris-Nantes, exit Beaujoire, then signs Le Housseau.

Although the Château du Housseau is located on the edge of Nantes, it is still in the country. The owner has just equipped the beautiful and very large guest rooms with all the modern amenities. They are handsomely decorated with furniture which is painted to match the curtains, bedspreads and carpets. Monsieur Jean-Luc Audonnet prepares the meals, which are served in a pleasant, rustic dining room, and in warm weather, breakfasts are served on the terrace facing the private park and the swimming pool. This is a beautiful place to stay for tourists as well as business people.

345
Domaine de la Morinière

44330 La Regrippière-Vallet
(Loire-Atlantique)
Tel. 40 33 61 64
Cécile and Michel Couillaud

Rooms 2 with shower and WC; rooms cleaned on request. **Price** 265F (2 pers.), 320F (3 pers.). **Meals** Breakfast incl. Special rates for stays of more than 5 days. No evening meals but kitchen available. **Restaurants** Les Voyageurs (7km), La Bonne Auberge (17km). **Facilities** Lounge, mountain biking, visits to wine cellar, hiking on property. **Pets** Dogs allowed on request. **Nearby** Riding, tennis, Clisson, banks of Loire. **Credit Cards** Not accepted. **Spoken** English. **Open** All year. **How to get there** (Map 15): 30km southeast of Nantes. Autoroute exit Ancenis, then towards Clisson to Vallet, then D756 towards Beaupréau; go 7km, then signs. Or RN249 exit Vallet, then D756.

This is a lovely small house surrounded by flowers and set in the midst of the vineyards belonging to Michel Couillaud and his brothers. The interior is immaculate and is decorated in a modern, simple style. The very pleasant bedrooms are paneled with white wood and brightened with colorful fabrics, while contemporary paintings and sculptures add a personal note. The breakfasts are excellent and the hosts are young and friendly.

346
La Plauderie

1, rue du Verdelet
44680 Sainte-Pazanne
(Loire-Atlantique)
Tel. 40 02 45 08
Mme Mignen

Rooms 3 with bath or shower and WC. Rooms cleaned every 2 days. **Price** 270-400F (2 pers.). **Meals** Breakfast 35F. No communal meal. **Restaurant** Le Col Vert in Fresnay-en-Retz. **Facilities** Lounge. **Pets** Dogs allowed on request. **Nearby** Tennis, seaside, golf, Breton marshes, Noirmoutier Island. **Credit Cards** Not accepted. **Spoken** English. **Open** May 1 – end-Oct. **How to get there** (Map 14): 28km southwest of Nantes via D751 towards Pornic. In Port Saint-Père left on D758 towards Bourgneuf-en-Retz.

Right beside the church, this beautiful house is hidden in a delightfully romantic garden. Madame Mignen's hospitality is reason enough to recommend La Plauderie, but you will also find very prettily decorated, comfortable accommodations. The bedrooms and baths are elegant, and you can make yourself a cup of coffee or tea there. This is a charming place with many interesting things to do nearby.

347
Château de la Jaillière

La Chapelle-Saint-Sauveur
44370 Varades
(Loire-Atlantique)
Tel. 40 98 62 54
Comtesse d'Anthenaise

Rooms 4 and 1 suite (4 pers.) with bath and WC. **Price** 650F (2 pers.), suite 850F (4 pers.). **Meals** Breakfast incl., evening meals at communal table 200F (wine incl.). **Facilities** Lounge, swimming pool, tennis, fishing. **Pets** Dogs not allowed. **Nearby** Riding (30km), golf. **Credit Cards** Not accepted. **Spoken** English, German. **Open** Mid-May – mid-Oct. **How to get there** (Map 15): 30km west of Angers via N23, then D30 before Varades; upon leaving La-Chapelle-Saint-Saveur head for Saint-Sigismond.

La Jaillière is an immense 19th-century estate decorated with beautiful parquet floors, paneled walls and antique furniture. The comfortably appointed bedrooms are magnificent. Evening meals are served in a lovely, spacious dining room, and Countess d'Anthenaise's kind, energetic hospitality lends further charm to the château.

348
Château des Briottières

49330 Champigné
(Maine-et-Loire)
Tel. 41 42 00 02
Fax 41 42 01 55
Hedwige and François de Valbray

Rooms 9 with bath, WC and telephone. **Price** 400-700F (2 pers.). **Meals** Breakfast 45F, half board 695F per pers. in double room. Evening meals (except Sunday) at communal table, by reservation 250F (everything incl.). **Facilities** Lounge, French billiards, heated swimming pool, boxes horse, fishing. **Nearby** Tennis, riding, golf, Solesme Abbey, Anjou. **Credit cards** Visa, Eurocard and MasterCard. **Spoken** English. **Open** All year (by reservation from Jan. 1 – March 1). **How to get there** (Map 15): 25km north of Angers towards Laval. At Montreuil-Juigné, right on D768 through Feneu, then Champigné.

The Château des Briottières is off the beaten track and merits a detour. You will be received with warm hospitality. The large reception rooms have retained many of their antique furnishings. Decorated with tasteful elegance, the bedrooms have luxurious bathrooms overlooking the park. The evening meal is excellent at this remarkable château.

349
Beauregard

22, rue Beauregard
Cunault
49350 Chênehutte-les-Tuffeaux
(Maine-et-Loire)
Tel. 41 67 92 93
M. and Mme Tonnelier

Rooms 1 suite (4 pers.) 2 bedrooms with bath and WC. **Price** 350F (2 pers.) +120F (extra pers.); suite 550F (4 pers.). **Meals** Breakfast incl. No communal meal. **Restaurants** La Toque Blanche, Le Val de Loire, Les Rosiers (5km). **Facilities** Fishing. **Pets** Small dogs allowed on request. **Nearby** Equestrian center, golf, walks, churches of Trèves-Cunault, Le Thoureil, Montreuil-Bellay, Saumur. **Credit Cards** Not accepted. **Spoken** English. **Open** Easter – Nov 1. **How to get there** (Map 15): 10km northwest of Saumur on D751 towards Gennes; before the village, on the Loire.

You leave Saumur on a small road which follows the river and grows prettier as it reaches this manor house, which is located on a slight rise and has a wonderful view. The well decorated bedrooms are very large, pretty, and overlook the Loire. Breakfast is served in the dining room, which is decorated with very beautiful Haute Epoque furniture. The owners are very friendly.

350
Le Domaine de Mestré

49590 Fontevraud-l'Abbaye
(Maine-et-Loire)
Tel. 41 51 72 32/41 51 75 87
Fax 41 51 71 90
M. and Mme Dominique Dauge

Rooms 11 and 1 suite (3 pers.) with bath and WC. **Price** 295F (2 pers.) +65F (extra pers.).
Meals Breakfast 35F, half board 297F per pers. in double room (1 week min.) Lunch and evening
meals by reservation (separate tables) 135F (wine not incl.). **Facilities** Lounge. **Pets** Small dogs
allowed. **Nearby** Tennis, riding, golf, Loire châteaux. **Credit cards** Not accepted. **Spoken** English,
German. **Closed** Dec 20 – Feb 1. **How to get there** (Maps 15 and 16): 12km southeast of Saumur
via D947 towards Chinon, then head for Fontevraud-l'Abbaye; between Montsoreau and
Fontevraud.

This beautiful house was once the farm of the monks of Fontevraud
Abbey. The comfortable bedrooms have been very prettily decorated,
while their traditional elegance has been conserved. Excellent, generous
dinners are served in a lovely dining room at elegant separate tables. (Their
price is based on the farm produce used, including meats, vegetables, and
dairy products). Perfumed soaps are also made here using an ancient process,
and they are for sale.

351
La Croix d'Etain

2, rue de l'Ecluse
49220 Grez-Neuville
(Maine-et-Loire)
Tel. 41 95 68 49
M. and Mme Bahuaud

Rooms 3 with bath and WC. **Price** 340F (2 pers.). **Meals** Breakfast incl., evening meals by
reservation 120F (wine not incl.). **Facilities** Lounge. **Nearby** Restaurants, golf (18 holes), fishing,
tennis, riding, houseboat rental, châteaux, vineyards. **Credit cards** Not accepted.
Spoken English. **Open** Easter – Nov 1. **How to get there** (Map 15): 3km southeast of Lion
d'Angers. N162 from Angers towards Laval. In Grez-Neuville, between church and La Mayenne.

This distinctive house in old Grez-Neuville has been entirely restored
and has pleasant modern amenities. The bedrooms are quite modern,
spacious and light because of their corner location; they are very tastefully
furnished. In good weather you can enjoy the large park behind the house
or stroll along the banks of the Mayenne, which is only a few steps away.
The owners are very pleasant.

352
Château du Plessis

49220 La Jaille-Yvon
(Maine-et-Loire)
Tel. 41 95 12 75
Fax 41 95 14 41
Paul and Simone Benoist

Rooms 8 (2 with balcony) with bath and WC. **Price** 720F (2 pers.). **Meals** Breakfast incl., half board 610F per pers. in double room. Evening meals (except Sunday) at communal table, by reservation 270F (everything incl.). **Facilities** Lounge, telephone, tennis, boxes horse, hot-air ballooning. **Pets** Dogs allowed on request. **Credit cards** All major. **Spoken** English, Spanish. **Open** March 1 – Oct 31. **How to get there** (Map 15): 11km north of Lion-d'Angers via N162. At Fleur-de-Lys take D189; sign at the crossroads.

Madame Benoist loves flowers, and fresh bouquets adorn the Château du Plessis throughout the seasons. Your hosts are naturally hospitable and Monsieur Benoist is expert at advising guests on touring the region. The bedrooms are very well decorated and the bathrooms irreproachable. You will enjoy delicious evening meals, which are served in a lovely dining room with 1930s frescos.

353
Préfontaine

49430 Lézigné
(Maine-et-Loire)
Tel. 41 76 97 71
Mme O'Neill

Rooms 3 and 2 suites with bath and WC. **Price** 350-400F (1-2 pers.), suite 400-550F (4 pers.). **Meals** Breakfast incl., evening meals at communal table 120F (wine incl.). **Facilities** Lounge, fishing in the lake. **Pets** Dogs allowed. **Nearby** Golf, swimming pool, tennis, bathing in the Loir. **Spoken** English. **Closed** Jan. and Feb. **How to get there** (Map 15): 30km northeast of Angers on N23 towards Durtal; signposted.

Préfontaine is a lovely house set in a large well-kept park with many trees. The interior is tastefully decorated with elegant furnishings. The bedrooms are pleasant, bright, and quiet despite the proximity of the road, which can only be heard outside. Good evening meals are served in an elegant dining room. You will receive a warm welcome.

354
Château du Goupillon

49680 Neuillé
(Maine-et-Loire)
Tel. 41 52 51 89
Monique Calot

Rooms 2 and 1 suite (5 pers.) with bath or shower and WC. **Price** 290-420F (2 pers.) +60F (extra pers.), suite 700F (5 pers.). **Meals** Breakfast incl. No evening meals. **Restaurants** Many in Saumur. **Facilities** Lounge. **Pets** Dogs allowed on request. **Nearby** Swimming pool, tennis, golf, Loire châteaux. **Credit cards** Not accepted. **Open** All year. **How to get there** (Map 15): 9km north of Saumur towards Longué direction. At the La Ronde traffic circle take D767 towards Vernantes for 2km, then left on D129 towards Neuillé. 1km before Neuillé take the Fontaine Suzon road, then follow signs.

Close to Saumur in the midst of luxuriant vegetation, this château seems completely preserved from the modern world. The decor is simple and beautiful, with antique wood paneling, bouquets of dried flowers, upholstered walls and beautiful antique furniture. Some bedrooms are small and charming, while others are immense; they are prettily decorated and have pleasant bathrooms. Your host is the model of kindness.

355
Moulin de Rabion

49490 Noyant
(Maine-et-Loire)
Tel. 41 89 32 80
Fax The same
Antonia and Edward Hoogewerf

Rooms 2 with bath or shower and WC. **Price** 300F (2 pers.). **Meals** Breakfast incl., evening meals at communal or separate tables 90F (wine incl.), 50F (children under 10). **Facilities** Lounge, river fishing and 2 horse stalls on property. **Pets** Dogs allowed in kennel. **Nearby** Tennis, swimming pool, water sports (10km), golf (18 holes, 15km), châteaux and vineyards of Loire, Sound and Light at Le Lude. **Credit cards** Not accepted. **Spoken** English, Spanish. **Open** All year (by reservation from Oct to April). **How to get there** (Map 16): 20km north of Saumur via D767 towards Le Mans; then go towards Noyant-Vernantes. After Vernantes, go 8km to Linières-Bouton intersection; then go straight ahead; house 1km farther on D767, on right.

The Moulin de Rabion is an authentic bed and breakfast which is run by an informal, very friendly English couple. Located in a large private park which is traversed by a small stream, the Moulin is decorated very elegantly with handsome old furniture and English-style wallpapers and fabrics. The house is very comfortable but lacks soundproofing in places. (The blue room is an exception). There is a pretty view of the trees and shrubs, and the communal dinners are very pleasant.

356
Le Verger
de la Bouquetterie

118, rue du Roi-René
49250 Saint-Mathurin-sur-Loire
(Maine-et-Loire)
Tel. 41 57 02 00 - Fax 41 57 31 90
Claudine Pinier

Rooms 4 with shower and WC. Special rates for more than 3 days. **Price** 190-240 (1 pers.), 250-300F (2 pers.). **Meals** Breakfast incl., evening meals at communal table by reservation 105F (wine incl.). **Facilities** Lounge. **Pets** Dogs not allowed. **Nearby** Fishing in Loire, swimming pool, tennis, riding, water sports, mountain biking, hiking; châteaux of Loire, troglodyte and sculptured caves, Route des Vins. **Credit cards** Not accepted. **Spoken** English, Italian. **Open** All year. **How to get there** (Map 15): 20km southeast of Angers via D952 (touristic route along Loire), towards Saumur; 1km before Saint-Mathurin-sur-Loire.

If it weren't for the road in front, Le Verger de la Bouquetterie would be right on the Loire. However, the sound of the traffic is not disturbing due to efficient double windows in the bedrooms. The great attractions here are the splendid view of the river and the interior decoration which includes charming 19th-century furniture. Behind the Verger, the lovely garden seems lost in the midst of an immense orchard. Monsieur and Madame Pinier will make you feel very much at home. And their breakfasts are excellent.

357
La Croix de la Voulte

Route de Boumois
Sainte-Lambert-des-Levées
49400 Saumur
(Maine-et-Loire)
Tel. 41 38 46 66
M. and Mme Jean-Pierre Minder

Rooms 4 with bath or shower and WC. **Price** 330-430F (2 pers.). **Meals** Breakfast 35F. No evening meals. **Restaurants** Le Relais, Les Forges de Saint-Pierre in Saumur (5km) and La Toque Blanche in Rosier-sur-Loire (9km). **Facilities** Lounge, swimming pool. **Pets** Dogs allowed on request. **Nearby** Golf, Saumur, Fontevraud, Langeais, Boumois, Montreuil-Bellay. **Credit cards** Not accepted. **Spoken** English, German. **Open** Mide-April – mid-Oct. **How to get there** (Map 15): 4km north of Saumur via D952, then D229; signposted after the railway.

This is a lovely group of houses made of native limestone; all are very old and have been beautifully restored. The bedrooms are tastefully decorated, with antique furniture lending each a special style. Breakfasts are truly delicious and are charmingly served on a flower-filled terrace, or in a small dining room. There is no lounge, but the bedrooms are spacious, and in good weather you can enjoy the park, which has plenty of garden furniture.

358
Domaine du Marconnay

Route de Saumur – Parnay
49400 Saumur
(Maine-et-Loire)
Tel. 41 67 60 46
Fax 41 50 23 04
M. and Mme Goumain

Rooms 3 and 1 suite (4 pers.) with bath or shower and WC. **Price** 250-300F (2 pers.), +65F (extra pers.). **Meals** Breakfast 30F; evening meals at separate tables by reservation 80F (wine not incl.). **Facilities** Lounge with TV; swimming pool, visit to wine cellar and tasting, troglodyte caves on property. **Pets** Dogs allowed on request. **Nearby** Golf (18 holes, 7km); banks of Loire (200m), Saumur, Montsoreau, Fontevraud, Ussé, châteaux of Loire. **Credit cards** Not accepted. **Spoken** English, German. **Open** April 1 – mid-Nov. **How to get there** (Map 15): 6km east of Saumur. In Saumur, D947 towards Chinon, then 6km and signs.

At the Domaine du Marconnay you will find the three characteristic features of Saumur and its region: beautiful red Saumur-Champigny wine; houses made of local white limestone and the famous troglodyte caves. The bedrooms are simple and pleasant and are located in the house facing the château. (Families will enjoy the rooms under the eaves.) The château, 15th- and 18th-centuries, is hollowed out in the rock, forming an incredible labyrinth of caves. The Domaine is located in a lovely private park surrounded by the old houses of this charming village on the banks of the Loire.

359
Mirvault

Azé
53200 Château-Gontier
(Mayenne)
Tel. 43 07 10 82
Brigitte and François d'Ambières

Rooms 2 with bath and WC, and 2 spare rooms. **Price** 300F (1 pers.), 350F (2 pers.). **Meals** Breakfast incl. No evening meals. Restaurant nearby, on other bank of river (1km). **Facilities** Lounge, pond and river (boating, swimming, sailing), bikes on property. **Pets** Dogs not allowed. **Nearby** Golf (18 holes, 30km), tennis (100m), swimming pool (100m), cruise boats on the Mayenne; church and museum of Château-Gontier, Tatin Museum. **Credit cards** Not accepted. **Spoken** English. **Open** Apr. 1 – Nov. 1. **How to get there** (Map 15): 1km from Château-Gontier, towards Laval via bypass; at last traffic circle follow signs. Road 50m from traffic circle.

It would be difficult to imagine a more beautiful location for this residence, surrounded by lush foliage on the banks of the Mayenne River and yet only a stone's throw from the picturesque 11th-century village of Château Gontier. You will be greeted with warm hospitality to Mirvault, which is furnished with good taste and imagination, very much in the spirit of the 18th-century. The bedrooms are beautiful and comfortable. (Those on the *second étage* are perfect for families). In the evening, you can enjoy a free boat ride to the good, small restaurant located on the opposite bank of the river.

360
Château du Bas du Gast

6, rue de la Halle aux Toiles
53000 Laval
(Mayenne)
Tel. 43 49 22 79
Fax 43 56 44 71
M. and Mme Williot

Rooms 3 with bath and WC, 1 suite (4 pers.) with bath and shower, WC. Price 550-650F (2 pers.); suite 1150F (2 pers.), +150F (children), +250F (extra pers.). **Meals** Breakfast 45F, 70F (English). No evening meals poss. snack avalaible on request. 5 good restaurants in Laval. **Facilities** Lounge. **Pets** Dogs allowed on request. **Nearby** Golf (27 holes, 4km), swimming pools, cruising, fishing, riding, tourist information at château. **Credit cards** Not accepted. **Spoken** English. **Closed** Dec., Jan. **How to get there** (Map 7): In Laval.

Built in the purest 18th-century classical style, this is a splendid mansion located in the heart of Laval, a pretty town on the banks of the Mayenne. Monsieur and Madame Williot are very friendly and will be delighted to tell you the history of their château. The bedrooms are very beautiful and comfortable with handsome family furniture, old engravings, and elegantly coordinated fabrics and wallpapers. The high windows of the suite look out over a formal garden which looks the way it did in the time of Louis XV.

361
Villeprouvé

53170 Ruillé-Froid-Fonds
(Mayenne)
Tel. 43 07 71 62
M. and Mme Davenel

Rooms 5 with bath or shower and WC. **Price** 150F (1 pers.), 220F (2 pers.). **Meals** Breakfast incl., half board 180F per pers. in double room, evening meals at communal table 70F (wine not incl.). **Facilities** Lounge, fishing. **Pets** Dogs allowed on request. **Nearby** Monasteries of Solesmes, La Trappe. **Credit cards** Not accepted. **Spoken** English. **Open** All year. **How to get there** (Map 15): 25km south of Laval via N162 to Villiers-Charlemagne, then D109; signposted in the village.

This farmhouse is as lovely as the natural surroundings in which it stands. The bedrooms are comfortable and large, with rustic furniture and pretty bathrooms. Only home-grown farm produce is used in the excellent evening meals, which are cheerfully served by Mme Davenel, and the *grog flambé au calvados* is spectacular (and delicious). You will find a lovely country atmosphere at Villeprouvé.

362
Le Logis
et les Attelages du Ray

53290 Saint-Denis-d'Anjou
(Mayenne)
Tel. 43 70 64 10
Fax 43 70 65 53
Martine and Jacques Lefebvre

Rooms 3 with shower and WC. **Price** 300-350F (2 pers.), 480F (3 pers.) +50F (extra pers.). **Meals** Breakfast incl. No communal meal. **Restaurants** Auberge du Roi René and La Calèche (800m). **Facilities** Lounge, riding, mountain bicycles; theme weekend with table d'hôtes, horsedrawn-carriage school (with picnic). **Pets** Dogs allowed on request. **Nearby** Golf, tennis, swimming pool (10km), fishing, Solesmes abbey, châteaux, river trips, medieval villages. **Credit cards** Visa, Eurocard and MasterCard. **Spoken** English. **Open** All year. **How to get there** (Map 15): 9km southeast of Sablé-sur-Sarthe via D27 towards Angers; in Saint-Denis-d'Anjou, follow signs "Chambres d'Hôtes."

In this old restored farmhouse you will find numerous pieces of beautiful country furniture: M. Lefebvre is a cabinet maker and antiques dealer. The bedrooms are very comfortable and have been decorated in good taste (especially the room with the canopied bed). In summer M. Lefebvre, an enthusiastic horseman, will invite you for a carriage ride. Unfortunately, there is, as of yet, no lounge for guests.

363
La Maison du Roi René

4, Grande-Rue
53290 Saint-Denis-d'Anjou
(Mayenne)
Tel. 43 70 52 30
Fax 43 70 58 75
M.-C. and P. de Vaubernier

Rooms 3 with bath and WC. Special rates for long stays. **Price** 400F (2 pers.). **Meals** Breakfast 50F; restaurant on property, menus: 90-250F, also à la carte. **Nearby** Tennis in village, swimming pool (5km), golf (27 holes, 5km), carriage rides (weekends); Malicorne pottery factory, Solesmes Abbey, Lion d'Angers stud farm, river boating. **Credit cards** Not accepted. **Spoken** English, Italian, German. **Open** All year. **How to get there** (Map 15): 10km south of Sablé towards Angers. In the village in front of antiques shop. Or TGV train to Sablé: 1 hour 15. mins. from Paris.

Located in a medieval village, this 15th-century house has three delightful bedrooms which are beautiful, comfortable an still have much of their old charm. There is an excellent restaurant on the park floor where a fire is permanently ablaze in the monumental fireplace. In the summer, drinks and meals are served in the flower-filled garden. You will be warmly received at "King René's House."

364
Le Chêne Vert

Chammes
53270 Sainte-Suzanne
Tel. 43 01 41 12
Fax 43 01 47 18
M. and Mme Morize

Rooms 6 with shower and WC. Rooms cleaned every 3 days. **Price** 210F (2 pers.). **Meals** Breakfast incl., half board 160F per pers. in double room (out of season, 3 days min.), evening meals at communal table 70F (cidre incl.). **Facilities** Library, walking path, swimming pool, children's play area. **Pets** Dogs allowed on request. **Nearby** Golf, Château de Mézanger, Solesmes Abbey, medieval village of Sainte-Suzanne. **Credit cards** Not accepted. **Spoken** English. **Open** All year. **How to get there** (Map 7): 45km west of Le Mans via A81 towards Laval, exit Vaiges. In Vaiges, left on D125 towards Sainte-Suzanne until Chammes.

Close to the medieval village of Sainte-Suzanne, this old farmhouse has been completely renovated. The three pretty guestrooms are attractive with colorful, fresh fabrics, handsome furniture and well-equipped shower rooms. Breakfast and evening meals are served in a large rustic room with a bar-kitchenette area. The owners are young and friendly.

365
Château le Grand-Perray

72500 La Bruère
(Sarthe)
Tel. 43 46 72 65
M. and Mme Thibault

Rooms 8 with bath or shower and WC. **Price** 320-450F (2 pers.). **Meals** Breakfast 35F, evening meals at communal table (price to be agreed). **Facilities** Lounge, elevator, fishing, golf practice. **Pets** Dogs allowed on request. **Nearby** Tennis, swimming pool, Loir Valley, visit to wine cellars, Château du Lude (sound and light show, June – Sept.). **Credit cards** Not accepted. **Spoken** English. **Open** All year. **How to get there** (Map 16): 40km south of Le Mans via N138 towards Tours, then right on D11 towards La Bruère-sur-Loir until Croix de Bonlieu (5km after Château du Loir); signs on D11.

This château, part of which is medieval, lies deep in the forest. The bedrooms are very beautiful and vary in size depending on which floor they are on. All have antique furniture and pretty fabrics. Those with a taste for the Middle Ages should ask for the bedroom in the tower. There is a pleasant lounge and a large dining room for breakfast and evening meals. The owners are very hospitable.

366
Garencière

72610 Champfleur
(Sarthe)
Tel. 33 31 75 84
Denis and Christine Langlais

Rooms 5 with bath or shower and WC. **Price** 150F (1 pers.), 220-250F (2 pers.). **Meals** Breakfast incl., half board 200F per pers. in double room. Lunch and evening meal at communal table 90F (wine incl.). **Facilities** Lounge, telephone, mountain biking. **Pets** Dogs allowed on request. **Nearby** Swimming pool, riding, fishing, Saint-Ceneri (historic village) Le Pin stud farm. **Credit cards** Not accepted. **Spoken** English. **Open** All year. **How to get there** (Map 8): 5km southeast of Alençon via N138 towards Le Mans, then left on D55 towards Champfleur.

Y ou will be warmly welcomed to this hillside farmhouse. The bedrooms are tastefully decorated with prettily colored fabrics and old-fashioned furniture. The small house is ideal for families; the ground floor is rustic and we especially loved the lovely upstairs bedroom. Breakfast and dinner are served in a bright dining room. The excellent cuisine is made with products from the farm.

367
Manoir du Ronceray

72220 Marigné-Laillé
(Sarthe)
Tel. 43 42 12 05
M. and Mme Madamet

Rooms 4 with bath or shower, all sharing WC. **Price** 350-380F (2 pers.). **Meals** Breakfast incl. No evening meals. **Restaurants** In Jupilles (4km). **Facilities** Lounge, boxes horse, fishing. **Pets** Dogs not allowed. **Nearby** Tennis, golf. **Spoken** English. **Open** Mid-April – mid-Nov. **How to get there** (Map 16): 30km south of Le Mans via N138 to Ecommoy, then Marigné-Laillé and D96 for 2km towards Pruillé-L'Eguillé.

R onceray is the perfect model of a manor house: small, very old, and very charming. The vaulted entrance hall is hung with hunting and old military trophies. The bedrooms, less austere, are comfortable and light, with lovely fabrics, antique furniture, beds in alcoves, and round bathrooms in the towers. Breakfast is served in an antique paneled room. The owners of this beautiful place are hospitable and friendly.

368
Château de Saint-Paterne

72610 Saint-Paterne
(Sarthe)
Tel. 33 27 54 71
Fax 33 29 16 71
Charles-Henry de Valbray

Rooms 3 and 3 suites (3 pers.) with bath or shower and WC. **Price** 450-750F (2 pers.), garret 450F 1800F the week, 4th night free. **Meals** Breakfast 45F, evening meals at communal table, by reservation 250F (wine incl.). **Facilities** Lounge, tennis, loose boxes. **Pets** Small dogs allowed on request. **Nearby** Swimming pool, riding, Mont-Saint-Michel. **Credit Cards** Amex, Visa, Eurocard and MasterCard. **Spoken** English. **Open** March 1 – mid-Dec. (by reservation out of season). **How to get there** (Map 8): 2km southwest of Alençon on D311 towards Mamers-Chartres; in Saint-Paterne.

The village of Saint-Paterne is on the edge of Alençon, but the château is secluded behind a beautiful walled park. With youthful enthusiasm, the owner has completely restored it and will welcome you warmly. The lounges and the huge, very comfortable bedrooms are decorated with beautiful antiques and lovely fabrics. There are beautiful, luxurious bathrooms. Dinner by candlelight further enhances the charm of this magnificent place.

369
Le Fresne

Route de Beaucé
72300 Solesmes
(Sarthe)
Tel. 43 95 92 55
Marie-Armelle and Pascal Lelièvre

Rooms 3 with bath or shower and WC. **Price** 230-260F (2 pers.), +70F (extra pers.). **Meals** Breakfast incl. (brunch); meals at communal table 100F (wine incl.). **Facilities** Fishing in pond on property. **Pets** Dogs allowed on request. **Nearby** Golf (27 holes, 14km), riding, boating on Sarthe River (600m), Asnières-sur-Vègre, Solesme Abbey, Malicorne pottery factory. **Credit cards** Not accepted. **Spoken** English, German. **Open** All year. **How to get there** (Map 15): 7km east of Sablé towards Solesmes; follow signs beginning at pharmacy. House in 3km. (TGV train station in 7km).

Le Fresne enjoys a peaceful country location near the Sarthe River not far from the village of Solesmes and its famous Benedictine Abbey. The owners are young, informal and refined, and they have just opened their comfortable residence to guests. The bedrooms are very tastefully decorated with colorful fabrics, light woodwork and terra cotta floors. The rooms have immaculate, beautifully tiled bathrooms which open directly onto the outside. The living room is pleasant and the prices are very reasonable.

370
Le Domaine du Grand Gruet

Route de Challes
72440 Volnay
(Sarthe)
Tel. 43 35 68 65/43 89 87 27
Mme Eveno-Sournia

Rooms 3 rooms and 2 suites with bath or shower and WC, 2 studios with kitchenette, shower and WC (for longer stays). Rooms cleaned on request. **Price** 350-550F (2 pers.) +70F (extra pers.). **Meals** Breakfast incl., brunch 35F, evening meals by reservation or restaurant nearby (6km). **Restaurant** In the village. **Facilities** Lounges. **Pets** Dogs not allowed. **Nearby** Equestrian center, lakes, tennis, golf, Loir valley. **Credit cards** Not accepted. **Spoken** German. **Open** Mid-Feb – end-Dec. (in winter on request). **How to get there** (Map 16): Chartres Autoroute A11, exit Ferté-Bernard towards Le Mans. At Connerré, towards Grand Lucé for 15km. At Volnay take D90 towards Challes. In 600m on left, dirt path.

A nne Sournia is a painter and has restored this beautiful house with an expert eye. Everything has been made by her artist friends, from the ashtrays to the enameled washbasins. The overall decor is bright, modern and comfortable. No two bedrooms are alike and each has a charm of its own. The lounge and dining room also serve as art galleries. This is a beautiful, quiet place where you will be warmly welcomed.

371
Manoir de Ponsay

Saint-Mars-des-Prés
85110 Chantonay
(Vendée)
Tel. 51 46 96 71
Fax 51 94 56 12
M. and Mme de Ponsay

Rooms 8 with bath or shower and WC. **Price** 350-550F (2 pers.), suite 600F (2-3 pers.). **Meals** Breakfast (brunch) 40F. Evening meals at communal or separate table 170F (wine incl.). **Facilities** Lounge, telephone. **Nearby** Swimming pool, tennis, seaside, golf, Ile d'Yeu, Poitou marshes. **Pets** Dogs not allowed. **Credit cart** Amex. **Spoken** English, German. **Open** April – Nov. 30 (on request in winter). **How to get there** (Map 15): 35km east of La Roche-sur-Yon via D948 and D949 bis to Chantonnay and Saint-Mars-des-Prés; signposted.

F ar out in the beautiful rolling countryside, amid pastures where horses and cows graze, you will find this perfect 17th-century manor house. Some bedrooms are simple, others luxurious, but all are comfortable and have beautiful bathrooms. Excellent breakfasts are served in a beautiful dining room.

372
Logis de Chalusseau

111, rue de Chalusseau
85200 Doix
(Vendée)
Tel. 51 51 81 12
M. and Mme Gérard Baudry

Rooms 2 with bath or shower and WC. Rooms cleaned every three days. **Price** 180F (1 pers.), 220F (2 pers.) +50F (extra pers.). **Meals** Breakfast incl. No evening meals (independent kitchen for guests). **Facilities** Lounge. **Pets** Dogs not allowed. **Nearby** Swimming pool, tennis, seaside (40km), riding, golf, Poitou marshes, Forest of Mervent, Romanesque art, Maillezais Abbey, Nieul-sur-L'Autize Cloisters. **Credit cards** Not accepted. **Open** April 1 – mid-Nov. (2 nights min.). **How to get there** (Map 15): 9km south of Fontenay-le-Comte via D938 towards La Rochelle, then left on D20 after 4km towards Doix.

The vast reception rooms in this very beautiful 17th-century Vendée house still have their original exposed beams and stone fireplaces. The bedrooms are very spacious, bright and are prettily decorated with charming regional furniture. The hearty breakfasts can be served in the pleasant garden. This is a special place in a lovely location where you will be made to feel at home.

373
Le Petit Marais des Broches

7, chemin des Tabernaudes
85350 L'Ile d'Yeu
(Vendée)
Tel. 51 58 42 43
Chantal and Jean-Marcel Hobma

Rooms 5 (2 with mezzanine) with shower and WC. **Price** 340F (2 pers.) +100F (extra pers.). **Meals** Breakfast incl.; meals at communal table 110F (wine incl.). **Facilities** Children's swimming pool, tennis, fishing, boat rides on property. **Nearby** Beach (300m), biking, mountain biking, water sports, riding, tennis, summer concerts, small museums. **Open** All year. **How to get there** (Map 14): northeast of island. 300m from Anse des Broches. Boat from Noirmoutier Island (information 51 39 00 00); or from Saint-Gilles Croix de Vie (information 51 54 15 15).

Le Petit Marais des Broches is located in a sublime protected site on the Ile d'Yeu near the sea. Newly decorated, the bedrooms are elegantly simple with cedar wardrobes, blue-and-white printed eiderdowns and pretty bathrooms. Two rooms have a mezzanine for children. The couple are very friendly and Madame Hobma is an excellent cook; her delicious fish dinners are made with the catch-of-the day and served on the terrace in good weather. You can rent bikes in Port Joinville and tour this beautiful island. This B&B is a true find.

374
Le Logis d'Elpénor

5, rue de la Rivière
85770 Le Gué-de-Velluire
(Vendée)
Tel. 51 52 59 10
Christiane Ribert

Rooms 5 with bath or shower, WC (TV on request). **Price** 190F (1 pers.), 250F (2 pers.) +60F (extra pers.). **Meals** Breakfast incl., evening meals at communal table 80F (wine incl.). **Facilities** Lounge, fishing in river on property. **Pets** Dogs not allowed. **Nearby** Hiking, tennis (5km), biking, boat rental, Poitou marshes, Maison du Petit Poitou, Mervent National Forest, villages of Nieul-sur-Autize, Vouvrant (historic site) and Maillezais. **Credit cards** Not accepted. **Closed** Dec. 1. to March 1. **How to get there** (Map 15): 45km southwest of Niort and 30km northeast of La Rochelle. From Niort N148 towards Fontenay-le-Comte, then D938 ter, towards La Rochelle. From La Rochelle, N137 towards Nantes, then in Marans D938 ter, towards Fontenay-le-Comte.

L e Logis, which is located on a quiet village street, is simple and charming. There are terra cotta floors (particularly lovely on the stairway), antiqued wood doors, wide-board parquet floors, and the bedrooms are bright, cheerful and generally quite large. There is a pleasant walled garden behind which a path runs along the waters of the Vendée. The Marais Poitevin, (Poitou marshes) truly merits a stay. The family cooking is delicious and the hosts are very friendly.

375
Chez Mme Bonnet

69, rue de l'Abbaye
85420 Maillezais
(Vendée)
Tel. 51 87 23 00
Mme Liliane Bonnet

Rooms 4 with shower and WC. **Price** 310F (2 pers.), 400F (4 pers.). **Meals** Breakfast incl. No evening meals. **Restaurants** L'Auberge Maraîchère in Mazeau and farmhouse-auberge in Saint-Michel-de-Cloucq. **Facilities** Lounge (library), children's swimming pool, tennis, fishing, boating trips, private enclosed parking. **Pets** Dogs not allowed. **Nearby** Riding, Forest of Mervent-Vouvant, Maillezais and Nieul Abbeys, Coulon, La Rochelle, Ile de Ré. **Spoken** English, Spanish. **Open** All year (2 nights min.). **How to get there** (Map 15): 28km northwest of Niort via N148 towards Fontenay-le-Comte, then left on D15 to Maillezais.

T his elegant Vendée house is hidden in a splendid park bordered by a canal where you will find a boat waiting to take you through the marshes. The comfortable bedrooms are charming, with old furniture and lovely bathrooms. There is also a pretty dining room where excellent breakfasts are served – they are served outside in summer – and a spacious lounge. Madame Bonnet is very hospitable.

376
Le Logis de la Cornelière
85200 Mervent
(Vendée)
Tel. 51 00 29 25
Lise and Jean–Raymond
de Larocque Latour

Rooms 3 and 1 suite (4 pers.) with bath and WC. **Price** 400-500F (2 pers.) +100F (extra pers.); suite 600F (3 pers.). **Meals** Breakfast 40F (brunch); meals at communal table by reservation ab. 120F. **Facilities** Lounge, mushroom gathering in forest (12,355 acres), mountain biking on property. **Nearby** Riding (5km), Mervent Lake, rock climbing, Poitou marshes, villages of Vouvant and Foussais. **Spoken** English. **Open** All year. **How to get there** (Map 15): 13km northeast of Fontenay-le-Comte; in Fontenay, towards Bressuire, then road to Mervent; go through Mervent and continue to Les Ouillières; then towards La Châtaigneraie for 3km; signs.

The Cornelière, a stunning spectacle with its old roofs and golden stones, lies in a lovely valley on the edge of a beautiful forest. The interior has retained all of its old charm, with antique furniture, family objects and beautiful sculpted fireplaces. The bedrooms are vast, comfortable and very tastefully decorated. The owners will make you feel at home in their beautiful residence.

377
Le Château
85450 Moreilles
(Vendée)
Tel. 51 56 17 56
Fax 51 56 30 30
Mme Danièle Renard

Rooms 8 with bath or shower, WC and telephone. **Price** 350F (1 pers.), 400-450F (2 pers.). **Meals** Breakfast 45F, half board 400-450F per pers. in double room, evening meals (separate tables) 185F (wine not incl.). **Facilities** Swimming pool. **Pets** Dogs allowed on request. **Nearby** Tennis, riding, fishing, golf (18 holes, 25km), La Rochelle, Poitou marshes. **Spoken** English. **Open** All year (on request Oct – March). **How to get there** (Map 15): 35km north of La Rochelle via the Nantes road N137; on N137 at the entrance to the village on the right.

In this large, welcoming house the bedrooms are cozy and prettily decorated with period furniture. If you reserve in advance, you can sleep in the deliciously old–fashioned bed of "Belle Otero", the queen of Maxim's in the Belle Epoque. In the dining-room, breakfast and dinner are served under the benevolent eye of Mme Renard. There is a pretty garden, but some traffic noise can be heard here. The staff is particularly friendly.

378
Le Castel du Verger

85670 Saint-Christophe-du-
Ligneron
(Vendée)
Tel. 51 93 04 14/51 93 10 62
Telex 700 846 chamco F
M. and Mme H. A. Gouon

Rooms 6 and 1 suite with bath and WC. **Price** 300-350F (2 pers.) +50F (extra pers.).
Meals Breakfast 35F, half board 600-660F per couple in a double room (2 days min.), evening
meals and lunch at separate tables 120-180F (wine not incl.). **Facilities** Lounge, bikes, heated
swimming pool, fishing in the lakes. **Pets** Dogs allowed (extra charge). **Nearby** Tennis (500m),
riding, golf (15km), Islands of Noirmoutier and Yeu. **Spoken** English. **Open** All year.
How to get there (Map 14): 10km southeast of Challans on D948; 30km before La Roche-sur-
Yon.

From the courtyard of this imposing Vendée château, you will enjoy a view of the beautiful lawn, flowers, and the swimming pool, and you will forget there is a road below. Protected by thick walls, the bedrooms are quiet and comfortable, and decorated in antique style. (We preferred the ones with Jouy fabrics on the walls.) M. and Mme Gouon are very welcoming and serve excellent evening meals made with fresh farm products. The guest book is filled with compliments for the cook.

379
Château de la Millière

85150 Saint-Mathurin
(Vendée)
Tel. 51 22 73 29
Claude and Danielle Huneault

Rooms 4, incl. 1 suite, with bath and WC. 2 rooms heated. **Price** 500F (2 pers.), +100F (extra
pers.); suite 750F (4 pers.). **Meals** Breakfast 40F; evening meals by reservation before noon
(poss. separate tables) 170F (wine incl.). **Facilities** Lounge, swimming pool, lake, French
billiards, poss. horse boxes on the property. **Pets** Small dogs allowed on request. **Nearby** Golf
(18 holes); salt marshes, Saint-Gilles, La Rochelle, Noirmoutier. **Spoken** English. **Open** May
through Sept. incl. **How to get there** (Map 14): 8km north of Les Sables d'Olonne via N160 on
the La Mothe-Achard-Les Sables d'Olonne road; 1km on right before Saint-Mathurin.

You will enjoy a splendid view from the beautiful 19th-century Château de la Millière which overlooks a private park with large trees and a lake. The interior has been newly restored, combining various kinds of furniture with a profusion of carpets. The very comfortable bedrooms are vast, the bathrooms are luxurious and the château, where you will be warmly welcomed, is beautifully quiet.

380
Le Fief Mignoux

85120 Saint-Maurice-des-Noués
(Vendée)
Tel. 51 00 81 42
M. and Mme Schnepf

Rooms 2 sharing bathroom with shower and WC. Rooms cleaned every three days. **Price** 250F (2 pers.) +50F (extra pers.). **Meals** Breakfast incl. No evening meals. **Restaurant** Auberge de Maître Pannetier. **Pets** Dogs not allowed. **Nearby** Tennis, riding, lake, golf, Forest of Mervent, Poitou marshes, Maillezais Abbey. **Credit cards** Not accepted. **Spoken** English, German. **Open** May 1 – Nov 1. **How to get there** (Map 15): 25km northeast of Fontenay-le-Comte via D938 towards La Châtaigneraie. In L'Alouette take D30 towards Vouvant. After Saint-Maurice-des-Noués right on D67 towards Puy-de-Serre.

L e Fief Mignoux is a charming 17th-century Vendée house which is filled with light and surrounded by two gardens full of flowers. The main bedroom is immense, bright, and very pleasantly furnished in country style; there is a private shower room opposite. For families or groups, it is possible to annex a second bedroom which is large and beautiful. The owners are very welcoming.

381
Château de la Cacaudière

85410 Thouarsais-Bouildroux
(Vendée)
Tel. 51 51 59 27
Fax 51 51 30 61
M. and Mme Montalt

Rooms 5 (2 with twin beds) and 2 suites (3-4 pers.) with bath or shower, WC; telephone in 3 rooms, TV on request. **Price** 400F (1 pers.), 450-650F (2 pers.), 750F (3 pers.). **Meals** Breakfast incl. Evening meals at communal or separate tables 170F (wine incl.). **Facilities** Lounges, billiards, bar, piano, telephone. **Pets** Small dogs only allowed on request. **Nearby** Tennis, riding, lake fishing, golf (18 holes, 45km); Vouvrant, Maillezais, Le Puy-du-Fou, Poitou marshes. **Credit cards** All major. **Spoken** English, German, Spanish. **Closed** From Sept. 30 to May 1. **How to get there** (Map 15): 20km north of Fontenay-le-Comte via D 23 towards Bressuire; 4km after Saint-Cyr-des-Gâts, take GC39 on right towards Thouarsais-Bouildroux. Château in first small village in front of the barn.

L a Cacaudière is a small, charming 19th-century château set in a lovely park filled with trees. It is furnished with antiques, and the salon, billard room and dining room are at your disposal. The bedrooms have been entirely renovated; they are extremely comfortable and subtly decorated with English wallpapers, elegant fabrics and very tasteful furniture. You will find a romantic atmosphere here, and very friendly hosts.

382
La Ferme de Léchelle

Hameau de Léchelle
02200 Berzy-le-Sec
(Aisne)
Tel. 23 74 83 29
Fax 23 74 82 47
Nicole and Jacques Maurice

Rooms 2 with bath or shower and WC; 2 rooms share 1 shower and WC. **Price** 180-220F (1 pers.), 200-250F (2 pers.). **Meals** Breakfast incl. Half- and full-board poss. for 2 days min.; evening meals at communal table by reservation 90F (wine not incl.). **Facilities** Lounge, pool, bikes on property. **Nearby** Golf (18 holes, 30km), tennis, forest, riding, Romanesque churches, archaeological tours, Château de Longpont. **Credit cards** Not accepted. **Spoken** English, Spanish **Open** All year (by reservation from Nov. to April). **How to get there** (Map 2 and 10): 10km south of Soisson via N2 towards Paris. At Cravançon intersection, turn left on D172 towards Oulchy-le-Château for 4km, then go left on D177 towards Lechelle; in the village.

Built on a 12th-century foundation, this opulent farm is outstanding in many ways, including its magnificent garden, its harmonious, elegant interior decoration and the owners' warm hospitality. The guest rooms are homey, comfortable and look out over a beautiful wooded countryside. The excellent, very generous breakfasts are served in a bright room with a beautiful, large fireplace and antique fruitwood furniture. Superb dinners are prepared with poultry and vegetables from the farm.

383
Le Clos

Chérêt
02860 Bruyères-et-Montberault
(Aisne)
Tel. 23 24 80 64
M. and Mme Simonnot

Rooms 1 with bath and WC, 3 sharing shower and WC, and 1 suite (2-5 pers.) with bath and WC. **Price** 200-250F (2 pers.) +80F (extra pers.). **Meals** Breakfast incl., evening meals at communal table 80F (wine incl.). **Facilities** Lounge. **Pets** Dogs not allowed. **Nearby** Tennis, swimming pool, golf, medieval town of Laon, Saint-Gobain forest. **Credit cards** Not accepted. **Open** Mid-April – mid-Oct. **How to get there** (Maps 3 and 10): 8km south of Laon via D967 towards Fismes, then D903; signposted.

Surrounded by lovely countryside, Le Clos is a 17th-century house which once was where were brought to be crushed for wine. The family atmosphere is friendly, cultured and countrified. Evening meals are jovially hosted by M. Simonnot. The house is furnished throughout with beautiful antiques. A long corridor, which is being renovated, leads to the bedrooms; the suite is very pleasant, the Blue room has just been added, and the others are much simpler, with no private bath. The owners are very welcoming.

384
Domaine des Jeanne

Rue Dubarle
02290 Vic-sur-Aisne
(Aisne)
Tel. and fax 23 55 57 33
M. and Mme Martner

Rooms 5 with shower, WC and TV. **Price** 310-3500F (2 pers.) according to season. **Meals** Breakfast incl., evening meals (separate tables) 90F (wine not incl.). **Facilities** Lounge, telephone, swimming pool, tennis. **Pets** Dogs allowed on request. **Nearby** Golf, châteaux of Pierrefond, Compiègne, hunting museum in Senlis. **Credit cards** Visa, Eurocard and MasterCard. **Spoken** English. **Open** All year. **How to get there** (Map 2 and 10): 16km west of Soissons on N31 towards Compiègne; signposted.

The grounds of the estate begin in the town and stretch right to the river's edge. All the bedrooms overlook the park. They are very comfortable and well decorated, with impeccable bathrooms, and the lounge and dining room are also very pleasant. Excellent evening meals and a very friendly welcome add further charm to the Domaine des Jeanne.

385
Les Patrus

L'Epine-aux-Bois
02540 Viels-Maisons
(Aisne)
Tel. 23 69 85 85
Fax 23 69 98 49
Mme Royol

Rooms 3 and 2 suite (2-4 pers.) with bath or shower, WC and telephone. **Price** 280-330F (2 pers.), suite 330-450F (2 pers.), 530-810F (4 pers.). **Meals** Breakfast incl., evening meals at communal or separate table 90-130F (wine not incl.). **Facilities** Lounge, telephone, boxes horse, fishing in the lakes. **Pets** Small dogs allowed on request (+50F). **Nearby** Golf, Château Thierry. **Credit cards** Visa, Eurocard and MasterCard. **Spoken** English, German. **Open** All year. **How to get there** (Map 10): 10km west of Montmirail via D933 towards La-Ferté-sur-Jouarre. At La Haute-Epine, D863 towards L'Epine-aux-Bois; signposted.

This splendid farmhouse is very pleasantly decorated and surrounded by green countryside where several saddle horses are pastured. The bedrooms are comfortable and very elegant with white walls and antique furniture. The Blue bedroom is magnificent. There is a charming dining room decorated with antique objects. You will enjoy homemade preserves for breakfast and good family cooking. The atmosphere is very pleasant.

386
Ferme du Château

02130 Villers Agron
(Aisne)
Tel. 23 71 60 67
Fax 23 69 36 54
Christine and Xavier Ferry

Rooms 4 with bath or shower and WC. **Price** 330-390F (2 pers.). **Meals** Breakfast incl., evening meals at communal table, by reservation 160F (wine incl.). **Facilities** Lounge, tennis, trout fishing, Champagne golf course (18 holes). **Pets** Dogs allowed on request. **Nearby** Swimming pool, riding (10km), canoeing, Champagne wine route, forest walks, châteaux and abbeys. **Credit cards** Not accepted. **Spoken** English, German. **Open** All year. **How to get there** (Map 10): 30km north east of Château-Thierry. A4, leaving it at Dormans, then D380, then D801 towards Golf de Champagne; signposted.

You will be very cordially welcomed to this old (13th-18th-century) house whose verdant park extends to a golf course traversed by a small river. The interior is very tastefully decorated, elegant and comfortable. The beautiful bedrooms have cheerful fabrics on the walls and are furnished with antiques. Game in season and other local products are served at the excellent dinners, hosted by the friendly young owners.

387
Chez Mme Gittermann

26, rue Nationale
60110 Amblainville
(Oise)
Tel. (16) 44 52 03 22
Mme Gittermann

Rooms 3 with bath or shower and WC, and 1 extra room without bath. **Price** 170-200F (2 pers.) +80-85F (extra room per pers.). **Meals** Breakfast incl. No evening meals. **Restaurants** In Méru (4km). **Facilities** Lounge. **Pets** Well-behaved dogs allowed. **Nearby** Swimming pool, tennis, riding, golf, Auvers-sur-Oise, Beauvais. **Open** All year. **How to get there** (Map 9): 50km northwest of Paris via A15, exit Pontoise, then D27 and D927 towards Amblainville (4km before Méru).

This house on the edge of the road has been richly and imaginatively decorated down to the last detail. The bedrooms are pleasant and good breakfasts are served in the extraordinary lounge with its accumulation of sculptures, paintings and exotic plants, along with dogs, parrots, cats and toucans. You will be very warmly welcomed to this unique, charming place.

388
Chez M. and Mme Bernard

4, rue de Gomerfontaine
60240 Chambors
(Oise)
Tel. (16) 44 49 77 28
M. and Mme Jean Bernard

Rooms 1 with bath, WC and child's room (under 5 years old), and 1 bedroom with shower and WC. **Price** 210F (1 pers.), 260F (2 pers.) +50F (child's room). **Meals** Breakfast incl., no evening meals. **Restaurants** Many in Gisors (4km). **Pets** Dogs not allowed. **Nearby** Golf (18 holes), riding (8km), walks, Gerberoy, Giverny, Lyons-la-Forêt, Château-Gallard. **Credit cards** Not accepted. **Open** All year. **How to get there** (Map 9): 35km north east of Vernon (A13), then D181 towards Gisors; 4km south east of Gisors. **No smoking**.

This inviting house, set in a pretty Norman hamlet of old stone walls and brown roofs, has a lovely, quiet garden bordered by a stream. The bedrooms are delightful, with eiderdowns matching the curtains and English wallpapers. Breakfast, including several different kinds of bread and excellent preserves, is served in the guests' dining room with a fireplace, or outside in summer. This is a a very pleasant place to stay.

389
La Bultée

60300 Fontaine-Chaalis
(Oise)
Tel. (16) 44 54 20 63
Fax (16) 44 54 08 28
Annie Ancel

Rooms 5 with shower, WC and TV. **Price** 300F (2 pers.) +80F (extra pers.). **Children** under 7 not allowed. **Meals** Breakfast incl. No evening meals. **Facilities** Lounge, parking. **Pets** Dogs not allowed. **Nearby** Restaurants, swimming pool, riding, golf, Chantilly, Compiègne, Pierrefond, Jean-Jacques Rousseau Park. **Credit cards** Not accepted. **Spoken** A little English. **Open** All year. **How to get there** (Map 9): 8km south east of Senlis (A1) via D330a towards Nanteuil- le-Haudouin; house after Borest and before Fontaine-Chaalis. (Roissy Airport, 20km)

The inner courtyard of this farmhouse has great character, with its large living room and fireplace. Breakfast is served here when the weather is not good enough to use the tables outside. Entirely renovated, the bedrooms are beautiful, comfortable, simple and impeccably well-kept, as are the bathrooms. They all overlook a pretty flower garden. This is a very restful place and the owners are friendly and informal.

390
Abbaye de Valloires

Valloires – Service Accueil
80120 Rue
(Somme)
Tel. 22 29 62 33
Fax 22 23 91 54
Association de Valloires

Rooms 6 (of which 4 with bedroom annex) with bath, WC and telephone. **Price** 340F (1 pers.), 400F (2 pers.), 470F (3 pers.) +70F (child suppl.). **Meals** Breakfast incl. No evening meals. **Facilities** Lounge, tour of the abbey. **Pets** Dogs not allowed. **Nearby** Restaurants, golf (18 holes, 6km). **Credit cards** Not accepted. **Spoken** English. **Open** All year. **How to get there** (Map 1): 31km north of Abbeville via N1 to Nampont-Saint-Martin, then D192 towards Argoules.

Built in the 17th-century, Valloires is an enormous abbey. A large gallery leads to the six beautiful bedrooms, formerly used by the Abbot and his guests; large, comfortable and prettily decorated, most of them have the paneling and recessed beds. There is a beautiful view over the very lovely gardens. Breakfast is served at separate tables in the vast old refectory. During the day, groups of tourists come to visit the Abbey and gardens.

391
Château des Alleux

Les Alleux
80870 Behen
(Somme)
Tel 22 31 64 88 (after 7.30PM)
M. and Mme René-François de
Fontanges

Rooms 4 with bath or shower and WC, 1 for children. **Price** 230F (1 pers.), 280F (2 pers.); +75F (extra pers.). **Meals** Evening meals and lunch at communal table 110F (drinks incl.). **Facilities** Lounge, pony riding, boxes horse, bicycles, living room with fireplace and independent kitchen for guests. **Pets** Dogs not allowed. **Nearby** Golf, tennis, seaside (20km), Somme bay, Marquenterre park. **Credit cards** Not accepted. **Spoken** English, Spanish. **Open** All year. **How to get there** (Map 1): 10km south of Abbeville, exit Autoroute 28, towards Blangy-sur-Bresle on D928. Signs begin at Les Croisettes.

Lying secluded in a lovely 30-acre park, this château offers impeccable guest rooms in small annexes. (The beautiful Empire bedroom, however, is in the château.) They are pleasant and well decorated. You will enjoy a very well-tended flower garden, a friendly and cheerful atmosphere, and excellent evening meals. This is a charming place, and reasonably priced.

392
Château de Foucaucort

80140 Oisemont
(Somme)
Tel. 22 25 12 58
Mme Mackay

Rooms 1 and 1 suite bath or shower and WC, and 1 bath and 1 WC for 2 rooms. Rooms cleaned every two days. **Price** 300F, 350F and 400F (2 pers.). **Meals** Breakfast incl., lunch and evening meals at communal table 60 or 110F (wine not incl.). **Facilities** Lounge, telephone, equestrian centre, boxes horse. **Pets** Dogs allowed on request. **Nearby** Golf, tennis (5km), boating center, Somme Bay, Tréport. **Credit cards** Not accepted. **Spoken** English. **Open** All year. **How to get there** (Map 1): 25km south of Abbeville via N28 to Saint-Maxent, then D29 to Oisemont and D25 towards Senarpont.

This charming 18th-century château is set in attractive grounds outside the village. The reception rooms still evoke the past, and the lounge has a happy mixture of furniture from different periods. The suite is pleasant and the two bedrooms on the park have private baths. The two other rooms share a bathroom which has just been redone. You will find a friendly, family atmosphere, but the quality of the meals, unfortunately, varies.

393
Le Bois de Bonance

80132 Port-le-Grand
(Somme)
Tel. 22 24 11 97
Fax 22 31 63 77
M. and Mme Jacques Maillard

Rooms 3 with bath and WC, and 1 suite of 2 bedrooms (4 pers.) with bath, WC, kitchen and sitting room (except July and Aug.). **Price** 300F (1 pers.), 380F (2 pers.) +100F (extra pers.), suite 400F (2 pers.). **Meals** Breakfast incl. No evening meals. **Restaurants** In Saint-Valéry-sur-Somme and Favières. **Facilities** Lounge, swimming pool, boxes horse. **Pets** Small dogs allowed in kennels. **Credit cards** Not accepted. **Nearby** Golf (5km), seaside (10km). **Spoken** English, German. **Closed** Dec 25 – Jan 1. **How to get there** (Map 1): 8km northwest of Albertville on D40 towards Saint-Valéry-sur-Somme; signposted at the entrance to the village.

Standing alone in the countryside, this welcoming family house is surrounded by lovely grounds. The interior is very elegant. Each beautiful, comfortable bedroom is furnished with antiques, mostly Louis XVI. Breakfast is served in a very attractively decorated dining room furnished with graceful "lyre" chairs. There is a small TV-lounge for guests.

394
Ferme du Bois de Bonance

80132 Port-le-Grand
(Somme)
Tel. 22 24 34 97
M. and Mme Benoit Maillard

Rooms 2 (twin beds) with bath or shower and WC. **Price** 300F (2 pers.) +100F (extra pers.).
Meals Breakfast incl. No evening meals. **Restaurants** In Saint-Valéry-sur-Somme and Favières.
Pets Dogs allowed on request. **Facilities** Swimming pool, boxes horse, riding. **Nearby** Golf (5km),
Le Crotoy, Saint-Valéry, Somme Bay, Marquenterre Park. **Credit cards** Not accepted. **Spoken**
English. **Open** All year. **How to get there** (Map 1): 8km northwest of Albertville via D40 towards
Saint-Valéry-sur-Somme; sign at the entrance to the village.

This large Artois farmhouse has two comfortable, elegant guest bedrooms. The owners are young, informal and friendly. There is a swimming pool in a beautiful garden and breakfast is served outside in good weather. We recommend a summer visit, as there is no guest lounge.

395
La Grande Métairie

Oyer
16700 Bioussac-Ruffec
(Charente)
Tel. 45 31 15 67
M. and Mme Moy

Rooms 1 room and 1 suite (4 pers.) with shower and WC. Rooms cleaned on request. **Price** 150F (1 pers.), 200F (2 pers.), 260F (3 pers.), 320F (4 pers.). **Meals** Breakfast incl., half board 165F per pers. in double room, evening meals at communal table, by reservation 65F (wine incl.); poss. vegetarian meals (or use of kitchen by guests). **Facilities** Lounge, swimming pool, bicycles. **Pets** Small, well-behaved dogs allowed. **Nearby** Tennis, riding, fishing, canoeing, Nanteuil-en-Vallée, Château de Cibioux, Verteuil. **Credit cards** Not accepted. **Spoken** English. **Open** End of March - Nov. 1. **How to get there** (Map 23): 6km west of Ruffec via D740. At Condac, D197 towards Bioussac then left for Oyer; signs before Oyer.

Set in the countryside, this old farmhouse has been well renovated and offers one pleasant guest room and one suite. The suite in the main house is very attractive, with flagstones and stone alcoves. The Louis-Philippe beds are very comfortable and the bathrooms are well kept. Evening meals are based on nutritious, fresh farm fruits, vegetables and meats. Excellent breakfasts are served.

396
La Breuillerie

Trois-Palis
16730 Fléac
(Charente)
Tel. 45 91 05 37
Mme Bouchard

Rooms 1 with bath, WC and TV, 2 with washbasin sharing bath and WC; TV. **Price** 180-230F (1 pers.), 200-250F (2 pers.), 300F (3 pers.). **Meals** Breakfast incl. No evening meals. **Restaurant** Le Pont de La Meure (500m) and in Angoulême. **Facilities** Bicycles. **Pets** Dogs not allowed. **Nearby** Tennis, swimming pool, riding at Angoulême. **Spoken** English. **Open** All year. **How to get there** (Map 22): 5km west of Angoulême via D699. At Nersac, D41; signs "Chambres d'hôtes".

The outskirts of Angoulême are badly spoiled but La Breuillerie is far enough away to be in beautiful countryside. The guest bedrooms are comfortable, well kept and prettily decorated. (Unfortunately, only one has a private bath.) Good breakfasts are served in a charming dining room with an imposing fireplace. There is a pleasant and cordial atmosphere.

397
Logis de Romainville

16440 Roullet-Saint-Estèphe
(Charente)
Tel. 45 66 32 56
Fax 45 66 46 89
Francine Quillet

Rooms 3 with private baths (private WC for 2 rooms, communal WC for the other), and 1 spare room without bath. Rooms cleaned every day, except beds (guests' responsibility). **Price** 250F (1 pers.), 280F (2 pers.) +70F (extra pers.). **Meals** Breakfast incl; evening meals at communal table 100F (wine incl.). **Facilities** Lounge; swimming pool, bikes on property. **Nearby** Golf (9 holes, 10km), tennis, riding, fishing, Romanesque churches, Cognac distilleries. **Credit cards** Not accepted. **Spoken** English, Italian. **Open** All year. **How to get there** (Map 22): 12km south of Angoulême via bypass towards Bordeaux, N10 exit Roulet, go through village via D42; house in 2km, signs.

We love the Logis de Romainville and its comfortable, pretty rooms, soft carpets, white or patchwork bedcovers and its soft pastel wallpapers. The rooms are immaculate and have lovely bathrooms. Breakfasts and succulent dinners are served in a vast, spacious room with antique furnishings. In summer, meals are served outdoors so that you can enjoy the splendid panoramic view here, where the hosts are friendly and informal.

398
Les Granges

16410 Vouzan
(Charente)
Tel. 45 24 94 61
Mme Lousie Le Mouée

Rooms 1 in separate building (2-3 pers.) and 1 suite (4 pers.) with shower and WC. **Price** 210-230F (1 pers.), 240-270F (2 pers.), 310-330F (3 pers.), 380F (4 pers.). **Meals** Breakfast incl., No evening meals. **Restaurants** In the vicinity. **Facilities** Lounge, telephone, locked parking, painting and yoga lessons for beginners. **Pets** Dogs allowed on request. **Nearby** Swimming pool, tennis, golf courses (9 holes and 18 holes), Brantôme, Périgord vert, Romanesque art, châteaux. **Credit cards** Not accepted. **Open** All year. **How to get there** (Map 23): 16km south east of Angoulême via D939. At Sainte-Catherine, D4. At La Petitie, first road on the right after 1.6km. **No smoking.**

A pretty house between Angoulême and Brantôme, Les Granges is surrounded by a lovely garden. Both bedrooms have a private terrace. (We preferred the bedroom in the small separate building.) Comfortable and well decorated with antique furniture, the house has a living area and a mezzanine. You can have breakfast outside in the sunshine. The owners are friendly and discreet, and you will feel very much at home.

399
Le Maurençon

10, rue de Maurençon
Les Moulins
17400 Antezant
(Charente-Maritime)
Tel. 46 59 94 52
Pierre and Marie-Claude Fallelour

Rooms 1 with shower and WC, 2 shared bath or shower and WC. Rooms cleaned twice a week on longer stays. **Price** 220-240F (2 pers.) +65F (extra pers.). **Meals** Breakfast incl., half board 180F per pers. in double room (3 nights min.). Evening meals at communal table (not Sundays and holidays), 85F or farmhouse-auberge Antezant (200m). **Facilities** Lounge, fishing, billiards. **Pets** Dogs not allowed. **Nearby** Golf, swimming pool, riding, tennis, Saintes, Cognac, Poitou marshes, châteaux, Romanesque churches. **Credit cards** Not accepted. **Open** All year. **How to get there** (Map 22): 6km north of Saint-Jean-d'Angély via D127 towards Dampierre; house at the entrance to the village.

The River Boutonne once powered the mill but is now simply a romantic border to the garden. The bedrooms, which are furnished with handsome old furniture, are light and pleasant. The lounge has a billiards table. Excellent breakfasts are served outside in good weather. Mme Fallelour is a very welcoming hostess.

400
Le Logis

17610 Dompierre-sur-Charente
(Charente-Maritime)
Tel. 46 91 02 05/46 91 00 53
Mme C. Cocuaud

Rooms 2 with bath and WC, 2 with bath and shared WC, and 1 child's room. **Price** 440F (2 pers.). **Meals** Breakfast 50F, half board 450F per pers. in double room (3 days min.), evening meals at communal table, by reservation 200F (wine incl.). **Facilities** Lounge, telephone. **Pets** Dogs not allowed. **Nearby** Restaurants, golf, tennis, fishing, equestrian centre, seaside (30km), Saintes, Cognac, Romanesque churches. **Credit cards** Not accepted. **Spoken** English. **Open** March 1 – Oct 30. **How to get there** (Map 22): 13km south east of Saintes via D24 (through the Charente Valley).

Built in the 18th-century on a rise near the Charente River, Le Logis is a truly beautiful house. The principal reception rooms are open to guests and have handsome furniture and spacious proportions. The bedrooms are light, prettily decorated and comfortable. Mme Cocuaud enlivens the dinner table conversation and her cooking is outstanding.

401
La Jaquetterie

17250 Plassay
(Charente-Maritime)
Tel. 46 93 91 88
Michelle and Jacques Louradour

Rooms 1 and 2 suites (4 pers.) with bath or shower and WC. **Price** 220-260F (2 pers.). **Meals** Breakfast incl., half board 180-190F per pers. in double room, evening meals at communal table 75F (wine incl.). **Facilities** Horse boxes. **Pets** Dogs allowed on request. **Nearby** Fishing, swimming pool, tennis, riding, golf, Romanesque churches, châteaux. **Credit cards** Not accepted. **Spoken** German. **Open** All year. **How to get there** (Map 22): 13km northwest of Saintes (A10) via N137 towards Rochefort for 11km. Then right on D119 towards Plassay for 2km.

La Jaquetterie is a charming farmhouse located just outside of the village. The bedrooms are intimate and have many charming personal touches. There are comfortable beds and lovely 18th-century wardrobes. A beautiful family suite has just been added. If the weather permits, breakfast is served outside. Evening meals are prepared with excellent produce from the farm and you will enjoy a pleasant, rustic atmosphere here.

402
Le Logis de l'Epine

17250 Plassay
(Charente-Maritime)
Tel. 46 93 91 66
M. and Mme Charrier

Rooms 2 with bath or shower and WC, 2 with washbasin and shared WC. **Price** 190-280F (2 pers.). **Meals** Breakfast incl. No evening meals. **Facilities** Lounge. **Pets** Dogs allowed on request. **Nearby** Restaurants, swimming pool, tennis, riding, seaside, golf, Romanesque Saintonge. **Credit cards** Not accepted. **Spoken** English. **Open** All year. **How to get there** (Map 22): 10km northwest of Saintes via N137, then D119; house on the way out of the village.

This 18th-century house in its large and shady garden seems sheltered from the modern world. M. and Mme Charrier are very hospitable. The bedrooms contain antique furniture and wide ship's bunks brightened with pretty fabrics. Breakfast is served outside under the oak trees, or in a magnificent room covered with 19th-century frescos of leafy scrolls and fruit. The Logis is very charming.

403
33, rue Thiers

33, rue Thiers
17000 La Rochelle
(Charente-Maritime)
Tel. 46 41 62 23
Fax 46 41 10 76
Mme Maybelle Iribe

Rooms 6 with bath or shower and WC. **Price** 380-400F (1 pers.), 480-510F (2 pers.).
Meals Breakfast incl., evening meals (separate tables) 120F (wine not incl.). **Facilities** Lounge,
telephone, cooking courses. **Pets** Dogs not allowed. **Nearby** Sailing, golf, Ile de Ré, Poitou
marshes. **Credit cards** Not accepted. **Spoken** English. **Open** All year. **How to get there** (Map 22):
In La Rochelle follow the Centre Ville signs and go around the main square; in front of the
cathedral at the traffic lights, take first right, rue Gargoulleau, which becomes rue Thiers further
on.

This house in the very pretty town of La Rochelle has a pleasant inner
garden where breakfast is served in summer. The bedrooms, on two
floors, are quiet, very comfortable, and remarkably decorated with pictures
and family objects. There is an elegant lounge-library for guests. Don't miss
the evening meal because Madame Iribe is an outstanding gourmet cook.
This is a very beautiful place.

404
Château des Salles

17240 Saint-Fort-sur Gironde
(Charente-Maritime)
Tel. 46 49 95 10
Fax 46 49 02 81
Sylvie Couillaud

Rooms 5 with bath or shower and WC. **Price** 350-450F (2 pers.). **Meals** Breakfast 50F, half
board 350-420F per pers. in double room (3 days min.), evening meals by reservation (separate
tables) 160F (wine not incl.). **Facilities** Lounge, telephone and fax. **Pets** Dogs not allowed.
Nearby Tennis, seaside, Cognac, La Rochelle. **Credit cards** Visa, Eurocard and MasterCard.
Spoken English, German. **Open** Easter – end Sept. **How to get there** (Map 22): 14km from the
A27 Mirambeau-Royan exit; at the crossroads of D125 towards Saint-Fort-sur-Gironde and D730
towards Royan.

Built in the 15th century and renovated in the 19th, the château has five
pleasant guest bedrooms with views over the park. The tasteful decor
is quite classic. (Some bedrooms have just been entirely redone with pretty
fabrics). Watercolors painted by the owners add further aesthetic appeal.
Breakfast is served in the bedrooms or in the dining room (no smoking).

405
Chez Monsieur et Madame Howarth

6, rue Rose
17400 Saint-Jean-d'Angely
(Charente-Maritime)
Tel. 46 32 03 00
Jack and Margaret Howarth

Rooms 2 with bath or shower and WC, and 2 spare rooms. **Price** 350F (2 pers.). **Meals** Breakfast 35F. No evening meals. **Restaurants** Le Scorpion (2 min. walk) and others. **Pets** Dogs not allowed. **Nearby** Swimming pool, lake, tennis, riding center, golf practice, golf (18 holes, 20km), La Rochelle, Royan, Rochefort, Cognac, Ile d'Oléron and Ile de Ré, Romanesque churches. **Credit cards** Not accepted. **Spoken** English, German. **Closed** Nov. 1 – Easter. **How to get there** (Map 22): 2km from Autoroute A10, exit 24, in the center of Saint-Jean-d'Angély. **No smoking.**

Set in the heart of the old village of Saint-Jean-d'Angély, this old mansion belongs to an English family who divide their time between their native country and this charming town. The interior is comfortable and decorated in English style. The bedrooms are all the same price and therefore we recommend the two largest ones. The bathrooms are beautiful and there is a lovely garden where you can enjoy the gentle climate of the Charente-Maritime region.

406
Rennebourg

Saint-Denis-du-Pin
17400 Saint-Jean-d'Angely
(Charente-Maritime)
Tel. 46 32 16 07
Michèle and Florence Frappier

Rooms 3 with bath or shower and WC, and 1 suite of 2 bedrooms (3-4 pers.) with 1 bath and WC. **Price** 250-270F (2 pers.). **Meals** Breakfast 25F, evening meals (separate tables) 90F (table wine incl.). **Facilities** Lounge, swimming pool, equestrian centre, horse boxes, pony-cart rides. **Pets** Dogs not allowed. **Nearby** Tennis, golf, La Rochelle, Romanesque Saintonge. **Credit cards** Not accepted. **Spoken** English and German understood. **Open** All year. **How to get there** (Map 22): 7km north of Saint-Jean-d'Angély (A10 exit 24), via N150; signposted.

In the heart of the Saintonge countryside, this traditional house has several rooms with 18-century paneling, fine old provincial furniture and, throughout, antique curi and paintings. The bedrooms are lovely (the Blue Room is our favorite) and there is a beautiful swimming pool. You will also find a summer lounge in the converted barn. Excellent evening meals are charmingly served by Michèle Frappier.

407
Bonnemie

49, route départementale
17310 Saint-Pierre-d'Oléron
(Charente-Maritime)
Tel. 46 47 22 57
Mme Chassort

Rooms 3 with shower and WC, 2 with TV. **Price** 210-240F (2 pers.). **Meals** Breakfast incl., half board 175F per pers. in double room, evening meals (separate tables) 75-85F (wine not incl.; fish specialties on 24-hour notice) **Pets** Cats not allowed. **Nearby** Swimming pool, tennis, riding, sea fishing, sailing, golf. **Spoken** English. **Open** All year. **How to get there** (Map 22): On the way out of Saint-Pierre-d'Oléron towards Saint-Gilles Saint-Denis.

Though located on a busy road in an unappealing setting, Bonnemie is fortunately sheltered by a pretty garden. Once inside, you will enjoy the very friendly hospitality of a retired couple who will make every effort to please you. The comfortable bedrooms are located in the manor house and a small annex. We prefer those which are upstairs in the manor. There is a flower-covered veranda. The magnificent shellfish dinners must be ordered in advance.

408
Le Clos

La Menounière
17310 Saint-Pierre-d'Oléron
(Charente-Maritime)
Tel. 46 47 14 34
Micheline Denieau

Rooms 3 with shower, WC and mezzanine for children. Rooms cleaned every week for long stays. **Price** 230F (2 pers.) +40F (extra pers.). **Meals** Breakfast incl. No evening meals. **Restaurants** Chez François in Saint-Pierre d'Oléron, L'Ecailler in La Cotinière. **Pets** Dogs allowed on request. **Nearby** Golf (9 holes), fishing, bicycle rental, riding, tennis, seaside (500m), salt marshes, bird sanctuary. **Credit cards** Not accepted. **Spoken** English, Spanish. **Open** All year. **How to get there** (Map 22): 4km west of Saint-Pierre d'Oléron via D734; at Saint-Pierre turn left at the traffic lights after the Shell station, then follow signs for La Menounière.

This small house, surrounded with vines, lies at the entrance to the village and has a flower garden. The bedrooms are simple, pleasant and well kept. Each has a mezzanine (which will please families) and a small terrace at ground level. This is a good and economical place to stay.

409
Château de la Tillade

17260 Saint-Simon-de-Pellouaille
(Charente-Maritime)
Tel. 46 90 00 20
Vicomte and Vicomtesse
Michel de Salvert

Rooms 3 with bath or shower and WC. **Price** 350F, 400F and 450F (2 pers.). **Meals** Breakfast incl., meals at communal table 150F (wine incl.). **Facilities** Lounge. **Pets** Dogs not allowed. **Facilities** Drawing and painting lessons, poss. horseback riding with owner, bikes lent on property. **Pets** Dogs not allowed. **Nearby** Swimming pool (4km); Romanesque Saintonge, Saintes, Talmont. **Credit cards** Not accepted. **Spoken** English. **Open** All year. **How to get there** (Map 22): 4km north of Gemozac on road to Saintes on left.

The Château de la Tillade is a vast wine-growing estate located in very quiet surroundings where you will be charmingly welcomed. The interior is elegant and decorated as it was in the past; there are modern amenities. Upstairs, the bedrooms have just been renovated and decorated with 18th- and 19th-century furniture, soft pastel colors on the walls, and shimmering fabrics; all are exemplary of Madame de Salvert's artistic tastes (she gives courses in watercoloring). The bathrooms are impeccable; The communal meals are mouthwatering.

410
Aguzan

Rue du Château
La Sauzaie
17138 Saint-Xandre
(Charente-Maritime)
Tel. 46 37 22 65
M. and Mme Langer

Rooms 3 with washbasin sharing 1 bathroom and WC. **Price** 200F (1 pers.), 250F (2 pers.); 2 nights min. **Meals** Breakfast incl. No evening meals. **Facilities** Lounge. **Pets** Dogs allowed on request (+30F). **Nearby** Riding, seaside, golf, La Rochelle, Poitou marshes, Romanesque Saintonge, Ile de Ré. **Credit cards** Not accepted. **Open** March 1 – mid-Sept. **How to get there** (Map 22): 9km northeast of La Rochelle via D9 towards Luçon through Villedoux. Telephone for directions.

Surrounded by fields in the countryside behind La Rochelle, this house looks almost Provençal and has lovely gardens. The inside is well kept, and the bedrooms are all very comfortable and classic. While they share a bathroom, each room has a very pretty, modern washroom. If the excellent breakfasts are not served in the garden, they are served in the very attractive lounge. The owners are charming.

411
La Treille Marine

8, rue des Rosées
Ile de Ré
17740 Sainte-Marie-de-Ré
(Charente-Maritime)
Tel. 46 30 12 57
Alain and Danielle Fouché

Rooms 1 bedroom (3 pers.) with bath, WC and TV. Rooms cleaned every 2 days. **Price** 295F (1 pers.), 350F (2 pers.), 400F (3 pers.). **Meals** Breakfast incl. No communal meal. **Facilities** Lounge. **Pets** Dogs allowed on request. **Nearby** Restaurants, golf (25km), mudtherapy and saltwater swimming pool (1km), little ports of La Flotte and Saint-Martin-de-Ré. **Credit cards** Not accepted. **Open** All year; 2 nights min. **How to get there** (Map 22): On the Ile de Ré (reached by bridge from La Rochelle), in the center of the village.

Peacefully situated in a small, white, flower-filled village, this former wine cellar has a beautiful guest bedroom. Decorated in blue and white, it is very comfortable and charming, with old furniture, pretty objects and fabrics, eiderdowns and a modern bathroom. Breakfast is served with a smile in a large and handsome dining room. It is best to reserve far in advance.

412
Château de la Roche

79290 Argenton-L'Eglise
(Deux-Sèvres)
Tel. 49 67 02 38
M. and Mme Keufer

Rooms 8 and 1 suite (4 pers.) of 2 bedrooms with 1 bath and WC. **Price** 250F (1 pers.), 400F (2 pers.). **Meals** Breakfast incl., evening meals 150F (wine incl.). **Facilities** Lounge, telephone, riding (+suppl.), horse-drawn carriage, boating. **Pets** Dogs allowed on request. **Nearby** Golf. **Credit cards** Not accepted. **Spoken** English. **Open** All year. **How to get there** (Map 15): 35km south of Saumur via N147. At Montreuil-Bellay take D938. At Brion-près Thouet take D162 towards Taizon.

Essentially Renaissance in style, this château is situated in the countryside and has huge, quiet, very well furnished guest bedrooms with exemplary bathrooms. It overlooks Argenton. On the ground floor, charmingly old-fashioned lounges and dining rooms open onto a beautiful terrace. Horses and carriages can pick you up at the station.

413
La Talbardière

86210 Archigny
(Vienne)
Tel. 49 85 32 51/49 85 32 52
M. and Mme Lonhienne

Rooms 3 (2-3 pers.) with bath or shower and WC, and 1 studio (5 pers.) with bath, WC, kitchen, telephone and TV. **Price** 250F (2 pers.), studio 1100-1750F per week for 5 pers. (depending on the season). **Meals** Breakfast incl. (except the studio). No evening meals. **Facilities** Fishing (with permit). **Pets** Dogs not allowed. **Nearby** Restaurants, riding, tennis, golf, swimming, Chauvigny, Angles-sur-Anglin, Saint-Savin. **Spoken** English, German, Italian, Russian. **Open** All year. **How to get there** (Map 16): 18km southeast of Châtellerault via D9 towards Monthoiron, then D3 towards Pleumartin; signs after 1km.

We were immediately enchanted by this spacious, old fortified house. The bedrooms are beautiful and well furnished, and they vary in size. Those in the main building are very elegant, while the room in the right wing is more rustic. Breakfast includes homemade preserves and home-baked bread. The gentle, rolling countryside is ideal for walks. The owners are very friendly.

414
Château d'Epanvilliers

Epanvilliers
86400 Brux-Civray
(Vienne)
Tel. 49 87 18 43
M. Lorzil

Rooms 1 with shower and WC, and 2 suites (2 pers.) with bath, WC and 1 child's bed. **Price** 250F (2 pers.), suite 400F (2 pers.) +50F (extra pers.). **Meals** Breakfast incl. No evening meals. **Restaurant** In Chaunay. **Facilities** Lounge, carriage rides (suppl.), tour of the château. **Pets** Dogs allowed on request. **Nearby** Swimming pool, riding. **Spoken** English. **Open** All year. **How to get there** (Map 23): 41km south of Poitiers via N10 to Couhé, then D7 towards Civray; signposted.

Monsieur Lorzil is restoring his château with good taste and determination. The charming bedrooms are very well furnished– some have a small museum-room–and all overlook the park. The bathrooms are being renovated. A huge, inviting lounge-library is available to guests, and the owner is very friendly.

415
La Veaudepierre

8, rue du Berry
86300 Chauvigny
(Vienne)
Tel. 49 46 30 81/49 41 41 76
Fax 49 47 64 12
M. and Mme J. de Giafferri

Rooms 5 and 1 suite (3 pers.) with bath or shower and WC (1 room with bath outside room). **Price** 180-250F (1 pers.), 230-300F (2 pers.) +60F (extra pers.). **Meals** Breakfast incl., half-board; 10% reduction after 7 days; evening meals at communal table 80F (wine incl.), 60F (children under 12). **Facilities** Lounge; cultural stays in Poitou organized. **Pets** Dogs not allowed. **Nearby** Golf (18 holes, 16km), tennis and swimming pool (village), Romanesque abbeys and churches, Saint-Savin, châteaux, visit of Fort Chauvigny (50m). **Credit cards** Not accepted. **Spoken** English. **Closed** Nov. 1 – Easter. (Open on request in winter). **How to get there** (Map 16): In the village.

La Veaudepierre is a Directoire house which is located in a medieval village surmounted by an imposing fortress. The owners are warm and helpful. The house is richly furnished with antiques while retaining provincial charm. The pleasant bedroom open onto a lovely garden which is surrounded by the old walls of the village. This is a very delightful place and a good base for discovering the hidden treasures of the Poitou region.

416
Moulin de la Dive

Guron
Payré
86700 Couhé
(Vienne)
Tel. 49 42 40 97
M. and Mme Vanverts

Rooms 2 with bath or shower and WC. **Price** 315-330F (1 pers.), 355-375F (2 pers.). **Meals** breakfast incl. No evening meals. **Restaurants** In Couhé and Vivonne. **Facilities** Lounge, telephone, fishing. **Pets** Dogs not allowed. **Nearby** Equestrian centre, golf, châteaux (La Roche-Gencay and Epanvilliers). **Credit cards** Not accepted. **Open** July and Aug. (on request). **How to get there** (Map 16): 34km south of Poitiers via N10, then D29 towards Anché.

The Dive River meanders through a beautiful garden and under several little bridges before disappearing beneath the mill. M. and Mme Vanverts will receive you in a beautiful lounge-dining room and let you choose between two comfortable guest bedrooms. The Seville bedroom has old Spanish furniture, and the Nohant room is decorated in homage to George Sand. Breakfast is served in the garden or the lounge.

417
Les Godiers

86800 Lavoux
(Vienne)
Tel. 49 61 05 18
M. and Mme Rabany

Rooms 1 with bath and WC, and 1 room with private washroom, communal bath and WC. Rooms cleaned twice a week. **Price** 210-240F (1 pers.), 260-290F (2 pers.); 10% reduction beginning 2nd day. **Meals** Breakfast incl., communal meals by reservation 100F (wine incl.), 40F (children under 10). **Facilities** Lounge and library, tennis on property. **Pets** Dogs not allowed. **Nearby** Riding, fishing, golf, hunting, Romanesque churches, Châteaux of Touffou, Dissay and Vayres. **Credit cards** Not accepted. **Spoken** English. **Open** All year. **How to get there** (Map 16): Autoroute A10 exit Poitiers North, then towards Toulouse, exit Bignoux. In 2km on right, towards Château du Bois-Dousset, 1st house on right.

Set in the midst of fields and woods, Les Godiers is an old farm which has been lovingly restored. All the bedrooms are pleasant, but we recommend the one located in a small outbuilding because it has its own bath. The living room is very tastefully decorated with pretty objects, antique furniture and paintings and has a large fireplace. There is a lovely small dining room and the hosts are delightful.

418
Le Logis du Château du Bois Dousset

86800 Lavoux
(Vienne)
Tel. 49 44 20 26
Vicomte and Vicomtesse
Hilaire de Villoutreys

Rooms 3 with bath and WC (1 with bath outside room); 1 bedroom not heated in winter. **Price** 300F (2 pers.) +50F (extra pers.). **Meals** Breakfast incl. No evening meals. **Facilities** Lounge. **Pets** Dogs allowed on request. **Nearby** Restaurants, golf (18 holes, 5km), riding, sailing (20km), canoeing, kayaks, Roman Poitou, Brenne lakes, châteaux. **Credit cards** Not accepted. **Spoken** English, Spanish. **Open** All year. **How to get there** (Map 16): 12km east of Poitiers. Autoroute A10 exit Poitiers North, towards Limoges, then in 5km towards Brignoux. Logis on D139 between Brignoux and Lavoux.

The Logis is an outbuilding of a superb château admirably located in the heart of an immense private park. In a small, newly restored wing, there are two comfortable guestrooms with tasteful decoration and beautiful bathrooms. The large (450 sq. ft.) third room upstairs is magnificently furnished and lighted by tall windows, but its bath facilities are old-fashioned. Breakfasts are pleasant and are served in a sunny room looking out on the beautiful 17th-century park.

419
Château de Vaumoret

Rue du Breuil-Mingot
86000 Poitiers
(Vienne)
Tel. 49 61 32 11
Fax 49 01 04 54
M. and Mme Vaucamp

Rooms 3 with bath and WC. **Price** 300-350F (1 pers.), 350-400F (2 pers.), 450F (3 pers.).
Meals Breakfast incl. No evening meals. (Guests may may use kitchen). **Restaurants** In 2km
and in Poitiers (8km). **Facilities** Lounge, bikes on property. **Nearby** Golf (18 holes, 5km); all
sports nearby, Roman Poitou, châteaux, Old Poitiers. **Credit cards** Not accepted. **Spoken** English,
Spanish. **Closed** Nov. 1 – Easter (open on request in winter). **How to get there** (Map 16): 8km
east of Poitiers via east bypass, then D 3 towards La Roche-Posay; then on right, towards Sèvres-
Anxaumont; entrance to château in 2.5km on right.

The small, 17th-century Château de Vaumoret is located on the outskirts
of Poitiers but it is nevertheless still in the country. One wing is reserved
for the guestrooms, which are lovely and have superb bathrooms. Each very
comfortable room has its own style, which is created by a tasteful choice of
furniture, paintings and fabrics. Breakfast is served in a salon decorated with
old engravings, many depicting hunting scenes. This is a welcoming and
elegantly luxurious place to stay.

420
Le Bois Goulu

86200 Pouant
(Vienne)
Tel. 49 22 52 05
Mme Marie-Christine Picard

Rooms 2 with bath or shower and WC (poss. rooms in suite for child). **Price** 240-250F (2 pers.)
+60F (child's room). **Meals** Breakfast incl. No evening meals. **Restaurants** In Pouant and
Richelieu. **Facilities** Lounge, bike rentals. **Pets** Dogs allowed on request. **Nearby** Swimming
pool, fishing, golf, hunting, châteaux of the Loire, Richelieu. **Credit cards** Not accepted. **Open**
All year. **How to get there** (Map 16): 15km east of Loudun towards Richelieu via D61; on leaving
village, avenue of linden trees.

The Bois Goulu is a large farmhouse built around a flower-filled courtyard
There are two vast bedrooms with retro decoration. Joined by a large
hall with a lovely parquet floor, the rooms are comfortable, light and
cheerful. Breakfasts include good homemade preserves and are served in
the newly built living room, which is reserved for guests. There are no
dinners on the property, but there is a good restaurant nearby. You will
be cordially welcomed to Le Bois Goulu.

421
Château de la Roche du Maine

86420 Prinçay
(Vienne)
Tel. 49 22 84 09
Fax 49 22 89 57
M. and Mme Neveu

Rooms 4 in annexes with shower and WC, 2 in the château with bath and WC. **Price** 420-990F (2 pers.). **Meals** Breakfast 60F, half board 490-725F per pers. in double room (3 days min.), evening meals at communal table, on reservation 280F (wine incl.). **Facilities** Lounge, swimming pool, gym, tour of the château. **Pets** Dogs not allowed. **Nearby** Tennis, riding, golf, Loire châteaux, wine route. **Credit cards** Not accepted. **Spoken** English. **Open** April 1 – Nov 1. **How to get there** (Map 16): 33km south of Chinon via D749 after Richelieu. After 2km go right on D22 towards Monts-sur-Guesnes, then D46; signposted.

In this exceptionally beautiful château, guests are offered two extraordinary medieval bedrooms (with luxurious bathrooms) and four others which are simpler but comfortable. The gardens are the views are magnificent. Evening meals are served in the superb vaulted, colonnaded dining room. This is an exceptional place and the owners are very hospitable.

422
Château de Prémarie

86340 Roches-Prémarie
(Vienne)
Tel. 49 42 50 01
M. and Mme Jean-Pierre de Boysson

Rooms 5 with bath or shower and WC. **Price** 400-450F (2 pers.). **Meals** Breakfast incl. No evening meals. **Restaurant** In Saint-Benoit (8km). **Facilities** Lounge, swimming pool, tennis. **Pets** Dogs not allowed. **Nearby** Equestrian center (12km), golf (18 holes, 10km), Romanesque art. **Credit cards** Not accepted. **Spoken** English. **Open** Easter – Nov 1. **How to get there** (Map 16):. 14km south of Poitiers via D741 towards Smarves-Confolens.

Once an English fortress, this small château is inviting and comfortable, and you will be very warmly welcomed. The rooms are very charming and cheerful, as are the bathrooms. Everything is admirably well kept. and there are excellent breakfasts. The heated swimming pool is open from springtime onwards.

423
Château de Ternay

Ternay
86120 Les Trois–Moutiers
(Vienne)
Tel. 49 22 92 82/49 22 97 54
Marquis and Marquise de Ternay

Rooms 3 with bath and WC. **Price** 500-600F (2 pers.). **Meals** Breakfast incl., evening meals in the château at communal table 250F (wine incl.). **Facilities** Lounge. **Pets** Dogs not allowed. **Nearby** Golf, Fontevrault abbey, Loire châteaux. **Spoken** English. **Open** Easter – Nov 1. **How to get there** (Map 15): 30km south of Saumur via N147. At Montreuil-Bellay head towards Les Trois-Moutiers, then Ternay.

Built in the 15th century around an even older dungeon, the Château de Ternay was somewhat refurbished in the 19th century but retains an impressive character. It has a beautiful inner courtyard and the rooms are handsomely decorated. The bedrooms are quiet, huge, and have beautiful fabrics and antique furniture, while the pleasant bathrooms are modern. Evening meals are pleasant and served in a friendly atmosphere.

424
La Malle Post

86260 Vicq–sur–Gartempe
(Vienne)
Tel. and fax 49 86 21 04
Mme de Kriek

Rooms 3 with independent entrance (2 with kitchen) with bath or shower and WC. **Price** 250-340F (2 pers.); set price for 7 days 1490-1960F (2 pers.). **Meals** Breakfast incl., evening meals by reservation at communal table 80F (wine incl.). **Facilities** Lounge, bicycle hire, boats for fishing. **Nearby** Riding, golf. **Credit cards** Not accepted. **Spoken** English, German. **Open** All year (on request in winter). **How to get there** (Map 16): A10 exit Châtellerault Nord towards La Roche-Posay, then 8km to Vicq-sur-Gartempe.

Situated on a small square near the lovely Gartempe River, this converted 18th-century postal relay station is very prettily decorated. The bedrooms are large and the beds are comfortable. You can also enjoy a lounge has a very friendly corner bar. Marion de Kriek takes great care of her guests and her dinners are excellent.

425
Le Pigeonnier

Rue du Château
04280 Céreste
(Alpes-de-Haute-Provence)
Tel. 92 79 07 54
Fax 92 79 07 75
Mme Exbrayat

Rooms 2 with bath or shower and WC, and 1 room with private shower and WC upstairs.
Price 230-295F (2 pers.). **Meals** Breakfast incl. No evening meals. **Restaurants** L'Aiguebelle
(gourmet) in 500m and L'Auberge de Carluc (regional specialties). **Facilities** Lounge; private,
lighted parking lot. **Pets** Dogs allowed on request. **Nearby** Swimming pool and tennis in village,
riding, hiking, golf (18 holes, 20km), Lubéron Regional Park, Gordes, Bonnieux, Roussillon,
Lacoste. **Credit cards** Not accepted. **Spoken** English. **Closed** Nov. 1 – April 1. **How to get there**
(Map 33): 20km from Manosque via N100 towards Apt.

"The Pigeon Loft" is a very old village house with especially lovely
interior decoration which compensates for the absence of a garden.
Each bedroom has its own color scheme for the bedcovers, lampshades,
paintings and objects, all of which are prettily set off by the white walls.
The bathrooms are immaculate. Good breakfasts are served in a beautiful
living room with a beautiful view of the village and the countryside. This
is a beautiful place to stay.

426
Le Vieux Castel

04500 Roumoules
(Alpes-de-Haute-Provence)
Tel. 92 77 75 42
M. Allègre

Rooms 5 with bath and WC. Rooms cleaned guests' responsibility. **Price** 110F (1 pers.), 185F
(2 pers.) +50F (extra pers.). **Meals** Breakfast incl., half board 160F per pers. in double room,
evening meals at communal table 70F (wine incl.). **Facilities** Telephone, enclosed parking.
Pets Dogs not allowed. **Nearby** Verdon gorges, lakes of Sainte-Croix and Esparron. **Credit cards**
Not accepted. **Open** Easter – Nov 1. **How to get there** (Map 34): 3km from Riez via D952 towards
Moustiers; signposted "Gites de France".

Le Vieux Castel presents a slightly austere 17th-century façade which has
been made more inviting by numerous modifications. You will be
welcomed by the young owners, who are restoring the house themselves.
The bedrooms are on the first floor and their monastic appearance, softened
by turn-of-the-century furniture, is not without charm. The beds are
comfortable and the small shower rooms have been completely refurbished.
This is a quiet place, except when there is a great amount of traffic.

427
Le Pi-Maï

Hameau de Fréjus
Station de Serre-Chevalier
05240 La Salle-les-Alpes
(Hautes-Alpes)
Tel. 92 24 83 63
M. and Mme Charamel

Rooms 1 with bath and WC, 3 with washbasin sharing shower and WC. **Price** 290-360F (2 pers.). **Meals** Breakfast incl. in low season, half board 300-320F per pers. in double room. Lunch and evening meal in the restaurant on site. **Pets** Dogs not allowed. **Nearby** Skiing, golf, mountain bikes. **Credit cards** Visa, Eurocard and MasterCard. **Spoken** English. **Open** Dec. 1 – May 1 and July 1 – mid-Sept. **How to get there** (Map 27): 10km northwest of Briançon via N91. At Villeneuve Lasalle, Hauts- de -Fréjus; 7km by road passable except when there is heavy snow (telephone and the owner will pick you up).

Isolated in the countryside on a mountain slope 6000 feet up, this modern house is built in the style of a Swiss chalet. The restaurant and terrace are intimate and charming. The four guest bedrooms are small but pretty and (like the rest of the house) entirely paneled in wood; the largest has a balcony. There is a sporting but sophisticated atmosphere, and good, refined cuisine.

428
L'Alpillonne

Sigottier
05700 Serres
(Hautes-Alpes)
Tel. 92 67 08 98
M. and Mme Moynier

Rooms 5 with bath and WC. **Price** 200-250F (1 pers.), 250-300F (2 pers.) +60F (extra pers.). **Meals** Breakfast incl.; evening meals 80F or restaurants (5km). **Facilities** Library and TV, swimming pool, fishing, river swimming. **Nearby** Tennis, lake, wind surfing, golf (18 holes, 40km). **Credit cards** Not accepted. **Spoken** English. **Open** Mid-June – mid-Sept. **How to get there** (Map 33): 3km north of Serres via N75 towards Grenoble.

This 17th-18th-century house standing at the foot of the mountains is charmingly decorated with old regional furniture. The bedrooms are pretty, comfortable and light, and those with bathrooms are large; the two small ones are ideal for children. Breakfasts are served in a huge vaulted barn with a bar and lounges. The only drawback to the Alpillonne is the Grenoble-Marseille National Highway, which is not far way and can be heard when there is heavy traffic. You will receive a very pleasant welcome.

429
Château de Montmaur

Montmaur
05400 Veynes
(Hautes-Alpes)
Tel. 92 58 11 42
M. and Mme Raymond Laurens

Rooms 5 suites (3 pers.) with bath, shower and WC. Rooms cleaned on request. **Price** 400F (2 pers.), +50F (extra pers.); 15% reduction for 1-week stay. **Meals** Breakfast incl. No evening meals. **Restaurants** In Veynes (1.5 to 4km). **Facilities** Lounge, tel., park on property. **Nearby** Tennis in front of château, lake in Veynes, hiking, riding in Veynes, golf (18 holes, 20 km), ski run in Superdevolvy, Gap Museum, natural sites, summer concerts. **Credit cards** Not accepted. **Spoken** English. **Open** All year (on reservation only in low season). **How to get there** (Map 27): 20km northwest of Gap via D 994 towards Valence, then towards Veynes and Montmaur. In village, château indicated.

Facing a magnificent countryside between Provence and the Alps, the historic château is surrounded by the pretty little houses of the village. Although the bedrooms are located in the oldest, 13th-century part of the château, they are unfortunately somewhat drab. (The bathrooms are small, and the installations are modern). The other rooms have the nostalgic but somewhat melancholy charm of châteaux that are too vast to be inhabited and too old to be renovated well. Fortunately, the owners are so fond of th is château that they give it life.

430
La Bastide du Bosquet

14, chemin des Sables
06600 Antibes
(Alpes-Maritime)
Tel. 93 67 32 29/93 34 06 04
Sylvie and Christian Aussel

Rooms 3 with bath or shower and WC, and 2 spare rooms without bath. Rooms cleaned every 3 days. **Price** 350-390F (2 pers.) +80F (extra pers.), +100F (extra room). **Meals** Breakfast incl. **Pets** Small dogs only allowed. **Nearby** Golf (18 holes, 15km); beach (5 min. walk), all water sports, old villages, Picasso Museum, Jazz Festival in Juan-les-Pins, (July). **Credit cards** Not accepted. **Spoken** English. **Open** All year; 3 nights min. in July, Aug. **How to get there** (Map 35): From Cannes via Jean-les-Pins, ask at the Palais des Congrès (at bottom of Chemin des Sables); number 14 is in front of the synagogue. Or Autoroute exit Antibes, towards "Centre Ville", then Cap d'Antibes. On the seafront, take towards Juan-les-Pins (not Antibes). In Cap d'Antibes, follow signs.

This 18th-century Provençal house is located some distance from the busy streets of Antibes even though it is in the heart of the city and a short walk to the beaches. It is a family house which is as beautiful inside as out. The bedrooms are bright, quiet, brightened with pretty Provençal fabrics and tastefully furnished. The bathrooms are very pleasant and are decorated with large, colorful pottery motifs. Breakfasts are served in a pretty dining room or on the terrace. The young owners are very friendly.

431
La Bergerie

77, chemin de l'Hermitage
06160 Juan-les-Pins
(Alpes-Maritime)
Tel. 93 67 97 15
M. and Mme Patrick Dereux

Rooms 5 rooms with bath, WC, telephone, TV, and 1 studio (4 pers.) with bath, WC; 1 living room with beds and 1 bedroom, telephone, TV. Price 430-900F (dep. on room and season), 975-1200F (dep. on season). **Meals** Breakfast incl. No evening meals. **Facilities** Lounge, swimming pool on property; water-skiing lessons by M. Dereux and stain-board rides (suppl.). **Pets** Small dogs allowed on request. **Credit cards** All major. **Spoken** English. **Open** All year; 2 nights min.; no children under 12. **How to get there** (Map 35): In Cap d'Antibes. **No-smoking.**

The owners discovered La Bergerie in their search for a pretty bed- and- breakfast and they have designed it throughout for your pleasure and comfort. Located five minutes from the center of Antibes with its old quarter and market, the house is set in a private park with a swimming pool and tennis court, and thus it is well protected and isolated from the neighboring apartment blocks. Only the stone exterior reflects the name, "The Shepherd's Hut." Inside, the decoration is luxurious with occasional bright colors, such as in the yellow bedroom and the dining room with its rose patinas and trompe l'œil moldings. The overall effect is lovely.

432
Domaine du Paraïs

La Vasta
06380 Sospel
(Alpes-Maritimes)
Tel. 93 04 15 78
Mme Marie Mayer

Rooms 4 with shower and WC. **Price** 240-280F (1 pers.), 290-400F (2 pers.) +100F (extra pers.); 2 nights min. **Meals** Breakfast incl., evening meals by reservation, at communal or separate table 90-120F. **Facilities** Lounge. **Pets** Small dogs allowed on request. **Nearby** Golf (29km), riding, tennis, footpaths, canoeing, Sospel, Roya valley. Open All year no children under 12; non-smokers only. Open All year; 2 nights min.; 2 nights min, no children under 12; non-smokers only. **Credit cards** Not accepted. **Spoken** English, German. **Open** All year. **How to get there** (Map 35): 21km from Menton; in Sospel take the Moulinet road for 1.9km starting from the town hall, then left on the La Vasta road for 1.3km.

A family of artists has brought this beautiful 19th-century Italianate house back to life. Frescos of intertwined flowers have been restored and the sober bedrooms have a magnificent view of Mercantour Park. The Domaine is surrounded by luxuriant vegetation, and it is decorated with delightful paintings and sculptures. The owners are charming.

433
La Burlande

Le Paradou
13520 Les Baux de Provence
(Bouches-du-Rhône)
Tel. 90 54 32 32
Mme Fajardo de Livry

Rooms 3 and 1 suite (2-4 pers.) with bath or shower, WC; patio or terrace and TV. **Price** 260-360F (2 pers.), suite 560F (2 pers.). **Meals** Breakfast 45F, evening meals at communal or separate table 135F (wine not incl.), in summer lunch in the garden 100F. **Facilities** Lounges, telephone, laundry service, baby sitting, swimming pool. **Pets** Dogs allowed on request. **Nearby** Tennis, riding, golf, fishing, climbing, bicycle hire. **Credit cards** Not accepted. **Spoken** English. **Open** All year. **How to get there** (Map 33): 12km southwest of Avignon on Autoroute 7, exit Novès; N7 towards Orgon, D26 on left, towards Cabannes.

La Burlande stands at the end of a long rocky road. A veritable oasis full of flowers, the house has numerous bay windows and a beautiful swimming pool. The very quiet bedrooms all look onto the garden and are tastefully decorated. You will enjoy a very friendly welcome and excellent breakfasts.

434
Mas du Barrié

Grand Chemin du Barrié
13440 Cabannes
(Bouches-du-Rhône)
Tel. 90 95 35 39
M. Michel Bruel

No children. Rooms 2 with shower or bath and WC. Rooms cleaned every 2 days. **Price** 400F (2 pers.); 2 nights min. **Meals** Breakfast incl., evening meals at communal table 150F (wine incl.). **Facilities** Lounge. **Pets** Dogs not allowed. **Nearby** Festivals. **Credit cards** Not accepted. **Spoken** English. **Open** All year. **How to get there** (Map 33): 12km southeast of Avignon A7 exit Noves; N7 towards Orgon then left on D26 towards Cabannes.

Michel Bruel fell in love with this peaceful 18th-century Provençal farmhouse, which is shaded by two 250-year-old plane trees and surrounded by fruit trees. He has restored it elegantly and tastefully, adding modern accommodations to the beautiful old rooms. One guest room is decorated in shades of blue and white, while the other has a canopied bed and a red and white decor. There is also a guest lounge with a fireplace. Breakfast is served in the lounge or, in good weather, on the terrace.

435
Le Mas de l'Ange

Petite route de saint-Rémy
13940 Mollegès
(Bouches-du-Rhône)
Tel. 90 95 08 33
Fax 90 95 48 69
Bruno and Hélène Lafforgue

Rooms 5 with bath and WC. Rooms cleaned every 2 days. **Price** 390F (2 pers.). **Meals** Breakfast 45F. No evening meals. **Restaurants** Many nearby; Les Micocouliers... **Facilities** Lounge. **Nearby** All sports; golf (18 holes, 15km), Ile-sur-Sorgue antiques shops, Les-Baux-de-Provence, Les Antiques de Saint-Rémy, the Camargue. **Credit cards** Not accepted. **Spoken** English, Spanish. **Open** All year. **How to get there** (Map 33): 25km southwest of Avignon. Autoroute du Sud, exit Cavaillon towards Saint-Rémy-de-Provence; on leaving Plan-d'Orgon, towards Mollegès, then, in front of the "Postes", towards Saint-Rémy for 2km, and follow signs.

Surrounded by a luxuriant shady garden, the Mas de l'Ange is a small paradise which has been designed and decorated by a very friendly young couple. The interior looks like a Provençal painting with its warm colors, lovely fabrics, terra cotta and *faïences,* and regional furniture. Every comfortable bedroom recreates an atmosphere of the past and yet they are all very contemporary. "The Angel's House" is a very beautiful place to stay.

436
Château de Vergières

13310 Saint-Martin-de-Crau
(Bouches-du-Rhône)
Tel. 90 47 17 16
Fax 90 47 38 30
Jean and Marie-Andrée Pincedé

Rooms 6 with bath and WC. **Price** 750F (1 pers.), 800F (2 pers.). **Meals** Breakfast incl., evening meals by reservation at communal table 300F (drinks incl.). **Facilities** Lounge, telephone. **Pets** Dogs not allowed. **Nearby** Swimming pool, tennis, golf, the Camargue. **Credit cards** Amex, Visa, Eurocard and MasterCard. **Spoken** English. **Open** All year. **How to get there** (Map 33): 17km east of Arles via N113 towards Saint-Martin-de-Crau, then D24 towards La Dynamite and *le mas des Aulnes*; signs.

The vast plain of the Crau and the closeness of the Camargue marshes are enough to attract you to this château, but you will also enjoy its late 18th-century elegance, its beautiful old furniture and M. and Mme Pincedé's charming hospitality. The comfortable bedrooms retain their traditional charm and each has a style of its own, complementing the beautiful antique furniture. The Provençal dinners are excellent.

437
Les Cancades

Chemin de la
Fontaine-de-Cinq-Sous
Les Cancades
83330 Le Beausset (Var)
Tel. 94 98 76 93
Mme Zerbib

Rooms 1 with bath and WC, 1 with bath, shared WC and terrace, and 1 studio (4 pers.) with shower and WC (consists of 1 large room and 1 small). Room cleaning up to guests. **Price** 350-400F (2 pers.), studio 1800-2500F the week (1-4 pers.). **Meals** Breakfast incl. No evening meals (poss. summer cooking). **Restaurants** In Le Beausset. **Facilities** Lounge, swimming pool. **Pets** Dogs not allowed. **Credit cards** Not accepted. **Open** All year. **How to get there** (Map 34): 20km northwest of Toulon via N8 towards Aubagne; opposite Rallye supermarket Fontaine-de-Cinq-Sous road for 1.3km then dirt road on the left; 50 metres after the 90° turn.

After passing through a small housing development, you will discover this large Provençal-style villa standing in a landscape of pine and olive trees. Recently built and tastefully decorated, it has two beautiful guest bedrooms, one with a private terrace opening onto the garden and swimming pool; the other, somewhat smaller, has been prettily redecorated with lovely Provençal fabrics. You can also rent the studio by the week.

438
Domaine du Riou Blanc

Le Grand Chêne
83440 Callian
(Var)
Tel. 94 47 70 61
Fax 94 47 77 21
Mme Micheline Delesalle

Rooms 4 with bath or shower and WC; 1 studio (4 pers.) with 1 room, bath, kitchen and lounge (convertible). **Price** 380-450F (2 pers.),+120F (extra pers.); studio 4000F the week (2-4 pers.). **Meals** Breakfast incl. No evening meals. **Facilities** Lounge, swimming pool (at certain hours). **Pets** Small dogs only. **Nearby** Restaurants, riding, tennis, mountain biking, Saint-Cassien Lake (fishing, sports); golf (18 holes, 25km); Montauroux, Caillan, Tourrettes, Seillans, Saint-Paul-en-Forêt. **Credit cards** Not accepted. **Spoken** English, German, Spanish. **Closed** Sept. – May 1 (or on request). **How to get there** (Map 34): 20 west of Grasse towards Draguignan on D562. Turn left towards Les Coulettes d'Alongues for 1.3km and follow signs.

The renovated Domaine du Riou Blanc is a large old farmhouse made of the warm stone typical of this region of the south. Surrounded by fields and forests, it is not easy to reach via the rocky path leading to it. The interior decoration is irregular: Some bathrooms are not separated from the bedrooms and some of the furniture is ordinary. With its beautiful swimming pool, terrace and enchanting country setting, the Domaine is best for those who like to spend their time outdoors.

439
L'Ormarine

14, avenue des Grives
L'Eau Blanche
83240 Cavalaire - (Var)
Tel. 94 64 39 45
(in winter) 76 80 66 88
Heidi and Gérard Léopold

Rooms 1 suite (2-4 pers.) with bath and WC. **Price** 300F (2 pers., 1 night), +100F (extra pers.); 280F reduction beginning the 2nd night. **Meals** Breakfast incl. No evening meals. **Facilities** Heated swimming pool, barbecue, sailing trips (for longs stays). **Pets** Dogs allowed on request. **Nearby** Restaurants, golf, sports, Saint-Tropez, Gassin, Ramatuelle, Verdon gorges, Carthusian monastery of la Verne. **Spoken** German. **Open** April 1 – mid-Dec. **How to get there** (Map 34): Map will be sent.

L'Ormarine is a Provençal-style house built in the residential area of Cavalaire but is sheltered by a magnificent, aromatic, flower-filled garden. The small guest suite is very simple, with twin beds and white wood furniture, but it has a very comfortable bathroom. Guests have their own terrace to relax on. Heidi and Gérard are charming hosts and occasionally Gérard takes guests for a day's cruise at sea.

440
Château d'Entrecasteaux

83570 Entrecasteaux
(Var)
Tel. 94 04 43 95
Fax 94 04 48 46
M. Lachlan Mc Garvie Munn

Rooms 1 suite with shower, WC and telephone; 1 room "Chambre de la marquise" with bath, WC and telephone. **Price** 950F (2 pers.) +250F (extra pers.); 1250F, + 500F (extra room, 36m^2). **Meals** Breakfast incl. No evening meals. **Restaurants** Lou Picatou in Entrecasteaux (100m), Chez Bruno in Lorgues (15km). **Facilities** Swimming pool, exhibitions. **Credit card** Amex. **Pets** Dogs not allowed. **Credit cards** Not accepted. **Spoken** English, Spanish. **Open** All year by reservation. **How to get there** (Map 34): 31km west of Draguignan via D562 towards Lorgues, then D31. **No smoking.**

Entrecasteaux has a panoramic view of the village. The modern paintings and antique furniture go together perfectly. The suite, which is on the ground floor, is very comfortable and has a magnificent view. Upstairs, the *Chambre de la Marquise* is extraordinary, with gilt furniture and a splendid marble bathroom with white arches. An adjacent room in the same style can also be rented. Generous breakfasts are served in a bright dining room.

441
Le Mazet des Mûres

Route du Cros d'Entassi
Quartier Les Mûres
83310 Grimaud
(Var)
Tel. 94 56 44 45
Mme B. Godon

Rooms 5 studios (1-4 pers.) with shower, WC, kitchenette and TV. **Price** 380F (2 pers.), 450F (3 pers.). **Meals** Breakfast incl., evening meals on request. **Nearby** Restaurants, beaches, sailing, golf, equestrian center, tennis, Grimaud, Port-Grimaud, Gassin, Saint-Tropez. **Credit cards** Not accepted. **Spoken** English, German. **Closed** Mid-Oct. – mid-Dec. and mid-Jan. – mid-Feb. **How to get there** (Map 34): N98 between Sainte-Maxime and Saint-Tropez; at the traffic circle, follow Les Mûres signs.

Though close to Saint-Tropez, le Mazet des Mûres is in surprisingly unspoiled surroundings. There are several terraces for breakfast in summer. All the bedrooms overlook the garden and are prettily decorated with cane furniture and colored fabrics; the kitchenettes are decorated with Salernes tiles. Unfortunately, some rooms are not well soundproofed. You will enjoy the relaxed atmosphere and reasonable prices.

442
La Calanco

Rue du Docteur Rayol
83131 Montferrat
(Var)
Tel. and fax 94 70 93 10
Mme Katrin Kuhlmann

Rooms 6 with bath or shower and WC. **Price** 220-360F (1 pers.), 260-400F (2 pers.). **Meals** Breakfast incl.; half-board in addition to room; meals at communal or separate tables by reserv. 120-150F (wine incl.). **Facilities** Lounge. **Nearby** Tennis in village, riding clubs (4 and 7kms); Montferrat Falls, 12th-century chapel, Gorges du Verdon, museums on Coast. **Credit cards** Visa, Eurocard and MasterCard. **Spoken** English, German. **Open** All year. **How to get there** (Map 34): 15km north of Draguignan. In Draguignan, take Ave. de Montferrat towards Dignes via D955. In Montferrat, house after "boulangerie" on left.

At La Calanco, one ground-floor bedroom opens onto a small garden; the others are upstairs and have small fireplaces and ingenious bathrooms with pretty tiles. Our favorite room is the one with floral wallpaper (somewhat yellowed), which is bathed in light at sunset. Katrin, the owner, has decorated the house with a combination of charming old objects from her grandmother, and modern furniture, creating an amusing and lighthearted decor. Régis is in charge of the very good cuisine; it is unfortunate that he doesn't cook more often, but he will advise you on the best restaurants nearby.

443
La Maurette

83520 Roquebrune–sur–Argens
(Var)
Tel. 94 45 46 81
M. and Mme Rapin

Rooms 4 and 5 studios (2 pers.) with bath or shower, WC and telephone. **Price** 350-450F. **Meals** Breakfast 45F, evening meals for residents only by reservation. **Facilities** Lounge, swimming pool. **Pets** Dogs not allowed. **Credit cards** Visa, Eurocard and MasterCard. **Spoken** English, German. **Open** Easter – mid-Oct. **How to get there** (Map 34): 10km west of Fréjus via N7 between Le Muy and Le Puget-sur-Argens, then D7 towards Roquebrune; signposted.

Perched on the top of a small mountain, La Maurette enjoys an exceptional view over the Esterel and Maures Mountains. The comfortable bedrooms have direct access to the garden; their decor is pleasantly rustic Meals are served by the windows of the very large living room. You will enjoy the panoramic views from the swimming pool and the new veranda where, beginning in May, meals are served .The owners are charming.

444
Vasken

Les Cavalières
83520 Roquebrune–sur–Argens
(Var)
Tel. 94 45 76 16
M. and Mme Kuedjian

Rooms 3 with bath or shower and WC. 1 studio (2 pers. + 2 children), with shower, WC and 1 bedroom/living room. TV on request. Rooms cleaned on request. **Price** 350F (1 pers.), 400F (2 pers.); studio500F. **Meals** Breakfast 35F. No evening meals. Restaurants in 2 and 7km. **Facilities** Lounge, swimming pool. **Pets** Dogs not allowed. **Nearby** Water skiing, riding and tennis (2 km), hiking, mountain biking, golf (18 holes, 2km), Roquebrune (traditional glassworks), Nice, Fréjus. **Credit cards** Not accepted. **Open** All year (by reservation in low season). **How to get there** (Map 34): 12 km west of Fréjus via N7 between Le Muy and Le Puget-sur-Argens, then D7 towards Roquebrune. In the village, 1st right. At the cemetery, Blvd. du 18 Juin for 1.5km and then follow Vasken signs.

Monsieur Kuerdjian, a retired pastry chef, makes fresh croissants for your breakfast at Vasken, a house which he built himself. Made of the warm red stones of the region, his pretty, L-shaped house is set amidst the aromatic shrubs and trees of Provence. Decorated in simple, rustic style, the ground-floor bedrooms open onto the garden and each has a private terrace. Madame Kuerdjian will welcome you with enthusiastic and friendly hospitality.

445
Le Jardin d'Ansouis

Rue du Petit-Portail
84240 Ansouis
(Vaucluse)
Tel. and fax 90 09 89 27
Arlette Rogers

Rooms 2 with bath and WC. Rooms cleaned once a week. **Price** 230F (1 pers.), 290F (2 pers.), 350F (3 pers.), 450F (4 pers.). **Meals** Breakfast incl., evening meals on separate tables by reservation 50-200F. **Restaurant** L'Auberge du Cheval Blanc (12km). **Facilities** Lounge. **Pets** Dogs allowed. **Nearby** Swimming pool (8km), riding, tennis (5km), beach, water sports, Château d'Ansouis, Luberon villages, lake la Bonde. **Credit cards** Not accepted. **Spoken** German, Dutch. **Open** All year. **How to get there** (Map 33): 35km north of Aix-en-Provence via A51, exit Pertuis, then D56.

L ocated in a delightful medieval village dominated by an imposing château, Ansouis is on a charming little street behind a flower garden. Inside there is a pleasing blend of modern works of art and furniture of various styles. The bedrooms are inviting and comfortable and you will be very well looked after.

446
La Ferme Jamet

Ile de la Barthelasse
84000 Avignon
(Vaucluse)
Tel. 90 86 16 74
Fax 90 86 17 72

Rooms 4 with bath or shower and WC, 3 bungalows and 4 suites (2-4 pers.) with bath or shower, WC, kitchenette or kitchen. **Price** 350F (2 pers.), suite 400F (2 pers.), bungalow 350F (2 pers.) +50F (extra pers.). **Meals** Breakfast 40F. No evening meals. **Restaurant** La Ferme (150m). **Facilities** Lounge, swimming pool, tennis. **Nearby** Golf, Avignon, festivals. **Spoken** English, German. **Credit cards** Visa, Eurocard and MasterCard. **Open** March 1 – Nov. 1 (by reservation in winter). **How to get there** (Map 33): In Avignon, head for Villeneuve-lès-Avignon via Daladier bridge; signposted.

J amet is a very old farmhouse on a quiet, verdant island outside Avignon. It is a perfect base for both touring the region and relaxing. The bedrooms are mostly suites; those in the house have old Provençal furniture. The bungalows are simpler and each has a private terrace. This is a very peaceful and comfortable place to stay, and the owners are young and friendly.

447
Château de Saint-Ariès

Route de Saint-Ariès
84500 Bollène
(Vaucluse)
Tel. 90 40 09 17
Fax 90 30 45 62
Michel-Albert de Loÿe

Rooms 4 with bath, WC and sitting room, and 1 suite with bath, WC and 2 sitting rooms. **Price** 630-740F (2 pers.) +120F (extra pers.), suite 990F (2 pers.), 1090F (3-4 pers.). **Meals** Breakfast 50F, evening meals on request, at communal table 240F (wine incl.). **Restaurants** In Mondragon (4km). **Facilities** Swimming pool, equestrian centre, bicycles. **Pets** Small dogs allowed on request. **Nearby** Tennis, golf, gorges of the Ardèche, Suze-la-Rousse, Mont Ventoux. **Credit card** Visa, Eurocard and MasterCard. **Spoken** English, Italian. **Open** March 2 – Jan. 2 (2 nights min.). **How to get there** (Map 33): 3km from A7 exit Bollène; town center, then towards Mondragon. On the way out of Bollène turn left for Saint-Ariès, then go 1.5km.

Saint-Ariès, built in 1820 and modeled on the villas of Tuscany, stands in a huge park. The interior is beautiful. From the reception rooms to the bedrooms, family furniture, coloured fabrics and paintings create a marvelously harmonious ensemble. Michel de Loye will greet you warmly and is a charming host at his excellent dinners. The château is a splendid place.

448
Bonne Terre

Lacoste
84480 Bonnieux
(Vaucluse)
Tel. and fax 90 75 85 53
M. and Mme Lamy

Rooms 6 with bath or shower, WC, TV and terrace. **Price** Depending on season 390F and 420F (1 pers.), 450F and 480F (2 pers.); +120F (extra pers.); 3 nights min. **Meals** Breakfast incl. No evening meals. **Restaurants** In Lacoste and nearby (7-8km). **Facilities** Telephone, swimming pool. **Pets** Dogs allowed (+40F). **Nearby** Golf, tennis, riding, music festivals, theater, Luberon villages. **Credit cards** Visa, Eurocard and MasterCard. **Spoken** English, German and Italian. **Open** March 1 – Oct. 30. **How to get there** (Map 33): East of Cavaillon via N100 towards Apt, then D106 towards Lacoste; opposite the Renault garage.

At the entrance to the very beautiful village of Lacoste, this elegant house is peaceful, and the very comfortable bedrooms are prettily decorated; each opens onto a private, ground-floor terrace where you can have breakfast. The garden is on several levels, with a swimming pool and a beautiful view of Mont Ventoux.

449
La Bouquière

Quartier St Pierre
84480 Bonnieux
(Vaucluse)
Tel. 90 75 87 17
Françoise and Angel Escobar

Rooms 4 with bath or shower, WC and terrace. Rooms cleaned every 2 days. **Price** 360F (2 pers.) +60F (extra pers.). **Meals** Breakfast incl. No evening meals. **Restaurants** Le Fournil and Les Cavernes in Bonnieux (3km). **Facilities** Lounge and small kitchen. **Pets** Dogs allowed on request. **Nearby** Hiking in Lubéron National Park. **Credit cards** Not accepted. **Spoken** English, Spanish. **Open** All year. **How to get there** (Map 33): 3km from Bonnieux via D3 towards Apt; signs after 2.5km .

Surrounded by verdant countryside, La Bouquière enjoys a magnificent view of Mont Ventoux and has four comfortable guest bedrooms, very prettily decorated in Provençal style. Each bedroom has an independent entrance and opens onto a terrace where breakfast can be served. You will be pleasantly welcomed by Françoise and Angel Escobar and their young son.

450
Clos Saint-Vincent

84410 Crillon-le-Brave
(Vaucluse)
Tel. 90 65 93 36
Fax 90 12 81 46
M. and Mme Vazquez

Rooms 5 with shower and WC, and 1 small house (4 pers.) with 2 rooms, bath, WC, lounge, kitchen, terrace, TV and telephone. **Price** 410-460F (2 pers.); 750F (2 pers.); 950F (4 pers.), +110F (extra pers.), 70F (children). **Meals** Breakfast incl.; evening meals occasionally 140F (wine incl.). **Restaurants** In 500m and 12km. **Facilities** Lounge, swimming pool and pétanque court on property. **Pets** Not allowed. **Nearby** Tennis, riding (2.5km); Carpentras Synagogue, Mechanical Instruments Museum in Crillon. **Credit cards** Not accepted. **Spoken** English, Spanish. **Closed** Mid-Nov. – mid-Feb. **How to get there** (Map 33): 12km from Carpentras, road to Bedouin, then towards Crillon-le-Brave. Clos Saint-Vincent indicated.

Madame Vazquez loves her house and will share her enthusiasm with you. The decoration is tasteful, original and pleasant with its antique furniture and materials which she has found in the region. Don't miss the breakfasts, which include homemade preserves and pastries. If dinner is suggested, don't miss that either! You'll meet the family and guests/friends who are happy regulars at the Clos Saint-Vincent.

451
Au Ralenti du Lierre

Les Beaumettes
84220 Gordes
(Vaucluse)
Tel. 90 72 39 22
Mme Deneits

Rooms 5 with bath or shower and WC. **Price** 350-500F (2 pers.) +80F (extra pers.). **Meals** Breakfast incl. No evening meals. **Restaurants** La Remise and Le Mas des Lavandes. **Facilities** Lounge, swimming pool. **Pets** Dogs not allowed. **Nearby** Golf, walks, fishing, tennis, riding, canoeing, climbing, villages of Gordes, Lacoste and Bonnieux, Senanque abbey. **Credit cards** Not accepted. **Open** Mid-March – Nov.1. **How to get there** (Map 33): 15km east of L'Isle-sur-la-Sorgue. Avignon-Sud Autoroute, exit towards Apt; in the village of Les Beaumettes.

This village house is beautifully decorated, with colors, fabrics and furniture creating a lovely harmony throughout; the bedrooms are very comfortable. For those with a taste for the unusual, there is an extraordinary suite of two vaulted rooms, one of which is very dark. A pretty garden slopes down the hillside. The breakfast is excellent and the owner is charming.

452
La Méridienne

Chemin de la Lône
84800 L'Isle-sur-la-Sorgue
(Vaucluse)
Tel. 90 38 40 26
Fax 90 38 58 46
Jérôme Tarayre

Rooms 4 with bath, WC and terrace. Rooms cleaned every 3 days. **Price** 250-300F (2 pers.) +80F (extra pers.). **Meals** Breakfast incl. No evening meals. **Restaurant** Les Jardins de la Gare in L'Isle-sur-la-Sorgue. **Facilities** Lounge, swimming pool. **Nearby** Riding, canoeing, kayaks, golf courses (9 and 18 holes, 6km); villages of Lubéron, Avignon and Gordes Festivals, antiques dealers in L'Ile-sur-la-Sorgue. **Credit cards** Not accepted. **Spoken** English, Spanish. **Open** All year. **How to get there** (Map 33): 27km east of Avignon via N100 towards Apt. 3.5km after the center of L'Isle sur-la-Sorgue, go 500m after fork, towards Lagnes; discreet blue sign on left.

In this small house, typical of the beautiful Lubéron region, the comfortable bedrooms are prettily decorated with regional wicker furniture as well as lacquered pieces in the warm colors of Provence. Each room is on the ground floor and opens directly onto a private terrace where breakfasts are served. At La Méridienne, you will enjoy rest and relaxation in a beautifully quiet setting which is enhanced by Jérôme Tarayre's friendly hospitality.

453
Sous Les Canniers

Route de la Roque
Saumane
84800 L'Isle-sur-Sorgue
(Vaucluse)
Tel. 90 20 20 30
Mme Annie Marquet

Rooms 2 with shower and WC. **Price** 250F (2 pers.) +100F (extra pers.). **Meals** Breakfast incl., evening meals at communal table 100F (wine incl.). **Facilities** Lounge. **Pets** Dogs allowed on request. **Nearby** Golf (3km), walks, tennis, swimming pool, riding, abbeys and villages of Luberon. **Credit cards** Not accepted. **Spoken** Italian, Spanish. **Open** All year (by reservation in winter). **How to get there** (Map 33): 7km east of L'Isle-sur-Sorgue via D938 and D25 towards Fontaine-de-Vaucluse, then left on D57 towards Saumane; Route de La Roque, then signs in the village.

This small Provençal house is set in a beautiful garden which is surrounded by countryside. The bedrooms open directly onto the outside; they are pleasant and pretty, with bits and pieces of furniture collected from antique shops. One room has a mezzanine. Madame Marquet is very welcoming and prepares good dinners which are often served at a communal table on the terrace. Sous les Canniers has many attractive qualities.

454
Mas du Grand Jonquier

Route départementale 22
84800 Lagnes
(Vaucluse)
Tel. 90 20 90 13 - Fax and
answering machine 90 20 91 18
Monique and François Greck

Rooms 6 with shower, WC, TV, telephone. **Price** 450-500F (2 pers.) +100F (extra pers.). **Meals** Breakfast incl., evening meals at separate tables 130F (wine not incl.). **Facilities** Lounge, swimming pool. **Credit Cards** All major. **Pets** Dogs not allowed. **Nearby** Riding, canoeing, kayaks, golf courses (9 and 18 holes, 5km); villages of Lubéron, Gordes and Avignon Festivals, antiques dealers in L'Ile-sur-la-Sorgue, Vaucluse Fountain. **Credit cards** Not accepted. **Spoken** English, Italian, German, Spanish. **Open** All year. **How to get there** (Map 33): 10km east of Cavaillon. On D22 between Avignon, Sud and Apt. Coming from Avignon: 1.5km after the sign indicating the village of Petit Palais.

A screen of lush foliage shields this Provençal *mas* from the noise of the road. Entirely renovated, it has lovely, very comfortable bedrooms named *Olivier, Thym, Basilic* (very quiet), and also *Amandier* and *Figuier,* which we especially like. The guest book is filled with compliments for the dinners and breakfasts, which are served in a rustic room or outdoors in the shade of an enormous chestnut tree. The Grecks are very welcoming and pleasant.

455
Saint-Buc

Route de l'Isle
84800 Lagnes
(Vaucluse)
Tel. 90 20 36 29
Mme Delorme

Rooms 4 with bath and WC; no children. **Price** 400F (1-2 pers.). **Meals** Breakfast incl. No evening meals. Kitchen for guests' use. **Facilities** Lounge, telephone, swimming pool, bicycles. **Pets** Animals not allowed. **Nearby** Restaurant, golf (18 holes), Luberon, Gordes, Avignon Festival, Fontaine-de-Vaucluse. **Credit cards** Not accepted. **Spoken** English. **Open** June 1 – early Sept. **How to get there** (Map 33): 23km east of Avignon via N100 towards Apt. At Petit-Palais head for Fontaine-de-Vaucluse. At Lagnes take D99 towards Isle-sur-la-Sorgue.

Saint-Buc is a modern house a few minutes from L'Isle-sur-la Sorgue. The comfortable bedrooms are at garden level and are pleasantly and simply decorated; the bathrooms are large and functional and have sunken baths. There is a vast lounge decorated with antique objects. Breakfast is served outside under an awning. There is a swimming pool and a small kitchen in the garden for guests. The atmosphere is informal.

456
Domaine de la Lombarde

BP32, 84160 Lourmarin
(Vaucluse)
Tel. 90 08 40 60
Fax 90 08 40 64
M. and Mme Gilbert Lèbre

Rooms 4 with shower, WC, fridge and terrace, and 1 studio (2 pers. + 2 children) with shower, WC, kitchen and terrace. Rooms cleaned every 3 days. **Price** 300-340F (2 pers.) +100F (extra pers.), studio 2400F weekly. **Meals** Breakfast incl. (except studio). No evening meals. **Facilities** Restaurants, swimming pool, bicycles. **Pets** Dogs not allowed. **Nearby** Tennis, riding, golf, walks, Luberon, many festivals. **Credit cards** Not accepted. **Spoken** English, Spanish. **Open** Easter – Nov 30. **How to get there** (Map 33): 30km north of Aix-en-Provence via N556 towards Pertuis and D973; it's between Cadenet and Lauris; signposted.

La Lombarde is a lovely Provençal house set among fields and vineyards. Each bedroom has an independent entrance with a wooden canopy forming a terrace. The bedrooms are comfortable and attractively decorated. Good breakfasts are served on an old convent table in a long, white, vaulted room.

457
Villa Saint Louis

35, rue Henri de Savornin
84160 Lourmarin
(Vaucluse)
Tel. 90 68 39 18
Fax 90 68 10 07
Michel and Bernadette Lassallette

Rooms 5 with bath or shower and WC. Rooms cleaned on request. **Price** 300-400F (2 pers.). **Meals** Breakfast incl. No evening meals. **Restaurants** Many in village. **Facilities** Lounge, mountain-bikes. **Nearby** Skiing, golf (25km), tennis, fishing, riding, canoeing, Luberon Natural Park, Luberon villages, summer festivals. **Credit cards** Not accepted. **Spoken** English. **Open** All year. **How to get there** (Map 33): 50km east of Avignon via N7 and D973 towards Cavaillon, then Cadenet and left on D943 towards Lourmarin.

This beautiful 17th-century house, secluded in a walled garden, is located on the edge of Lourmarin. Designed by Michel Lassallette, the interior decoration is an exceptional combination of different periods (18th to 20th centuries) with a profusion of furniture, paintings, objects and wall fabrics. Breakfast is served in the lounge–dining-room, and occasionally on the terrace. The Villa is very comfortable and you will receive a marvelous welcome.

458
Château Unang

Route de Méthamis
84570 Malemort-du-Comtat
(Vaucluse)
Tel. 90 69 71 06
Fax 90 69 92 80
Marie-Hélène Lefer

Rooms 4 with bath and WC. **Price** 390-550F (2 pers.). **Meals** Breakfast 50F, evening meals at communal or separate table 150F (wine not incl.). **Restaurants** Les Remparts in Vénasque (6km). **Facilities** Lounge, swimming pool. **Pets** Dogs not allowed. **Nearby** Tennis, equestrian centre, golf (15km), ski ing (30km), Gordes, Senanque Abbey, Luberon villages. **Credit cards** Not accepted. **Spoken** English, Spanish. **Open** All year (on request in Jan. and Feb.). **How to get there** (Map 33): 12km south east of Carpentras via D4 towardsVénasque for 6km, then left for Malemort.

Château Unang is a beautiful 18th-century residence with a formal French garden facing the Vaucluse Mountains. Inside there is a pleasing blend of different styles. The lounge is very inviting, and the bedrooms are extremely elegant. We prefer the *Fontaine* Room; *Vignes* is equally beautiful but the view is less beautiful. Excellent breakfasts are served outside when the weather is good. The owner is young and extremely friendly.

459
Mas de Capelans

84580 Oppède
(Vaucluse)
Tel. 90 76 99 04
Fax 90 76 90 29
Jacqueline and Philippe Poiri

Rooms 6 with bath and WC, and 2 suites (4 pers.) with bath and WC., of which 1 with 2 bedrooms and 1 with mezzanine. **Price** 400-900F (2 pers.) +120F (extra pers.), suite 600-1000F. **Meals** Breakfast 50F, half board 400-600F per pers. in double room, evening meals at communal table 155F (wine not incl.). **Facilities** Lounge, library, TV, heated swimming pool. **Pets** Dogs not allowed. **Nearby** Golf, tennis, fishing, riding, mountain biking. **Credit cards** Amex, Visa, Eurocard and MasterCard. **Spoken** English, German. **Open** 15 Feb. – 15 Nov. 3 nights min. **How to get there** (Map 33): 23km east of Avignon Sud on N100 towards Apt until Coustelet, then 1st road on the right.

Surrounded by lavender fields, this lovely old house has a pleasant inner courtyard where meals are served in summer. The bedrooms are large, very comfortable, decorated with pale wood and pretty fabrics, and have an exceptionally beautiful view. The sitting room is high and beamed, with comfortable wooden furniture and painted objects.

460
Mas de Lumière

Campagne Les Talons
84490 Saint-Saturnin-lès-Apt
(Vaucluse)
Tel. 90 05 63 44
M. and Mme Bernard Maître

Rooms 2 with bath and WC, 1 with shower and WC. **Price** 400-550F (2 pers.) +100F (extra pers.). **Meals** Breakfast incl. No evening meals. **Restaurants** Ferme de la Huppe and La Bartabelle. **Facilities** Lounge, swimming pool. **Pets** Dogs not allowed. **Nearby** Golf (25km), riding, tennis, Luberon villages. **Credit cards** Not accepted. **Spoken** English, Spanish. **Open** All year. No children under 5. **How to get there** (Map 33): 10km west of Apt via N100 towards Gordes, and D4 towards Roussillon-Murs, then at the crossroads with D2 go 500m on D4, then turn right at the Les Talons sign.

Standing on a slight rise above a tiny hamlet, Mas de Lumière is a lovely, both outside and within its cool walls. The bedrooms are luxurious and beautiful, with decor in soft colors. Several outside terraces offer guests privacy and comfort; (the terrace facing east is ideal for breakfast). There is a beautiful swimming pool overlooking the Luberon Plain. The owners are friendly and refined.

461
L'Evêché

Rue de l'Evêché
84110 Vaison-la-Romaine
(Vaucluse)
Tel. 90 36 13 46/90 36 38 30
Fax 90 36 32 43
M. and Mme Verdier

Rooms 4 with bath or shower, WC and telephone. Rooms cleaned on request. **Price** 300-360F (1 pers.), 360-400F (2 pers.). **Meals** Breakfast incl., no evening meals. **Restaurants** In Vaison. **Facilities** Lounge. **Pets** Dogs allowed on request. **Nearby** Swimming pool, tennis, riding, golf (miniature and practice) in the village, walks, Vaison-la-Romaine. **Credit cards** Not accepted. **Open** All year. **How to get there** (Map 33): 29km north east of Orange via D975; in Vaison-la-Romaine follow Ville Médiévale signs.

This former Bishop's Palace in the medieval part of Vaison-la-Romaine was built in the 17th-century and is very charming. The austere façade hides a comfortable, well decorated house, with two terraces (one used for breakfasts) which have a magnificent view. The bedrooms are delightful; the largest is the one with a tub in the bathroom. You will receive a pleasant welcome.

462
La Fête en Provence

Place du Vieux Marché
Haute Ville
84110 Vaison-la-Romaine
(Vaucluse)
Tel. 90 36 16 05/90 36 36 43
M. and Mme Christiansen

Rooms 2 duplex (3-4 pers.) with bath, WC, kitchen area, telephone and TV, 4 studios (2 pers.) with bath or shower, WC, kitchen area, telephone and TV, and 1 apartment (2 pers. and 1 child) with sitting room, kitchenette, bath and WC. **Price** Studio 300F (2 pers.), duplex 600-650F (3-4 pers.), apart. 450F. Room cleaning on request. **Meals** Breakfast 40F, restaurant for lunch and dinner (except Wednesday and Thursday lunch out of season) 90F and 150F or à la carte (wine not incl.) **Nearby** Swimming pool, tennis, 18-hole golf, Merindol les Oliviers. **Credit cards** Amex, Visa, Eurocard and MasterCard. **Spoken** German. **Closed** Nov. and Feb. **How to get there** (Map 33): 27km north east of Orange via D975.

This is one of the loveliest medieval villages in the Midi, and La Fête en Provence is on the picturesque market square. A beautiful patio leads to the bedrooms. We recommend the duplexes, which have a terrace with a beautiful view. They are comfortable and have modern olivewood furniture. Neither a hotel nor a bed and breakfast, this is a charming place in a very good location.

463
Mastignac

Route de Taulignan
84600 Valréas
(Vaucluse)
Tel. 90 35 01 82
Mme Nicole de Precigout

Rooms 1 with bath and WC and 4 with shower sharing 3 WCs. **Price** 300-450F (2 pers.). **Meals** Breakfast incl. No evening meals. **Facilities** Lounge, swimming pool. **Pets** Small dogs allowed. **Nearby** Restaurants, tennis, swimming, golf, festivals. **Credit cards** Not accepted. **Spoken** English. **Open** June 1 – Oct 10. **How to get there** (Map 33): 37km south east of Montélimar via A7, exit Montélimar Sud, then N7 towards Donzère, and D541. In Valréas, left on D47, the Taulignan road; signposted.

Two kilometres from Valréas you will come upon this big old 18th-century farmhouse. It is well restored and immaculate, with an inner courtyard, an English lawn and a lovely swimming pool. The five tastefully decorated bedrooms are large and light, each with a bathroom but four share three toilets. Breakfast is served outside whenever possible, or in the lounge or the large kitchen. You will enjoy a pleasant and peaceful atmosphere.

464
La Maison aux Volets Bleus

84210 Vénasque
(Vaucluse)
Tel. 90 66 03 04
Fax 90 66 16 14
Mme Martine Maret

Rooms 5 with bath and WC (of which 1 with shower and bath). **Price** 315-385F (2 pers.) +120F (extra pers.). **Meals** Breakfast incl., evening meals (separate tables) 120F (wine not incl.). **Facilities** Lounge, telephone. **Nearby** Tennis, bicycles, footpaths, Sénanque Abbey, Fontaine-de-Vaucluse, Avignon, Luberon. **Credit cards** Not accepted. **Spoken** English. **Open** Mid-March – mid-Nov. **How to get there** (Map 33): South of Carpentras via D4; signposted.

"The House With Blue Shutters" is tucked away in the pretty village of Vénasque, perched on top of a rock. It is built of stone and is quite delightful, with a small shady courtyard full of flowers. The lounge is large, pleasantly decorated, with antique furniture and dried flower arrangements. The bedrooms are big, comfortable and tastefully decorated. There are beautiful bathrooms and a magnificent, panoramic view. The owners are friendly, the cuisine is excellent and breakfast is served on the beautiful terrace.

465
Manoir de Marmont

01960 Saint-André-
sur-Vieux-Jonc
(Ain)
Tel. 74 52 79 74
Henri and Geneviève Guido

Rooms 2 with bath or shower and WC, and 1 spare room with washbasin. **Price** 400F (1 pers.), 450F (2 pers.), 700F (4 pers.); 10% reduction beg. 3rd night. Children under 13 free. **Meals** Breakfast incl. No evening meals. **Restaurants** At golf course (400m), and La Rotonde (3km). **Facilties** Lounge. **Pets** Dogs allowed on request. **Nearby** Golf (18 and 6 holes); Lakes of the Dombs Route, Chatillon-sur-Charonne, Pérouges, Bird sanctuary in Villars-les-Dombes. **Credit cards** Not accepted. **Spoken** English, Italian. **Open** All year. **How to get there** (Map 26): 14km southwest of Bourg-en-Bresse via N83 towards Lyon to Servas. At traffic light on right towards Condeissiat (D 64) for 5km, and take the road with plane trees on left.

Located next door to a beautiful golf course, this late 19th-century manor house has conserved all its traditional charm, including the original wallpapers and handsome old furniture. Mme Guido puts all of her incredible energy and good nature into pleasing her guests. You will find books in the vast bedrooms and innumerable pretty details in the bathrooms–your hostess has overlooked nothing. The delicious breakfasts are served in the salon and on the charming patio just outside.

466
Le Jeu du Mail

07400 Alba-la-Romaine
(Ardèche)
Tel. 75 52 41 59
M. and Mme Maurice Arlaud

Rooms 4 with bath or shower and WC, and 1 suite (4-6 pers.) of two bedrooms (with mezzanine) with 2 showers, 2 WCs and fridge. Rooms cleaned every 2 days. **Price** 220-290F (2 pers.), suite 500F (4 pers.). **Meals** Breakfast incl. No evening meals. **Facilities** Lounge, swimming pool, mountain bikes. **Pets** Dogs allowed on request (+30F). **Nearby** Restaurants, tennis, riding, golf, medieval villages, Romanesque churches. **Credit cards** Not accepted. **Spoken** English, Italian. **Open** All year. **How to get there** (Map 26): 18km west of Montélimar via N102. At Buis-d'Aps, D107 towards Viviers; it's 200m from the château.

Alba-la-Romaine is a lovely village built of volcanic rock. This old house, just outside the village, has thick walls which keep it cool and quiet. The bedrooms are charming, comfortable and well decorated with old furniture and amusing prints. Breakfast is served on a large table in the beautiful sitting room. The owners are delightful.

467
Maison Icare

Faugères
07230 Lablachère
(Ardèche)
Tel. 75 39 48 66
M. Bruno Harmand

Rooms 1 suite (2-3 pers.) with private bath and communal WC, 1 duplex (4 pers.) with bath and WC. Rooms cleaned by guests. **Price** 230F (2 pers.) +60F (extra pers.); duplex 250F (2 pers.), 380F (4 pers.). **Meals** Breakfast incl., half-board min. 2 nights 190F(per pers.), evening meals at communal table 80F (wine incl.). **Facilities** Lounge. **Pets** Small dogs only allowed. **Nearby** Fishing, tennis, swimming pool, hiking; old villages, Verdon Gorges, Romanesque churches, Thines. **Credit cards** Not accepted. **Closed** Dec. 1 – April 1. **How to get there** (Map 32): 32km southwest of Aubenas via D104 towards Alès. In Lablachère, D4 on right to Planzolles, then D250 on left and signs.

This very old village house is surrounded by low stone walls and lovely terraces. The bedrooms are comfortable, very charming and furnished with numerous antiques (except for the loft and its solarium/terrace). There is a very good communal meal which is served is various places according to the weather. The atmosphere is warm and friendly and the prices are very reasonable.

468

Mounens

07270 Lamastre
(Ardèche)
Tel. 75 06 47 59
Max Dejour and
Mayèse de Moncuit-Dejour

Rooms 3 with bath or shower, and WC. Rooms cleaned on request; linens changed every 5 days. **Price** 290F (1 pers.), 330F (2 pers.) +95F (extra pers.). **Meals** Breakfast incl., meals at communal table 110F (wine incl.). **Facilities** Lounge, swimming pool. **Pets** Small dogs allowed on request. **Nearby** Golf (18 holes, 35km); tennis, fishing, riding, cross-country skiing, Le Mastrou touristic train, villages (Desaigues, Chalencon). **Credit cards** Not accepted. **Spoken** English, Spanish. **Open** All year. **How to get there** (Map 26): 6km south of Lamastre via D578 towardsLe Cheyland. After Lapias, straight ahead for 800m; on left, take small uphill road; signs Mounens.

Built on a hillside, Mounens is composed of two old houses connected by a lovely flower garden. One house has just been renovated for guests and is beautifully tasteful and comfortable with lovely printed cottons, elegant antique furniture, thick carpets and watercolors. The dinners are mouthwatering and the breakfasts, too, are delicious. The owners are very friendly; this part of the Ardèche is particularly beautiful with its gentle hillsides covered with chestnut trees, terraced farms and verdant orchards.

469
Chez Marcelle and Jean-Nicolas Goetz

07000 Pourchères
(Ardèche)
Tel. 75 66 81 99/75 66 80 22
M. and Mme Goetz

Rooms 3 with shower and WC, and 1 suite (3 pers.) with bath, shower, and WC. Rooms cleaned every 4 days. **Price** 200-280F (2 pers.) +70F (extra pers.). **Meals** Breakfast incl., evening meals at communal or separate tables 95F (wine incl.). Vegetarian meals poss. **Pets** Well-behaved dogs allowed. **Credit cards** Not accepted. **Spoken** English, German. **Closed** 15 days in winter and 15 days mid-season. **How to get there** (Map 26): At Privas head for Les Ollières, at Petit Tournon 2nd left towards Pourchères; signs. **No smoking.**

This old house is built on a lava flow that is today covered with flowers. The dark stone contrasts with the verdant countryside. The pleasant bedrooms are furnished in regional style, and some are in a recently converted shepherd's cottage. Good dinners are served outside in good weather, and you will enjoy a breathtaking view. The austere countryside will please those who love traditional Ardèche.

470
Chez Claire

Cros-la-Planche
07310 Saint-Martial-de Valamas
(Ardèche)
Tel. 75 29 27 60
Mme Claire Gélibert

Rooms 3 with shower and WC. **Price** 220F (2 pers.) +60F (extra pers.). **Meals** Breakfast incl., half board 190F per pers. in double room, lunch and evening meals at communal table, on request 80F (wine incl.). **Facilities** Lounge, fishing, swimming in river and lake. **Nearby** Tennis, cross country skiing, lake, Ray-Pic waterfall. **Credit cards** Not accepted. **Spoken** English. **Open** All year. **How to get there** (Map 25): Autoroute A7, exit Loriol, towards La Voulte–Beauchastel, take D120 towards Le Cheylard and Saint-Martin-de-Valamas.

In a wild and mountainous part of Ardèche, this is an inviting house in which Claire and Roger have arranged several lovely, small, chalet-type guest bedrooms. There is a profusion of plants in the skylit lounge. The good evening meals (the children are served first) are happy occasions. There is a beautiful stream below with natural swimming pools in the rock hollows. This is a relaxing place far from civilization.

471
La Ferme du Pic d'Allier

Quartier la Rivière
07400 Saint-Martin-sur-Lavezon
(Ardèche)
Tel. 75 52 98 40/75 52 94 69
Fax 75 52 93 37
Dominique and Alain Michel

Rooms 2 with bath or private shower, and 1 room with washroom; communal WCs. **Price** 310F (1 pers.), 360F (2 pers.) +50F (extra pers.). **Meals** Breakfast incl. Restaurant-auberge on property, by reservation 140F (wine not incl.), and restaurants nearby. **Facilities** Lounge, fishing and swimming in river on property. **Pets** Dogs not allowed. **Nearby** Golf (18 holes, 18km), hiking, lake (7km), tennis, riding, villages of Ardèche, Cruas, Château de Rochemaure. **Credit cards** Not accepted. **Spoken** English, Italian, German. **Open** All year. **How to get there** (Map 26): 18km northwest of Montélimar. Autoroute exit Montélimar Sud, towards Le Teil (or Montélimar Nord, then towards Rochemaure); then N86 towards Meysse. In village, take D2 towards Privas, then D213 towards Saint-Martin-sur-Lavezon: signs.

Bordering a small river, this old farm is surrounded by the magnificent Ardèche countryside. Behind the volcanic-rock walls of La Ferme, you will find a charming patio and a very pleasant interior. The farmhouse is lovely with its beautiful patinated furniture, a large fireplace, and comfortable, prettily decorated bedrooms. This is a lovely place to stay, and your hosts are very hospitable.

172
Scarlett's

Bonnemontesse
Beaulieu
07460 Saint-Paul-le-Jeune
(Ardèche)
Tel. 75 39 07 26/75 39 32 49
M. and Mme Munari

Rooms 3 with bath or shower and WC. **Price** 400F (2 pers.). **Meals** Breakfast 45F, evening meals (separate tables) 100-120F (wine not incl.). **Facilities** Lounge, swimming pool, riding. **Pets** Dogs on request. **Nearby** Golf courses (6 and 18 holes, 3km and 30km), tennis, bicycles, gorges of the Ardèche, Thines, old villages. **Credit cards** Not accepted. **Spoken** Italian. **Open** All year. **How to get there** (Map 32): 35km south of Aubenas via D104 towards Alès, then left on D111 after Maison-Neuve towards Ruoms, then 1st road on the right; signposted.

Standing alone on a small hill, this old house and its swimming pool jut out into the plain like the prow of a ship, offering beautiful, vast views. Very comfortable bedrooms (one with a terrace) are well decorated and furnished in old-fashioned style. A charming lounge with a fireplace is reserved for guests. Breakfast and dinner are served beneath a pergola in good weather. The owners are very welcoming.

473
Ferme de Prémauré

Route de Lamastre
07240 Vernoux-en-Vivarais
(Ardèche)
Tel. 75 58 16 61
Claudine and Roland Achard

Rooms 7 with bath or shower and WC. Rooms cleaned on request. **Price** 240F (2 pers.) +70F (extra pers.). **Meals** Breakfast 35F, evening meals at communal or separate table 95F (wine not incl.). **Facilities** Lounge, stabling, mountain bike rentals, boules court. **Pets** Dogs not allowed. **Nearby** Golf (35km), riding, swimming pool, tennis, botanical trails, châteaux, village of Chalançon. **Credit cards** Not accepted. **Spoken** English. **Open** Easter – Nov 11. **How to get there** (Map 26): Autoroute exit Valence Nord or Sud then towards Saint-Peray-Le Puy. In Vernoux-en-Vivarais, go 8km on the Lamastre road, (D2); lane with signs on right

Clinging to the hillside, this ancient farm has an exceptional view over the Ardèche mountains. The owners are friendly and welcoming. Pleasant, well-kept, small bedrooms are embellished with old furniture. Excellent cuisine is served in the dining room-lounge or on a flowery terrace looking out over the countryside.

474
Grangeon

Saint-Cierge-la-Serre
07800 La Voulte
(Ardèche)
Tel. 75 65 73 86
Mme Paule Valette

Rooms 3 with bath or shower and WC, and 2 suites (3-4 pers. and 5 pers.) with bath, shower and WC. **Price** 280-350F (2 pers.) +150F (extra pers.). **Meals** Breakfast 36F, half board starting at 280F per pers., evening meals (separate tables) 150F (wine not incl.). **Pets** Small well-behaved dogs allowed. **Nearby** Golf, Ardèche châteaux. **Credit cards** Not accepted. **Spoken** English, Italian. **Open** April 1 – early Nov. **How to get there** (Map 26): 35km south of Valence via A7 exit Loriol, then N104 towards Privas. At Fonts-du-Pouzin, right on D265 towards Saint-Cierge-la-Serre; signposted.

Grangeon lies in a remote valley at the end of a long rocky path. All the bedrooms are simple, charming, and well equipped. Excellent dinners are served at separate tables, and almost all the produce comes from the property. Outside, the flower-filled terraces provide superb views. This unique, very isolated place is perhaps not recommended if you are travelling with small children.

475
Domaine Saint-Luc

26790 Baume-de-Transit
(Drôme)
Tel. 75 98 11 51
Ludovic and Eliane Cornillon

Rooms 5 with bath and WC. **Price** 240F (1 pers.), 280F (2 pers.). **Meals** Breakfast incl., evening meals at communal table 130F (wine not incl.). **Facilities** Lounge, telephone, wine tasting. **Pets** Dogs allowed on request (+12F). **Nearby** Swimming pool, golf, château de Grignan, villages of Saint-Restitut, La Garde-Adhémar. **Credit cards** Not accepted. **Spoken** English. **Open** All year. **How to get there** (Map 33): From Bollène head towards Nyons; at Suze-la-Rousse, D117 towards Grignan for 5km; it's on the left before Baume-de-Transit.

A very pretty, traditional 18th-century farmhouse built in the shape of a square for protection against the *mistral*, the Domaine is tastefully decorated with beautiful stone and wood. The comfortable bedrooms are well renovated. Excellent meals are accompanied by wine produced on the property and are served at a communal table. The owners are attentive and professional hosts.

476
Les Grand' Vignes

Mérindol-les-Oliviers
26170 Buis-les-Baronnies
(Drôme)
Tel. 75 28 70 22
François and Chantal Schlumberger

Rooms 1 with shower, WC, TV and fridge, and 1 studio (2 pers.), with bath, WC, TV and fridge. Rooms cleaned twice weekly. **Price** 210F (1 pers.), 250F (2 pers.), studio 300F (2 pers.) +60F (extra pers.); 2 nights min. **Meals** Breakfast incl. No evening meals. **Restaurant** In 100m. **Facilities** Swimming pool. **Pets** Small dogs allowed. **Nearby** Walks, tennis, riding, skiing, Vaison-La-Romaine, wine cellars. **Credit cards** Not accepted. **Spoken** English. **Open** All year. **How to get there** (Map 33): In Vaison, D938 towards Nyons then D46 towards Puyméras and D205. In Mérindol, D147; 1st house on the right on the Mollans road.

In a rolling countryside of vineyards and olive groves, this very pretty house reflects the gentle Provençal way of life. There are pleasant and comfortable bedrooms with white walls and lovely colored fabrics; the larger room has its own entrance but both are near the swimming pool. In good weather, you can enjoy breakfast outdoors with a view of the countryside.

477
Domaine du Grand Lierne

26120 Châteaudouble
(Drôme)
Tel. 75 59 80 71
M. and Mme Charignon-Champel

Rooms 2 and 2 suite (of whith 1 with terrace, lounge and TV) with bath or shower and WC. **Price** 230-250F (1-2 pers.); suite 250-450F (2-4 pers.); 2 nights min. **Meals** Breakfast incl. No evening meals. **Pets** Dogs not allowed. **Nearby** Resaturants, tennis, fishing, riding club, golf, cross country skiing, clay pigeon shooting, walks, Vercors Bach festival (July 20 – Aug 15.). **Credit cards** Not accepted. **Spoken** English. **Open** All year. **How to get there** (Map 26): 15km east of Valence via D68 towards Chabeuil; at the roundabout at the entrance to Chabeuil go towards Romans; at the 2nd roundabout 1.5km later, go right towards Peyrus; 1st house on the left after Les Faucons.

This old stone farmhouse with its square tower typical of the Dauphiné region lies on the plain of Chabeuil, with the silhouette of the Vercors Mountains in the distance. The house, surrounded by corn fields, has a very traditional atmosphere. The bedrooms and one suite are on the first floor. The other suite, on the ground floor, is more attractive and opens onto the pretty courtyard. Breakfast is served outside in summer and includes homemade jams.

478
Le Balcon de Rosine

Route de Propiac
26170 Mérindol-les-Oliviers
(Drôme)
Tel. and fax 75 28 71 18
Jean and Jacqueline Bouchet

Rooms 1 with bath, WC, TV and kitchen, and 1 with shower, WC, TV, lounge, terrace, kitchen and telephone. Rooms cleaned twice weekly. **Price** 200F (1 pers.), 240F (2 pers.); 300F (2 pers.), 350F (3 pers.). **Meals** Breakfast incl. No evening meals. **Restaurant** La Gloriette (1km). **Pets** Dogs allowed. **Nearby** Cross-country skiing and ski slopes, tennis, riding, baths, Vaison-la-Romaine, wine route. **Credit cards** Not accepted. **Spoken** English, Italian. **Closed** In Feb and August. **How to get there** (Map 33): 10km northeast of Vaison-La-Romaine via D938 towards Nyons, then D46 towards La Tuillière for 4km, then left on D205. In Mérindol D147 towards Propiac for 1km.

Le Balcon de Rosine has an exceptional position overlooking the plain of Ouvèze, with a view of Mont Ventoux. The old farmhouse has a lovely garden and two simple but pleasant bedrooms with their own entrances (one is in a small building next door). Breakfast is served outside on the terrace or in the lounge. The owners are informal and friendly.

479
Ferme de Moutas

Saint-Pons
Condorcet
26110 Nyons
(Drôme)
Tel. 75 27 70 13
M. and Mme Taelman

Rooms 2 with shower, WC and fridge. Rooms cleaned on request. **Price** 230F (1 pers.), 250F (2 pers.). **Meals** Breakfast incl., evening meals "campagnard" on request or restaurants in 6km. **Facilities** Swimming pool., visit to angora goat farm (angora sweaters made). **Pets** Small dogs allowed. **Nearby** Fishing, riding, Drôme Provençale. **Credit cards** Not accepted. **Spoken** Dutch, English. **Open** May 1 – end Sept. **How to get there** (Map 33): At Nyons, D94 and D70. At Condorcet, D227 towards Saint-Pons; after Saint-Pons, take the road on the right after 600m.

The approach to the Ferme de Moutas is down a long narrow road edged with broom. M. and Mme Taelman receive their guests with obvious pleasure. The two large bedrooms have white walls and are comfortable, each with a simply and tastefully decorated living area, as well as a private, flowery terrace, which is lovely for breakfast. In summer, the rooms are pleasantly cool. This is a marvelous place set in superb countryside.

480
Les Tuillières

26160 Pont-de-Barret
(Drôme)
Tel. 75 90 43 91
Fax 75 90 40 75
Mme Williams

Rooms 6 with bath and shower, WC. Price 280F (1 pers.), 300F (2 pers.) or 350F in July-August less than 3 nights; +80F (extra pers.). **Meals** Breakfast incl., half-board 280F (per pers.), meals at communal table 130F (wine incl.). **Facilities** Lounge, swimming pool. **Pets** Dogs allowed on request. **Nearby** Riding (5 min.), tennis (5 min.), golf (18 holes, 15km), Silk Museum, medieval villages, Dieulefit potteries. **Credit card** Amex. **Spoken** English. **Open** All year. **How to get there** (Map 26): 24km east of Montélimar, exit Montélimar Sud (Mézanc), towards Dieulefit. In La Begude, go left to Charols; then right, towards Pont-de-Barret. 3km on right before village.

The oldest parts of this redecorated farm date from the 16th-century. Over the years, parts have been added and integrated harmoniously into the main building. Today, the English owners extend friendly hospitality to guests from all over the world. Set in a 40-acre private park, Les Tuillières is very quiet and peaceful. We prefer the bedrooms located under the eaves, which have beautiful beamed ceilings and old stone walls. The other rooms are more impersonal.

481
Mas de Champelon

Hameau de Saint-Turquois
26790 Suze-la-Rousse
(Drôme)
Tel. 75 98 81 95
Christiane and Michaël Zebbar

Rooms 4 with bath or shower and WC (1 has private terrace). **Price** 220F (2 pers.). **Meals** Breakfast incl., half board 200F per pers. in double room, evening meals at communal table. **Pets** Dogs not allowed. **Nearby** Gorges of the Ardèche, châteaux of Suze-la-Rousse and Grignan, Vaison-La-Romaine. **Credit cards** Not accepted. **Spoken** English, Italian. **Open** April 1 – Sept 30. **How to get there** (Map 33): From Bollène head towards Nyons; at Suze-la-Rousse head for Saint-Paul-Trois-Châteaux and Grignan via D117; the house is at the beginning of Saint-Turquois.

This small traditional farmhouse, very peaceful and completely renovated, is set back from the road and hidden between rows of vines and a small forest. The simple, comfortable bedrooms are hung with Provençal fabrics and overlook a flowering garden; each has a modern shower. Breakfast is generally served outside in the shade and includes a large choice of homemade preserves; the evening meals, based on local recipes, are very good. There is a friendly, family-style atmosphere.

482
La Ferme des Collines

Hameau Notre-Dame
38260 Gillonay
(Isère)
Tel. 74 20 27 93
Marie and Jean-Marc Meyer

Rooms 2 and 2 suites (4 pers.) with shower and WC. **Price** 250-270F (2 pers.) +70F (extra pers.). **Meals** Breakfast incl., meals at communal table 100F (wine incl.); gourmet restaurant (4km). **Facilities** Lounge. **Pets** Small dogs allowed on request. **Nearby** Swimming pool, mountain biking, Paladru and Charavines Lakes (water sports), tennis, Berlioz Museum, Chartreuse cellars, Saint-Antoine Abbey, Facteur Cheval House. **Credit cards** Not accepted. **Spoken** English. **Open** All year. **How to get there** (Map 33): 4km east of La-Côte-Saint-André. In La-Côte-Saint-André, go towards Grenoble, then follow signs in Gillonay.

We love this old farmhouse which is charmingly perched on one of the many hills of this rolling countryside. The interior has just been very tastefully and comfortably redecorated, with some antiques and modern paintings. The beams have been finished in soft pastel tones, and the walls are white or subtly painted; adding to the charm are pretty floral bedcovers, drapes in coordinated or eggshell colors, beautiful bathrooms and a magnificent view.

483
Le Val Sainte-Marie

Bois-Barbu
38250 Villard-de-Lans
(Isère)
Tel. 76 95 92 80
Fax 76 96 56 79
Dominique and Agnès Bon

Rooms 3 with shower and WC. Rooms cleaned every 2 days. **Price** 200F (1 pers.), 250F (2 pers.). **Meals** Breakfast incl., half board 205F (2 night min., per pers); dinner at communal table 85F (wine not incl.). **Facilities** Lounge. **Pets** Dogs not allowed. **Nearby** Cross-country and alpine skiing, swimming pool, tennis, caving, mountain biking, golf, Vercors National Park. **Credit cards** Not accepted. **Spoken** English. **Open** All year. **How to get there** (Map 26): 32km southwest of Grenoble via A 48, exit Veurey-Voroise, then N532 and D531 towards Villard-de-Lans, then towards Bois-Barbu, then at Centre de Ski de Fond, 1st lane on left. **No smoking.**

L e Val Sainte-Marie is a restored old farmhouse surrounded by fields and pine groves, just next to the cross-country skiing departure area. The bedrooms are intimate, comfortable and prettily decorated, and all look out on the countryside. Good dinners feature regional specialties. The atmosphere is very pleasant, and there is an extensive library along with numerous card games.

484
Château–Auberge de Bobigneux

Bobigneux
42220 Saint-Sauveur-en-Rue
(Loire)
Tel. 77 39 24 33 – Fax 77 39 25 74
M. and Mme Jacques Labere

Rooms 5 with shower and WC. **Price** 195F (1 pers.), 225F (2 pers.) +65F (extra pers.). **Meals** Breakfast incl., half board 180F per pers. in double room (3 days min.), evening meals and lunch (separate tables) 65-125F (wine not incl.). **Facilities** Telephone. **Pets** Dogs allowed on request. **Nearby** Lake, riding center, mountain biking, golf (8km), cross-country skiing. **Credit cards** Visa, Eurocard and MasterCard. **Spoken** English and Danish. **Open** Easter – Nov 1. **How to get there** (Map 26): 18km northwest of Annonay towards Bours-Argental, then D503 towards Saint-Sauveur; on the left before the village.

T his small château built of local granite is in the Pilar National Park. The bedrooms are simple but pretty, comfortable and quiet. Tables are set in a beautiful room with 18th-century paneling. You will seldom be alone because this small auberge is very popular locally and it is particularly economical for families.

485
Château de Bois-Franc

69640 Jarnioux
(Rhône)
Tel. 74 68 20 91
Fax 74 65 10 03
M. Doat

Rooms 1 with shower and WC, and 2 suites (1-6 pers.) with bath or shower and WC. **Price** 300F; suites 400-900F; 2 nights min. between Nov. 15 and March 15. **Meals** Breakfast incl. No evening meals. **Facilities** Lounge. **Pets** Dogs allowed on request. **Nearby** Restaurants, tennis (1km), riding (6km). **Credit cards** Not accepted. **Spoken** English, German. **Open** All year. **How to get there** (Map 26): 7km west of Villefranche-sur-Saône via D38 towards Tarare-Roanne, then on D31, 4km after Chervinges.

Bois-Franc is in the countryside not far from the villages constructed of golden stone from the Beaujolais region. Madame Doat will receive you with kind hospitality. (Her dog is less welcoming). The interior still has all its traditional old charm. Ask for the *Chambre Jaune* which is the most expensive but is absolutely magnificent and beautifully furnished. The *Mireille* suite is less comfortable. Breakfast is served in a pretty dining room. There is an immense park.

486
Saint-Colomban Lodge

7, rue du Hêtre-Pourpre
69130 Lyon-Ecully
(Rhône)
Tel. 78 33 05 57
Fax 72 18 90 80
Annick and Michaël Altuna

Rooms 5 with bath, WC, telephone and satellite TV. **Price** 350F (1 pers.), 390-450F (2 pers.). **Meals** Breakfast incl.; evening meals at communal table, by reservation 90-120F (wine incl.) or restaurants in 200m. **Facilities** Lounge, locked parking lot. **Pets** Dogs not allowed. **Nearby** Golf (18 holes, 5km), tennis in village, all entertainment in Lyon (5km), visit of Old Lyon, Dombes National Park, Lyon Mountains, gastronomy. **Credit cards** Not accepted. **Spoken** English. **Open** All year. **How to get there** (Map 26): 5km west of Lyon. Autoroute exit Ecully, then Ecully-Centre; after church, go towards Tassin (straight ahead), 2nd street on left (fire station).

The Saint-Colomban Lodge is a very special place to stay in a residential suburb just outside Lyon. The house is surrounded by a private park which is very pleasant in good weather. The very beautiful bedrooms have ultra-modern conveniences like a direct telephone and satellite television, and lovely bathrooms. There is a tasteful combination of fabrics, eiderdowns and honey-colored English pine furniture. Excellent breakfasts are served at a beautiful table in the salon or outdoors in sunny weather.

487
La Javernière

69910 Villié-Morgon
(Rhône)
Tel. 74 04 22 71
M. François Roux

Rooms 7 with bath or shower and WC, and 1 suite (4 pers.) of 2 bedrooms with bath or shower and WC each. **Price** 540-580F (2 pers.), suite 950F (4 pers.). **Meals** Breakfast 55F. No evening meals. **Facilities** Lounge, swimming pool, fishing. **Pets** Dogs allowed (+30F). **Nearby** Restaurants, riding, golf, Romanesque churches. **Credit cards** Amex, Visa, Eurocard and MasterCard. **Open** All year. **How to get there** (Map 26): Take Belleville exit from autoroute, D68 between Morgon and Villié-Morgon; the road is 600m from Morgon.

All the bedrooms overlook the Beaujolais countryside, with vineyards stretching as far as the eye can see. The interior is elegant and immaculate. In the bedrooms and the lounge there is handsome old furniture set off by beautiful curtains and carpets. Our favorite bedrooms are under the lovely beamed eaves. The breakfasts are good and the owners are pleasant.

488
La Revardière

Hameau de Saint-Victor
Trévignin
74100 Aix-les-Bains
(Savoie)
Tel. 79 61 59 12
Madame Jackline Rocagel

Rooms 1 with bath, WC and TV; 2 with shower (sharing WC), sitting room and TV. Rooms cleaned every 5 days. **Price** 360F (2 pers.); 185F (1 pers.), 275F (2 pers.) +100F (extra pers.). **Meals** Breakfast incl. No evening meals. **Facilities** Lounge. **Pets** Dogs allowed on request (+18F). **Nearby** Restaurants, golf, ski slopes and cross country skiing, Lake of Le Bourget, Hautecombe Abbey, Chartreuse. **Credit cards** Not accepted. **Open** All year. **How to get there** (Map 27): 7km east of Aix-les-Bains via D913, the Revard road. After Trévignin, turn right; signs close to the stone roadside cross; left on small road towards Saint-Victor. **No smoking.**

On the slopes of Mont Revard, this modern chalet overlooks the countryside between Le Bourget and Annecy Lakes. The bedrooms are comfortable, meticulously well kept, have paneled walls and share a pleasant small lounge. We especially liked the room upstairs with a large bed and floral fabrics. The other room is less pleasant, and we felt that the suite was too expensive. You will be warmly welcomed with a glass of Savoy wine.

489
Le Selué

Le Cernix
73590 Crest-Voland
(Rhône)
Tel. 79 31 70 74
Anne-Marie Gressier

Rooms 1 with shower and WC and 2 with shared bathroom, shower and WC. **Price** 150F (1 pers.), 240-260F (2 pers.). **Meals** Breakfast incl. No evening meal. **Restaurants** In the village. **Facilities** Lounge, telephone. **Pets** Dogs not allowed. **Nearby** Alpine skiing (ski lift in 100m), cross-country skiing, bike rentals, hiking, riding, hang-gliding. **Credit cards** Not accepted. **Open** All year on request. **How to get there** (Map 27) 16km southwest of Mégève via N212.

Located in a quiet village of the Savoy region, this modern chalet has three very comfortable guestrooms which are especially well kept and prettily decorated with beautiful furniture, charming engraving and antique mirrors. The bathrooms also are charming. In the lovely salon, breakfast is served with homemade preserves. The owner is very friendly.

490
Chez M. and Mme Coutin

73210 Peisey-Nancroix
(Savoie)
Tel. 79 07 93 05
M. and Mme Maurice Coutin

Rooms 2 sharing bath and WC. **Price** 135-150F (1 pers.), 190-210F (2 pers.) +75F (extra pers.). **Meals** Breakfast incl., evening meals at communal table 75F (wine incl.). **Facilities** Telephone. **Pets** Dogs allowed on request. **Nearby** Alpine skiing (ski lift 500m, connection with Les Arcs) and cross-country skiing, Vanoise National Park. **Credit cards** Not accepted. **Open** All year. **How to get there** (Map 27): At Moutiers, head towards Bourg-Saint-Maurice. After Bellentre leave N90 and go right on D87 towards Peisey; in front of Maison Savoyard, at the top, car park and road on the right; signposted.

This old farmhouse with its flowery balconies and slate roof is just outside the still unspoiled village of Peisey. It has two guest bedrooms with a shared balcony overlooking the valley and the Alliet (3080m) and Bellecôte (3415m) peaks. Breakfasts are served in a large and inviting dining room. There is an informal atmosphere which would appeal to families.

491
Les Chataîgniers

Rue Maurice Franck
73110 La Rochette
(Savoie)
Tel. 79 25 50 21
Fax 79 25 79 97
Anne Charlotte Rey

Rooms 3, 1 suite and 1 apartment with bath, WC and telephone. **Price** 390-950F (2-4 pers.). **Children** Under 10 not allowed. **Meals** Breakfast 65F served 7:45-10:00, lunch and evening meals (separate tables) 130-270F (wine not incl.). **Facilities** Lounge, piano, swimming pool. **Pets** Dogs not allowed. **Nearby** Golf, tennis, skiing, Château de Miolans, Grande Chartreuse Convent. **Credit cards** Visa, Amex, Diners. **Spoken** English, German, Italian, Swedish. **Closed** Jan 2– 15 and Saturday noon,Sunday evening and Monday in low season (by reservation Oct 15 – March 15). **How to get there** (Map 27): 30km north of Grenoble, take Autoroute 41, exit Pontcharra, then D925. In La Rochette, in front of "Hôtel de Ville", towards Arvillard, 200m on left.

A beautiful, exquisitely decorated family house, a captivating hostess, and a poet–cook combine to make Les Châtaigniers a very special place. At guests' request, theme dinners can be organized. The bedrooms are spacious, luxurious and comfortable, and most overlook the pretty grounds, where there is a swimming pool. The lounges are lovely, with beautiful furniture and many decorative objects.

492
La Maison des Gallinons

Les Gallinons
74130 Ayze
(Haute-Savoie)
Tel. 50 25 78 58
Mme Alice Rosset

Rooms 1 with small shower and WC; 2 rooms with communal bath and WC; and 2 spare rooms Rooms cleaned on request. Price 150F (1 pers.), 200-250F (2 pers.) +150F (extra room) +75F (extra pers.). **Meals** Breakfast incl., occasional meals at communal or separate tables 60-100F (wine incl.); barbecue at guests' disposal or restaurants (5km). **Facilities** Lounge. **Pets** Dogs only. **Nearby** Golf (25km), cross-country and alpine skiing (1/2 hour); Chamonix, Annecy, Lake Geneva. **Credit cards** Not accepted. **Spoken** English, Italian. **Open** May 15 – Sept. 15; year round for long stays by advance reservation. **How to get there** (Map 27): 5km north of Boneville towards Marignier-Ayze. Turn left after school and town hall, towards Chez Jeandets; go up the hill to Gallinons.

P erched on the side of a mountain 2100 feet up, this beautiful chalet offers you a truly panoramic view. Inside, the antique furniture, decorative objects, paintings, upholstered walls and lovely carpets create a warm and very elegant atmosphere. The Maison des Gallinons is charming, very well kept and the owner is the model of friendliness.

493
La Girandole

46, chemin de la Persévérance
74400 Chamonix Mont Blanc
(Haute-Savoie)
Tel. 50 53 37 58
M. and Mme Pierre Gazagnes

Rooms 3 (of which 2 with washbasin) sharing 1 bath and 1 WC. **Price** 260F (2 pers.).
Meals Breakfast incl., meals 120F (wine incl.). **Restaurants** La Tartifle and Le National.
Facilities Lounge. **Pets** Dogs allowed on request. **Nearby** Golf, all winter sports, all summer
sports, Aiguille du Midi, music weeks in summer. **Credit cards** Not accepted. **Spoken** English,
German. **Open** All year. **How to get there** (Map 27): At Chamonix-sud, head for Bravent funicular,
then towards Les Moussoux; signposted.

Built on a mountain side, this chalet is magnificently located facing the
Aiguille du Midi, Mont Blanc and the Bossons Glacier. The small,
pretty bedrooms and the balcony share this breathtaking view, which you
can enjoy with a telescope. M. and Mme Gazagnes are very welcoming;
they have an intimate knowledge of the area and will be delighted to help
you to explore it. This is a beautiful place to stay.

INDEX

A

B

ALSO IN THE RIVAGES SERIES

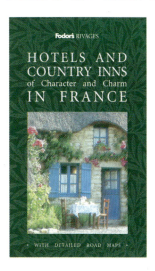

Fodor's RIVAGES

HOTELS AND COUNTRY INNS
of Character and Charm
IN FRANCE

· WITH DETAILED ROAD MAPS ·

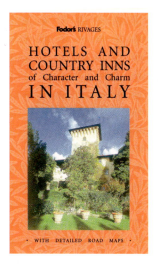

Fodor's RIVAGES

HOTELS AND COUNTRY INNS
of Character and Charm
IN ITALY

· WITH DETAILED ROAD MAPS ·

Hotels and Country Inns of Character and Charm in France

The flagship of the series, with over 400 hotels and inns that are as different as can be—from small hotels in country towns to inns in simple farm-houses, to sumptuous châteaux—and share a devotion to traditional French hotel-keeping. Delightful color photographs and no-nonsense text team up to depict each property. Color maps abound.

**$20.00 ($27.95 Canada)
ISBN: 0-679-02872-2**

Hotel and Country Inns of Character and Charm in Italy

Over 400 of the most charming places to stay all over Italy are included in this guide, from small hotels in country towns to inns in farmhouses and villas alike. There is an appealing color photograph and an unfussy description of each hostelry, along with a delightful section of brief restaurant reviews and detailed color road maps.

**$18.00 ($25.00 Canada)
ISBN: 0-679-02874-9**

Printed in CEE